Listening to Music

Singing boys in the Choir Gallery of the Cathedral Museum in Florence

DELLA ROBBIA

Listening to

Music

Creatively

EDWIN J. STRINGHAM

Professor of Music
Queens College of the City of New York

Werner Laurie : London

Table of Contents

CHAPTER   PAGE

I. MUSIC AND THE DANCE –   –   –   1

Discussion of the place dance music has in our living and a study of the basic characteristics of this type of music.

Essential Listening: A popular dance record, Turkey in the Straw (Guion), Beautiful Blue Danube (Johann Strauss), Slavonic Dance No. 1 (Dvorák), Amaryllis (Ghys), Suite No. 2 in B minor (Bach).

Additional Suggestions for Listening: Waltz in C-Sharp Minor (Chopin), Golliwog's Cakewalk (Debussy), "Rhumba" movement from Harl McDonald's Symphony No. 2.

RHYTHM: THE HEARTBEAT OF MUSIC. Discussion of rhythm and integration with painting and poetry.

II. MUSIC AND CEREMONY –   –   –   11

How music serves in various formal ceremonies of life.

Essential Listening: Marche Militaire (Schubert), Pomp and Circumstance (Elgar), Stars and Stripes Forever (Sousa), Polonaise Militaire (Chopin), Triumphal March from "Aida" (Verdi), Wedding March from "Midsummer Night's Dream" (Mendelssohn), Wedding March from "Lohengrin" (Wagner), and Funeral March (Chopin).

Additional Suggestions for Listening: Slow movement from the "Eroica" (No. 3) Symphony (Beethoven), and the third movement from Tchaikovsky's "Pathetique" (Sixth) Symphony.

MELODY AND HARMONY. Discussion of those two elements in music.

III. MUSIC AND RELIGION –   –   –   18

Place and function of music in our religious worship. Brief résumé of the subject in Protestant, Catholic and Jewish faiths, with typical examples from each.

Essential Listening: "A Mighty Fortress is Our God"; selected Jewish Kaddish Chants; Gregorian (Catholic) Chants: "Kyrie," "Gloria," or "Tenebrae factae sunt"; "Sanctus" and "Gloria" from the Pope Marcellus Mass

CONTENTS

CHAPTER   PAGE

III
(continued) (Palestrina); Lutheran Chorales, "Jesu Joy of Man's Desiring" (Bach), "Credo," "Crucifixus," "Et Resurrexit," and "Sanctus" from The B-minor Mass (Bach).

Additional Suggestions for Listening: Excerpts from "Parsifal" (Wagner), Finale from the "Reformation" Symphony (Mendelssohn), and Finale from the Ninth Symphony (Beethoven).

VOLUME AND SPEED AS ELEMENTS IN EMOTIONAL EXPRESSION: Brief discussion of the part dynamics, accent, and tempo play in music.

IV. MUSIC, WORK AND PLAY: THE TRADITIONAL FOLK SONG   –   –   –   30

Discussion of traditional folk songs from many nations. Elementary phrase structures. Basic elements of the Ternary (three-part), A-B-A, form. The Strophic form. Some scales.

Essential Listening: Barbara Allen, Marlborough, Home on the Range, John Henry, Drink to Me Only, and Comin' Through the Rye.

Additional Suggestions for Listening: Selected folk songs from Germany, France, Italy, Spain, and Russia.

V. THE COMPOSED FOLK SONG: THE ARCHITECTURE OF MUSIC   –   –   42

Differentiation between the "traditional" and the "composed" folk songs. Period and Binary structures and forms.

Essential Listening: Lullaby (Brahms). The Birch Tree (Russian folk song), and the Finale from Tchaikovsky's Fourth Symphony.

THE ARCHITECTURE OF MUSIC: FORM AND STRUCTURE. Discussion of a few basic concepts of the function of form and structure in the allied fine arts. Integration with poetry and painting. The Rondo form in music and poetry.

Essential Listening: Rondino (Beethoven-Kreisler).

VI. MUSIC AS PERSONAL EXPRESSION: THE ART SONG (LIED)   –   –   –   55

Historical sketch of the rise of the Art Song. The Strophic versus the Thorough-composed song. Important function of the poem.

CONTENTS

Essential Listening: Study of the following art songs with their English translations of the foreign words: Serenade (Schubert), Der Erl König (Schubert), Ich Grolle Nicht (Schumann), Minnelied (Brahms), Ich Liebe Dich (Grieg), The Flea (Moussorgsky), and The Sea (MacDowell).

Additional Suggestions for Listening: Selected songs by Wolf, Franz, Richard Strauss, César Franck, Gabriel Fauré, Duparc, Debussy, Bond, Cadman, Carpenter, and others.

SENTENCE STRUCTURE IN MUSIC: THE PHRASE, PERIOD AND CADENCE. Further study of these aspects as they are found in simple songs.

Essential Listening: London Bridge Is Falling Down, the Farmer in the Dell, and Swanee River.

VII. THE OPERA — — — — — — — 75
PART ONE: OPERETTA AND LIGHT OPERA. History of Opera. Description of different types. Typical examples of arias.

Suggestions for Listening: Selections from various popular works in this form, including Show Boat (Kern), Rose Marie (Friml), Mlle. Modiste (Herbert), Porgy and Bess (Gershwin), The Mikado (Sullivan), and others.

THE OPERA BUFFA:

Suggestions for Listening: Excerpts from the Marriage of Figaro (Mozart), and The Barber of Seville (Rossini).

PART TWO: GRAND OPERA. History and description of various types of Grand Opera. Outstanding composers and their principal works in this form. Discussion of French, Italian and Wagnerian types, with pertinent suggestions for optional listening.

Essential Listening: The opera Carmen by Georges Bizet; its story and dramatic action, act by act, and descriptive study of the principal arias, ensembles, and instrumental numbers as they appear in each act.

Additional Suggestions for Listening: Selections from various Wagnerian operatic works. Selections from Aida (Verdi), La Bohème (Puccini), Pagliacci (Leoncavallo), Cavalleria Rusticana (Mascagni), Boris Godunoff (Moussorgsky), and reference to other works by Verdi, Richard Strauss, Massenet, Charpentier, Gruenberg, Hanson, Taylor, Hageman, Herbert, Menotti, and Giannini.

VIII. THE ORATORIO — — — — — 104
Survey of the backgrounds of this form. Biographical sketch of George Frideric Handel. Outline of "The Messiah," with a complete list of numbers in this work.

CONTENTS

CHAPTER   PAGE

VIII   *Essential Listening:* Indicated selections from "The Mes-
(*continued*)   siah," either complete, or with two alternate reduction
          plans to meet time allowance.

          Additional Suggestions for Listening: Works by Bach, Haydn,
          Beethoven, Mendelssohn, Liszt, Berlioz, Franck, Parry,
          Stanford, Stainer, Elgar, Walton, Delius, Holst, Paine,
          Parker, Stillman-Kelley, Loeffler, Shelley, Smith, d'Indy,
          Wolf-Ferrari, Pierné, and Honegger.

IX. MUSIC IN THE THEATRE: INCIDENTAL
    MUSIC: THE SUITE   --   --   --   --   114

          Brief outline of the history pertinent to the subject.

          Essential Listening: Valse Triste (Sibelius), Peer Gynt Suite
          No. 1 (Grieg), Midsummer Night's Dream Suite (Men-
          delssohn), the "Indian" Suite (MacDowell).

          Additional Suggestions for Listening: "Through the Looking
          Glass" Suite (Taylor) with words of Lewis Carroll pertin-
          ent to each movement of the Suite. Music for the Cinema,
          with a few typical examples cited.

X. MUSIC AND THE BALLET --   --   --   128

          Brief résumé of the history of this form.

          Essential Listening: Description and analysis of Ritual Fire
          Dance from "El Amor Brujo" (Falla), Petrouchka
          (Stravinsky), Skyscrapers (Carpenter), "Mother Goose"
          Suite (Ravel).

          Additional Suggestions for Listening: Selected and appro-
          priate works by Tchaikovsky, Delibes, Offenbach,
          Glazounov, Milhaud, Ravel, Gliere, Stravinsky, Shosta-
          kovitch, and Aaron Copland.

XI. TONE COLOUR IN MUSIC --   --   --   141

          PART ONE: THE INSTRUMENTS OF THE
          ORCHESTRA

          A study of the history, description, range, transposition,
          and tonal characteristics of the many instruments compris-
          ing the modern symphony orchestra; musical illustrations;
          orchestra seating plans; the Art of Orchestration; the
          complete orchestra score.

          Essential Listening: Peter and the Wolf (Prokofieff);
          "Instruments of the Symphony Orchestra" from available
          commercial recordings of string, woodwind, brass and
          percussion instruments; Introduction and Allegro for
          Strings (Elgar).

CONTENTS

CHAPTER   PAGE

PART TWO: THE ORCHESTRA IN ACTION
Essential Listening: The "Nutcracker Suite" (Tchaikovsky).
Additional Suggestions for Listening: Carnival of the Animals
(Saint-Saëns).

XII. CLASSIC AND ROMANTIC ELEMENTS
IN ART – – – – – – – – 171

Analysis and discussion of these two typical categories, or
tempers, and comparisons with similar tempers in painting, poetry, and architecture. General historical implications.

THE ROMANTIC MOVEMENT IN MUSIC and its historical backgrounds; Programme music. Biographical sketch of
Tchaikovsky.

Essential Listening: Minuet from the Symphony in E-flat
(Mozart), the Liebestod music from "Tristan and Isolde"
(Wagner), and the Overture-Fantasy, Romeo and Juliet
(Tchaikovsky).

XIII. THE SYMPHONIC POEM: TONE PAINT-
ING – – – – – – – – 195

Narrative and mood depiction through musical means.
Definitions of terms involved. Romanticism and the injec-
tion of the literary element into musical forms.

Essential Listening: Detailed analysis of Danse Macabre
(Saint-Saëns), Night on Bald Mountain (Moussorgsky),
and The Sorcerer's Apprentice (Dukas).

Additional Suggestions for Listening: the tone-poem, The Isle
of the Dead (Rachmaninoff).

XIV. NATIONALISM IN MUSIC – – – 212

Nationalism as an expression of Romanticism; biographical sketches of Smetana and Sibelius.

Essential Listening: Minute study of the Moldau (Smetana),
the Overture Solennelle 1812 (Tchaikovsky), and Finlandia (Sibelius).

Additional Suggestions for Listening: Works by Sibelius,
Albeniz, Grieg, Smetana, Kodály, Rimsky-Korsakoff,
Liadov, German, Grofé, Enesco, and McDonald.

XV. EXOTICISM IN MUSIC: RIMSKY-
KORSAKOFF – – – – – – 227

Romanticism and exoticism in poetry, painting, and
music. Biographical sketch of Nicholas Rimsky-Korsakoff.

CONTENTS

CHAPTER   PAGE

XV   *Essential Listening:* The "Scheherezade" Symphonic Suite
(*continued*) (Rimsky-Korsakoff); analysis of narrative and music.

Additional Suggestions for Listening: Other works by Tchai-
kovsky, Saint-Saëns, David, Massenet, Verdi, Puccini,
Cui, Borodin, Rimsky-Korsakoff. The Caucasian Sketches
(Ippolitov-Ivanov).

XVI. THE SYMPHONIC POEM: FRANZ LISZT --   242

The Romantic spirit and the composer Liszt; biography
of the composer and a list of his works in the symphonic
poem form; his use of the "germinal motif" and thematic
metamorphosis as a means of musical narrative.

Essential Listening: Les Préludes, described and analysed
in detail.

Additional Suggestions for Listening: Other works by Liszt to
be chosen from the number of symphonic poems mentioned in the early paragraphs of this chapter.

XVII. RICHARD WAGNER AND THE LEIT
MOTIF TECHNIQUE   --   --   --   --   251

Biography of Wagner and his general historical background. Enumeration of his works and statement of his
ideals. The *leit motif* technique as developed by Wagner;
as a means of musical narrative.

Essential Listening: The Overture to "Tannhäuser" described and analysed from a literary as well as musical
standpoint.

Additional Suggestions for Listening: Other appropriate
works by Wagner to be selected from: The Prelude to
"Die Meistersinger," Prelude and Entrance of the Gods
into Valhalla from "Das Rhinegold," Magic Fire Scene
and Ride of the Valkyries from "Die Walküre," Forest
Murmurs from "Siegfried," the Rhine Journey from
"Götterdämmerung," the Good-Friday Spell from
"Parsifal," Siegfried's Funeral March, and the Siegfried
Idyl.

XVIII. RICHARD STRAUSS AND REALISM IN
MUSIC   --   --   --   --   --   --   --   263

Biographical sketch of the composer. The "Expressionist"
composers and their ideas concerning programme and
descriptive music.

Essential Listening: the Symphonic Poem, the Merry Pranks
of Till Eulenspiegel, with detailed analysis showing how
Strauss uses the "descriptive" themes and transforms
them in musical development.

CONTENTS

CHAPTER   PAGE

Additional Suggestions for Listening: Selections to be made
from other works by Strauss, including Don Juan, Don
Quixote, Death and Transfiguration, Heldenleben, and
Thus Spake Zarathustra.

XIX. THE SONATA AND THE SYMPHONY –   275

A ROMANTIC SYMPHONIST: ANTONIN DVORAK.

Comparisons between so-called "absolute" and "programme" music. History and application of the sonata
form to the symphony. Each movement of a typical work
outlined and explained. The symphony as a realization
of combined forms. Antonin Dvorák: his biography and
his ideals.

Essential Listening: Symphony in E Minor, "From the New
World" (Dvorák), with musical and formal analysis.

SCHEMATIC OUTLINE OF A SYMPHONY AS A WHOLE: The
internal characteristics of each of the usual four movements of a "composite" or conventional type of symphony,
with special emphasis upon the sonata-allegro form and
its application. A skeletal diagram of general style and
design of each movement.

XX. BEETHOVEN: CLASSICISM AND
ROMANTICISM IN IDEAL BALANCE –   301

An early Romantic symphony (the Symphony No. 5 in C
Minor). Biography and general historical background of
the composer and his time; his achievements and general
characteristics of Beethoven's style.

Essential Listening: Symphony No. 5 in C Minor, with
musical and formal analysis.

Additional Suggestions for Listening: Beethoven's Third,
Sixth, Seventh, and Ninth Symphonies.

XXI. BRAHMS: THE CLASSICAL ROMANTI-
CIST–   –   –   –   –   –   –   ·   –   317

Biography and general historical background of the composer.

Essential Listening: Symphony No. 2 in D Major, with
musical and formal anaylsis.

Additional Suggestions for Listening: In addition to the remainder of Brahms' four symphonies, selections may be
made from : the "Unfinished" Symphony (Schubert), as
well as his C-Major Symphony; Tchaikovsky's Fifth and
Sixth Symphonies; Symphony in D Minor (Franck); the

CONTENTS

CHAPTER   PAGE

XXI
(continued) "Italian" and the "Scotch" Symphonies of Mendelssohn; the "Spring" and "Rhenish" Symphonies of Schumann; the Second Symphony in E Minor, Op. 27, by Rachmaninoff; the First, Second Fourth, or Fifth Symphonies of Sibelius; the "Symphony Fantastique" by Berlioz; and the "London" Symphony by Vaughan Williams.

XXII. THE CLASSICAL SYMPHONY: TWO VIENNESE MASTERS: MOZART AND HAYDN – – – – – – – 329

Discussion of the salient characteristics of the Classical temper in painting, poetry, sculpture, and music. The Rococo versus the Classical styles. Biography and general historical background of Mozart.

Essential Listening: Symphony in G Minor, No. 40 (Mozart), with musical and structural exposition of each movement. Biography of Haydn; his style and general historical background.

Essential Listening: Symphony No. 6, in G Major, the "Surprise" (Haydn), with musical and structural analysis.

Additional Suggestions for Listening: the "Jupiter" and E-flat Major Symphonies by Mozart; and the "Oxford," "Paris," "Clock," and "Drum-Roll" Symphonies by Haydn.

REVIEW OF SALIENT CHARACTERISTICS OF THE CLASSICAL TEMPER as they may be discovered in all the fine arts, with special emphasis upon those characteristics and traits in music.

XXIII. CLASSICAL FORM AND ROMANTIC CONTENT IN THE OVERTURE – – 356

The historical background of the overture; Gluck and the Classical overture; the so-called "Italian" and "French" forms of the overture; "absolute" versus "programmatic" content in the overture; the Romantic overture; the potpourri type.

Essential Listening: Overture to the opera "Der Freischütz" by Weber and the Overture "Leonora" No. 3 by Beethoven; detailed musical and formal analysis of both works.

Additional Suggestions for Listening: Overture to The Marriage of Figaro, The Magic Flute, and Don Giovanni by Mozart; the Egmont and Coriolanus Overtures by Beethoven; the Oberon and Euryanthe Overtures by Weber; and the Hebrides and Fingal's Cave Overtures by Mendelssohn.

CONTENTS

CHAPTER   PAGE

XXIV. THE CONCERTO FOR SOLO INSTRU-
MENT AND ORCHESTRA   –   --   --   369

Musical and historical backgrounds of the Solo Concerto.
Biography of Robert Schumann.

Essential Listening: Concerto for Piano and Orchestra in A
Minor, Op. 54, by Robert Schumann, with historical
sketch and analysis of the concerto.

Biographical review of Felix Mendelssohn.

Essential Listening: Concerto in E Minor, Op. 64, for
Violin and Orchestra, by Felix Mendelssohn, with analysis of the concerto.

XXV. CHAMBER   MUSIC: THE   STRING
QUARTET   –   --   –   –   --   –   384

History and discussion of chamber music, especially that
for the string quartet. Comparisons between the orchestra
and the string quartet as performing and compositional
media, and their peculiar demands upon the listener.
Some parallels between this type of music and the arts of
drawing, painting, and sculpture.

Essential Listening: "Ein kleine Nachtmusik" by Mozart;
the "Andante Cantabile" movement from String Quartet
Op. 11 by Tchaikovsky; the complete String Quartet in
F Major, Op. 96 (the "American"), by Antonin Dvořák.
Detailed analysis of all three works.

Additional Suggestions for Listening: Selected string quartets
by Haydn, Mozart, Beethoven (with representations from
each of his "three periods"), Brahms, Schubert, Debussy,
and Ravel, and the quintets of Schumann, Brahms,
Franck, and Ernest Bloch.

XXVI. THE PIANO SOLO AND THE VIOLIN
AND PIANO SONATA   –   –   –   –   398

The emergence of the solo performer and the complex
relationship between the composer, performer, listener,
and instrument maker.

THE PIANO: Its history and musical characteristics. Biography of Frederic Chopin; discussion of his compositional
style and output.

Essential Listening: Ballade No. 3, in A-Flat Major, Op. 47,
by Chopin, with detailed analysis of its contents and form.

Additional Suggestions for Listening: To be chosen from a
large number of additional works of Chopin as listed in
the text, together with piano compositions by Schumann,

CONTENTS

CHAPTER   PAGE

XXVI   Mendelssohn, Schubert, Beethoven, Mozart, Rachmani-
(*continued*)   noff, MacDowell, Grieg, Debussy, Ravel, Franck, Scriabin, Schönberg, and others.

THE VIOLIN: THE VIOLIN AND PIANO SONATA: THE TRIO:
Historical sketch of the violin; essential characteristics of
the instrument and its tone. Biography of César Franck,
with a discussion of his style and compositional idioms.
The nature of the "idée-fixe."

Essential Listening: Sonata in A Major for Violin and
Piano (Franck), with minute analysis and explanation.
The three "germinal motives" underlying the entire
sonata.

Additional Suggestions for Listening: A rather large list of
violin and piano sonatas by Bach, Beethoven, Brahms,
Corelli, Dvorák, Grieg, Handel, Mozart, Schubert, and
others. Also a list of TRIOS FOR PIANO AND STRINGS by
Mendelssohn, Mozart, Beethoven, Schubert, Tchaikovsky,
Dvorák, and Brahms.

XXVII. BACH AND THE POLYPHONIC STYLE:
THE   REFORMATION   AND   THE
BAROQUE   –   –   –   –   –   –   423

Survey of the history of the contrapuntal style of music.
Comparisons between homophonic and polyphonic
styles. Instrumental versus vocal means of muscial expression. Bach and the Reformation. Bach and the Baroque,
with extended integration and explanation of Baroque
characteristics in painting, sculpture, architecture, and
literature, and parallels with music. Descriptive analysis
of the chorale, the chorale prelude, the fugue, the Well-
Tempered Clavichord, the passacaglia, the chaconne, and
the concerto grosso.

Essential Listening: Choral preludes: "Christ Lay in the
Bonds of Death" and "Come Sweet Death"; the so-called
"Little" Fugue in G Minor, with a general explanation
of the fugue form and a specific application to this particular work; the Passacaglia in C Minor, with explanation
of its derivation and general, as well as specific, characteristics and form; the Chaconne in D Minor in its original
and orchestral versions; transcription of Bach's organ
works.

Additional Suggestions for Listening: Rather extended list of
Bach's works to choose from in the forms of the Invention
and the Prelude and Fugue. The "Kunst der Fuge," the
CONCERTO GROSSO, with brief descriptions of the six
"Brandenburg Concerti" by Bach. Additional works by
Corelli, Locatelli, Vivaldi, and Bloch, and six Concerti
Grossi by Handel.

CONTENTS

CHAPTER   PAGE

XXVIII. IMPRESSIONISM -- -- -- -- -- 453

Derivation of the term and relationship to Realism, Symbolism, Classicism, and Romanticism. Impressionism in painting, literature, and music. Impressionism in France, England, Italy, and America. Synthesis of the arts. Biography of Claude Debussy.

Essential Listening: Prelude to "The Afternoon of a Faun" by Debussy; analysis from literary and musical standpoints. Brief sketch of Maurice Ravel.

Essential Listening: Daphnis and Chloé, Suite No. 2, for orchestra, by Maurice Ravel. Programme for choreography as a ballet. Ottorino Respighi and Impressionism in Italy.

Essential Listening: "The Fountains of Rome," a symphonic poem, by Ottorino Respighi, with literary programme and musical analysis.

Additional Suggestions for Listening: In addition to other compositions by Debussy, Ravel, and Respighi, the suggested listening includes works by Manuel de Falla, Delius, Loeffler, Griffes, and Carpenter.

XXIX. EXPRESSIONISM AND OTHER MODERN TRENDS -- -- -- -- -- -- 472

Native and contemporary composers have been discussed throughout previous chapters without discrimination. The present is a part of the past as well as of the future. It is difficult to appraise contemporary works, either pro or con. Classicism, Romanticism, Realism and Symbolism co-exist now as in the past; but the manner and means of expressing them may be different. The manner of using techniques of music is as important as the musical idioms themselves—often more so. Neo-classicism, neo-romanticism, realism, and primitivism. Expressionism: integration with painting. Study of pictures by Vytlacil, Picasso, and Gris. "Abstract" and non-representational art. Surrealism; Cubism. Integration of Expressionism with literature: "Ulysses" by James Joyce, "The Hairy Ape" by Eugene O'Neill, and "Rhapsody on a Windy Night" by T. S. Eliot. Some modern techniques in music: Atonality, the twelve-tone system, the "Schönbergian Row," polytonality, poly-rhythms, modern contrapuntal techniques such as the canon, the fugue and the Canon Cancrizans. Contributors to renewed and sustaining life of art. Responsibilities of listeners; personal choices and biases inevitable and necessary.

Essential Listening: Ballet-suite, "Sacre du Printemps", by Igor Stravinsky; "Pierrot Lunaire" by Arnold Schönberg:

CONTENTS

CHAPTER   PAGE

XXIX   "Mathis der Maler Suite" by Paul Hindemith; and
(continued)   Symphony No. 4 in A Minor, Op. 63, by Jean Sibelius.

Additional Suggestions for Listening: An extended list of
works by native and foreign composers to select from as a
beginning and a foundation for building the listener's
own personal list of recordings; and a list of works to be
heard in the concert room, as well as by radio.

POSTSCRIPT TO THE LISTENER –   –   491

Acknowledgments

*It is not possible here to mention the names of all, or even many,
of the persons who have contributed to the text in its many stages of
development; but we would be ungrateful indeed if we failed to acknowledge our gratitude to President Paul Klapper of Queens College,
to whom this book is dedicated, for his sympathetic interest and support; and above all others, to my wife, Alta Morrill Stringham, for
her tireless and active aid and unceasing encouragement, without which
this book could never have been realised. To the many unnamed others
who have contributed directly or indirectly, including the students in
my classes during the past score or more years, we offer our sincere
thanks and appreciation.*

E.J.S.

Illustrations

PAGE

SINGING BOYS FROM CHOIR GALLERY. Della Robbia. (*University Prints, Newton, Mass.*) – – – – *Frontispiece*

DANCING PEASANTS. Brueghel. (*University Prints, Newton*) – – 3

PRIMAVERA. Botticelli. (*University Prints, Newton*) – – – 8

CORONATION OF NAPOLEON AND JOSEPHINE. David. (*University Prints, Newton*) – – – – – – – – 12

A MEDIEVAL MANUSCRIPT. (*Metropolitan Museum, New York*) – 20

MADONNA DELLA SEDIA. Raphael. (*University Prints, Newton*) – 24

THE FORGE. Goya. (*Copyright, Frick Museum, New York*) – – 33

THE TOMB OF GIULIANO DE' MEDICI. Michelangelo. (*Metropolitan Museum, New York*) – – – – – – – 38

THE VISITATION WITH TWO SAINTS. Piero di Cosimo. (*National Gallery of Art, Washington, D.C.*) – – – – – – 45

SCHOOL OF ATHENS. Raphael. (*University Prints, Newton*) – – 51

THE CAPITOL BUILDING IN WASHINGTON. (*University Prints, Newton*) 52

FROM THE ORIGINAL MS. OF THE SONG "HEIDENRÖSLEIN". Schubert. (*Juillard School of Music, New York*) – – – – – 61

SCENE FROM THE OPERA "AÏDA" Verdi. (*Metropolitan Opera Company*) – – – – – – – – – – 85

SCENE FROM THE OPERA "CARMEN" Bizet. (*Metropolitan Opera Company*) – – – – – – – – – 92

MILAN CATHEDRAL. From a photograph. (*University Prints, Newton*) 105

GEORGE FRIDERIC HANDEL. From a rare old print. (*New York Library*) – – – – – – – – – 108

PORTRAIT OF EDWARD MACDOWELL – – – – – 119

BALLET REHEARSAL ON STAGE. Degas. (*Metropolitan Museum of Art, New York*) – – – – – – – – 129

A SCENE FROM THE BALLET "PETROUCHKA" Stravinsky. (*The Ballet Theatre, presented by S. Hurok*) – – – – – 134

DOODLE-SACK PLAYER. Dürer. (*Metropolitan Museum of Art, New York*) – – – – – – – – – 148

A NOVEL SEATING PLAN FOR THE SYMPHONY ORCHESTRA – – 160

A CONVENTIONAL SEATING PLAN FOR THE SYMPHONY ORCHESTRA – 161

FIRST PAGE OF SCORE OF "DER FREISCHÜTZ" OVERTURE. Weber – 163

ILLUSTRATIONS

PAGE

THE PARTHENON FROM THE NORTH-WEST. From a photograph.
(*University Prints, Newton*) - - - - - - 172

ORPHEUS AND EURYDICE. Poussin. (*Metropolitan Museum of Art,
New York*) - - - - - - - - - 174

ABDUCTION OF REBECCA. Delacroix. (*Metropolitan Museum of Art,
New York*) - - - - - - - - - 177

ISLE OF THE DEAD. Böcklin. (*Metropolitan Museum of Art, New York*) 197

MICKEY MOUSE AS THE SORCERER'S APPRENTICE. From "Fantasia".
(*Walt Disney Productions*) - - - - - - 209

MIDNIGHT RIDE OF PAUL REVERE. Grant Wood. (*Permission of Mrs.
C. M. Gooch*) - - - - - - - - 213

THE GIRL IN THE PURPLE ROBE. Matisse. (*Etta Cone Collection,
Baltimore*) - - - - - - - - - 228

PORTRAIT OF GEORG GISZE. Holbein. (*University Prints, Newton*) - 264

BOSTON SYMPHONY ORCHESTRA, SERGEI KOUSSEVITSKY, CONDUCTOR.
(*Boston Symphony Orchestra*) - - - - - - 279

BIRTHPLACE OF LUDWIG VAN BEETHOVEN AT BONN (ON THE UPPER-
MOST FLOOR). (*New York Public Library*) - - - - 303

PORTRAIT OF JOHANNES BRAHMS - - - - - - 318

THE PURSUIT. Fragonard. (*Frick Museum, New York*) - - - 331

PIETÀ. Michelangelo. (*Metropolitan Museum of Art, New York*) - 333

DOUBLE VIRGINAL. (FLEMISH, ABOUT 1600). Ludovicus Grovvelus.
(*Metropolitan Museum of Art, New York*) - - - - 371

GIRL IN FEATHERED HAT, AN INK DRAWING. Matisse. (*Museum of
Modern Art, New York*) - - - - - - - 387

STRING QUARTET. Levine. (*Metropolitan Museum of Art, New York*) 392

ECSTASY OF ST. THERESA. Bernini. (*University Prints, Newton*) - 431

TOLEDO. El Greco. (*Metropolitan Museum of Art, New York*) - 433

ORIGINAL MANUSCRIPT OF AN ORGAN PRELUDE. J. S. Bach. (*New
York Public Library*) - - - - - - - 436

ROUEN CATHEDRAL. Photograph. (*University Prints, Newton*) - 455

ROUEN CATHEDRAL. Monet. (*Metropolitan Museum of Art, New
York*) - - - - - - - - - - 456

NOCTURNE, A CANAL IN HOLLAND. Whistler. (*Freer Gallery, Washington, D.C.*) - - - - - - - - 462

STILL LIFE WITH FRUIT. Vytlacil. (*Permission of the Artist*) - 482

THE THREE MUSICIANS. Picasso. (*Paul Rosenberg & Co.*) - - 483

STILL LIFE. Gris. (*Museum of Modern Art, New York*) - - 487

Chapter One

⊚∿∿∿∿∿∿∿∿∿∿∿∿∿⊚

Music and the Dance

SINCE music does not attempt to reproduce the exact shapes and images of the real world in the tangible way that literature and painting do, many persons have come to think of the art of sound as being remote and divorced from life. As a matter of fact, from its very beginnings in savage and primitive society, music has been an integral part of the daily life of the individual and the group. Whether to express triumph over the enemy or thanksgiving for the harvest, the praise of heroes or the pleasures of the hunt, religious feelings, incantation against evil spirits, tenderness for the beloved or lament for the dead, music is called upon to convey and at the same time to heighten the emotional side of man's experiences. Let us, by way of introduction, examine some of these uses of music, and by so doing perceive more clearly the relation of the art of music to our daily lives and its place in society as a whole.

In all times and places music has been a necessary part of the dance. On the one hand, it serves the immediate purpose of keeping the dancers in step. More important psychologically, it helps to create and sustain that mood of joy and physical well-being that finds its natural expression in rhythmic bodily movement. Wherever people come together for social purposes they require music to create the proper festive atmosphere. Naturally, the music differs with each country and century, reflecting the tastes and needs of the particular social environment. But the basic emotional responses are more or less the same everywhere.

We may begin our study and our first listening by playing a *popular dance record*, any one of the current hits. How eloquently the abrupt rhythms, the spicy harmonies and instrumental effects express the feverish tempo of modern life! This is the music of a sophisticated urban culture, breathing an air of restless gaiety and movement, awakening in the listener an almost irresistible physical response. One is immediately struck by the fact that in this modern equivalent of folk-dance music, rhythm is immeasurably more important than melody. From the first pulsation of the drums and double basses, we are in a world of ecstatic rhythm. Clarinet, saxophone, and trumpet alternate and unite in dazzling improvisations that completely wipe out the original tune. Only the harmonies and rhythm remain to make the blood run faster and the muscles flex more vigorously.

The traditional folk dance makes its appeal in somewhat simpler fashion. Try listening, as our second essential study, to our own *Turkey in the Straw*, as arranged by David Guion. The melodies go along merrily, with clusters of rapid notes and clearly marked accents, in a manner dear to generations of village fiddlers. This music, too, conjures up a definite way of life: the boisterous jollity of hard-working agricultural folk, the barn dance on Saturday night, with much clapping of hands and stamping of feet. Before long you will find yourself beating time, with a "down-up" of the hand or foot, in what is the simplest of rhythmic patterns: ONE-two, ONE-two—an accented or strong beat alternating with an unaccented or weak beat (the musical equivalent of the pattern we get when we stand marking time with LEFT-right, LEFT-right). This rhythmic grouping is known as two beats in a measure, or duple metre.

The lilting waltzes of Johann Strauss (1825-1899) sing of still another milieu, of a nineteenth-century dream city that has become the symbol of an era. Listen to his *Beautiful Blue Danube*. How well these flowing melodies combine urbanity and tenderness, gaiety and longing, the spirit of the dance with the nostalgic! Again you will find yourself beating time with the music. But the rhythmic movement is broader here, more flowing. This is waltz time, to which we can count ONE-two-three, ONE-two-three: a pattern consisting of an accented beat followed by two unaccented beats, giving us three beats in a measure, or triple metre. (This is our third essential listening project.)

Since dancing and singing are such deep-rooted human impulses and are among all people so close to the life of the folk, it was natural that each nation should develop its own musical idiom, as characteristic as its spoken language. The great composers found inspiration in the rich literature of native folk song and attempted in their art to capture and express the spirit of their homelands. The national dances that they wrote vary in mood from gentle melancholy to joyous abandon, but all breathe the spirit of the folk, the vigorous peasant rhythms, the melodic richness and pungent flavour of the countryside. And all speak the simple language of the heart, which knows no barriers of nation, race, or time.

Fine examples of this folk-dance genre within the literature of "composed art music," to distinguish it from the traditional type,

Dancing Peasants   *Brueghel*

are the SLAVONIC DANCES of Anton Dvořák, of which we should now hear the first, that in E minor. Dvořák (1841-1904), himself of peasant stock, was an ardent nationalist and stands in European music, together with his compatriot and guide, Bedrich Smetana (1824-1884), as the voice of the Czech nation—musically speaking. (This is to be used as the fourth essential listening project of the chapter.)

The *Slavonic Dance No. 1*, originally written for piano duet, has become very popular in the orchestral version as well as in Fritz Kreisler's arrangement for violin solo. The opening section brings us a poignant melody in triple metre, with that undercurrent of melancholy so often found in the folk music of Central and Southeastern Europe, and with a strong Gipsy colouring. (As in Hungary and Rumania, the Gipsies left their imprint on the musical idiom of Bohemia.)

In the middle section the mood brightens; the pace becomes animated. A playful theme appears, followed by a broad lyrical melody, serene and folklike in character. Then we return to the sombre mood of the opening theme. This music has warmth and forthrightness and is rooted—as its composer wished it to be—in the soil of his native land.

Notice how clear-cut is the contrast in mood between the opening section and the two themes in the middle part. Having achieved a pleasant diversity of effect, the composer returns to his original melody, which balances and unifies the structural scheme of the composition.

A popular dance form of the eighteenth-century composers was the *Rondo*, based upon the old French round dance (much like our ring-around-the-rosy type of dance), in which the leader's tune alternates with that sung by the dancing ring. This form might be basically described as A^1-B-A^2-C-A^3, and so on, although many variants are possible. The distinguishing feature is the recurrence throughout of the main, or first, theme, separated by episodes, or contrasting material. An excellent variant of this type is the old French rondo, *Amaryllis* (Ghys). Haydn, Mozart, Beethoven, and countless other composers have used this type of dance form in their symphonies, chamber music, and other works. Listen to *Amaryllis* and try to recognize the principal theme when it recurs.[1]

---

[1] Mozart and Haydn are generally referred to as the two outstanding masters of the "Classical Period." In this connection it might not be amiss to clear up some misconceptions surrounding the use of the word *classical*. In colloquial speech, the term is generally used to denote art music as opposed to popular music, or "jazz." For the musician, *classical* refers to an art style distinguished from *romantic*, the classical spirit seeking to recapture the qualities of serenity, universality, restraint, and perfection of form associated with the art of Greece in classical antiquity. The historian often applies the term "Classical Period" to the second half of the eighteenth century when the spirit of classicism was very much to the fore in European art, as distinct from the "Romantic Period," which is generally considered to have begun after the French Revolution and to have lasted for the greater part of the nineteenth century. (For a detailed discussion of the two styles and the two periods, see Chapter XII.) The schematic phrase design of *Amaryllis* is A-A-B-A-A-C-C-B-C-A-A.

(See also Chapter V, page 52.) (This is the fifth essential listening project of the chapter.)

What Mozart and Haydn did for the dance of the Classical Period, the great Johann Sebastian Bach (1685-1750) did in the early part of the eighteenth century. In his DANCE SUITES, as in those of his contemporaries, we find characteristic dance rhythms of the various nations of Europe brought together. There is the *Allemande*, or German dance, a moderately slow movement in quadruple metre; the French *Courante*, which as its name implies contains running passages and simple rhythms; the stately *Sarabande*, of Spanish or Moorish ancestry, in slow triple metre; the *Bourrée* and *Branle*, rollicking French peasant dances in vigorous duple metre; the *Polonaise*, a martial Polish dance, almost like a march, in a broad, strongly accented triple metre; the dignified but vivacious *Gavotte*, a French court dance with four beats to a measure; and the lively Italian *Giga* (*Gigue*), allied to the English *Jig*, with three or six rapidly paced beats to a measure. Let us

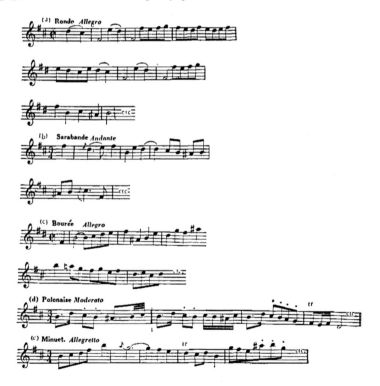

listen to Bach's *Suite No. 2 in B minor*, for flute and strings, which contains a rondo, sarabande, bourrée, polonaise, and minuet. The suite opens with an overture, and ends with a section called *Badinerie*, which, as the title implies, is full of playfulness and mischief. Here is merry, heart-warming music, rich with the spirit of the dance. If time does not permit the playing of all the records of this suite, select accordingly. (This is the sixth, and last, listening suggestion for this chapter.)

ADDITIONAL SUGGESTIONS FOR LISTENING

The "masters" often wrote in idealized dance forms—that is, they sought to capture the spirit of the dance in art music rather than to create music for actual dancing. Thus, Frederic Chopin (1810-1849), one of the most distinctive of the Romanticists, transformed the rhythms of the waltz into something altogether personal and subtle, what the critic, James Huneker, called "a dance of the spirit rather than of the body." Listen to his *Waltz in C Sharp Minor*, a poetic idealization of this dance form, tinged with gentle sadness. Notice the clearly defined sectional construction, similar to that found in the *Slavonic Dance*, each section introducing a melody and mood of its own. The hauntingly lovely opening theme is followed by a caressing melody in running notes. Then comes a broad, flowing theme of quiet lyricism and serenity. By introducing new melodic material, Chopin sustains our interest and achieves a pleasantly varied effect. By repeating the old, at judicious intervals, he gives coherence and unity to his structural scheme, a sense of orderly and symmetrical arrangement.

In *Golliwog's Cakewalk*, Claude Debussy (1862-1918) makes delightful use of the rollicking American dance rhythm that was popular at the turn of the century. The piece was written for piano, one of a set of five known as THE CHILDREN'S CORNER. Golliwog is an imaginary figure who, in the middle of the dance, becomes romantic, at which point the composer introduces with sly satire the opening notes of the love theme from Wagner's TRISTAN AND ISOLDE. Save for this brief interlude, the music struts and bounces along with gusto—and cleverness.

Also listen to the "Rhumba" movement from Harl McDonald's *Symphony No. 2.*

Rhythm: The Heartbeat of Music

The compositions we have just heard differ in style and content, but they all share certain basic elements. There is the melody, or tune, which caught and held our attention, and the harmony, the chords that accompany and support the melody. There is the steady pulse of the rhythm (to which some of the listeners may have responded by beating time quite unconsciously with the music). Each performing instrument has a distinctive tone colour, which either blends with that of the other instruments sounding simultaneously or stands out by itself. The various themes alternate, as we saw, in accordance with a definite structural pattern. In addition, the music grows softer or louder at various times, and travels at a faster or slower pace. Let us begin with the element that plays so decisive a part in all dance music—the rhythm.

"In the beginning was rhythm," Johannes Brahms is reported to have said. Unquestionably, rhythm is one of the basic elements in music, and one with universal appeal. One has only to watch people fall into step or nod their heads as the band plays to realize how irresistible is its power. In primitive society, the rhythmic beating of the drums takes on a ritualistic or magical potency. Some writers on music go so far as to ascribe the origin of the art to the stamping, clapping, and beating that accompanied the work and play activities, the harvesting, threshing, ceremonial dances, and sacrificial rites of the primitive tribes. In any case, when we hear a haphazard succession of sounds coming at irregular intervals, we remain more or less indifferent. But as soon as these sounds are arranged in a regular sequence of accented and unaccented beats, repeated over and over, we become aware of a rhythmic pattern and respond accordingly. We begin to expect the accent in a definite place, and receive a pleasant sense of security from having our expectation fulfilled. Rhythm is the heartbeat, the pulse, of the music. The word in Greek means "flow" or "flowing." Rhythm may be defined as the element of music that regulates its forward movement through the regular recurrence of accented and unaccented beats in a pattern.

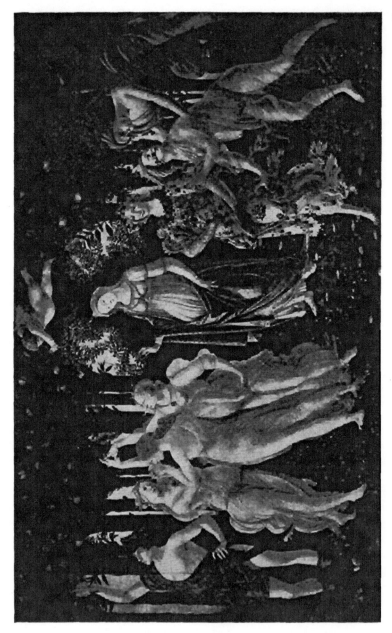

Primavera

Actually, rhythm is not restricted to music. It enters into painting and all the arts of design, where the subtle repetition of a decorative pattern reinforces the relationship of the parts to the whole, balancing and unifying the composition. The great painters were masters of spatial rhythm. See (on page 8) in the "Primavera" of Sandro Botticelli (1447-1510), how subtle are the internal rhythms uniting the individual figures and the groups to the total design. Within the rectangular framework, the movement is carried in a vast oval from the figure of the wind on the right, along the curve of the trees, to the cherub on top and down again along the raised arm of the figure on the left. Within this oval are three smaller ones taking in the two groups of figures arranged symmetrically on either side, and the central figure of Spring, framed so dramatically by the arching trees and the cherub overhead. Notice how rhythmically the movement flows from one end of the canvas to the other, from the male figure on the left, along the billowing draperies and raised arms of the nymphs, curving gently over the central figure, and sweeping on to the group at the right. Synchronized with this movement is the vertical rhythm of the trees in the background and the positions of the individual figures, the whole melting in a harmonious interplay of rhythmic design.

Rhythm figures no less prominently in the art of poetry, where the arrangement of the lines in metrical patterns adds a strange power to the music of the words. Through these patterns poets have achieved a marvellous diversity of effect and have mastered the most subtle musical cadences of which language is capable. The simpler metrical combinations are familiar to all. The sonnets of Shakespeare are superb examples of the *iambic pentameter*, two beats to a measure, accent on the second, five measures (or feet, as we call them in scanning poetry) in each line:

> Shall *I* com*pare* thee *to* a *sum*mer's *day?*
> Thou *art* more *love*ly *and* more *tem*pe*rate.*

Robert Browning in his "Song" used two beats to a measure, accent on the first, four measures to a line (*trochee*):

> *Nay* but *you*, who *do* not *love* her,
> *Is* she *not* pure *gold*, my *mis*tress?

Three beats to a measure, accent on the first, three measures to a line, characterize Longfellow's "Evangeline" (*dactyl*):

> *This* is the *for*est prim*æv*al,
> The *mur*muring *pines* and the *hem*locks.

Three beats to a measure, accent on the third, mark Byron's "Sennacharib" (*anapaest*):

> The A*ssy*rian came *down* like a *wolf* on the *fold;*
> And his *co*horts were *gleam*ing in *pur*ple and *gold.*

We see, then, that in all ages, no matter in what medium he works, man derives untold pleasure and satisfaction from the simple, orderly arrangement of the accented and unaccented pulsations upon which rhythm depends. In the ideal world that he has created for himself through art, these pulsations assume the importance of a vital force, a dynamic principle. They constitute the very heartbeat of the art of music.

Chapter Two

Music and Ceremony

MUSIC plays its part not only in moments of festivity and recreation, but also at occasions when a more lofty mood, whether of triumph, exaltation, or grief, is appropriate. From earliest times men have relied on music to heighten the impressiveness of ceremonies marking the important events of their existence as individuals and as members of the social group.

The military march, with its stirring trumpet and drum passages, its simple melodies and steady beat, has always served to arouse a festive and martial mood. An example of what this type of music can become in the hands of a great artist is the *Marche Militaire* by Franz Schubert (1797-1828). The spirited opening theme, in strongly accented duple metre, is vibrant with energy and movement.

Notice the contrast with the quieter middle section, where the music takes on grace and lightness, after which it returns (in simple, symmetrical, A-B-A formation) to the opening theme.[1] Notice, too, that the music seems to be laid out in simple symmetrical sections, a type of architecture highly appropriate to "outdoor" music.

The ceremonial march often creates an effect of great dignity, pomp, and patriotic fervour. For an example of this type, play Edward Elgar's *Pomp and Circumstance*, which has become almost

---

[1] This A-B-A basic formation may be taken to mean, for the moment, first a statement of the principal theme, then an appearance of a contrasting section, and finally the restatement of the main theme after the contrast. Mutations and adaptations of this form will be noted in subsequent pages.

11

a national march for Britain. Marches of this kind are most often in a rather slowly paced four-four time, which imparts a broad span to the measure. For a good example of the more rapid (quick-step) type of march, listen to *Stars and Stripes Forever*, by our own "March King," John Philip Sousa. Such marches are likely to be in a fast two-four or six-eight time, with the last mentioned given only two beats to a measure.

Coronation of Napoleon and Josephine   *David*

The march, like the dance, depends upon rhythmic bodily movement, upon music with a strong pulse and with catchy melodies that are easy to whistle and hum. March and dance come together in the broad triple metre of the *Polonaise*, the stately processional dance in which the Polish nobles filed past the throne of their kings. Chopin's *Polonaise Militaire* brings us this march dance in its proudest and most military mood. Notice here, too, the layout of the music in simple symmetrical sections and the effective contrast between the brusque opening theme and the broad second theme.[2]

---

[2] The smooth, connected style that we heard in the second theme, where every tone melted into the next, is known as *legato*, in contrast to *staccato*, a short, sharp, and disconnected manner of playing the notes.

For ceremonial music on the grand scale, we turn to the *Triumphal March* from Giuseppe Verdi's opera, AÏDA. Here is the perfect setting for pomp and pageantry as trumpets and drums roar a welcome to the victorious Radames, general of the Egyptians, and his army at the gates of Thebes. Note particularly the effect of the rich massive chords at the opening, the brilliant tone colour of the brass in the second theme, and the imposing effect of the melody supported by a full running accompaniment in the final section.[3]

Music figures no less prominently in ceremonies of a more personal character. The *Wedding March* from Wagner's LOHENGRIN has become part of the heritage of all nations. Listen to this in the *Bridal Chorus* version, as it contains beautiful choral writing.

The steady duple metre (a metre divisible by two) has nobility and breadth. When played in the correct tempo, this music is an

---

[3] For supplementary processional music of similar character, listen to the majestic *War March of the Priests* from Mendelssohn's ATHALIE, the *Grand March* from Wagner's TANNHÄUSER (Entrance of the Knights), or the *Coronation March* from Giacomo Meyerbeer's LE PROPHÈTE.

exalted, fiery processional, instead of the languid, drawn-out distortion that too often is heard at weddings.[4]

As universal in scope is the sombre music that accompanies the rites for the dead. Chopin's magnificent *Funeral March* is known all over the world.

How eloquently the solemn opening chords create the atmosphere of grief! The music surges with despair. Then, as if emotion had worn itself out, comes the benign legato melody of the middle part, a song of resignation and tenderness. But the surcease is brief and we are plunged back again into the darkly quivering chords of the opening. Here indeed music says all the things that language would, but cannot.

From the structural standpoint, it is hardly necessary to call attention to the A-B-A form, contrast between the chord theme and the legato melody of the middle part, and the spacious quadruple metre.[5]

ADDITIONAL SUGGESTIONS FOR LISTENING

As in the case of the dance, the diverse moods of ceremonial music found expression, on a more abstract plane, in the symphonies of the great composers. One of the noblest of all funeral marches is the slow movement from Beethoven's THIRD SYMPHONY, the *Eroica*. The simple, marchlike theme, announced by the violins, has that quality of intense feeling and sublimity of expression which is truly Beethovenian. The movement sweeps on in lonely grandeur until we come to the second theme, which is rich in courage and humanity. The themes are worked

[4] Different in mood is the gay and fanciful *Wedding March* from Mendelssohn's MIDSUMMER NIGHT'S DREAM that so well captures the spirit of Shakespeare's fantasy. Other examples of this type of ceremonial music that you should be acquainted with are the *Norwegian Bridal Procession* of Grieg, and the *Bridal Cortège* from Nicholas Rimsky-Korsakoff's fairy opera COQ D'OR.

[5] The essential listening for this chapter includes: *Marche Militaire* by Schubert, *Pomp and Circumstance* by Elgar, *Stars and Stripes Forever* by Sousa, *Polonaise Militaire* by Chopin, *Triumphal March* from AÏDA by Verdi, *Wedding March* by Wagner, and the *Funeral March* by Chopin. The other works mentioned may be considered optional.

out in rich symphonic style, steadily mounting in intensity. Then the
sorrowful first theme re-enters. If the Chopin *Funeral March* is an outpouring of grief for an individual, the slow movement of the *Eroica* is a
lamentation for all mankind.

The mood of the triumphal march has been sublimated, with memorable effect, in the third movement of Tchaikovsky's SIXTH SYMPHONY,
the *Pathétique*. The violins and woodwinds bustle about in the mazes of
a complex orchestral web. There are traces of dancelike gaiety, which
float across the scene for an instant and disappear. Presently a march
tune in four-four time enters unobtrusively on the oboe:

The music gathers strength, the theme is passed from one instrument
to the other; it grows steadily from its modest beginnings, becomes a
swift, driving force. Now it achieves its full splendour, bursting forth
from the brass in shattering clarion call, a feverish march movement
that sweeps all obstacles before it, a veritable tornado of clashing cymbals and drums.

Melody and Harmony

If rhythm is the heartbeat of music, melody is its soul. It is the
melody that projects much of the emotional message of the music
to the usual listener; it is the melody that he will most likely
remember, and sing or whistle with all the joy of recollection.
True, in modern sophisticated dance music the rhythm seems at
times to overshadow the melody. True also that, in contemporary
music, long, lyrical melody no longer plays quite so important a
part as it did in the music of the Classic and Romantic periods.
Despite all this, as far as most music lovers are concerned, nothing
quite equals the power of melody to captivate the human heart.

c

Actually, there is no need to contrast or separate rhythm and melody, since the two most often exist together in the music. As we sing the melody, we are at the same time responding to its rhythm. If we change the rhythm, the effect of the melody is changed as well.

Melody may be defined as a succession of musical tones arranged in a meaningful pattern. We do not "get" the melody until we have grasped the meaning of the pattern. We saw, in the case of rhythm, that haphazard or isolated beats bear no special significance for us. It is only when these beats are arranged in definite, easily recognizable patterns that they evoke in us an emotional response. So, too, with melody. A single tone tells us little. It is only when one tone leads to another, and still another, when each takes on a definite relation to the pattern as a whole, that a melody assumes fullest significance. The tones rise and fall, communicating meanings to us that far transcend the power of words, and can only be expressed through and by themselves.

In this process, everything depends upon the ease with which the listener grasps the connection of the tones, the meaningfulness of the pattern. Folk songs and popular tunes usually present no great problem. The pattern more often than not is so simple and obvious that everybody gets it after the first or second hearing. Other melodies may be more sophisticated; they demand more expertness on the part of the listener. Still others are like those forbidding individuals whom one has to meet again and again before they will open up and reveal their true characters. How often it happens that, through repeated hearings, we grasp the significance of a melodic pattern which in the beginning altogether eluded us! As we continue to listen to great music, we broaden our experience in grasping tonal relationships, we become more and more sensitive to their implications, until a melody of Brahms or Debussy may come to be as lucid and comprehensible as one by Stephen Foster.

We have called melody the soul of music. Harmony is its body, its substance. The harmony supports the melody and serves as a background for it. Sometimes the two are as one. Harmony, in its simplest form, consists of chords; these are clusters of tones sounded simultaneously within the rhythmic pattern, and providing an accompaniment for the melody—the "um-pah-pah" that the left hand sounds while the right hand plays the tune, or that the banjo player thrums on his instrument while he sings. Notice, in the following example—the first phrase of *Long, Long Ago*—how the cluster effect of the chords and the curvilinear quality of the melody are indicated in the two staves of adapted piano music:

Just as in a painting, the background harmonizes with and brings out the figures, sometimes even revealing them in a new light, so harmony colours and enriches the melody.

Various chords have distinctive personalities of their own. Some, sweetly harmonious, give an effect of rest and fulfilment. Others are harshly dissonant, clangorous, restlessly seeking completion. There are chords softly sensuous and caressing—how well Wagner knew their secret!—or grim with foreboding, or feverish and unstable. For the moment, suffice it to say that harmony not only adds support and third dimension to melody, but also, through its chords, reinforces the rhythm. We saw at the beginning of this section that in our system of music melody does not exist without rhythm. Nor does it exist without harmony, either actual or implied. Even when we whistle or sing only the melodic line, we may "hear" the harmonic background in our imagination.

Like melody, rhythm, tone colour, and form, harmony has a special contribution to make to the total musical effect. In a love song, where the melody holds the centre of the stage, the harmony is likely to remain discreetly in the background. In the dance, where rhythm is important, the harmony comes to the fore as thumping chords. In religious music, the swelling harmonies of organ and choir attain prime importance in creating the lofty, devotional mood.

Chapter Three

Music and Religion

OF ALL the ceremonies in human society, those concerned with religious worship are the most profound. They express the depths of man's noblest and sublimest emotions. Above all else, religious worship is a universal expression of man's devotion to the ideals he envisages in his fellow men and his God.

From time immemorial art has been the handmaiden of religion, shedding all its lustre upon the rites through which men worship. Architecture contributed the majestic cathedral with its vaulted arches soaring gracefully heavenward. The greatest painters and sculptors vied with one another to decorate the altarpieces and chapels. Master craftsmen gave their best in stained glass, in chalices of gold, in tapestries and vestments. In this atmosphere of splendour, a solemn ritual developed, designed to induce in the worshipper a mood of religious exaltation and to turn his thoughts to the fundamental problems of his spiritual life. It is hardly necessary to add that, in this union of the arts, music occupied a very important place. Indeed, because of its power over the hearts of men, music became one of the indispensable components of the divine service. And some of the most sublime measures ever written were inspired by religious feeling. Music serves either to create a mood or to be expressive of a mood that already exists.

Perhaps the most universal expression of the religious emotion is to be found in the hymn, which has become as much a part of our cultural heritage as the folk song. Since hymns were intended for performance by the entire congregation, they had to be tunes that could be easily remembered and easily sung; they had to function within a limited vocal range, to avoid rhythmic complexities and wide skips, to reflect faithfully the devotional spirit of the poetry, and to follow the metrical cadence of the words in so direct a fashion that the congregation would stay together in the singing. One has only to recall *A Mighty Fortress Is Our God*,

Christ Lay in the Bonds of Death, Jesu Joy of Man's Desiring, or *Lead Kindly Light* and *Onward Christian Soldiers* to realize that the restrictions we have enumerated did not hamper the form, but on the contrary aided it. What emerged was a body of enduring melody, profoundly expressive, that summed up the hopes and visions of many generations of men. Of the hymns just mentioned, it is suggested that you listen now to *A Mighty Fortress Is Our God,* which served as a battle hymn of the Reformation.[1]

Notice that the melody proceeds in short units and then pauses, as though to draw breath. We call these melodic units *phrases,* and the stopping places are the *cadences.* It goes without saying that when words are set to music the melody is moulded, as it were, to the metrical patterns of the verse, so that both become indissoluble parts of a greater whole. Notice, too, that the rhythm moves in regular pulses, and the chords supporting the hymn are simple but sonorous and full-bodied, as befits music of steadfastness and solemn purpose. Let us consider several types of chants and hymns.

Of remote antiquity are the Hebrew chants, a living art in the synagogue handed down from one generation to the next for well over 2,000 years. Naturally, these melodies underwent many changes as they assimilated various foreign elements. From its birthplace in the Orient, the Hebrew chant has retained some characteristics akin to those of the religious song of the Arabic world; but, at the same time, through the constant interchange between Greek and Hebrew culture at the beginnings of the Christian era, it undoubtedly assimilated many elements of Greek music. To these were added, centuries later, the influences stemming from close contact with Western European culture. Listen to the *Kaddish* (Chant for the Dead), a particularly impressive example of Hebrew religious song. Better known is *Kol Nidrei,* the traditional melody that the Jews of Spain sang during the terrors of the Inquisition in the reign of Ferdinand and Isabella, and that has become part of the solemn service for the Day of Atonement.

The Christian service, which owes much to Hebrew and Greek

---

[1] Or use the *Doxology* on page 425. Essential listening for this chapter includes: *A Mighty Fortress is Our God;* Jewish Chant *Kaddish; Kyrie, Gloria,* or *Tenebrae factae sunt* from Gregorian Chants; *Sanctus* and *Gloria* from Pope Marcellus Mass by Palestrina; Chorale: *Jesu, Joy of Man's Desiring,* by Bach; *Credo, Crucifixus, Et Resurrexit,* and *Sanctus* from Bach's B-Minor Mass—reduce to the Sanctus only if necessary. Other works mentioned are optional.

A Medieval Manuscript

cultures, naturally combined the heritage of both in its early liturgical chants. These religious songlike expressions evidenced themselves in many styles and directions until codified in the latter part of the sixth century under the official ægis of Pope Gregory the Great (540-604), and they remained the predominant form and style of European sacred music throughout the Middle Ages; yes, they have continued quite unchanged right into our own day and are still a regular part of church services of the Roman faith (and others too) the world over. The Gregorian chants, as we now identify them, are, like those of ancient Greek and Hebrew styles, of a pure vocal line without harmonic accompaniment and are usually sung in unison. In the words of one of the greatest authorities on the chant, Dom André Mocquereau, "... it appeals to what is highest in the soul; its beauty, its nobility, come from the fact that it borrows nothing, or as little as possible, from the world of the senses."

The Gregorian chant is based upon a melodic and rhythmic system quite different from the church tunes of our own time. Listen to some characteristic examples—the *Kyrie* and *Gloria* from the *Ordinary of the Mass*, or the *Tenebrae factae sunt*, which describes the death of Christ on the Cross.[2] This music has about it a strange quality of otherworldness, of timelessness, of spirituality. (Note the apparently unmetrical and asymmetrical character of these old chants.)

From approximately 1200 to 1700, composers of Western Europe experimented with combining two or more voices, or melodic lines, simultaneously. From these early beginnings an art style, that was both religious and secular, grew and reigned supreme in Western Europe for centuries. Some contemporary composers find inspiration in this old style. The art of combining several independent voice lines into a whole is called the art of *polyphony* (from the Greek *poly*, "many," and *phonē*, "sound"). Polyphonic music, or as it is often called, contrapuntal music, is distinguished from the prevailing style of more recent times, *homophonic*, or monodic music, in which an individual melody stands out from its harmonic, or supporting, background. (See also page 424.)

[2] The reader is advised to listen to the records of Gregorian chants prepared by the monks of the Abbey of Saint-Pierre de Solesmes and issued by Victor as *Masterpiece Album M-87*.

A long line of composers explored the manifold possibilities of combining many voices and developed an amazing technique that could weave as many as thirty or more vocal parts into an intricate polyphonic composition. One of the greatest of these masters of church music in the polyphonic style was Giovanni Pierluigi Palestrina (1524-1594), who, in the period of the Counter-Reformation, brought this type of music to its highest perfection. It is with good reason that the period of Palestrina and of his great contemporary, Orlando Lassus (1532-1594), has gone down in music history as the "golden age of choral music."

Now listen to the *Sanctus* and *Gloria* from the MASS FOR POPE MARCELLUS, by Palestrina. Note how smoothly the vocal texture flows along, how beautifully the different voices are blended and contrasted. There is in the music of Palestrina the note of true religious fervour, of contemplation and purity, that marks it as one of the high points in the history of religious art.

In the early sixteenth century Luther, in carrying through his religious reforms, substituted for the intricate polyphonic church music that could be performed only by a choir of highly trained singers, simple hymn tunes with texts in the vernacular that the whole congregation was able to sing—the *chorales*. In the course of two centuries a rich choral literature sprang from the very roots of the religious life of the nation. This was Bach's heritage. Upon it he reared the structure of his art. The spirit of the chorale permeates his church cantatas, chorale preludes, hymns and sacred songs, and receives its ultimate expression in the ST. JOHN and ST. MATTHEW PASSIONS.

By a *cantata* is meant a choral work of comparatively modest dimensions, either sacred—in which case it is generally intended as part of the church service—or secular, as a short lyric drama or story adapted to music but not intended to be acted. Bach, as Cantor of St. Thomas' Church, wrote cantatas for each Sunday of the church year, besides works for festivals and special occasions. The cantata was generally named after the chorale upon which it was based, and consisted of several sections for solo voices, with ensemble numbers and choruses interspersed, accompanied by organ and groups of instruments. The form was extremely flexible, and varied with the particular resources at the disposal of the composer. Passages from the Bible and religious texts were strung together to illustrate or expand upon different aspects of the thought embodied in the chorale text. The spirit was mystical and prayerful. Bach's settings of the familiar chorale tunes, as well as his presentation of original melodies, are masterpieces of imagination, his bold harmonies and rich counterpoint revealing the beauties of the famous chorale, *Jesu Joy of Man's Desiring*, from CANTATA No. 147, with its quality of naïve joy and faith.[3]

From the *preluding* (extemporization) of the organist, when he announced to the congregation the chorale to be sung, arose the art of the instrumental chorale prelude, in which the tune of the hymn to be sung served as the basis for the improvisation.[4]

Most imposing of Bach's religious works, in grandeur and scale of conception, are the PASSION ACCORDING TO ST. MATTHEW, which we shall consider later, and the B-MINOR MASS. Although the Mass was written to the Latin text of the Catholic service— Bach sent the *Kyrie* and *Gloria* to the Catholic Elector of Saxony, whom he hoped to make his patron—the music is quite Lutheran in outlook and spirit. Indeed, some of the material was borrowed by Bach from his earlier Protestant masses and cantatas. In addition, the use of an orchestral accompaniment makes the *Mass* impractical to perform during the regular church service. It is, in reality, a festival piece.

The B-MINOR MASS represents the apex of the polyphonic tradition which had nurtured generations of church composers, and which had received such polished expression two centuries before in the music of Palestrina. Yet, beside the "seraphic

---

[3] It is earnestly suggested that the listener hear *both* the original choral form of the chorale and the instrumental version.
[4] See Chapter XXVII, for fuller exposition of chorale prelude.

Madonna Della Sedia *Raphael*

harmonies" of the Roman master so close in spirit to the smiling madonnas of Raphael, the B-Minor Mass appears stern and rugged, a song of strength attained through suffering and grief. The sorrow of Christ, the soul tormented and longing for union with God, salvation and life eternal—those were the issues that fired the imagination of Bach to the crowning glory of his art. Listen to the soaring phrases of the *Credo*, the mournful *Crucifixus*, in which the reiterated descent of the bass and the motive of grief in the strings give a vivid tone painting of Christ's suffering on the cross, the joyous and hopeful *Et Resurrexit*, and the massive polyphonic architecture of the *Sanctus*. The music throughout is an eloquent expression of deep religious feeling and conviction. (Reduce to the *Sanctus* if time is limited.)

ADDITIONAL SUGGESTIONS FOR LISTENING[5]

So profound an impulse as the religious naturally made itself felt in many works of the great composers that were not intended for use with any actual church service. Although Richard Wagner (1813-1883) wrote for the opera house, certainly the *Prelude* to Lohengrin, depicting the descent of the Holy Grail from Heaven, breathes a spirit of devotion and faith. Celestial harmonies steal upon the air from out the highest register of the strings. Gradually the music descends, growing ever richer in colour; the crescendo builds unerringly toward an overpowering climax; now the Grail theme is intoned in all the sonorities of the brass, as though to envelop the worshipper in its splendour. Then the music withdraws and fades away.

Religious legend receives an even more mystical expression in Wagner's *Prelude* to his last work, the festival drama, Parsifal. Here the motives symbolize the Last Supper of Christ and the Apostles, the Lance that pierced the side of the Saviour, the Good Friday Spell, the Grail theme based upon the *Dresden Amen*, and the powerful Faith theme. Wagner believed that art could have as purifying an influence on the souls of men as religion, and that the music drama could achieve the same spirituality as the rites of a church. The *Prelude* to Parsifal is a convincing example of his attempts in this direction.

Among symphonic movements, the *Finale* of Mendelssohn's "Reformation" Symphony builds up to a stirring climax on the Lutheran hymn *A Mighty Fortress Is Our God*. Mendelssohn was the composer who rescued Bach from the neglect into which the old master had fallen in the half century after his death. It was fitting that in this

[5] Further discussion of religious music may be found in Chapter VIII.

FIFTH "REFORMATION" SYMPHONY Mendelssohn should have returned
to the chorale which had been so vital an inspiration to the composer
whom he admired above all others.

And certainly one of the most eloquent expressions of the religious
spirit—using the term in its broadest sense—in all music is to be found
in the exalted setting of Schiller's "Ode to Joy" in the *Finale* of
Beethoven's last symphony, the *Ninth*:

Praise to Joy, the God-descended Daughter of Elysium!
Ray of mirth and rapture blended, Goddess, to thy shrine we come . . .
O ye millions, I embrace ye, with a kiss for all the world.
Brothers, o'er yon starry sphere surely dwells a loving Father.
O ye millions, kneel before Him; World, dost feel thy Maker near?
Seek Him o'er yon starry sphere, o'er the stars enthroned, adore Him![6]

Volume and Speed as Elements in Emotional Expression
Dynamics and Tempo

We have seen how the composer uses rhythm, melody, and
harmony to achieve his musical effects. Closely associated with
these is *dynamics* (from the Greek *dynamis*, "power" or "strength"),
the element of power and volume in music, of softness or loudness
of tone. From the whisper of the muted violin or of a single voice
to the thunderous jubilation of the *Et Resurrexit* chorus of the
B-MINOR MASS, music is capable of innumerable gradations, each
producing a different emotional effect. Sorrow, joy, mystery,
triumph—every emotion expressed in music calls for its appropriate dynamic scheme. Needless to say, the effect of the other
musical elements is interwoven with the dynamics in closest
degree. If we were to play the *Triumphal March* from AÏDA, in a
subdued tone, the entire effect would be changed, even if melody,
harmony, and rhythm remained the same.

The broader emotional implications of loudness and softness are
fairly obvious. A mood of triumph, power, or jubilation generally
calls for brilliant sonority and volume. Sadness, dreamy lyricism,
or introspection usually calls for subtle shadings within a more subdued range of volume. The emotional meaning of the music automatically imposes the proper dynamic scheme.

[6] The English translation generally used in performances in this country is by
Natalia Macfarren, published by Novello and Company Ltd., London (New York: the
H. W. Gray Company, agents). Printed by permission.

In ordinary speech, the word *dynamic* pertains to energy, accent, and action. It is evident that in an art such as music, which moves forward steadily through time, the driving force and energy behind that forward movement are of paramount importance. For this reason rhythm, which regulates the forward flow of the music, is so basic a factor in music. But rhythm depends upon the recurrence of accent; and accent depends upon playing certain beats louder than others. Thus, rhythm is the most potent application of the principle of dynamics in music.

Dynamics enters into the general emotional projection of the mood in a larger sense. Music, like the motion pictures, exists as a series of impressions following each other in rapid sequence. Such an art must make the listener feel that it is headed somewhere, and should carry him along on the current. Otherwise he will lose interest. Music impinges upon the listener a ceaseless alternation between movement and rest. Between the points of rest, the movement must be inexorable, compelling. We shall see in subsequent chapters how melody, harmony, rhythm, and form all contribute to this supremely important forward drive. Dynamics plays here an exceedingly important part. The music undulates forward between a succession of high points or climaxes. After each peak there is a relaxing of emotional intensity, and a gradual building-up to the next. (Graphically this movement resembles the rising and falling line of a series of mountain peaks.) Dynamics help to regulate this steady undulation. The music accumulates force in a gradual *crescendo*. It reaches the peak. Then there is a gradual *decrescendo*, or lessening of volume, until we begin to approach the next climax.

In subtler fashion, dynamics enter into the composition as a means of highlighting or shading the musical line. By varying the volume of sound, the composer achieves an effect analogous to what the painter achieves through the brush. The musical canvas at times is painted in broad vigorous strokes, at others, the composer turns to vague outlines and subtle shadings. Through changes in dynamics, the composer is able to highlight certain parts of his composition, and to relegate others to relative obscurity; to achieve, in other words, a tonal equivalent of perspective and depth. Dynamics thereby become a potent factor in the total artistic scheme of musical composition.

It is plain that dynamics exist in two aspects: first, as a number of distinct levels of tonal volume; and second, as a series of nuances, or changes from one volume to another while the music is playing, that are part of the very life stream of the music. We have already met the two terms that indicate the nuances—*crescendo* and *decrescendo*. One cannot listen to a piece of music of any length without encountering either one or the other. The principal dynamic indications, going from soft to loud—that is, arranged in a *crescendo*—are:

> *pianissimo (pp):* very soft
> *piano (p):* soft
> *mezzo piano (mp):* medium soft
> *mezzo forte (mf):* medium loud
> *forte (f):* loud
> *fortissimo (ff):* very loud

Closely associated with dynamics is the element of *tempo*, or speed in music. This, too, has a part to play in the total effect. A light-hearted dance requires a brisk tempo. A stately march goes at a moderate rate of speed. A song of sorrow is slow. Changes in mood require corresponding changes in tempo. The principal nuances are *accelerando*, a faster tempo that, with its resemblance to a quickened pulse, produces an effect of emotional intensification upon the listener; and *ritardando*, a retarding or slowing up, that suggests a slackening of emotion.

The reader should take care at this point to distinguish between *metre* and *tempo*. *Metre* refers to the time measurement, specifically to the number of beats in the measure—duple, triple, quadruple, sextuple, and so forth. *Tempo* refers to the speed at which the metre is counted. Thus, a fast waltz and a stately minuet are both in triple metre; Chopin's *Funeral March* and the *Battle Hymn of the Republic* are both in quadruple metre. In fine, both metre and tempo are involved in regulating the forward movement of the music.

Tempo is subtly connected with dynamics in building up the climax. If the music, as it grows louder, also increases in speed, there will be marked accumulation of forward driving power. We shall frequently meet the two associated in the brilliant climax at the end of a piece, as in the *Finale* of Mendelssohn's "ITALIAN" SYMPHONY. Conversely, the *ritardando* is frequently used in conjunction with the *decrescendo* to produce the fadeout or dying-away effect so often met with at the end of a composition, as at the end of the *Prelude* to LOHENGRIN.

A climactic effect of another kind is achieved by having the *crescendo* accompanied by a marked broadening out in tempo, giving an effect of great dignity and strength. The climactic entrance of the final theme in the *Triumphal March* from AïDA illustrates this. Also, the final climax in Tchaikovsky's OVERTURE 1812 and in Franz Liszt's LES PRÉLUDES show how effective a *crescendo-ritardando* can be.

The principal tempo indications, going from slow to fast—that is, arranged in an *accelerando*—are:

> *largo:* broad and stately
> *adagio* or *lento:* slow
> *andante:* fairly slow
> *andantino:* a little faster than *andante*
> *moderato:* moderately fast
> *Allegretto:* fairly fast
> *allegro:* fast
> *vivace:* lively
> *presto:* very fast[7]

[7] One of the most scholarly expositions in the English language on the functions of the elements of expression in the art of music is the book *On the Elements of Expression in Music* by Professor Donald N. Ferguson, published by the University of Minnesota, Minneapolis, Minn., 1944.

Chapter Four

Music, Work and Play
The Traditional Folk Song

LONG before music became an art practised by trained composers and performers, song and dance flourished among the people as a vital, expressive folk art. In all the corners of the earth tunes sprang up, some to accompany dances, others to express every shade of personal emotion; and from these humble sources a magnificent literature grew that, together with folk tales, myths, and sagas, constitutes an enduring monument to the inexhaustible creativeness of the human race.

Folk song is, in the truest sense, a product of the national group from which it springs. A singer or fiddler in some hamlet makes up a song. His neighbours like it and sing it over and over, changing a phrase here, adding a verse there. In the course of time, the song spreads to the neighbouring village and through the entire countryside. It is polished by many talents, passed down from one generation to the next, until it becomes a crystallization of the emotions of the entire group, expressing its innermost feelings, its profoundest aspirations and insights, and at the same time capturing the essential spirit of its national song and speech, the very contour of its fields and valleys.

In a broader sense, however, folk song transcends national boundaries. It is the musical equivalent of the folk tale; it has that quality of simplicity and universality that sums up human experience in a few strokes, as do the myth and legend. The folk song springs out of man's primal need to give personal expression to his feelings—his devotion to home and fatherland, his rapture in love, his longing for the beloved, his sadness at parting and death. It addresses itself straight to the heart in a language that all mankind understands.

We may well begin our listening with a romantic folk song, in many versions, both in England and in parts of America

Barbara Allen.[1] The poem, taken from an ancient ballad found in *Percy's Reliques*, relates how Jemmy Grove lay dying for love of Barbara Allen, and how she, hard-hearted, repulsed him until it was too late. The melody is a North Country tune, one of the most beautiful of English airs. In his *Studies in Modern Music*, the eminent critic W. H. Hadow calls it a perfect example of the power of simplicity, "with each strain more beautiful than the one before, till it culminates in the perfect sweetness and pathos of its final cadence." The short melody is repeated with each stanza, a type of song construction that is called *strophic*.

The melodic symmetry is reinforced by the recurrence, at the end of every other line of poetry, of a distinctive rhythmic pattern used on the words "dwell-in'," "swell-in'," and "Allen": a short note on the beat (sixteenth note) followed by a longer note off the beat (a quarter note). This rhythmic figure was probably associated with a little hopping step off-the-beat in the country dances of North England. In Scotland this off-the-beat, or syncopated, rhythm became even more pronounced, the first note being shortened to a sixteenth note in value, and it has appeared so frequently in native folk tunes that it has become known as the "Scotch Snap." (Another good example of its use is *Comin' Through the Rye*, which is heard later in this chapter.) Here is the English version of *Barbara Allen*.[2]

---

[1] Essential listening for this chapter includes: *Barbara Allen, Marlborough, Home on the Range, John Henry, Drink to Me Only,* and *Comin' Through the Rye*. All other works mentioned are to be optional.

[2] Note the simple, symmetrical structure of this song, very obvious and easy to grasp at first hearing, yet most pleasing. The repetitions only seem to intensify the effectiveness of the "story-telling"—one of the basic reasons for folk songs.

D

The following jolly drinking song well exemplifies the changes in fortune that a song may undergo through the centuries; and, even more important, it shows how easily a melody may transcend the barriers of language and race. The melody appeared, according to good authority, first in the Holy Land during the period of the Crusades as the *Chanson de Mambron*, in praise of a French knight who lost his life near Jerusalem. It became so firmly rooted in the Orient that it is sung today in Egypt and Arabia and is mistakenly considered to be an old Egyptian folk tune. The "Mambron" in the title changed to "Malbrooke," and the song ultimately became the popular French *Malbrooke s'en va-t-en Guerre*, sung in England as *Marlborough Is Going to the War*, and for a long time supposed to have referred to the famous Duke. The song had disappeared for some time when Marie Antoinette heard a nursemaid sing it to the Dauphin. She took it up, the melody became enormously popular in Paris, was a favourite tune of Napoleon, and was used by Beethoven in his "BATTLE" SYMPHONY, written to commemorate Wellington's victory at Vittoria. After all these transformations, the pious lay of the medieval Crusader ended, in England and America, as the indispensable ditty of carousal.

A glance, however cursory, at the rich panorama of American folk song reveals the most varied influences. Subsidiary to the English are traces of Scottish, Irish, and Welsh folk-song idioms. Along the Northern border the French-Canadian influence predominates; in the Southwest, there is a strong Spanish tradition; in the Louisiana region, Spanish, French, and Negro influences blend in the Creole songs. In addition, there are the folk-song idioms of the various national groups—German, Bohemian, Hungarian, Italian, Jewish, Scandinavian, Negro, and Indian, all flowing together in a veritable melting pot of song.

The actual work song, or recreational song about work, plays a smaller though not less important part in American folklore. From the Northwest come lumberjack and shantyboy tunes, such as *The*

The Forge   *Goya*

Logger's Boast and *Driving Saw-Logs on the Plover.* From the Appalachian and Southern region come hillbilly tunes, and such famous songs as *The Ground Hog* and *High Up on Old Smoky.* From songs and ballads of the railroad, we have the saga of *Casey Jones, The Train That Never Pulled In,* and *Mama Have You Heard the News.* Cowboy songs are distinctive: the day-herding songs with loud refrains, sometimes based on cattle calls, to keep the herds moving; and the night-herding songs, with soft and soothing "dogie" refrains. *The Old Chisholm Trail, Git Along Little Dogie, Goodbye, Old Paint, Bury Me Not on the Lone Prairie*—these are simple tunes, varying in mood from the sentimental to the adventuresome, with easy-going, graceful rhythms. Typical of these traditional cowboy songs is *Home on the Range,* which we shall now hear.

Notice the simple structural design of *Home on the Range,* the unifying effect of repetition, the refreshing character of the first part of the "refrain" where there is a contrasting change of melody and rhythm, and, finally, the feeling of completeness and unity brought about by the recurrence of the first phrase—with a closing cadence, of course.

Among work songs, *John Henry,* who pitted his strength against the steam hammer, is the very essence of American folklore.[3] The melody, consisting of only four tones (D-F sharp-A-B), is a rare example of economy of tones. Note the interesting variety of rhythmic designs, no two measures being exactly alike. Yet in spite of this emphasis on variety, a definite feeling of unity and

[3] See *America Sings,* by Carl Carmer, with music by Edwin John Stringham and illustrations by Betty Carmer (New York: Alfred A. Knopf, 1942).

coherence exists, due, in large measure, to the character of the melodic scale structure. There is in this song a strong descriptive element; note the hammering strokes and the downward tendency of the melody, here and there, as though the rail spike were being driven home with each stroke of the sledge hammer swung by the mighty John Henry.

Cap - tain said to big, old John Hen - ry, "That old drill keeps a - com - ing a - - round. Take that steam drill out and start it on that job, Let it whop, let it whop that steel on down, Let it whop, let it whop that steel on down."

Close in spirit to folk songs are folk dances, practically all of which display the same general characteristics we noted in the chapter on music and dance—simple, catchy tunes, symmetrical phrase structure, and vigorous rhythms. The boundary between song and dance, in this case, is indeed a tenuous one. Many folk dances were sung long before they were played. Conversely, many folk songs were first danced. One might say that in many instances the two continued hand in hand. Both from Old-World and native sources a rich store of American folk dances has accrued: Virginia reels, square dances, Morris dances, country dances, and the like. Typical are such tunes as *Mississippi Sawyer, Arkansas Traveller, Irish Washerwoman, Turkey in the Straw, Pop Goes the Weasel,* and *Polly Put the Kettle On.*

Every nation has a more or less comparable body of folk music, responsive to the language and folkways of the particular group, with a characteristic flavour wholly indigenous to the soil out of which it grew. These songs and dances have served as a source of inspiration to the great composers and constitute one of the treasures of the nation, revealing eloquently its characteristic mode of thinking and feeling in music.

One qualification, however, may be added here: there are not many unique and exclusive characteristics in the so-called national strains of folk music in any country. It would be difficult indeed to point to any one characteristic and label it as exclusively American, for example; but there are generally a sufficient number of distinctive traits in a people's music to justify some kind of nationalistic designation. Only where a people have been really isolated and removed from extraneous influences can there be truly unique features in their musical idiom. Such national isolation in culture is very uncommon. More likely than not, alongside the characteristic national tunes will be found others with mixed antecedents betraying all sorts of outside influences that might easily belong to any one of several nations.[4]

Of the various national idioms, however, the English seem to be closest to our own. The melodies are usually forthright and without superfluous accent, conforming to the simple patterns of English speech. Many songs are based on, or make use of, the old Church Modes (see article "Mode" in Grove's *Dictionary of Music and Musicians*) and are four or five hundred years old. In the Hornpipe, Maypole, and Morris dances, vigorous four-four and six-eight metres abound. The balanced and symmetrical structure of the English folk song is well exemplified by the old tune which has become associated with Ben Jonson's lovely lyric, "Drink to Me Only With Thine Eyes," which is illustrated on page 37 and offered as the next subject for study.

Notice that each phrase, or unit, of this song consists of four measures, with a pause or cadence at the end of each. (This cadence consists of a melodic or harmonic formula imparting a feeling of a slight, partial, or complete close—quite as grammatical punctuation.) The first phrase is repeated, as though to take root firmly in the hearer's mind. The third phrase is somewhat new and different and provides the necessary contrast; and the fourth phrase returns to the original and opening phrase, to bring about a feeling of balance and unification. This may be diagrammed as follows, by giving each phrase a letter: A (A repeated) -B-A. This three-part form (sometimes called *ternary*) is a favourite

[4] Apropos of *national* versus *borrowed* musical characteristics, it might be pointed out that some Kentucky and Appalachian tunes are more truly in the early English manner of the sixteenth and seventeenth centuries than are the same tunes to be found today in England itself. They have been preserved in their original state by comparatively isolated mountain folk; in England, later influences crept in.

type of construction to be found in some of our best-known songs. In fact, it is the most common and basic of all musical structures, and is found in instrumental as well as in vocal music. Elaborated and developed, it is the basis for many of the larger and more pretentious musical forms used in chamber music, the symphony, the overture, the suite, as well as in works for solo instruments. But more of this matter in subsequent chapters. It is enough for the moment that this three-part structure be noticed, and that the reader recognize, also, that this A-B-A structure is a basic one in all the fine arts, for it best satisfies our aesthetic desire for balanced variety within unity—a result of securing a well-balanced disposition of the internal elements of compositional design, whether it be a painting, a sculpture, a poem, a sermon, a dance ensemble, a novel, or a piece of music. With these ideas in mind, study the picture of the "Tomb of Giuliano de' Medici" by Michelangelo on page 38; also note the play of binary and ternary elements within the scheme as a whole.

This is a truly graceful and dignified song, with its "dipping and bowing" eighth-note figure found in the first beat of so many measures, as though this were once a court dance.

The Tomb of Giuliano de' Medici   *Michelangelo*

We have already pointed out the rhythmic figure peculiarly known as the "Scotch Snap." This was, according to some authorities, originally characteristic of an old national dance, the Strathspey, but later found its way into all kinds of folk tunes with astonishing frequency. Notice, for example, how often the figure of the "snap" occurs in the next song we shall study, *Comin' Through the Rye*. (The words are by Robert Burns.) We have indicated these figures with a star.

Gin a bod-y meet a bod-y, Com-in thro' the rye.

Gin a bod y kiss a bod-y, need a bod-y cry?

Il-ka las-sie has her lad-die, Nane they say have I, Yet

a' the lads they smile at me, When com-in thro' the rye.

ADDITIONAL SUGGESTIONS FOR LISTENING[5]

The poet Thomas Moore played an important part in creating the folk songs of Ireland, most familiar among which are: *The Harp that Once Through Tara's Halls, Believe Me if All Those Endearing Young Charms*, and *The Last Rose of Summer*. Other Irish folk songs are popular in this country, especially *The Wearing of the Green* and *Londonderry Air*.

German folk song has much in common with English: regular formations, forthright melodies, simple lyricism, homely sentiment, and not a great deal of ornamentation. The songs are often sentimental and of much emotional fervour, yet there is something solid and foursquare about them. Some of this "solidity" comes from the fact that German folk tunes restrict themselves, as a rule, to the tones that belong to the scale of the moment. Also, German folk tunes are usually in simple rhythmic patterns, in which vigorous duple and triple metres predominate; a favourite type is the *Landler*, the peasant dance in three-four time that was the ancestor of our waltz. *Ach du lieber Augustin* is such a landler.

[5] To be used as fully as desired or as time will permit.

The folk songs and folk dances of the German people have had a great influence on the composers of that nation. We saw in the chapter "Music and Religion" how Bach was indebted to the chorale and what effect that form and style had on his music. In a similar way, the national heritage echoes through the works of Haydn, Mozart, Beethoven, Schubert, Schumann, Mendelssohn, and Brahms, to name only a few, all of whom either used folk songs outright in their works, or translated the spirit and idiom of them in their compositions. Some of the German traditional airs are almost as well known in this country as in Germany; for example: *Der Tannenbaum* (the melody of our own *Maryland, My Maryland*), *Die Lorelei*, and the student song, *Gaudeamus Igitur*. Brahms used this last song in his ACADEMIC OVERTURE.

French folk songs have the cool, limpid quality associated with the Gallic spirit—generally speaking, of course. Many of the songs are of great antiquity and bear marks of the influence of the troubadours and trouvères of the twelfth and thirteenth centuries. Many of the children's songs are well known in this country; among them we might mention: *Sur le pont d'Avignon, Il Etait un Bergère, Ah! que Vous Dirai-je, Maman*, and the two most popular songs of the Revolution, the *Carmagnole* and *Ça Ira*.

Italian songs, so often gay and impetuous, reflect the fiery temperament of the Southerner, the passionate abandon to the mood of the moment. Neapolitan street songs, Venetian boat songs, Sicilian serenades—these stem from an intensely musical people for whom song is as natural, almost, as speech. *Santa Lucia* has attained much popularity in America, and it is a good example of the Neapolitan folk style.

Spanish folk songs reflect the dance rhythms of the various provinces —*sequidillas, jotas, boleros, sevillanas*, and the like. Outstanding are the passionate flamenco songs, the idiom of the Spanish Gipsy, a rhapsodical, ornate vocal melody which bears the character of an improvisation. Such a song is *Saetas*, one of the flamenco songs used in Holy Week festivals. The rapturous incantation of the voice over the steady beating of the drums and the blare of cornets releases a flood of emotion as only the greatest of music is able to do.

Russian music is extremely variegated, including all the strains of a territory that occupies one-sixth of the earth—Greek, Slav, Tartar, Norse, Gipsy, German, Mongolian, the tribal songs of the Caucasus, and the melancholy tunes of the Siberian Steppes. Cossack dance songs are extremely rhythmic and vigorous, as are the Ukrainian peasant tunes.

Many currents meet in the richly imaginative folk music of Central, Northern, and Southeastern Europe—Scandinavian, Slavonic, Gipsy, Magyar, Czech, Teutonic, Croat, Bulgar, and Turkish. Those farther east and south across the Mediterranean Sea are outside the scope of this book. One cannot leave this array of nationalistic and racial expressions without further comment upon the Gipsy influences in Southeastern Europe. Their rhapsodical improvisations have become a real part of western music. These highly ornate melodies of the Gipsy fiddlers and singers, passing abruptly from one mood to the next, with their capricious rhythms and emotional fervour, seem strange in comparison with our more staid English and American folk songs; but with a few repeated hearings, we can learn to embrace them into our liking, if we will. In fact, if one has the time and the proper gramophone recordings, a pleasant and profitable excursion might well be made into these more or less exotic musical expressions. It has been well said, "I care not who makes the laws if I can make the songs."

Chapter Five

The Composed Folk Song
Architecture of Music[1]

BETWEEN the folk song and the so-called "art song" stands what is known, somewhat paradoxically, as the composed folk song. Certain composers are so thoroughly imbued with the spirit of their people and with their native musical idioms that their own original creations become so beloved and so generally used among the people that they achieve the status of traditional folk song. Dvořák, Sibelius, and Grieg, to name but a few, have often been charged with using actual traditional folk-song material, and they have had to refute such charges with the statement that the melodies were their own—a high compliment indeed to these composers when one comes to analyse the situation!

The composed folk song, being the product of a single creative personality, allows for wider ranges of subject emotion and aesthetic perfection than does the traditional folk song. Although well within the universality of the folk style, it will nonetheless bear the mark of a more personal approach to life and to the tenets of art. Then too, since the creator of the composed folk song may be a musician of considerable background and training, there may be a smoothness of style, a subtlety of effect in his compositions which would normally not be present, at least not to such a great degree, in the true folk art.

It may be said, therefore, that the composed folk song crystallizes within the span of a single career and through the medium of a single personality what it might take generations of spontaneous growth to achieve. In any case, the composed folk songs of

[1] Essential listening for this chapter includes: *Lullaby* by Brahms, *The Birch Tree*, Russian folk song, and *Finale* of Tchaikovsky's FOURTH SYMPHONY (in part, to show use of *The Birch Tree* song). Other works mentioned may be considered supplementary and optional listening.

42

a nation are as much a part of its national lore as the pure folk songs, in that they are actually used as such by the people. Indeed, it is entirely possible that had the composers of such songs as *O Sole Mio*, or *La Paloma*, or *My Old Kentucky Home* lived in a somewhat earlier age, they might have been numbered among the vast forgotten company of gifted village singers and players who had some part, however small, in the creation of the immortal literature known as traditional folk music—just as we now do not know the architects who actually conceived the original designs of most of the great Gothic cathedrals of Europe.

One of the first names that comes to mind, in connection with the composed folk songs of our own country, is that of Stephen Foster (1826-1864), whose songs have in the truest sense become part and soul of the heritage of the people of the United States. Foster's songs actually represent the essence of the American folk idiom in music. His was a fresh and untutored genius, which touched the hearts of his countrymen as no other composer's creations have done. Some of his songs, such as *Old Black Joe, Swanee River, My Old Kentucky Home, Massa's in de Cold, Cold Ground, Jeanie with the Light Brown Hair*, to name but a few, are deeply loved and sung throughout our country and beyond. And how much poorer the English-speaking peoples, especially those of America, would be without the immortal song by Sir Henry Bishop, *Home Sweet Home*, the words of which were penned by the New Yorker, John Howard Payne (1792-1852).

In this category may also be mentioned a number of national anthems which, through long association, have become symbols of patriotic emotion. Here the intimate folk style is superseded by a vigorous martial tune which the nation as a whole is able and eager to accept. Typical of these anthems are *The Star-Spangled Banner*, an old English song known as *To Anacreon in Heaven*, to which Francis Scott Key adapted his poem; *America*, or *God Save the King*, an old English song attributed to one of a number of composers; the *Battle Hymn of the Republic*, a hymn tune for which Julia Ward Howe wrote the words we now use; Rouget de Lisle's *Marseillaise*, written overnight in the heated atmosphere of the French Revolution; *Rule Britannia*, by Thomas Arne; and the hymn of the old Austrian Empire, *God Preserve Our Gracious Emperor*, by Joseph Haydn, one of the few national anthems composed by a great master.

As we might expect, the nineteenth-century composer's approach to folk song was more romantic than that of contemporary musicians. Often the simple folk idiom was dressed up with all the tricks of the composer's craftsmanship. Characteristic among such are the HUNGARIAN RHAPSODIES of Franz Liszt, in which the native tunes (it must be said that he was more prone to use Gipsy than "pure" Hungarian melodies) were treated in a dramatic and brilliantly technical manner often bordering on the bombastic. Some of these virtuoso piano pieces have received a new lease of life in brilliant orchestral arrangements. Try, sometime, listening to his Second, Sixth, or Twelfth Hungarian Rhapsody, and note how a highly charged romantic composer can treat his folk material.

Many of the great composers betray a startling closeness to their native soil. Many melodies of Schubert and Brahms, for example, evince the characteristics of true German folk song. Brahms carried the folk spirit into some of his original songs so successfully that two of them, at least, have become virtual folk songs—the universally loved *Lullaby*, and the delightful *Vergebliches Standchen* (Futile Serenade), with its irresistible lilting tune.

The *Lullaby* by Brahms possesses a number of characteristics that we are prone to associate with the folk-song genre. Its simple and straightforward internal structure consists of four phrases, each of four measures in length, with a salient cadence at the close of each; the sincere and deep feeling is presented with simplicity and economy of means; and the unity, contrast, and symmetry are secured in an inevitable yet unpretentious manner. Let us study it; but first let us listen to it.

We might express simply the structural formula of the melodic pattern thus: four phrases (marked "a," "b," "c," and "d," or two basic periods marked "I" and "II"—often called the *Binary*, or two-part, form). Note the melodic and rhythmic figures that are repeated more or less identically, and observe the process of building a work out of small units. Note the unifying effect of such a simple method of construction. Now put all this technical matter to the background of your mind and listen to the music with the

The Visitation with Two Saints   *Piero di Cosimo*

Observe that this picture is divided into two balanced parts. Note also the wavelike contour described by the heads of the four figures. The first characteristic corresponds to the two balanced periods of the musical form known as two-part or binary, while the graphic curve is analogous to the rising and falling tonic-dominant key relationship that exists in the true binary musical structure. It is almost needless to add that these objective facts are very secondary to the subjective and aesthetic considerations.

idea of enjoying it to the full. The same basic plan of study might well apply to all our efforts.

It would take far more pages than we have at our disposal simply to enumerate other worthy instances of the uses many great composers have made of the folk song in their larger works; and the same is true of the composed folk song and the original folk-songlike themes composers sometimes create. The listener will enjoy discovering such instances rather than having them pointed out for inspection. It is enough, we believe, merely to indicate the general principles involved and typical examples of such principles. Thus, the listener is in possession of a "tool" that will enable him to pursue this subject further.

As a further challenge, listen to the *Finale* of Tchaikovsky's FOURTH SYMPHONY. In this work, the composer uses the following Russian folk song known as *The Birch Tree*, with its curious phrase structure of three (not four) measures each, with a cadence at the end of each phrase, and a repetitious design that is very simple and almost primitive:

Compare that traditional folk song with the following version of it that Tchaikovsky evolved. Note the regular two-measure figure, four-measure phrase, and the repetitions that are more exact than are those in the original folk song:

Upon this tune and a contrasting theme is built a mighty symphonic development. The movement advances precipitously. Powerful fanfares in the brasses pronounce the ominous Fate motive, heard at the onset of the first movement. The work builds up, the gay opening theme returns, and the mood of triumph is powerfully reaffirmed. The movement closes in a blaze of colour and animation.

The Architecture of Music: Form and Structure[2]

We have seen in our earlier discussion on rhythm and melody that the essential element of both is pattern or design, and that through the discernment of such a pattern, the listener perceives that there is a meaning and inter-relationship of the small parts, first to each other and then to the whole. This desire to achieve design and order out of chaos, to balance unity with diversity, receives its ultimate expression in that basic element of the art of music known as *form*.

Form results from the attempt of the artist to achieve the most effective arrangement and balance of the material and the most coherent relation between the parts and the whole. Actually, the urge to secure unity and variety, symmetry, balance, contrast, and climax is not limited to art. It appears in one guise or another in all the activities of life, whether in the laying out of a garden, the setting of a table, or the embroidering of a dress. Children playing in the sand lay out elaborate structures in symmetrical patterns. Dancers go through elaborate sequences in movement that are coherent, balanced patterns. Both in the spatial arts—painting, sculpture, architecture—and in the sequential or time arts— poetry, drama, motion pictures, music—the material must not only say something significant to the beholder, it must say it to him in a coherent and intelligible—more, in an alive and interesting—way. This need to be coherent, intelligible, and interesting

---

[2] The following exposition of certain aspects of the creative artist's craft, as with all such technical and academic matters discussed *throughout this book*, is presented for its own extra-musical, scholarly, and interest-arousing values. It is not given with a mistaken notion that it is indispensable to the aesthetic appreciation of music. A good general rule to bear in mind is that all matters ABOUT MUSIC are just that and no more; and that the real appreciation OF MUSIC is quite a different matter. Further, that technical and academic knowledge is neither essential to nor a substitute for the listening appreciative process.

E

will lead the artist to seek the most appropriate, the one inevitable, form for his content.

If an artist is overflowing with something worth saying, the form in which it can best be said will come out of the materials themselves. Conversely, if he has nothing significant to say, no amount of perfection of form will breathe life and meaning into his art work. Whether he is dealing with word patterns or tone patterns, with shape and line and colour, or with great architectural masses, he will mould his materials to the form that they themselves demand. The content will lead him to a certain form.

However, we cannot look upon form as purely functional, a convenient means to an end. The pillars of the Parthenon had not only to help support the edifice; but they also had to become important contributors to the general beauty of the building. We cannot think of form as a thing in itself, a convenient mould into which the artist pours his meaning. The artist wishes his content to be clear and easily grasped. He wants to keep his audience interested in what he is saying. The artist desires his message to have a powerful, unified effect, and yet at the same time to have novelty, suspense, variety, climax. Also, being an artist, he must have beauty of outline in the external shape of his message. If he has felt his material deeply, if he has been endowed with creative imagination, and if he has achieved mastery in his medium, the requisite forms that will best enable him to achieve all these will come to him.

The artist would have a difficult task if he had to start from "scratch." Actually, he is working in an art that has a history and a tradition. He inherits a body of techniques, the cumulative achievement of generations of artists, of centuries of trial and error, to help him solve his aesthetic problems. The principles of form are timeless; but the actual forms that enable artists to carry out those principles change from one age to the next. The artist studies the forms at hand; alters them to suit his personal needs. Sometimes he abandons them altogether and turns in a new direction, blazing a trail for those who will come after him. Thus, when viewed dynamically, forms in art are living, growing organisms, adapting themselves to the needs and tastes of each successive generation of artists—they are so many diverse manifestations, in one century or another, of that eternal quest for law and order, for harmony and coherence, that seems to be one of the immanent characteristics of the human mind.

Since the particular form employed by the artist springs out of the materials he is working with, every art develops its own principles of construction. Nevertheless, certain underlying principles seem to be common to them all. First and foremost is that of unity: the desire to organize all the components of the art work into one cohesive design, so that each part of the cathedral, the novel, the painting, or the symphony will function organically within the total framework. In this connection, Poe's celebrated dictum on the short story—"In the whole composition there should be no word written of which the tendency, direct or indirect, is not to the established design"—shows a fine insight into this basic factor in form.

Closely allied to unity is the need for symmetry and balance, which make more easily perceptible the fundamental unity of the pattern. Man seems to take great pleasure in orderly arrangement, in the repetition of familiar quantities, in balancing one side against another. It is almost as if he found refuge in the orderliness of art from the chaos, the unpredictable accidents of life. As in the case of rhythm, he begins to expect certain things to happen in a certain order within the art pattern, and achieves a deep satisfaction, a pleasant sense of fulfilment and security, when his expectation is realized.

But security alone would soon grow wearisome, were it not enlivened with novelty and surprise within the pattern. And so the unity of the art form must be adroitly alternated with variety and contrast. From man's psychological need for both safety and adventure—seemingly irreconcilable elements—springs the basic aesthetic problem of the artist. If he were continually to introduce new material into his work, the result would be chaos. If, on the other hand, he were to continue to repeat the same motif again and again—like a child, or a member of a primitive tribe who sings a snatch of melody over and over for hours on end—he would become fearfully boring. Form results from the artist's attempt to achieve a satisfying balance between the two, from repeating enough of the old to give us a sense of pattern, while introducing enough of the new to achieve variety and sustain our interest.

In addition, the artist introduces into the material an element of suspense, of movement and growth toward a culminating point or climax. Whether it be the soaring dome in architecture, the denouement in drama, the crescendo and peak in melody, the climax carries the spectator aloft to the high point of intensity, after which the movement subsides or ends. Thus the art work takes on shape and form: a beginning, a middle, and an end.

The arrangement of the material is naturally of crucial importance in the space arts. Painting, sculpture, architecture, interior decoration—all place the utmost emphasis upon the problems of organizing space into a unified whole. One has only to look at Raphael's celebrated "School of Athens" (page 51) to see how masterfully the painter has arranged his material with an eye to formal unity and structure. The rectangular space is bound together by the curve of the arch, reinforced by the three concentric arches. These, like a reiterated climax in music, frame the central figures of Socrates and Plato. Notice how effectively the figures on either side of the two philosophers focus the movement upon them. The canvas presents a central group flanked on either side by two symmetrical groups, the balance accentuated by the two statues. Although analogies between different arts must be made only in a general way, the reader will have no difficulty in recognizing in this design an equivalent of the A-B-A structure in music. The larger rhythms of the three areas are subtly varied with all kinds of cross rhythms within the groups, and by the gentle elliptical movement between the figures in the middle distance and those in the foreground. The canvas of this most classical of the Renaissance masters presents an extraordinary example of the utmost diversity within a unified pattern, with symmetry, balance, climax, and richly variegated rhythms all contributing to the monumental effect. Note the crescendo effect of the four expanding arches.

Even more important is the problem of form in architecture, where the artist is faced with the task of organizing great expanses of mass and space into a coherent pattern. He does not begin with a definite form into which, as into a mould, he pours his conception. Rather, he considers the use to which the building will be put—whether it is to be a cathedral, a courthouse, or a villa; the materials available, whether marble, stone, or brick; the engineering problems involved. Out of this consideration grows the particular form that he will use. Notice, for example, in the Capitol at

School of Athens

Raphael

Washington, how appropriate is the serene, majestic form for a building intended as a seat of government. The magnificently climactic dome towering over the two symmetrical wings at either side is an architectural equivalent to the A-B-A structure in music. Considered in detail, without the dome, the building presents three similar façades—the repetition of an idea—which are brought out dramatically by means of the steps, the pillars, and the cornice, alternating with two sections—the contrast—which

The Capitol Building in Washington

are fairly well in the background. Here is a kind of A-B-A-B-A structure, which is precisely what we shall soon discover the classical rondo form to be. As in the painting of Raphael, we have unity and variety, symmetry, balance, climax, and diversified rhythms, expressed in appropriate architectural values.

These values, which depend on space measurements in the plastic arts, are translated into time measurements in the sequential or time arts. In the dance, the performer takes four steps in one direction followed by four in another. In poetry, the stanzas are symmetrical in length—the very word *length* being equally applicable to time and space—and the lines are symmetrical in the number and arrangement of the metrical pulses. The *rondo*, with its subtle reiteration of a unifying element, is one of the most effective lyric forms in poetry. Notice, in Jean Froissart's "Rondel," how the reiterated phrase takes on new meaning with each repetition, at the same time giving strength to the delicate pattern. We have here an A-B-A-C-A pattern, with the repetition of the first two lines in the middle of the poem and at the end:

> Love, love, what wilt thou with this heart of mine?
> Naught see I fixed or sure in thee!
> I do not know thee,—nor what deeds are thine:
> Love, love, what wilt thou with this heart of mine?
> Naught see I fixed or sure in thee!
>
> Shall I be mute, or vows with prayers combine?
> Ye who are blessed in loving, tell it me:
> Love, love, what wilt thou with this heart of mine?
> Naught see I fixed or sure in thee![3]

At this point, we should listen to Beethoven's *Rondino* as arranged by Fritz Kreisler for violin and piano. We should like to leave the discovery of the internal structure to the listener, and we shall do so with one admonition: watch for the recurrent theme and the episodes that alternate with that theme, then compare the form you have discovered with the general design of Froissart's rondeau. Bear in mind that the composer may have as many alternations as he deems necessary.

So, too, the other literary arts—the novel and the drama, as well as the cinema—have their problems of organization and structure, of tempo and transition, climax and denouement. One need only watch a well-directed movie as it unfolds from its leisurely beginning, gradually accelerating its pace, piling up suspense in a steady crescendo, yet adhering to the firmest kind of unity up to the inexorable climax, to realize how all-pervading are the basic elements of design and structure, tempo and dynamics, no matter what the particular art form or medium may be.

If these compositional values are of such importance in the static arts, where the spectator may linger at will over every detail of the painting, sculpture, the building, or the printed space, how much more important they are in an art where all is flow and movement, where the landscape rushes past before the listener has had a chance to grasp the details, where the tone lives but for an

---

[3] Translated by H. W. Longfellow. A rondel proper generally contains 13 or 14 lines.

instant before dissolving in air, where unity and coherence of form are perceived mainly in retrospect—or in anticipation. Indeed, no sooner has the listener become aware of one tone than another is on its way. It took composers centuries of groping, of trial and error, to develop the techniques of form as we now know them; but they gradually learned how to achieve in an art that exists as a rapid succession of impressions in time all the solidity and orderly arrangement of structure in space. Through mastery of form they succeeded in creating extensive works that, although they have their being only in the momentary billowing of the air, nevertheless communicate to the listener that sense of organic growth and towering strength found in the most imposing edifice—veritable cathedrals in tone, enduring monuments to the matchless resourcefulness and power of man's imagination.

In the folk songs that we have heard, one observed that the phrases were combined in several variants of the unity-and-variety, or A-B-A, pattern. In subsequent chapters we shall discover the many variations of this and other patterns in the most familiar forms, analysing both their external structure—the relation of the individual sections to each other and to the composition as a whole—as well as the internal structure of the units within the section.

Chapter Six

‿‿‿‿‿‿‿‿‿‿‿‿‿‿‿‿‿‿‿‿

Music as Personal Expression

The Art Song; "Sentence" Structure in Music[1]

THE same diversity of mood and immediate emotional appeal that we noticed in folk song animates its city cousin, the art song. Here, too, we meet with every shade of human feeling projected through beautiful melody and through the most personal of all musical instruments, the human voice. But whereas the folk song more often breathes of the soil and is racy with the life and humour of the peasantry, the art song usually has its being in urban culture and is the flower of a carefully nurtured tradition. Thus, for the simple universality of the folk song, the art song substitutes a more individualized idiom, the expression of a definite creative personality, subtly evocative in mood and atmosphere—an art form that has enlisted the talents of the most distinguished composers.

Although the two categories of song have flourished side by side since the days of the troubadours—we saw how such masters of art song as Schubert and Brahms captured the folk spirit in some of their works—some important points of difference between them exist. The art song is generally set to a high order of lyric poetry, instead of to a simple folk rhyme. Whereas the folk song is strophic in construction—that is, the tune is repeated over and over for successive stanzas—the art song, as often as not, follows the poem throughout, interpreting each new phase and nuance of the verse. This type of song is known as *durchkomponiert*, or "composed throughout," and it naturally captures the mood of the various stanzas more intimately than does the strophic type of song. (There are many strophic art songs, too, but by and large the

[1] Essential listening for this chapter includes: *Serenade* by Schubert, *Der Erlkönig* by Schubert, *Ich Grolle Nicht* by Schumann, *Minnelied* by Brahms, *Ich Liebe Dich* by Grieg, *The Flea* by Moussorgsky, and *The Sea* by MacDowell; for Part II, "Sentence Structure in Music," use *London Bridge Is Falling Down*, *The Farmer in the Dell* and Foster's *Swanee River*. All others are supplementary and optional.

55

through-composed type has predominated, particularly since the middle of the nineteenth century.)

The art song depends for its success on the perfect fusion of text and music. In some of our great songs this union is so complete that it is practically impossible for us now to conceive of the one existing without the other. Having picked a text with an emotional or poetic content that invites musical setting, the composer uses all the resources of his art to bring out every nuance, every hidden implication of the words. In this task all the elements of music that we have hitherto discussed play their parts. The rhythm not only conforms to, but also accentuates the metre of the poetry. The curve of the melody traces the rise and fall of emotion in the text. The important words and syllables are brought out by the musical accent. The harmonic background in the accompaniment provides a sympathetic commentary, ranging from lightness and gaiety to sombre drama. Timbre, too, is brought into play: the bright tinkling melody given to the brilliant soprano differs from the heroic ballad assigned to the baritone or the romantic love song of the tenor and lyric soprano. The themes alternate and reappear according to a formal scheme that matches the form of the poem. Tempo and dynamics underscore the mood, changing with each shade of meaning. Finally, all these factors combine to build up musically the emotional climax of the poetry. What emerges is a miniature tone poem, lyric or dramatic, that captures the innermost spirit of the poem.

The history of the art song goes back about eight hundred years to the works of the courtly Troubadours and Trouvères, and of their German counterparts, the Minnesingers (love singers) and the Master Singers who are so vividly satirized in Wagner's opera. The madrigals and airs of the Renaissance, cultivated in Italy, France, Germany, and England, were followed by a rich literature throughout the seventeenth and eighteenth centuries. The masters of the Baroque and Classical periods left a number of songs that are still part of the repertory. *If Music Be the Food of Love*, by England's great composer Henry Purcell (1658-1695), Haydn's *My Mother Bids Me Bind My Hair*, Mozart's *The Violet*, as well as a number of songs by the Italian masters, such as the frequently performed *Come Raggio di Sol* (As a Ray of Sunlight) by Antonio Caldara (1670-1736), and *Vittoria, Mio Core* (Victoria, My Love) by Giacomo Carissimi (1605-1674), are outstanding examples.

Yet, despite the excellence of these songs of the masters, when we say "art song" to a music lover he immediately thinks of the early nineteenth century and of the lyricism that welled out of the early Romantic Period through the transcendent genius of the greatest of song composers, Franz Schubert, who wrote well over five hundred. He was the first of a great line of writers who established the art song as one of the most fascinating forms in music, capturing the essence of the poem and translating it into its tonal equivalent with an almost clairvoyant insight. Although he left a legacy of first importance in every branch of music—symphony, chamber music, piano sonata, religious choral work—to the millions of his admirers, the composer of the *Serenade, Hark Hark the Lark, The Linden Tree, Death and the Maiden* remains, first and foremost, the inspired master of song.

In Schubert, the time, the place, and the man came together in more than fortuitous fashion. To begin with, a group of German lyric poets, headed by Goethe, had raised aloft the banner of Romanticism and created a new literary form, the intimate lyric of mood and emotion in which language was so surcharged with feeling as to cry for fulfilment in music. Then, too, the art of music as a whole was beginning to move ever closer to literature, a development that can be noticed throughout the whole of the nineteenth century. The short piece, lyrical in style and emotional in mood, was ready to take its place beside the large structural forms of the Classical Period. The piano had been sufficiently perfected to become a flexible, highly imaginative assistant to the voice. When all these influences had blossomed, there appeared the master who was able to bring them all to fruition in an art form so distinctive, so indissolubly associated with himself and his successors, that even today, when the art song has for decades been reproduced with the utmost felicity by French, Italian, Russian, English, and American composers, we still frequently call it, as Schubert did, the *Lied.*

Although the moods reflected in the art song are as diversified as those of the folksong, that of romantic love naturally holds first place. We may begin our listening study with one of the greatest of love songs, Schubert's *Serenade.* Over an accompaniment of simple chords there unfolds a melody so expressive, so attuned to the most intimate inflections of the human voice, that it conveys its message even if one does not understand the German in which it is usually sung. Here, the mood of tender longing, so characteristic of the early romantic movement in Germany, finds expression:

> Softly goes my song's entreaty
>   Thro' the night to thee,
> In the silent woods I wait thee,
>   Come, my love, to me.
>
> The whispering tree-tops shield us
>   From the light of the moon,
> Fear no intruding foot-steps coming,
>   Fear no spying eye.
>
> Hark! the nightingales are singing,
>   Ah, they plead with thee!
> With their notes so sweet, so ringing,
>   They would plead with me.
>
> Well they know a lover's longing,
>   Know the pain of love,
> With their silver-toned voices
>   Tender hearts they move.
>
> Ah, let thine, as well, grow tender,
>   Sweetheart, why so coy?
> Anxious, fevered, I wait thee,
>   Come and bring me joy![2]

We have had occasion, frequently, in discussing the folk song, to point out the regular construction of four measures in a phrase and four phrases (or two periods) in the melody. You will find an analogous construction in these verses—four lines in a stanza, four feet in a line (alternating with lines of three feet. When set to music, these shorter lines are filled out, so that they become equal in length to the others). Schubert has skilfully avoided an excessively four-square construction, first, by introducing short interludes in the accompaniment; second, by repeating certain lines of poetry, especially in the later stanzas.

Notice the characteristic introduction of the piano accompani-

---

[2] English version (except the second verse) by Henry G. Chapman, copyright 1911 by G. Schirmer, Inc. Copyright renewed 1939 by G. Schirmer, Inc. Quoted by permission of the publisher. Free and literal translation of second verse by the present author.

ment; the interplay between the regular phrases of the voice part and the piano interludes; the effective repetition of the melody to other words, in strophic style; the intensification of mood, building up to the wonderful climax in the last stanza, with the accompaniment subtly imitating the vocal line; and the rounding off of the design in a gentle subsiding of emotion, dying away in the tender piano postlude.

If the *Serenade*, written to verses by Rellstab, represents the lyric genius of Schubert, his setting of Goethe's narrative poem "Der Erlkönig" (The Erlking) reveals his dramatic powers. The song was composed in 1815, when he was but eighteen years old, and is considered by many the greatest lied ever written. Schubert's friend Spaun told how he and another companion went one afternoon to call on Schubert. They found him enthusiastically reading Goethe's dramatic ballad aloud. He walked up and down the room, book in hand, then sat down and, as fast as he could write, put the song on paper practically in its finished form.

Nothing is more characteristic of the first period of German romanticism than the sombre mood of this ballad, with its commingling of the supernatural and the strangely picturesque. Our second required listening in this chapter is, then, the immortal ballad-art song, *The Erlking*, by Franz Schubert:

> Who rides so late through night and wind?
> It is the father and his child.
> He holds the boy in his arms,
> He clasps him firmly, he keeps him warm.
>
> "My son, why do you hide your face in fear?"
> "See you not, father, the Erlking?
> The Erlking with his crown and train."
> "My son, that is but the mist trailing down."
>
> "Thou lovely child, come with me!
> And I'll play lovely games with thee,
> Where many gay flowers lie in the field,
> And my mother has many garments of gold."
>
> "Father! Father! don't you hear
> What the Erlking is softly promising me?"
> "Be calm, my child, have no fear,
> That is but the wind moaning through the leaves."

"Won't you go with me?
My daughters will wait upon you,
They will play in the evening
And they will sing and dance."

"Father! Father! don't you see
The Erlking's daughters in that dark place?"
"My child, I see it quite clearly—
Those are but the hoary willows so gray."

"I love thee, thy beautiful face arouses me,
And comest thou not freely, I shall use force!"
"My father, my father, he clasps me now,
His icy grasp hurts me!"

The father shudders, he rides on faster,
Clasping in his arms the ailing child.
He reaches home in dread and anguish—
In his arms the child lay dead!³

The octaves in galloping triplets with which the accompaniment opens, the ominous figure in the bass, at once set the atmosphere and the mood of the drama. The three protagonists—father, son, and seductive Erlking—are clearly differentiated through changes in tempo in vocal line, and in tonal register. (By *register* we mean the general location in regard to high or low; the "lie" of the music.) Thus, the father's tones are conspicuously lower than those of the child, while the Erlking sings a soft alluring strain, as if from another world. The cries of the child are abrupt and harrowing; the father's reassurance is sonorous, giving an impression of strength; the Erlking sings sirenlike in a broad, suave melody. As the father rides on in terror, we hear the galloping figure of the opening, leading to the dread climax. The final line is declaimed, with a dramatic pause before the two words at the end, "lay dead," followed by two simple chords. The effect is very impressive.

To get an inkling of Schubert's achievement in song, one should hear several of the masterpieces that music lovers the world over have come to treasure almost as a personal possession. *Hark Hark*

³ English version (except the fifth verse), by Arthur Westbrook. Copyright by Oliver Ditson Company, 1931. Quoted by permission of the publishers.

From the Original MS. of the Song "Heidenröslein"

Schubert

the Lark, written at one sitting on the back of a bill of fare, at a beer garden, after he had glanced through a volume of Shakespeare; *Ave Maria*, to the words from Walter Scott's *Lady of the Lake*; the dramatic masterpieces *Death and the Maiden*, *The Wanderer*, *The Phantom Double*; the folk-songlike *Heidenröslein* (Hedge-Rose); *Who Is Sylvia?*; *My Peace Thou Art*; *The Post*; *The Linden Tree* —each has become so integral a part of our song inheritance that it is almost inconceivable to think of the art without them. (See reproduction of manuscript of *Hedge-Rose* on page 61.)

Schubert's successor in the art song was Robert Schumann, one of the most original and striking figures among the Romantics. Schumann possessed unusual dramatic power and a deep sensitivity to poetry, which he projected into his songs by a melodic line and harmonies much more complicated, as a rule, than those of Schubert. He was not nearly so fertile, but his choicest works must be accounted as among the glories of literature of the lied.

For Schumann, the lyrics of Heinrich Heine provided the same inspiration that those of Goethe, Schiller, and the earlier Romantic poets of Germany had for Schubert. Unlike his predecessor, who set to music all kinds of poetry, good, bad, and indifferent—Schumann remarked of him that he could set even a placard to music—Schumann needed a really beautiful poem to be inspired to musical creation. As a result, the poetry in Schumann's songs is far more worthy of the music than is that in some of Schubert's songs.

Ich Grolle Nicht (I'll Not Complain), set to an exceedingly intense lyric of Heine, is one of the most powerful of Schumann's songs. The famous critic and scholar, H. T. Finck, has said that the best traits of Schumann's songs are united in this one, the third of our listening study:

> I'll not complain, even though my heart be breaking.
> O love for ever lost! O love for ever lost!
> I'll not complain, I'll not complain.
>
> Even tho' you shine with the splendour of a diamond,
> No rays of it brighten your dark heart.
> But I know full well I'll not complain.
> Even if my heart is breaking.

İ saw thee in my dream,
And saw the night within thy heart's abyss,
And saw the snake that on thy heart doth gnaw,
How all forlorn thou art, my love, I saw.
I'll not complain, I'll not complain.[4]

The brooding chords under the vocal line, with their acrid dissonances, communicate the emotion of the rejected lover. Very
gradually the music builds up to a climax on the line, "And saw
the snake that on thy heart doth gnaw." For emotional projection,
this song composed in 1840 remains one of the best of its type in
the full-blown German Romanticism.

Next in the dynasty of the masters of the lied was Johannes
Brahms, who united with the utmost lyricism a quality of inner
fervour and introspection that has given his songs a high place in
the literature. Brahms' songs have passion and intensity, a distinctive colouring in the vocal line and in the intricate piano
background, which stamp them as unmistakably his.

There is brooding melancholy in such songs as *May Night* and
Death is Like a Cool Still Night; contemplation and gentleness in
In Summer Fields; and fervid lyricism pervading the slow movements of his symphonies are matched in such a song as *Minnelied*
(Love Song). The flowing accompaniment that serves as the
introduction in the *Minnelied*—Brahms directed it to be played
"with much tenderness, but not too slowly"—leads into a vocal
melody of deep feeling and the intimate quality of inwardness that
is so peculiarly his own. Note the gloomy and despondent low-
pedal point (a sustained or reiterated tone) in the bass of the piano
throughout the verse beginning with "But for thee all joy were
dead." The eminent authority on the lied, H. T. Finck, whom we
have quoted before, has said that the *Minnelied* is the most inspired,
spontaneous, and delightful of Brahms' vocal works. The words of
our fourth study song follow:

Sweeter sounds the song of birds
When she roams the meadows,
When she comes with step so light
'Mid the woodland shadows.

[4] English version (except the second verse) by Arthur Westbrook. Copyright by
Oliver Ditson Company, 1931. Quoted by permission of the publishers.

F

Brighter is the blooming Spring,
Greener are its bowers,
When her tender fingers touch
Their countless flowers.

But for thee all joy were dead,
All earth's brightness faded.
E'en the glow of evening sky
Were for me o'ershaded.

Dearest sov'reign of my heart,
Never leave me, never,
Bloom sweet blossoms of thy love,
In my soul forever.[5]

Notice the richness of the chords in the piano part and the symmetrical structure of the voice part, and how both the melody and the piano accompaniment interpret and highly intensify the spirit and mood of the poem—a perfect wedding of the two arts! Each of the four stanzas is given to two four-measure phrases. Each stanza is separated from the next by a brief piano interlude. The first, second, and fourth phrases are similar in contour, the third is contrasting, outlining the phrase-period pattern we met so frequently in the folk song—A,A:B,A. The last line of the poem is repeated, bringing us to the peak of the melody and the climax of the emotion. It has often been pointed out that in Brahms profundity of emotion and intricacy of texture go hand in hand with the simplest structural formations. In the tender *Minnelied* we have a good example of this.

German Romanticism, in the second half of the nineteenth century, strongly influenced composers throughout the entire musical world; and even such ardent nationalists as Grieg, Tchaikovsky, and our own Edward MacDowell (1861-1908) came under its spell. In their songs they combined the lyricism of the lied with their own national idiom. A number of Grieg's songs, among them the beloved *Solvejg's Song*, are completely nationalistic in style and content; but one of the most famous, *Ich Liebe Dich* (I Love You), written when he was twenty-one and very much under the

[5] Translation (except the second verse) by Arthur Westbrook. Copyright, 1931, by Oliver Ditson Company. Quoted by permission of the publishers. The second verse is a literal translation by the present author.

influence of Schumann, is in the great tradition of the lied. Like Schumann, who turned to song in the year of his marriage to Clara Wieck, Grieg wrote *Ich Liebe Dich* as an outpouring of his love for his cousin Nina Hagerup, whom he later married. In a letter to the American critic, Henry Finck, he said, "My best songs were composed for her; they embody my personal feelings, and I could no more have stopped expressing them in songs than I could have stopped breathing." The sincerity of the songs, and the gentle lyricism which is so much a part of Grieg's musical personality, have established him as one of the most popular composers of song. This is our fifth listening study.

Grieg wrote the music of *Ich Liebe Dich* to the lyrics of Hans Christian Andersen; but the German words are almost always used. The lyrics follow:

> My thought of thoughts, my very inmost being,
> Thou only art my heart's felicity!
> I love thee more than all else under heaven,
> I love but thee, I love but thee,
> I love but thee thro' all eternity!
>
> For thee alone my thoughts are turning,
> My heart is happy only for thee!
> Where ever God wills that I go,
> I love but thee, I love but thee,
> I love thee only thro' all eternity![6]

It is not without reason that this has become one of the most popular of love songs. It has the spirit of a live and passionately expressive emotion, tuneful throughout and as spontaneous as the declaration itself. It also contains an excellent example of a climax. Unfolding itself in a gentle curve, it begins to rise in emotional intensity on the words "I love but thee," and increases, with each repetition, to the peak on the line, "I love but thee thro' all eternity!" The melody is then repeated for the second stanza.

Of Tchaikovsky's 107 songs, unquestionably the most popular, and certainly one of the finest among them, is his setting of Goethe's *Nur Wer Die Sehnsucht Kennt* (None But the Lonely

---

[6] Translation (except the second verse) by Auber Forestier. Copyright, 1936, by Oliver Ditson Company. Quoted by permission of the publishers. The second verse is a literal translation by the present author.

Heart), which he wrote in his twenty-ninth year, the same year that produced the ROMEO AND JULIET OVERTURE. (See Chapter XII.) He succeeded in capturing the essence of Goethe's poem. The song has come to be regarded as a characteristic expression of the melancholy that pervades so many of this composer's works, and that reaches its culmination in his last work, the PATHÉTIQUE SYMPHONY.

> None but the lonely heart
> Can know my sadness;
> Alone and parted far
> From joy and gladness.

> Heav'n's boundless arch I see
> Spread out above me.
> Ah! what a distance drear
> To one who loves me!

[The first stanza is repeated here.]

> My senses fail,
> A burning fire devours me.
> None but the lonely heart
> Can know my sadness.[7]

Both the choice of Goethe's lyrics and the manner in which they are handled stamp this song in the tradition of the lied, shot through with the same quality of *sehnsucht* that permeated so much of the German Romantic poetry of the early nineteenth century. The highly emotional vocal line, with the downward leap in the first two measures, projects a mood of lassitude and despair. The melody undulates in a broad curve, a true outpouring of feeling, until it works up to the climax. Notice how masterfully the emotion is carried to its peak in the accompaniment, after the voice has stopped, on the last line of the third stanza (that is to say, the first stanza repeated as third). After a dramatic pause, the voice droops in despair, while the piano mournfully intones the original melody. The intertwining of both parts is faultless and is achieved with rare eloquence.

Much more truly Russian in style are the songs of Tchaikovsky's countryman, Modeste Moussorgsky, one of the most original

---

[7] Translation by Arthur Westbrook. Copyright by Oliver Ditson Company.

creative spirits in nineteenth-century music. In his works we find a potent, highly personal idiom, dramatic and intense, but altogether free from the influence of the German lied. The composer seeks to discover the exact musical equivalent of the words, sometimes with an almost brutal realism. As Moussorgsky himself wrote to the critic Stassoff: "Life wherever it shows itself, truth no matter how bitter, courage and frankness above all, point blank — that's my object, the thing I hope to achieve."

For our sixth listening study, we present Moussorgsky's famous *Song of the Flea*, which is spoken by Mephistopheles in Goethe's *Faust*.[8] He used the text as a means for expressing his hatred and contempt for the sham and favouritism of the Russian court:

> Once upon a time there was a king
>> Who had a big flea;
>>> A flea? A flea!
> Whom he loved
>> As if 't were his own son.
>> The flea? Ha, ha, ha, ha, ha!
>>> The flea! Ha, ha, ha, ha, ha!
>>> The flea!
>
> The king called his tailor,
>> The tailor came.
> "Make clothes for my pet,
>> And trousers too!"
>> Trousers? Ha, ha, ha, ha, ha!
>>> The flea? Ha, ha, ha, ha, ha!
>>> The flea! Ha, ha, ha, ha, ha!
>>> Yes, trousers!
>
> In silks and satins
>> He was now arrayed,
> With ribbons across his chest,
>> And a star.
>>> The flea? Ha, ha, ha, ha, ha!
>>> The flea!
>
> He became Minister of State,
>> And received many decorations;
> And all his relatives
>> Were most important at court.
>> Ha, ha!

Faust, Part I, Scene in Auerbach's cellar.

> And the courtiers and their ladies
> > Were plagued by fleas,
> The queen and maids of honour
> Had quite a time of it!
>
> Not one of them dared scratch
> > Or kill the pests.
> Yet we ordinary folks are free
> To scratch whene'er we like, and kill
> > As soon as one bites us!
> > > Ha, ha, ha, ha, ha, ha, ha,
> > > Ha, ha, ha, ha, ha, ha, ha!

In view of his nationalism and the poetic quality of his lyric gift, Edward MacDowell has frequently been held up as the American counterpart of Grieg. Both men spent the formative periods of their careers in Germany, and both adapted the lied to the requirements of their native milieu. Although much less prolific a song writer than Grieg, MacDowell infused his works with the same richness of atmosphere and mood. They have all the melodic charm that has made his piano pieces so popular. The *Sea, The Swan Bent Low, Thy Beaming Eyes,* and *To the Sea* are among the best known. Notice, in *The Sea,* written in 1892 to the verses of William Dean Howells, how the six-eight time gives a gently flowing effect. MacDowell marked it "Broadly, with rhythmic swing." The rich chords limn the emotion of the poem:

> One sails away to sea, to sea,
> One stands on the shore and cries;
> The ship goes down the world, and the light
> And the light on the sullen water dies,
>
> The whispering shell is mute,
> And after is evil cheer;
> She will stand on the shore and cry in vain,
> Many and many a year.
>
> But the stately wide-winged ship lies wrecked,
> Lies wrecked on the unknown deep;
> Far under, dead in his coral bed,
> > The lover lies asleep.

This is the seventh, and last, essential listening in this section of the chapter.

ADDITIONAL SUGGESTIONS FOR LISTENING

Among the German composers who continued in the tradition of the lied, special mention must be made of Robert Franz (1815-1892), Hugo Wolf (1860-1903), and Richard Strauss (1864-1949). Franz never achieved great popularity in this country, but his melodies—among the best known are *Für Musik* (For Music), *Gute Nacht* (Good Night), and *Im Herbst* (In Autumn)—have an elusive lyric charm. Wolf, by far the most important song writer of the late nineteenth century, and an artist of highly individual gifts, achieved within the limited framework of the song a kind of miniature Wagnerian music drama. He was strongly influenced by Wagner in his harmonic idiom. With him, the piano part became a most complex web, out of which the vocal line emerged, with an extraordinary combination of emotional power, psychological acumen, and imaginative tone painting. Try listening to his *Anakreon's Grab* (Anacreon's Grave), *Auch Kleine Dinge* (Even Little Things), *Verborgenheit* (Secrecy), or *Zur Ruh, zur Ruh!* (To Rest, to Rest!). They stand among the great songs.

Richard Strauss, phenomenally successful in symphonic music and opera (see Chapter XVIII), has also enriched the song repertory with a number of compositions that have achieved world-wide fame. *Ständchen* (Serenade), *Traum durch die Dämmerung* (Dream in the Twilight), *Zueignung* (Devotion), and *Allerseelen* (All Souls Day) are among the works that have stamped him a contemporary master of the lied.

In France, the principal composers during the height of the Romantic Period—Hector Berlioz, Charles Gounod, Camille Saint-Saëns, Georges Bizet, and Jules Massenet—devoted their best efforts to either opera or instrumental music. It was not until the latter part of the century, when a group of French composers made a concerted attempt to break away from German influence and found a true national style, that the French art song came into its own. The leader in this movement was César Franck (1822-1890). Although he wrote few songs, they occupy a high place in the repertory, chief among them being *(La) Procession*, *Nocturne*, and *(Le) Mariage des Roses*. His followers were Gabriel Fauré (1845-1924), best known for such songs as *L'Automne* and *Clair de Lune* (Moonlight); and Henri Duparc (1848-1933), composer of the exquisite *L'Invitation au Voyage* and *Extase*. Although Duparc wrote only a few songs, they are among the finest in French literature.

But the most distinctive song composer of France, and the one who influenced the form most profoundly, was Claude Debussy (1862-1918), master of Impressionism (see Chapter XXVIII), that tenuous cool and fluid style to which European music turned for respite after the over-emotionalism of the Wagnerian music drama. Debussy subordinated his vocal line to the poetic declamation of the verse—he set to music the great French poets, François Villon, Baudelaire, Mallarmé, and Verlaine—with the result that melody as such disappeared from his songs. Instead there developed a vocal line of the most exquisite subtlety, demanding from the performer the utmost sensitivity to nuance, while the piano let float a background of wavering harmonies. When performed by two artists who understand the style, these songs produce an effect of sheer magic. A fine introduction to this idiom is afforded by the setting of Verlaine's *Mandoline*, in which the tinkling chords give the atmosphere of the "gallants who go serenading and fair dames who to them listen," as their shadows

> Whirl ecstatic where the moonlight
> Falls in rose and silver splendour;
> A mandolin softly tinkling
> Answers the wind, gay and tender. [9]

Here, and in such songs as *Harmonie du Soir* (Evening Harmonies), *Receuillement* (Meditation), and *La Mort des Amants* (Death of the Lovers) is to be found that exquisite sensibility and suggestiveness that we shall meet again and again when we study the works of the Impressionists.

In America, the song has always been a favourite form, running the gamut from the sentimental, popular kind to the highest type of art song. At one extreme are songs such as Carrie Jacobs Bond's *Just a Song at Twilight* and James Molloy's *Love's Old Sweet Song*, which have sold millions of copies. Then there is the romantic art song, such as Charles Wakefield Cadman's *At Dawning* and *From the Land of the Sky-Blue Water*, or Thurlow Lieurance's *By the Waters of Minnetonka*, which combine a charming lyricism with popular melodic appeal. Typical of this genre are such extremely successful works as *Love Went A-Riding*, by Edward Bridges; Ethelbert Nevin's *The Rosary*; *Trees*, the setting by Oscar Rasbach of Joyce Kilmer's poem; Richard Hageman's setting of Rabindranath Tagore's *Do Not Go, My Love*, and Ernest Charles' *When I Have Sung My Songs*. In the tradition of French Impressionism are such works as *By a Lonely Forest Pathway* by Charles Griffes (1884-1920), the gifted young American whose career was cut short by an untimely death, and the exquisite songs of Charles Alden Carpenter (1876-　　　), *When I Bring You Coloured Toys*, the *Serenade*, and *On a Screen*.

[9] Translation by Bliss Carman. Copyright, Boston Music Co. Reprinted by permission.

Sentence Structure in Music: Phrase, Period, and Cadence

The reader may have noticed, in the songs we just heard, that there were definite breaks or pauses in the musical thought where the singer paused to draw breath. These naturally corresponded to the breaks in poetic thought at the end of the verse or sentence. In reading or speaking, we all pause an instant, almost automatically, at the end of the thought, which is generally marked by a comma—or half stop—at the end of a phrase or clause, and by a period—full stop—at the end of a sentence.

It is apparent, from our discussion on musical architecture, that, although music may at first sight appear to us to be a continuous flow without shape or form, it is in reality built of well-defined structural units or sections—the equivalent, we might say, of paragraphs or stanzas in writing. In many of the compositions we have listened to thus far, these sections or paragraphs were fairly easy to recognize, since often a new theme appeared in each section and dominated the scene until followed by another theme in the next section. We saw also that these sections appeared and reappeared in conformity with general aesthetic principles of construction—symmetry, balance, contrast, climax—which obtained not only in music but also in poetry, painting, sculpture, and architecture.

The paragraph in literature is further subdivided into sentences, clauses, and phrases, as is also the stanza. So, too, the musical section is subdivided into definite groupings of thought, known to the reader as phrases and periods. These groupings have to be set off with punctuation, otherwise they could not function effectively as recognizable units. The first phrase generally ends with a half stop or comma, known in music as the incomplete or semicadence, which gives the impression that more is to follow. In many folk songs two phrases make a musical sentence, or period, which ends with a full stop, an authentic or full cadence. The word comes from the Latin *cadere*, "to fall," since the pause was indicated, in song as in speech, by a downward inflection of the voice.

The upward and downward inflections of the two types of cadence, and the relation of the two phrases in the period, are well illustrated in a simple musical sentence such as the tune of *London Bridge*. (See page 72.)

We have here two four-measure phrases which stand in a kind

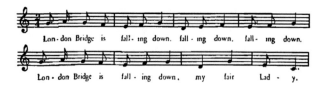

of question-answer relation. The first, ending with an upward
inflection on the semicadence, is answered by the second, ending
with a downward inflection on the full cadence. A similar relation
is observable in the two phrases that comprise the period in *The
Farmer in the Dell*:

Phrasing in both speech and song sprang up from an interplay
of two factors: first, an inherent need of the human mind for logical
organization in grouping its thoughts: second, the number of
words or tones that could be conveniently carried on one breath.
We phrase, or pause for breath, not only when we speak but also
when we read silently or write. Phrasing is just as important for
the instrumental player as it is for the singer, even though certain
instrumental performers are not restricted by breathing and
could go on playing indefinitely. In singing, we stop at the end of
the thought which, we noticed, comes simultaneously in both
words and music. In playing an instrument, the phrasing has to
be brought out just as carefully; and the wind instruments are
akin to the singer as regards breath. If a pianist or violinist does
not phrase properly he will be unable to indicate clearly the outlines of the musical structure. Incorrect phrasing in music is
equivalent to running sentences together in speech or writing. It
is symptomatic of confused thinking.

There is no fixed length for the phrase. Many folk songs, especially those that date back to the Middle Ages, when our system of
"measured music" was not yet as prevalent as it became in later
centuries, have quite irregular phrase lengths. The rhapsodical

outpourings of the Hungarian Gipsy or of the flamenco are apt to be very irregular in phrase structure. We noticed a three-measure phrase in *The Birch Tree* (page 46). Nonetheless, the music of Western Europe was strongly influenced, as we have seen, by folk-dance rhythms. And as soon as dance becomes a factor in music, we find a tendency to clearly defined, regular phrase structure. Also, the simple metres of poetry played their part in calling forth a regular phrase structure. Although we find innumerable exceptions and variants, the four-measure phrase, organized in a period of eight measures or in a double period of sixteen, seems to have been most attractive to folk and art musicians alike, in their search for simple, symmetrical patterns. Many of our best-loved tunes are built on a four-measure phrase structure.

Let us examine Stephen Foster's *Swanee River* for phrase, period, and cadence structure. The verse consists of four lines in two sentences:

Way down upon the Swanee River, far far away,
Dere's wha my heart is turning ever, dere's wha de old folks stay.
All de world is sad and dreary, ev'rywhere I roam,
Oh! darkies, how my heart grows weary, far from de old folks at home.

The first and third lines end in a comma (semicadence); the second and fourth in a period (full cadence). Each line is set to a four-measure phrase. (Notice the following musical example.)

It is apparent that we have here two musical periods, each equivalent to a sentence (two lines) of verse. Notice too that, of the four phrases, the second repeats the melody of the first, the third introduces contrasting material, and the fourth returns to the old phrase. Thus, we have here unity, variety, symmetry, and contrast achieved through that serviceable pattern, A-A:B:A.

Notice particularly, in the Foster song, that each of the four cadences occupies a full measure, giving a definite sense of pause. The break in the thought is indicated by the rest. The semicadence in the first line, an upward inflection on the word *away*, is balanced by the full cadence at the end of the second line, the downward inflection on *de old folks stay*. Similarly, the half pause at the end of the third line on *I roam* is answered by the full stop at the end of the fourth line, the final cadence on *at home*. Thus, we have a question-answer formation in the first two phrases, and a similar formation in the last two.

Chapter Seven

The Opera

I. Operetta and Light Opera[1]

LOOKING back upon the study we have made so far of vocal music, it becomes apparent that a song is an independent and self-contained work of art. Whether the song be a "traditional" or a "composed" folk song, an art song or a lied, the words and the music, between them, contain all there is to say for the moment, and only a singer is necessary to interpret and reveal the content. The listener has but to hear and react to the performance of the song itself to obtain the complete experience.

It is but a logical and easy step, now, to consider songs, for one or more singers, that require the addition of something outside themselves; that are an integral part of a more extended story, action, and environment. Let us think of the type of song that involves the action and participation of others, that is incomplete without the co-operation of the other arts—painting, drama, costuming, dancing, acting, and so on. Such a song is only a small portion of the whole, and thus a number of songs are required in succession for the unfolding of the drama of which each is a part; and as the moods and situations of the performers change, so must the songs change in the development of the story.

Such a type might well be considered an operatic song; and so a number of them in sequence and involving a number of persons might well be an opera—after a fashion, a simple type of opera. If the tale were a tragic one and sung and acted throughout (or almost), it might well be called a "grand" opera; if, on the other hand, there were spoken dialogue and action between the songs, and the plot of a cheerful, romantic, and even humorous nature, it might well be an *operetta* or a "light" opera. Thus the song, or *aria*, as we should now call it, is to be considered in the environment of a number of arts and a number of persons, all joined in

---

[1] Listening Study for this chapter is in Part II: excerpts from the opera CARMEN.

75

concerted action to tell a story—and we have a simple and general recipe for an elementary and hypothetical opera.

The combination of these different elements into one unified entertainment seems to answer some deep human need, for we find it persisting throughout history under all sorts of conditions. The Greeks and the Romans had elaborate dramatic performances with song and dance; the Middle Ages and Renaissance saw the emergence of various types of musical plays, sacred and secular. Nor is the genre confined to Western European civilization. We find dramatic spectacles with song and dance, some of great antiquity, in India, China, Japan, Java, and Persia, some obviously inspired by the spiritual and dramatic contents of the religious ritual, others quite secular, romantic, or humorous, and of high artistic order. Even primitive cultures have song-and-dance cycles, highly symbolic in character, that display in rudimentary form the elements of the musical-dramatic genre.

Of the various types of musical play that flourish in our culture, the comic opera, or operetta, is one of the most engaging. The comic opera (known in Italy as *opera buffa*, in France as *opéra bouffe*, and in Germany as *Singspiel*, or *song-play*) is a play in which songs and dances are interspersed with spoken dialogue, and which contains highly diverting situations that combine fantasy, romance, warm human sentiment, and racy, topical humour. This popular kind of opera is distinct from grand opera, which is sung throughout, is of a lofty nature, generally tragic in mood, and may be far removed, as far as plot and characters go, from the environment in which it is presented. The relation between comic opera or operetta and grand opera may be compared to that between popular song and art song. Where grand opera is formal in character, *opera buffa*, *opéra bouffe*, and *Singspiel* are delightfully informal. Where grand opera demands a lavish expenditure for soloists, chorus, ballet and orchestra, scenery and costumes, comic opera is fairly accessible to the common man. Where grand opera is aristocratic and cosmopolitan, subsidized in its early stages by kings and nobles, comic opera is plebeian and close to the soil, a worthy descendant of the song-and-dance plays presented at village fairs and in the market place by the itinerant musicians, jugglers, tumblers, and actors of the Middle Ages. Where grand opera, as often as not, deals with mythical or historical personages, comic opera bases itself on the personal experiences and interests of the audience, presenting them with rich satire and drollery. As happened with popular music and art music throughout the history of the art, the two genres flourished side by side and interacted on each other. In the eighteenth century, short comic operas were presented as *interludes* or *intermezzos* between the acts of grand opera. The popular opera took over some of the techniques and style characteristics evolved in grand opera. In return, whenever grand opera threatened to become excessively formalized and stilted, it found new life and vitality in the spirit of the folk opera.

The American stage has developed its own genre, the *musical comedy*, in which youth, beauty, and romance are intermingled with comedy, spectacular scenic effects, and a dancing chorus. Allied to this form is the *musical revue*, which presents the same elements either in a series of separate scenes and skits, or held together by the merest thread of plot or continuity. With the advent of the "talkies" came the motion-picture operettas, some of which presented song, dance, romance, and comedy in an even more lavish manner than was possible for the Broadway stage. All these types, with their appealing love songs sung by hero and heroine against a most romantic background, the rollicking antics and misadventures of the comedian, and the invariable happy ending, offer, through a combination of all the theatre arts with music, an irresistible type of entertainment which transports the spectator, in most compelling fashion, to the world of the imagination.

Since the essence of theatre is make-believe, we accept without question the convention whereby a character in an operetta suddenly switches from speech to song; pours out his feelings in a lyrical number, while the action pauses; and, after the applause has died down, resumes his role in the play. True, we know that he would never behave like this in real life. Yet in some mysterious way the music creates a reality and value of its own, lifting the action to the plane of pure emotion; and it is on this plane that we respond. When Shakespeare presents to us the jealousy of Othello or the anguish of Lear in the iambic pentameters of blank verse, we are aware that people do not express themselves in this fashion in everyday existence. Through the use of lofty and impassioned verse, the dramatist has lifted us into a world more intense, more "real" than the actual world, a realm of pure imagination in which our awareness of life is immeasurably heightened.

In the same way, when a character in a musical play sings of his love and longing for the heroine, even though he seems to violate every canon of realism, he communicates to us, as he could never have done through mere speech, the essence of romantic emotion. The music has added a new dimension, a new meaning, to the emotional impact of the drama. "It is better to invent reality than to copy it!" said Giuseppe Verdi, one of the great opera composers. There could be no better comment on both the poetic and the music drama.

The *romantic operetta*, or *light opera*,[2] which came into prominence all over Europe in the second half of the nineteenth century, has been cultivated with great success in America, and has enjoyed phenomenal popularity on our stage. The roster of gifted operetta composers includes such names as Victor Herbert (1859-1924), Reginald DeKoven (1859-1920), and later Rudolf Friml (1881-   ), Sigmund Romberg (1887-   ), and Jerome Kern (1885-1945). These men developed a style of smoothly flowing, sentimental melody of wide popular appeal, most appropriate to the picturesquely romantic plots of their operettas. Many of these musical plays are no longer given on the stage; but one or two songs from each seem to hold on year after year with astonishing vitality. Some even, as in the case of *Oh Promise Me* from De-Koven's ROBIN HOOD, and *Ol' Man River* from Kern's SHOW BOAT, are well on the way to becoming part of our stock of composed folk songs. A number have survived as favourite love songs: the *Indian Love Call* from Friml's ROSE-MARIE; *Will You Remember?* from Romberg's MAYTIME; the *Song of Love*—based on the second theme from the first movement of Schubert's UNFINISHED SYMPHONY—from BLOSSOM TIME, the musical romance of that composer's life; *Kiss Me Again* from Herbert's MLLE. MODISTE, as well as the *Gipsy Love Song* from his FORTUNE TELLER; and *Smoke Gets in Your Eyes* from Kern's ROBERTA.

In his short career George Gershwin (1898-1937) made an outstanding contribution to the tradition of American operetta. His gifts found apt expression in his "folk opera" PORGY AND BESS, a

---

[2] It is recommended that the specific songs mentioned in Part I, "Operetta and Light Opera," be considered as suggested and supplementary rather than assigned listening, and be indulged in as far as taste and time will allow. The "musts" for listening are in Part II of this chapter.

setting of DuBose Heyward's play. Technically, the work is on the borderline between operetta and opera, since some of the dialogue is spoken and some of it sung. The classification is immaterial. In PORGY AND BESS the conventions of the drama with music are invested with the colour and life of folk tale and folk speech. The result is a work of vivid imagination and effective as "good theatre." Listen to the following excerpts, which have become popular: the lullaby *Summertime*; *A Woman is a Sometime Thing*; Porgy's *I Got Plenty o' Nuttin'*, and his love song, *Bess, You Is My Woman Now*; Sporting Life's edifying sermon, *It Ain't Necessarily So*; the *Requiem*; and Porgy's final song, *Where is My Bess?*

In England the comic opera reached its apogee in one of the most amazing collaborations in dramatico-musical history, that between William S. Gilbert and Arthur Sullivan, which began in 1875 and lasted for over twenty years. Out of it came a type of operetta so original and distinctive that it has become something of a cult for hundreds of thousands of "Savoyards" throughout the English-speaking world. (The Savoy operas were so named after the theatre in which they first made their unparalleled success.) Here were fantasy and romance, whimsy and social satire, keyed to the rapierlike wit and astonishing verbal dexterity of Gilbert, and set off by the sparkling tunes of Sullivan.

The distinctive flavour of the Savoy operas is amply demonstrated in what has remained, in this country, the most popular of the series, THE MIKADO. A wonderful satire is levelled here against the English bureaucracy, through the symbolic figures of Ko-Ko, Lord High Executioner, and Pooh-Bah, Lord High Everything Else. In addition there are the lovers Nanki-Poo and Yum-Yum, the formidable Katisha, an elderly Lady in love with Nanki-Poo, and the Mikado, who humanely desires to "let the punishment fit the crime." It is futile to attempt to describe, in mere prose, the plot of a Gilbert and Sullivan operetta. Like *Alice in Wonderland*, it exists in a world of its own within which, through the magic of the verses and the music, it makes perfectly good sense. To transplant it out of that fantasy world is little short of fatal. See it on the actual stage if possible; if not, hear it through carefully selected records—and exercise your imagination a great deal.

G

Opera buffa

The spirit of comedy through music, which found such felicitous expression in the late nineteenth century, had reached its perfection of form and style a century earlier in the *opera buffa* of the Classical Period. This genre depended for its charm on a situation often extravagantly comical, keyed in the mood of the eighteenth-century comedy of manners; a light, playful style of music, and that pure vocal line that was the glory of the Classical masters; an ebullient ensemble number at the finale of each act; and the personality of the *buffo*, the chief comic character. Generally baritone or bass, the buffo not only was one of the protagonists in the play but, in the fashion of a master of ceremonies, he informally harangued the audience from the footlights, taking them into his confidence—as the Gilbert characters do—commenting slyly, in almost improvisational manner, on life, love, and politics, and keeping them in gales of laughter with his couplets: the living embodiment, in short, of the spirit of the *commedia dell' arte*. Between the arias, duets, and ensemble numbers, the action was carried on by a *secco* (dry recitation), a rapid-fire interchange of question and retort carried on in a manner bordering on speech, in which the musical line was subservient, in shape and rhythm, to the words, and supported by the flimsiest accompaniment of chords on the harpsichord. (These, in modern productions, are played by the orchestra.) Among the outstanding examples of this type are La Serva Padrona (The Maid-Mistress), by the short-lived Giovanni Pergolesi (1710-1736), which was revived in recent years at the Metropolitan Opera House; Il Matrimonio Segreto (The Secret Marriage) by Domenico Cimarosa (1749-1801), the delightful overture of which is still frequently performed; and the Barber of Seville by Gioacchino Rossini (1792-1868), which, for over a century, has remained a favourite with opera audiences. But the supreme example of opera buffa is Mozart's Marriage of Figaro, in which the spirit of eighteenth-century comedy is clothed in music eternally young and radiant that for sheer loveliness has never been equalled.

Incidentally, both the Rossini and Mozart operas are based on the satirical comedies of Beaumarchais (1732-1799), The Marriage of Figaro being the sequel to The Barber of Seville. Beaumarchais, who was a musician as well as a dramatist, intended the BARBER as a comic opera, with music by him based on the songs and dances he had heard in Spain. When the work was refused by the *Opéra Comique*, he submitted it, as a "comedy in prose interspersed with songs," to the *Comédie française*, where it was produced.

ADDITIONAL SUGGESTIONS FOR LISTENING

For excerpts from the MARRIAGE OF FIGARO, listen to the *Overture*, a delectable titbit of musical merriment which, although it does not use any of the themes of the opera itself, fully captures the spirit of what is to follow; the aria of Cherubino in the first act, *Non so più cosa son* (I Know Not What I am Doing), in which he pours out his love for the Countess; the Countess' aria in the second act, *Porgi amor* (Love, Thou Pure Impulse), in which she begs the God of Love either to bring her husband back to her or to let her find release from grief in death; the wonderful *Voi che sapete* (You Who Know, Tell Me), in which Cherubino expresses all his youthful ardour; the song of the Countess in Act III, *Dove Sono* (They are Over), in which she looks back with longing to her former days of happiness; and Susanna's beautiful *Deh vieni, non tardar* (Oh, Come, Do Not Delay), in the final act. Here is sparkling vocal melody, spontaneous and flowing, pure in form and luminous of texture. The listener might wish to include in his supplementary listening the vivacious and humorous aria from Rossini's THE BARBER OF SEVILLE, *Largo al factotum* (Room for the Factotum), sung by the leading male character, Figaro.

II. Grand Opera

In the operetta, we found, the plot is carried on through spoken dialogue which, at the lyrical moments, reverts to song. In the opera, the dialogue too is sung, in the free and flexible musical declamation or song-speech known as *recitative*, which gives way, at the lyrical high points, to the arias, the songs or airs. This procedure gives us a dramatic work set to music from beginning to end.

In view of what we have said about the theatre as a world of fantasy, and about the function of music or poetry in heightening the emotional intensity of the dramatic situation, it need not surprise us that generations of theatregoers throughout the world have accepted the conventions of the play that is sung instead of spoken. Indeed, for over three hundred years the opera has been one of the most popular forms of entertainment in Western European culture.

This acceptance of musico-dramatic art goes back much farther than is commonly supposed. We have already pointed out (in Chapter III) the role of music in religious ritual. It should be remembered that the formal theatre, whether in ancient Greek or medieval European civilization, probably sprang out of the spirit and dramatic elements of religious ceremonial. From the beginning of the Catholic Church, the supreme drama of Christendom —the life and death of Christ—has been presented within a framework of words and music. The ceremonial Mass of the Church became the supreme music drama of Europe. Magnificent vestments, sacred vessels, incense, an elaborate ritual, and music by the greatest composers, known and unknown, against a scenic background furnished by the finest artists in painting, sculpture, and architecture—all combined in a most imposing spectacle. In the later Middle Ages there sprang up the *Mystery* and *Miracle plays*, containing basic elements of both opera and poetic drama. Based on incidents in Scripture or in the lives of the saints, these plays were originally given either inside the church or in the open space before it, with such realistic props as calves, donkeys, and other Biblical animals, and used spoken dialogue as well as song. It can readily be supposed that such episodes as the lament of the mothers over the slaying of the Innocents or the repentance of Magdalene lent themselves to effective musical treatment. Thus, for centuries before the actual development of the opera, music had become an integral part of the most engrossing symbolic drama known to European man.

On the other hand, no less important elements of the opera came from secular sources. Dance, pantomime, scenic splendour, and certain musical characteristics were derived from the masques and spectacles which throughout the feudal period predominated at the entertainments of the princely courts. Musical declamation stemmed out of the experiments of a group of Florentine noblemen who, spurred on by the spirit of the Italian Renaissance, sought to revive the lost musical-dramatic art of ancient Greek tragedy. By the year 1600, all these elements were ready to be united, awaiting only the touch of the creative artists who would

fuse them into a new art form. This fusion was accomplished, in
the early stages, by Jacopo Peri (*c.* 1561-*c.* 1633) and Giulio
Caccini (*c.* 1588-*c.* 1615), and brought to completion by the first
great master of operatic style, Claudio Monteverde (1567-1643)
who, at about the same time that Shakespeare was carrying the
poetic drama to a higher level than it had ever before attained,
opened new vistas of dramatic expressiveness for music in the
theatre.

We are so accustomed to the naturalistic drama of today that
we think of opera and drama as poles apart. Actually, not only do
poetic drama and music drama go back to the same origin in the
medieval religious plays, but they also had many elements in
common during long periods of their development. The so-called
realistic drama of our contemporary theatre, which presents to us
characters and situations familiar to us from our everyday milieu,
is, strictly speaking, a comparatively recent innovation, having
come into its own only a little over a half century ago, with the
plays of Ibsen and Shaw. The theatre of the past, of Shakespeare
and Marlowe, of Corneille and Racine, of Calderon and Lope de
Vega, of Schiller and Lessing—it goes without saying, of Sophocles and Aeschylus—was a theatre of poetry and lofty declamation, of pageantry, musical interludes, songs, choruses, and stately
dances. (One has but to examine the stage directions in Shakespeare's plays to realize the extent of this "operatic" element.) It
is from this emotional-musical speech that musical declamation
arose in the theatre of antiquity, returning two thousand years
later to the theatre of the Renaissance. As the two genres developed, the literary element was subordinated to the musical in the
opera, while the poetic element was subordinated to the realistic
in the drama, with the result that we encounter them today as
completely contrasting types of theatre. But this should not blind
us to their common ancestry.

In the music drama, a number of elements come together within the musical framework: poetic mood, dramatic action, vocal
and orchestral music, singing and dancing, solos, ensembles and
choruses, scenery, and costumes and pageantry all held together.
The basic problem in operatic aesthetics is the need to fuse all
these elements into a harmonious whole. The fundamental differences between the several operatic styles, in all periods, have
sprung from the various ways in which this synthesis is accom-

plished, from the emphasizing of one or another, or several, of the different ingredients. Even the style of individual composers may be analyzed from this point of view.

The Italians, throughout the whole of operatic history, have been enamoured of the voice, and developed in their lyric theatre a style of *bel canto*, or beautiful singing, that has, in the opinion of many musicians, never been surpassed. Italian opera, consequently, is primarily vocal opera, depending for its appeal on the power and beauty of the human voice, to which all the other factors are subordinated. This preoccupation led, on the one hand, to showy exhibition pieces calling for prodigious technique on the part of the singer, and as often as not having very little to do with the mood of the drama out of which they were supposed to have sprung, and on the other, to the development of a style of flowing, sensuous vocal melody that is the glory of the Italian school. The tendency to subordinate drama to voice was pushed so far that in the classical opera of the eighteenth century the plot became little more than a meaningless, artificial framework for the brilliant arias and ensemble numbers of the chief performers. This was the so-called "prima donna opera," which was really little more than a vocal concert in costume.

By the beginning of the nineteenth century, the Italian opera had already begun to return to the dramatic principles with which it had started out. The start was made in the works of the three great masters of brilliant vocal melody who flourished in the first half of the century, the earliest composers of Italian opera whose works are still performed today: Rossini, whose masterpiece, THE BARBER OF SEVILLE, we mentioned earlier in the chapter; Gaetano Donizetti (1797-1848), known to us for his setting of Walter Scott's tragic story of "Lucy of Lammermoor" (LUCIA DI LAMMERMOOR), as well as the delightful comic operas DAUGHTER OF THE REGIMENT, DON PASQUALE, and ELIXIR OF LOVE; and Vincenzo Bellini (1801-1835), composer of NORMA. Their successor was Giuseppe Verdi (1813-1901), a great dramatic composer, who brought the Italian operatic style to its peak. He perfected a type of melody that was not only attractive to the ear and admirably shaped to the contours of the singer's voice, but essentially dramatic melody: that is, it sprang logically out of the situation on the stage, out of the personalities, the moods and inner conflicts, of the characters. The famous works of his middle period,

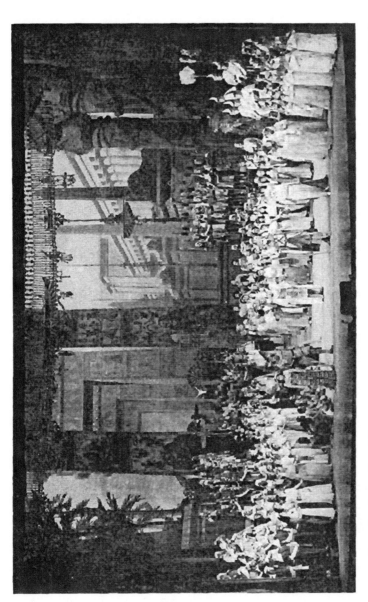

Scene from the Opera "Aida"

Verdi

RIGOLETTO, LA TRAVIATA and LA FORZA DEL DESTINO (The Force of Destiny), and the three masterpieces of his maturity—AÏDA, OTELLO and FALSTAFF—represent a superb fusion of the great *bel canto* tradition with dramatic truth and musical expressiveness.[4]

The French, on the other hand, loved not only the voice but also logic, literature, elegant diction—and the ballet. They insisted on understanding what the singers were singing. Consequently, pure vocal line could not gain complete ascendancy over dramatic coherence. Their composers stood in close contact with their literary men. As a result, the principles of French classical drama had some influence on operatic procedure. At the court of the Bourbons poetic drama, music, and the dance attained a greater homogeneity of style than anywhere else in Europe.

Opera in France had its roots in the elaborate ballet spectacles and masques performed at the entertainments of the nobility. It was an Italian, Jean Baptiste Lully (1632-1687), who introduced the new Florentine music drama to the court of Louis XIV and who, by adapting it to the tastes and needs of the French genius, became known to history as the "father of French opera." His successor in the period of Louis XV was Jean Philippe Rameau (1683-1764), a friend of Voltaire, several of whose librettos he set to music. Rameau was a theorist as well as a composer, author of several important treatises on harmony. He was, besides, a trenchant critic who carried on extensive polemics with Diderot, Jean Jacques Rousseau, and d'Alembert on the æsthetics of the opera.

In the reign of Louis XVI, it was a foreigner again who guided the destinies of French opera—the German, Christophe Willibald Gluck (1714-1787). Gluck, who achieved his greatest triumphs in Paris, under the patronage of his one-time pupil Marie Antoinette, attempted to lead the eighteenth-century opera back to the principles of sound dramaturgy, which had been espoused by Monteverde and the Florentine founders of the music drama. For this he is remembered as one of the reformers of the opera. His famous

---

[4] His successors followed in his footsteps, adapting the Italian vocal style to the exigencies of modern dramatic realism. Chief among them were Giacomo Puccini (1858-1924), composer of LA BOHÈME, TOSCA, and MADAME BUTTERFLY; Ruggiero Leoncavallo (1858-1919), known chiefly for the ever-popular I PAGLIACCI (The Clowns); and Pietro Mascagni (1863-1945), who wrote CAVALLERIA RUSTICANA (Rustic Chivalry). Although less gifted than the master, they and their confrères all had a flair for vocal-dramatic music that was the essence of their Italian heritage.

preface to his opera ALCESTE formulates his artistic creed and gives a clue to the significance of his reforms:

When I undertook to set this poem it was my intention to avoid all those abuses which had crept into Italian opera through the mistaken vanity of singers and the unwise compliance of composers, and which had rendered it wearisome and ridiculous instead of being, as it once was, the most beautiful and imposing spectacle of modern times. I endeavoured to reduce music to its proper function, that of seconding poetry by enforcing the expression of the sentiment and the interest of the situations without interrupting the action or weakening it by super-fluous ornament. . . . I also thought that my first and chief care as a composer was to aim at a noble simplicity; and there is no rule of composition which I have not thought it my duty to sacrifice in order to favour truthfulness of emotion and produce the proper effect.

The first half of the nineteenth century saw the triumph in Paris of grand opera, a type of heroic drama set in a background of orchestral and scenic splendour. Despite the intensity of its tragic moments and the lofty plane of the action, this genre strikes us today as being somewhat bombastic and pompous. In this period French grand opera reached its peak in the works of the German, Giacomo Meyerbeer (1791-1864), and the Italian, Gasparo Spontini (1774-1851), composer of LA VESTALE. Meyer-beer's works, enormously popular throughout the nineteenth century, are gradually disappearing from the repertory, although we still hear the *Coronation March* from LE PROPHÈTE, the aria *O Paradiso* from L'AFRICAINE, and that wonderful show piece for the coloratura soprano, the *Shadow Song* from DINORAH.

The reader will have noticed that, until this point, French grand opera was largely the work of Italians or Germans who adapted the international Italian opera style to Parisian tastes. Yet, side by side with this type of opera, there flourished the truly native *opéra comique*. Out of the combination of the two there came into being, about the middle of the nineteenth century, what we consider today the distinctive French contribution to opera, the *drame lyrique* or lyric drama, as typically French in its conception and execution as the opera of Verdi and Puccini is Italian. In the French lyric drama we have convincing dramatic situations; a type of musical declamation that grows out of the inflections of the French language; a certain literary quality in the libretto; and a sweet lyricism that is quite distinct from the dramatic melody of the Italians. The most popular of these French works are Charles Gounod's FAUST (1859), based on an episode from Goethe's drama, although completely Gallicized; Jules Massenet's MANON (1884), a setting of the appealing novel of Abbé Prevost; Camille Saint-Saëns' Biblical opera, SAMSON ET DELILAH (1877); and the finest of the French operas, Georges Bizet's CARMEN (1875), a masterful setting of Prosper Mérimée's exciting story. To these may be added two more recent works, Gustave Charpentier's LOUISE (1900), an opera of modern working-class life in Paris; and Debussy's memorable setting of Maeterlinck's symbolist drama PELLÉAS AND MÉLISANDE, the quintessence of the French spirit in modern music drama.

Just as the Italians emphasized vocal melody, and the French, musical declamation, the Germans tended to use the orchestra as the foundation of their music drama. With Richard Wagner this tendency became so pronounced that we may with justice speak of his works as symphonic operas. Yet already the first great composer of German opera, Mozart, had used his orchestra for dramatic characterization and theatrical effect as it had never been used before. When Napoleon asked Grétry the difference between the style of Mozart and that of Cimarosa, he replied: "Sire, Cimarosa puts his statue on the stage and the pedestal in the orchestra; Mozart puts his statue in the orchestra and the pedestal on the stage." We believe today that in Mozart statue and pedestal are one; but the remark provides some insight into the reactions of his contemporaries.

It must be remembered that Mozart was one of the outstanding symphonic composers of all time. He was heir alike to the Italian tradition of *bel canto* and the German instrumental style. The combination of the two produced, in DON GIOVANNI, a work that is coming more and more to be rated as one of the great music dramas, in which orchestra and voice fuse in a perfect unity, and in which the symphonic background interprets with the utmost psychological penetration and power every nuance of the action and characterization unfolding on the stage. In the Italian *opera buffa* tradition he produced the MARRIAGE OF FIGARO; and in the style of the native comic opera, the *Singspiel*, he wrote, three months before his death, the fairy opera, THE MAGIC FLUTE. With these works, as far as present-day audiences are concerned, German opera begins.

Carl Maria von Weber (1786-1826), generally called "the father of German romantic opera," is today chiefly remembered for the overtures to his three operas, FREISCHÜTZ, OBERON, and EURYANTHE. In him we find the beginnings of that ardent nationalism, the glorification of German folklore and myth, of German forest and mountain and river, which reached its culmination in the music drama of Richard Wagner (1813-1883). Outside of Germany, where his operas still hold the stage, Weber is considered of importance in operatic history mainly as having prepared the way for his illustrious successor.

Wagner, particularly in the music dramas of his mature period —TRISTAN AND ISOLDE, the cycle of THE RING OF THE NIBELUNG, and his comic masterpiece DIE MEISTERSINGER (The Master Singers)—represents the peak of German operatic style in the same way that Verdi does the Italian, Bizet and Debussy the French. In Wagner's works the chief protagonist, and the mainspring of the action, is the orchestra. The orchestra reminisces and warns of things to come; it comments on the action as did the chorus in Greek tragedy; it weaves a symphonic web that encases actors and audience alike. Out of this seething harmony rises the vocal line, which is declaimed by the singers in a kind of *sprechstimme*, or speaking song, geared to the German tongue as intimately as is Debussy's declamation to the French. This form Wagner, in his later works, called "endless melody," to distinguish it from the aria, the moulded and "set" tune of Italian opera. At high lyrical moments, the "endless melody" gives way to what might be considered equivalent to arias; yet these are always but strands in the rich symphonic texture. There are no pauses at the end of the songs to allow for applause; no ballets or *divertissements*, choruses, or ensemble numbers save those that are an integral part of the dramatic action.

Wagner believed that the poetic drama was worthy of the same reverence as a religious ceremonial. His life work represents an attempt, carried through with singular devotion to what he considered his mission, to purge the lyric theatre of the triviality into which it had fallen, and to restore it to the place of honour it had occupied among the Greeks. One of the most original figures in the history of art, he inaugurated a revolution in musical thinking comparable to that effected by his contemporary Darwin in the domain of scientific thought. (He has been called by so trenchant a critic as H. L. Mencken "one of the greatest geniuses in the history of man.") Yet, despite the elaborate aesthetic theory that he built up in his philosophical works—his prose writings fill twelve volumes—by making the orchestra more important than the voice in his dramas, he laid himself open to the charge of having misunderstood the fundamental nature of opera. (In any case, his theoretical writings do not always offer a trustworthy guide to what he achieved in his operas, for his practice often differed widely from his theory.) Excerpts from his music dramas are played continually at symphony concerts, where they sound effective without the voices—in the opinion of some, even more so. This means, in effect, that the voices are not indispensable to this type of performance, a condition that would be unthinkable in Italian or French opera. Whatever the merits of the controversy, the Wagnerian dramas remain with us, despite their many faults, as extended vocal-symphonic tone poems with passages of sweeping power and beauty; and the great moments in them rank unquestionably with the enduring achievements of musical-dramatic art.

As might be expected, German opera is somewhat slower in pace than is either Italian or French opera. The action is less externalized, and the music is less likely (especially in the later Wagner) to be a series of set-pieces, or arias. Rather, there is likely to be a continuous flow of song—either one song going imperceptibly into another, or assuming the half-lyric and half-declamatory style that Wagner used in his late music dramas. In the early •
Wagnerian operas, and those of his contemporaries, one finds the Italian traditions well established.

We have already referred to the *Prelude to Act I* of Lohengrin (see page 25) as an example of religious sentiment in music. (The function of the prelude to an act is to create in the audience the proper receptivity for the unfolding of the drama.) The motive reappears in the first act, in Elsa's great aria known as *Elsa's Dream*, in which the falsely accused Princess describes a vision that appeared to her of a knight in shining armour come to do battle on her behalf. The shimmering theme originally heard in the *Prelude* accompanies her recital in the aria, indicating that the deliverer of whom she dreamed is a knight of the Holy Grail. Then, softly, in the brass, we hear a chivalric motive that well describes the brave knight who is on his way to help her—the orchestra assuming the function of a commentator.

The *Prelude to the Third Act* of LOHENGRIN is an outburst of jubilation to celebrate the marriage of the Swan Knight of the Grail and Elsa. The tumultuous theme in the trombones sets a mood of festivity, which gives way, in the middle section, to tender lyricism and meditation; then the exuberance returns. At the very end, in the concert version, we hear the ominous theme of doubt, which is to prove Elsa's undoing—she had promised Lohengrin that she would never inquire into his identity. Then, softly, in the brass, we hear repeated the chivalric motive describing the brave knight.

If LOHENGRIN represents the German Romantic opera of Wagner's first period, TRISTAN AND ISOLDE belongs to the fully developed music drama of his maturity. Here, certainly, is a great paean of love between man and woman; love as seen by nineteenth-century Romanticism—love as escape, ecstasy, oblivion. The essence of this mood is captured in the magnificent duet in the second act, *Hymn to the Night* (O Descend Upon Us, Night of Love), sung by the two lovers in the garden of Isolde's palace. Never did dramatic music more eloquently capture the mood of rapture, of sheer sensuous beauty, the power of romantic passion, of wonder and ecstasy—and sustain it to such length!

We shall return to Wagner as a symphonic composer in a later chapter. (See page 251.) Suffice now to point out several other favourite excerpts from his operas that should be heard when time permits— and inclination directs. Among those selections, we name: *Song to the Evening Star*, the *Pilgrims' Chorus*, and Elisabeth's aria, *Dichteure Halle* (Oh! Hall of Song), from Wagner's opera TANNHÄUSER; the *Prize Song* from DIE MEISTERSINGER; Siegmund's *Love Song* from DIE WALKÜRE; Senta's *Ballad* and the *Spinning Chorus* from THE FLYING DUTCHMAN; and Isolde's hymn to love and death, the *Liebstod*, from the final scene of TRISTAN. Acquaintance with these will, we feel sure, lead the listener to others.

The opera "Carmen," by Georges Bizet (1838-1875)

The opera we have chosen for the essential listening project for this chapter is generally conceded to be one of the two or three most popular operas of the standard repertory, though its première in Paris in 1875 was a failure. Thus the listener has a likely chance of hearing it either on the stage or over the radio, or both.

Scene from the Opera "Carmen"

Bizet

CARMEN is filled with beautiful *recitatives*,[5] arias, and ballet tunes that are captivating on the first hearing.[6]

The underlying drama, based on the novel by Prosper Mérimée, is much more real and probable than that met in most operas; the general tempo of the opera is moving, vivacious, full of effective action, and tragically gripping from the brief overture, or prelude, to the fall of the final curtain, with hardly a dull moment in the entire work. It is a brilliant piece of operatic writing, with vocal parts that are so well conceived that they almost sing themselves; and the orchestration is so expertly executed that it stamps Bizet a master of that craft. There is in CARMEN musical characterization of a very high order, and a dramatic insight into the persons of the cast as people of real life and not merely stage appurtenances.

If the story of the opera is gone over carefully beforehand and held well in mind, the selections that we have indicated for listening will give a good idea of the continuity of the whole, and we hope will create a desire to see and hear a real stage presentation —for nothing can take the place of that. A large number of good recordings are available to choose from, all the way from separate pieces to a judicious and well-executed condensation of the opera as a whole. Only the listener's interest and available time can determine the limitations. In the author's opinion, no other opera adapts itself more naturally to a "record" performance than does CARMEN.

The characters of the opera are, in order of appearance:

Morales, an officer: *baritone*
Micaela, a peasant girl: *soprano*
Don José, a corporal of dragoons: *tenor*
Zuniga, captain of dragoons: *bass*
Carmen, a cigarette girl and Gipsy: *mezzo-soprano*

[5] A *recitative* is a kind of vocal declamation, free of the restrictions of regular and fixed rhythm, form, metre, or regularity of lyrical song, so as to follow more faithfully the accents and inflections of emotionalized speech, or rapidly changing moods in action. This "glorified speech" type of singing usually parallels the function of the monologue, dialogue, and speech accompanying action in the ordinary drama. The recitative usually precedes the lyrical and more static set-piece, the aria, throughout the opera; the arias being, more often than not, in the familiar three-part, or ternary, form.

[6] It should be noted here that Micaela's aria in Act III was "lifted" from GRISELIDIS, and the ballet scenes in Act III and IV were from ARLÉSIENNE and THE PEARLFISHER —a practice common enough among operatic composers. Also, it is interesting to note that when Bizet composed CARMEN he wrote it in *opéra comique* style with the dialogue spoken; these dialogues were replaced with recitatives, singing parts, composed by Ernest Guiraud (Paris, 1837-1892), thus transforming the work into a more truly "grand opera" type.

Gipsies, friends of Carmen: Frasquita, *soprano*; Mercedes, *contralto*
Escamillo, a toreador: *baritone*
Smugglers: El Remendado, *tenor*; El Dancairo, *baritone*
Innkeeper, guide, officers, dragoons, Gipsies, boys, cigarette girls,
    smugglers, etc.
Time: About 1820
Place: Seville and near-by mountains.

The brilliant *Prelude* to Act I introduces us to the music from
the final scene before the bull ring at Seville—music of riotous
colour and animation. Then we hear the famous *Toreador Song*
theme, and just before the curtain rises, the ominous Fate motive,
which will appear again and again in various guises throughout
the work, as the characters are swept to their doom. The Fate
motive follows:

"Fate Motif."

ACT I

The curtain rises, disclosing a guardhouse to the left, the cigarette factory to the right, an overhead bridge to the rear, and an
open square to the fore. Through the crowd, which has assembled
to watch the changing of the guard in the square at Seville, darts
the flirtatious Carmen, looking for the young and handsome
corporal, Don José.

Love is like an-y wild wood bird, That soars so high in a cloud-less sky.

She sings of love, as he understands it, to the seductive rhythms of
an "Habañera":

> Ah! love is like a wild wood bird,
> None may hope to tame his wings. . . .
> Often, deaf to threats and prayers alike,
> You refuse ardent homage,

> While the one who coldly slights you,
> You pick for a master. . . .
> If you love me, beware!
> If I love you, beware too!

Here, as in the music to come, we have not only a melody that is superb in its own right, but what is more—and this makes it great dramatic music—the melody reveals the essence of the character and of the situation. As the Gipsy sways hither and yon, circling about the simple, quiet soldier who has caught her eye, finally throwing him a rose, we have the beginning of that interplay of personality which is the essence of good theatre. Don José finally repulses Carmen, saying that he loves Micaela. The bell calls the girls back to work and José is left alone. Micaela appears with a letter from his mother, and he sings while she goes off stage. José sings (reading):

Tell him that his moth-er is lone-ly, pray-ing all the day for her son.

Presently a commotion is heard coming from the factory; the girls crowd upon the stage and report that Carmen has stabbed another girl in a fight. José is sent to arrest her. When apprehended, Carmen is tied to a chair for temporary safekeeping, until the Captain, Zuniga, can arrive. However, she continues to flirt with José and sings the captivating "sequidilla," *Near the Walls of Seville*, in which she promises to meet him at the inn if he will let her go free.

Near to the wall of Se - vil - - - - la.

There lives my friend Li - las Pas - tia,

The guards return to lead Carmen away, and in the scuffle that ensues, she makes her escape. Of course José is held to blame, arrested and led away to the guardhouse. (End of Act I.)

H

ACT II

The vivid and atmospheric introduction to Act II brings us the rhythmic music of the Dragoons of Alcala; then the curtain rises on the scene of the inn of Lillas Pastia outside Seville, where Carmen has gone to join a band of smugglers from the mountains. As she watches the dancers, she sings the gay *Gipsy Song* in praise of the wild, carefree Gipsy life:

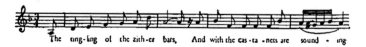

The ring-ling of the zith-er bars,   And with the cas-ta-nets are sound-ing

When the sound of gay guitars floats on the air,
The Gipsies spring forth in a merry dance,
Tambourines beat in time with the music,
And every voice repeats a merry song. . . .

The rhythm of the song, the curve of the melody, and the mysterious effect of plucked strings unite with the clicking of castanets in music that grows ever faster, ever more abandoned.

The shouting of the crowd announces the arrival of Escamillo, the popular toreador. In the famous *Toreador Song*, in which he

glowingly describes the life of the bull ring as one of swift action, reckless courage, applause, and love, we have another melody that not only is irresistible as pure melody, but one that paints the personality, the mood, and the manner of Escamillo in a sure and graphic fashion.

Don José arrives, looking for Carmen; he has just been released from his prison in the guardhouse. Fascinated by the Gipsy, Carmen, he overstays his leave. When she chides him for his eagerness to return to the barracks, he takes from underneath his coat the flower that she tossed to him in the first act, and gives vent to his feelings in the impassioned *Flower Song*:

I kept the flow'r you gave to me · Ev - en a - mid the pris - on walls.

> I kept the flower you gave to me
> Even amid the prison walls;
> Although faded, for me it still retained
> Its sweet perfume.
> Night and day I inhaled its lovely odour
> And wildly called to you—in vain. . . .
> Hoping only, beloved, to see you once again!

He is torn between his love and his deep desire to return to his duty; but the issue is decided by Fate. His superior officer, Zuniga, who has flirted with Carmen at the beginning of the act, returns to the inn. A fight breaks out between the two men, who are separated by the Gipsies. For José the life of a soldier— and of a law-abiding citizen—is over. He has no choice but to join Carmen and the smugglers.

ACT III

The *Intermezzo* that introduces Act III is of exquisite simplicity. A graceful shepherd tune played by the woodwinds and harp serves as a charming interlude in the mounting tensions. The curtain rises on the gathering place of the smugglers in the heights of the mountains; the *March of the Smugglers* gives a vivid tone picture of their stealthy movements as they clamber over the rocks to their camp.

Don José is tormented by remorse and jealousy; he quarrels with Carmen. She joins the Gipsy girls who are telling their fortunes with cards. Shuffling the pack, she draws the ace of spades. *Death—Always death!* she sings as the orchestra repeats the Fate motif a dozen times—a real dramatic stroke.

The smugglers leave on an expedition; the mountain pass is deserted. Micaela, Don José's sweetheart before his fatal infatuation with Carmen, arrives to look for her faithless lover. Micaela's aria—a prayer for Heaven's protection—is a superb example of the French equivalent of Italian dramatic melody. Here, too, we note Bizet's genius at delineating character and dramatic situation through the aria.

I swear that naught shall hin-der me,   I   say a   last I am eag-er for my part'

Following her prayer, Micaela spies José high above her on a cliff. She hails him, but he does not hear. Only a shot is heard, fired by José at Escamillo who has come to take Carmen. A duel takes place between the two rivals; but it is stopped by Carmen herself. Micaela is discovered hiding near by and is brought to José. She tells him that his mother is dying and pleads with him to return to the city with her. Of course Carmen urges him to leave, and as he exits, José threatens with, "We shall meet again!"; but Carmen is far too engrossed in listening to the Toreador's song that comes from the distance. The cards are flung to the winds, and as the curtain falls, Carmen's defiant laughing at Fate is heard above the hurried music of the orchestra.

ACT IV

The *Aragonaise* heard at the onset of this act provides a gay, tumultuous, and impassioned accompaniment for the colourful

ballet. The scene is at the entrance of the arena at Seville. Here is the hustle and bustle of gay pageantry in the square, just before the time set for the opening of the bullfight. The bullfighters march by in a jolly procession. A shout goes up on the entrance of the crowd's favourite, Escamillo, with Carmen at his side in the carriage. He takes affectionate leave of her to enter the ring. The crowd follows the procession into the entrance of the arena.

Just as Don José appears, the Fate motif is heard sounding from the orchestra and a sinister mood fills the scene. In the tragic final scene we see Carmen, in turn defiant, cruel, contemptuous of José, at last confessing that she loves Escamillo and has finished with the soldier. The drama mounts steadily to the climax where José draws his dagger and plunges it into Carmen. The Fate motif thunders forth from the orchestra. The crowd returns, as the shouts of "Bravo" to the victorious Escamillo come from the arena, mingled with the *Toreador Song*. José throws himself beside the lifeless form of the Gipsy and sobs, "O my Carmen, my adored Carmen!"—and the curtain falls.

ADDITIONAL SUGGESTIONS FOR LISTENING

Another of the three most popular operas in the standard repertory is unquestionably Verdi's spectacular AïDA, and we suggest the following numbers, which are readily obtainable in very good recordings: ACT I: *Celesta Aïda* (Heavenly Aïda), sung by Rhadames, tenor; *Ritorna Vincitor* (Return Victorious), sung by AïDA, soprano. ACT II: the opening *Balabili Dance* ballet music, the ballet from Scene 2, and the March of Victory. ACT III: O *cieli azzurri* (O Sky of Azure Hue), sung by Aïda; *Pur ti riveggo mia dolce Aida* (Again I See Thee, My Own Aïda), sung by Rhadames. ACT IV: O *terra addio* (Farewell, Oh Earth), duet sung by Rhadames and Aïda as the final curtain falls upon their impending death together in the sealed tomb. Aïda is often chosen to open an operatic season because of its spectacular and colourful pageantry, the large number of participants possible, the many opportunities for very impressive scenes on the stage—to say nothing of the countless beautiful arias, the superb choral writing throughout, and the timely and graceful ballets. As for potential scenic effects, Aïda has few equals. It is an excellent "first" for anyone who has never heard and seen an opera. This is Italian opera at its peak, composed by a master of the stage and traditional vocal styles, one who defies equality of comparison —yes, even with Wagner, in many respects.

Continuing our brief discussion of Italian opera at this point, it is fitting to follow Verdi by another of his countrymen who has, in many ways, departed from the older traditions and has taken up the more realistic type of thought and expression. We have in mind Giacomo Puccini (1858-1924), and mention first among his works his popular setting of Henri Murger's sketches of the life of young artists in Paris, LA BOHÈME (Première, Turin, 1896). Characteristic of Puccini's rich vocal line and appealing lyricism is the music of the love scene between

Rudolph and Mimi in the first act: Rudolph's vibrant aria, *Che gelida manima* (You Tiny Hand Is Frozen); Mimi's reply, *Mi chiamano Mimi* (My Name is Mimi); and the love duet *O soave fanciulla* (Oh Lovely Maiden). From Puccini's other works, the stirring aria from the second act of MADAME BUTTERFLY, *Un bel di vedremo* (Some Day He'll Come), in which the little Geisha affirms her belief that her American lover will return to her; Tosca's impassioned plea to Scarpia in the second act of LA TOSCA, *Vissi d'arte* (I've Lived for Art and Love), and Mario's song before his execution, in the third act, *E lucevan le stelle* (The Stars Were Shining) are favourites.

From the two outstanding examples of *verismo*, or dramatic realism, in Italian operas, Leoncavallo's PAGLIACCI and Mascagni's CAVALLERIA RUSTICANA, a number of excerpts have achieved great fame. From the first comes one of the most intense of operatic arias, Canio's anguished outcry that he must go on with his clowning before the audience while his heart is breaking with grief, *Vesti la giubba* (On With the Play):

> Put on your smock, smear your face with powder—
> The people pay you; they must have their fun.
> Even though Harlequin take your Columbine from you,
> Laugh loud, Pagliaccio,
> Hide your grief and play your part...
> Laugh, Pagliaccio, for your love that is destroyed,
> Laugh for the pain that is breaking your heart!

From CAVALLERIA RUSTICANA, the *Intermezzo*; the *Brindisi* or Drinking Song; and the *Siciliana*, the serenade of Turiddu in which he expresses his love for Lola (Thy Lips Like Crimson Berries), are most popular.

From the French lyric drama, a group of representative excerpts would include Delilah's seductive song, *Mon coeur s'ouvre à ta voix* (My Heart at Thy Sweet Voice), from the second act of Saint-Saëns' SAMSON AND DELILAH; the *Jewel Song* (*Air des Bijoux*) in which Marguerite expresses her delight at Faust's gift, from the third act of Gounod's classic, as well as the *Soldiers' Chorus* and the *Serenade of Mephistopheles* from Act IV, and the celebrated waltz, *Ainsi que la brise légère*, from the scene of the Fair in Act II; Juliet's *Waltz Song* from Gounod's ROMEO AND JULIET; Manon's farewell to the little table at which she and Des Grieux have been so happy, *Adieu, notre petite table*, from the second act of Massenet's MANON, as well as Des Grieux' aria later in the act, *Le Rêve* (The Dream), in which he describes the home he plans to share with her; from Massenet's THAÏS, the courtesan's passionate invocation to her mirror, *Dis-moi que je serais belle eternellement*

(Tell Me That I Shall Always Be Beautiful!), and the *Meditation*, symbolical of Thaïs' conversion, as famous an instrumental interlude as the *Intermezzo* from CAVALLERIA RUSTICANA; and the rapturous aria of Louise, *Depuis le jour* (Ever Since the Day), in which she expresses her happiness at being with her lover Julien, from the third act of Charpentier's opera, LOUISE.

The finest example of Russian operatic style unquestionably is Moussorgsky's BORIS GODOUNOV, one of the few Russian operas that have attained a permanent place in our repertory. Listen to the two excerpts from the magnificent final scene, the Farewell of Boris, *Farewell, My Son, I Am Dying*, and the Death of Boris, *Hark 'Tis the Passing Bell!* Boris, who had gained the throne by causing the rightful heir, Dmitri, to be assassinated, realizes that he has reached his end. He asks his nobles to withdraw, and remains alone with his son. With great feeling he bids the child rule justly, and protect his sister Xenia; he hopes the boy will never learn how his father came to the throne. Laying his hands on his son's head, he calls down Heaven's blessing upon him. Bells toll mournfully while the voices of the people outside the Kremlin rise in prayer for their Czar. The choral writing here, as in the Coronation Scene, is of surpassing beauty: with Moussorgsky, the emotional base of national opera lay in the chorus, the folk. The music, which depicts the anguish of the sick and tormented Czar, rises to a climax of great power, with something of the grim realism that we found in Moussorgsky's songs. A procession of priests files into the royal apartment, followed by the nobles. Boris, in his final struggle with death, points to his son: "Behold your Czar!" and falls back dead, the word "Mercy!" upon his lips.

Throughout the later nineteenth century German opera was wholly dominated by the Wagnerian music drama. A new note was introduced by Richard Strauss who, with the orchestral wizardry that was his heritage from the master, combined the lyricism and freshness of the lied, together with the sophistication and sensuous charm of French influences. The result was an idiom creating three works that made operatic history in the first decade of the twentieth century—the brilliant setting of Oscar Wilde's SALOMÉ; the stark and terrifying ELEKTRA, to the libretto of Hugo von Hoffmansthal; and the captivating comedy of eighteenth-century Vienna, DER ROSENKAVALIER (The Cavalier of the Rose). For the full flavour of Strauss' style, listen to the *Dance of the Seven Veils* from SALOMÉ, and the Princess' delirious exultation as she receives the head of the Prophet on a silver charger, *I Have Kissed Thy Lips, O Jokaanan.* The more wholesome side of Strauss' genius animates his immortal comedy. Listen to the enchanting waltzes; the resigned and world-wise *Soliloquy* of the Marschallin in the first act, as she realizes that soon her charms will fade, and she will no longer hold her youthful lover; the ecstatic *Presentation of the Rose* in the second act, when Octavian meets Sophie and forgets the Marschallin; the great trio in Act III, when the Marschallin unites the youthful lovers and graciously accepts her inevitable defeat; and the final duet of Sophie and Octavian, Mozartian in its limpid beauty and simplicity.

We have refrained from mentioning many of the larger ensembles to be found in opera, for they are likely to be quite unsatisfactory in records—they must be actually heard and seen on the stage to be fully effective, for dramatic action, the setting and the function of the ensemble are likely to be of prime importance. However, two very popular ensembles (not choruses) are pointed out here, as illustrating how the composer, by weaving together several threads of song, is able to pour out the emotions of several of his characters simultaneously, the voices joining in a single tonal web of power and effectiveness, though the individual emotions of the participating characters might differ widely.

Perhaps the most famous of ensemble numbers is the *Sextette* from Donizetti's LUCIA DI LAMMERMOOR. Although the broadly flowing melody is known to all the world, it requires some knowledge of the opera to realize how well the music expresses the dramatic situation in the play, and how adroitly each of the six voices reveals the conflicting emotions of the individual character. The *Sextette* is sung in the second act, when Edgar returns to the castle of his enemy, Lord Henry, to find that his beloved Lucy—sister of Lord Henry—has just married another. Edgar is swept by rage and hatred of Henry, yet realizes that he still loves Lucy; Henry, who has engineered the marriage for his own ends, fears for the success of his project; Lucy, who was led to believe by her brother that Edgar was faithless, is overcome with grief and shame when she realizes that she has wronged her lover; Raymond, the kindly chaplain, prays that Heaven will protect Lucy; Lord Arthur, the man whom Lucy has just married, is utterly bewildered; and Alice, Lucy's companion, shares her mistress' sorrow. The individual voices soar and intermingle in a rich harmonic pattern that constitutes one of the great moments in opera.

Equally effective is the *Quartet* from RIGOLETTO, one of the finest of Verdi's many ensemble pieces. Rigoletto, the hunchbacked court jester, attempts to cure his daughter of her love for the profligate Duke, who wooed her, won her, and has now forgotten her. He takes her to the inn where, peering through the door, she may watch the Duke making love to the barmaid Maddalena. The Duke sings a smooth amorous melody to Maddalena; the coquettish barmaid, wise in the ways of the world, retorts that she knows full well he is only trying to flatter her; Gilda, concealed in the darkness outside, pours forth the grief of her broken heart, while Rigoletto sternly vows to avenge his betrayed daughter.

Opera in this country has had, and is having, a difficult time to overcome the readiness of American audiences to bask in the Italian, French, and German heritage. Also, it has had to shake off the Old-World operatic traditions concerning essential characteristics, and it has been trying to work out native idioms of expressions. Then, too, the opportunities for hearing operas written by native composers are not many, and, consequently, the inspiration, encouragement, and tuition that would normally be derived from such performances are absent. However, a relatively small number of American composers have devoted their efforts in behalf of native opera. Among the outstanding composers and their works, obtainable in records, are:[7] Charles Wakefield Cadman's SHANEWIS (it is interesting to note that Cadman's Indian opera was the first American work to be performed for two consecutive seasons by the Metropolitan Opera Company); Louis Gruenberg's THE EMPEROR JONES; Howard Hanson's MERRY MOUNT; Deems Taylor's THE KING'S HENCHMAN and PETER IBBETSON; Richard Hageman's CAPONSACCHI; Victor Herbert's NATOMA; Gian-Carlo Menotti's AMELIA GOES TO THE BALL; and it is hoped that Vittorio Giannini's SCARLET LETTER will have been recorded by the time this book is published.

---

[7] According to the latest edition of the *Gramophone Shop Encyclopedia of Recorded Music* (New York: Simon and Schuster) at the time of writing.

Chapter Eight

The Oratorio

IN OUR introductory paragraph to the preceding chapter, we suggested the construction of a simple, hypothetical opera through the use of a series of songs having a common theme, or story, then the acting of them on a stage with the usual trappings. To carry the idea still further, we suggest that if those solo songs, ensembles, and choruses were built around a religious subject and the whole were sung, without actions, in a concert hall or a church instead of the theatre, we might have a fair representation of the basic idea of an oratorio. So the humble song of our early chapters assumes still greater importance. As a matter of fact, much of what has been said in the preceding chapter applies equally well in this; so let us discuss the immediate subject more precisely.[1]

We think of the oratorio as a dramatic poem, generally of a sacred or spiritual character, which is sung throughout by soloists and chorus to the accompaniment of an orchestra. It is distinguished from the mass and church cantata in that it is intended for concert or festival performance rather than as part of a regular religious service, and from the opera in that—at any rate in modern times—it is presented without scenery, costumes, and action. Its style and character make it ideally suited for performance by church choirs and choral societies.

Today the oratorio is considered as a type altogether distinct from the opera, although, from what we said in the preceding section about the origins of the music drama, it should be apparent that the two were derived from common sources. From the twelfth to the sixteenth centuries—a period that saw the brilliant flourishing, all over Europe, of the Miracle and Mystery plays—there developed in Italy, France, Germany, and England a species of musical drama based on incidents in the Old and New Testaments and the lives of the saints. These were intended to reinforce, on a popular basis and with strong emotional appeal,

[1] For essential listening, see section on THE MESSIAH, page 109.

the teachings of the church, and were generally performed under the supervision of the clergy, with scenery, acting, costumes, and all kinds of vivid dramatic effects. Often performers travelled from town to town in wagons, giving performances in public squares, palace courtyards or in the market place—a practice that may be seen in the episode of the strolling players in HAMLET, or in the "play within a play" in Leoncavallo's PAGLIACCI.

Milan Cathedral   *(From a photograph)*

This rare example of pure Gothic in marble, with its hundreds of pinnacles soaring towards the sky and whose exterior is adorned with more than 4,000 statues amidst incredibly delicate lacework carved in stone, was begun in 1386. To our day it remains one of the most beautiful works of man erected as an expression of homage to the divinity. Such great artists as Brunelleschi, Leonardo da Vinci, Pellegrini, and countless others lent their genius to its glorious realization.

Toward the end of the fifteenth century, at about the same time that the poets and musicians at the court of Florence were experimenting with the type of musical dramatic declamation that ultimately led to the opera, St. Philip Neri, founder of the congregation of the Oratorians at Rome, encouraged the performance of sacred musical dramatic allegories as a means of religious instruction. Since these performances were given in the oratory of his church, the sacred drama with music soon became known as *oratorio*, while the secular drama with music took the title of *opera*. At this point opera and oratorio differed from each other mainly in the choice of subject, for both used all the resources of the musical dramatic theatre. In 1600 Emilio del Cavalieri (*c.* 1550-1602) presented in Rome an elaborate allegory of the struggle between body and mind, LA RAPPRESENTAZIONE DI ANIMA E DI CORPO, a spiritual opera in the tradition of the Mystery and Miracle plays that is erroneously set forth, in histories of music, as the first oratorio. Since secular and sacred music drama were arising simultaneously from a common ancestry, it is difficult to mark clearly the first separation of their paths. For additional matter on the historical background, the reader is referred to a number of texts on musicology available in most libraries.

Opera and oratorio thenceforth developed side by side, borrowing from each other, and often crossing over into each other's territory. Thus, in our own time Saint-Saëns' Biblical opera SAMSON ET DELILAH has been performed in concert, without the trappings of the opera house, as an oratorio. Similarly, Mendelssohn's oratorio ELIJAH received a memorable performance in America with scenery, costumes, and acting. The two genres have, however, steadily gone farther and farther apart in character, style, and outlook. With opera we associate swift dramatic action, tense emotional climaxes, ardent romanticism, sensuous melody, and brilliant effect. With oratorio we connect vast harmonies, sublime choruses, lyricism of an introspective nature, and spiritual exaltation. Where opera remained a dynamic form, oratorio became increasingly static and contemplative. The last trace of dramatic action disappeared from the oratorio with the introduction of a narrator, whose function it was to relate the connecting incidents in the sacred play, instead of having them acted out. Above all, while the opera continued to rely for its emotional effect on the inner conflicts of individuals, the oratorio depended increasingly for its majestic effects on the chorus.

George Frideric Handel (1685-1759)

Interestingly enough, the composer who is considered to have played the decisive role in the oratorio as we know it today, George Frideric Handel, spent the greater part of his career in writing operas. For well on to twenty-five years, the great Saxon guided the destinies of opera in London. It was only when his audience began to tire of the conventional, artificial Italian opera of the period and turned with avidity to the freshness and charm of Gay's Beggar's Opera that Handel, sensing a competition he could no longer meet, turned his inexhaustible energies to the oratorio. With Handel the oratorio took on new life and colour; the chorus became the chief protagonist of the drama, much as the orchestra did, a century later, in the Wagnerian music drama. His great oratorios—The Messiah, Saul, Israel in Egypt, Judas Maccabaeus, Jephtha—are in effect choral tragedies, in which the lives and destinies of the individual heroes take on meaning and direction from the dynamic force embodied in the chorus. Master of a spacious architecture, of bold dramatic effect, of vivid musical characterization and of a variegated style of writing, Handel poured all the riches of his imagination into these works, which so perfectly hit off the taste of English Protestantism. For a century after his death, they completely dominated the musical life of his adopted land.

Handel and his great contemporary, Bach, represent the peak of that era in music which is known as the *Baroque*.[2] We shall have more to say of the Baroque in a later chapter. Suffice it for the present to point out that this term is used, in painting, sculpture, architecture, and music, to indicate the spirit of bold design and vigorous execution, of sweeping lines, richly imaginative ornamentation, imposing dimensions and dramatic effects, that characterized European art in the seventeenth and early eighteenth centuries. The Baroque was the counterpart, in the realm of art, of the spirit that pervaded the age: a spirit of bold questing for new horizons, of restless questioning of accepted norms, of exuberant self-confidence and achievement, and of intellectual inquiry throughout the period, in the far-flung religious and dynastic struggles, in the vigorous colonization of the New World, and in the steady, forward movement of the *bourgeoisie*—the "burgesses,"

[2] For extended discussion on the *Baroque*, see page 428.

George Frideric Handel   *From a rare old print*

the merchants and industrialists—as they consolidated their power
in their five-hundred-year-old struggle against the feudal agricultural aristocracy. This was a dynamic, rapidly changing world,
demanding pomp and external splendour, opulent façades riotous
with ornament, magnificent curves and stairways and candelabra:
a style that found its perfect expression in the palaces of the absolute monarchs of the seventeenth century, in the bold and teeming
canvases of a Rubens or a Caravaggio. It is the spirit of this world
that is immortalized, in music, by the sweeping recitatives, arias,
and ensembles, above all by the grandiose, stirring choruses of the
Handelian oratorio.

Handel's oratorio: "The Messiah"

We know of no better introduction to the oratorio style at its
best than the study of Handel's immortal work in that form, THE
MESSIAH, which he wrote in twenty-three days, in the early autumn
(August 22nd to September 14th) of 1741. The work consists of a
series of recitatives, arias, choruses, and orchestral numbers
arranged in three parts—analogous to the acts of an opera. There
is an overture and an instrumental interlude in the first part, the
latter known as the *Pastoral Symphony*. The text is made up of
appropriate verses from the Bible, some direct quotations, others
adapted to Handel's needs by the librettist, Charles Jennens. The
first part prophesies and anticipates the coming of Christ; the
second speaks of His sufferings and death; and the third tells of
His resurrection. In order to make the work more acceptable for
use during the Christmas season, a large part of sections two and
three are omitted.

Therefore, to enable the listener to follow the vagaries of concert as well as recorded performances of THE MESSIAH, we present
here the complete outline of the arias and choruses.[3] But for
practical reasons, we have indicated with one star (*) those numbers we should like to use as minimum essential listening for this
chapter. A further abridged series is reluctantly proposed for still
greater limitations of time. These are indicated with two stars (**)
before the title. (Other choices than these are possible.)

[3] As shown in the Schirmer Edition, edited and revised according to Handel's
original score by T. Tertius Noble.

Part the First:

      1. Overture.

* ** 2. Recitative (Tenor), "Comfort ye my people."

* ** 3. Aria (Tenor), "Every valley shall be exalted."

   * 4. Chorus, "And the glory of the Lord."

      5. Recit. (Bass), "Thus saith the Lord."

      6. Aria (Bass), "But who may abide the day of His coming?"

      7. Chorus, "And He shall purify."

      8. Recit. (Alto), "Behold, a virgin shall conceive."

      9. Aria (Alto) and Chorus, "O Thou that tellest good tidings."

  * 10. Recit. (Bass), "For, behold, darkness shall cover the earth."

  * 11. Aria (Bass), "The people that walked in darkness."

* ** 12. Chorus, "For unto us a child is born."

  * 13. Pastoral Symphony.

* ** 14. Recit. (Soprano), "There were shepherds abiding in the field."

        Recit. (Soprano), "And lo! the angel of the Lord."

     15. Recit. (Soprano), "And the angel said unto them."

     16. Recit. (Soprano), "And suddenly there was with the angel."

  * 17. Chorus, "Glory to God."

  * 18. Aria (Soprano), "Rejoice greatly, O daughter of Zion."

     19. Recit. (Alto), "Then shall the eyes of the blind be opened."

* ** 20. Aria (Alto), "He shall feed His flock like a shepherd."

  * 21. Chorus, "His yoke is easy, and His burden is light."

Part the Second:

  * 22. Chorus, "Behold the Lamb of God."

* ** 23. Aria (Alto), "He was despised."

* ** 24. Chorus, "Surely He hath borne our griefs."

     25. Chorus, "And with His stripes we are healed."

     26. Chorus, "All we like sheep have gone astray."

     27. Recit. (Tenor), "All they that see Him, laugh Him to scorn."

     28. Chorus, "He trusted in God that He would deliver Him."

  * 29. Recit. (Tenor), "Thy rebuke hath broken His heart."

  * 30. Aria (Tenor), "Behold, and see if there be any sorrow."

     31. Recit. (Tenor), "He was cut off out of the land of the living."

     32. Aria (Tenor), "But Thou didst not leave His soul in hell."

     33. Chorus, "Lift up your heads, O ye gates."

34. Recit. (Tenor), "Unto which of the angels said He."
35. Chorus, "Let all the angels of God worship Him."
36. Aria (Bass), "Thou art gone up on high."
37. Chorus, "The Lord gave the word."
38. Aria (Soprano), "How beautiful are the feet of them."
39. Chorus, "Their sound is gone out into all lands."
* ** 40. Aria (Bass), "Why do the nations so furiously rage."
41. Chorus, "Let us break their bonds asunder."
42. Recit. (Tenor), "He that dwelleth in heaven."
43. Aria (Tenor), "Thou shalt break them."
* ** 44. Chorus, "Hallelujah!"

Part the Third:

* ** 45. Aria (Soprano), "I know that my Redeemer liveth."
46. Chorus, "Since by man came death."
47. Recit. (Bass), "Behold, I tell you a mystery."
48. Aria (Bass), "The trumpet shall sound."
49. Recit. (Alto), "Then shall be brought to pass."
50. Duet (Alto and Tenor), "O death, where is thy sting?"
* 51. Chorus, "But thanks be to God."
52. Aria (Soprano), "If God be for us, who can be against us?"
* 53. Chorus, "Worthy is the Lamb," "Amen."

THE MESSIAH took England by storm and it was during the first London performance that the audience, carried away by the lofty sentiments, the impressive power and the noble character of the *Hallelujah Chorus,* arose in concert as though by prearranged signal. Ever since then audiences the world over express a similar respect by rising at the onset of this chorus and remaining standing until the conclusion of the section.[4]

ADDITIONAL SUGGESTIONS FOR LISTENING[5]

If Handel represents the pomp and splendour of the Baroque, Bach, as the reader will remember from our discussion of his religious music, stands for its other side—mysticism, introspection, passionate religi-

[4] Of course, there is usually no applause, and the listener is cautioned to be on guard for omissions throughout, but especially in Parts II and III, and transpositions of certain numbers from Part II to Part III, in order to effect a climax at the close. The complete outline provided above should be a helpful guide.

[5] In this chapter, we have had to relax the policy of restricting the references to recorded works because of the scarcity of the gramophone discs. Here, even more earnestly than elsewhere, we admonish hearing actual performances, and better still, that the reader participate as a singer in the chorus.

I

osity, and otherworldliness. Where Handel was at home in the glare of public life, in the atmosphere of royal courts and theatres, as artist, producer, and businessman all in one, Bach lived his life in the circle of his family, circumscribed by his duties as Cantor of St. Thomas', completely devoted to his religion and his art. Both by native temperament and mode of life he was eminently suited for the most eloquent projection, through his music, of the intense Pietism which pervaded his native Thuringia. Where Handel was fired by the dramatic conflicts in the Old Testament, Bach addressed himself almost exclusively to what was for him the supreme religious tragedy—the Passion of Christ. In the three Passion oratorios, by Bach, according to the Gospels of St. Luke, St. Matthew, and St. John, and in the Christmas oratorio, it is the reflective lyrical note that predominates, a brooding tenderness, a grandeur of resignation and peace rather than one of action; the spirit of evangelical mysticism rather than the spectacular dramatics of Handel. Throughout, there is that mingling of profound lyricism and pathos which makes Bach, for many listeners, the *sine qua non* among composers.

Of the two masters of the Classical Period in the late eighteenth century, Mozart devoted his best efforts to actual church music rather than to festive religious drama. Haydn, who achieved a triumphal success in England toward the end of his career, on the other hand, continued in the tradition of Handel with two works well calculated to please English taste—The Creation, after the first part of Milton's *Paradise Lost*; and The Seasons, after the famous poem of James Thomson. Haydn was a devout Catholic, writing for a Protestant audience on the heels of the Enlightenment; the result was a beautiful hymn to the Creator couched in language that men of all creeds and loyalties could understand. Haydn applied well, to his own idiom, the lessons he learned from his great predecessor; in England and in this country, The Creation has remained second only to The Messiah in popularity. The reader should also be acquainted with characteristic examples from The Creation, the exciting choruses *Achieved Is the Glorious Work* and *Rolling in Foaming Billows*; also, the touching *Dove Aria* for soprano.

The nineteenth century saw intense cultivation of the oratorio, even though the spirit out of which it had come into being no longer held undisputed sway over the souls of men. Neither Beethoven's Mount of Olives nor Schubert's Victory Song of Miriam have retained their hold on the musical world; the genius of these composers flowed in other channels. It is in Mendelssohn who, like Handel and Haydn, met his greatest success in England, that we have a continuation of the "great choral tradition." His Elijah and St. Paul have taken their places in the literature along with The Messiah and The Creation. The cycle of German oratorio closes with Brahms' GERMAN REQUIEM. Brahms was perhaps the last of the great masters to express the religious emotion of the late nineteenth century with something of the profundity and passion of the masters of the Baroque.

In France, the Catholic revival, which was part of the Romantic movement, created an atmosphere most favourable for the oratorio. The finest examples are Liszt's CHRISTUS and ST. ELISABETH, Berlioz's sacred trilogy THE CHILDHOOD OF CHRIST, and César Franck's THE BEATITUDES. The oratorio has always been most popular in England, where outstanding works are presented in all forms. Among the better known examples of English oratorio are Charles Hubert H. Parry's JUDITH and SAUL; Charles Villiers Stanford's THE HOLY CHILDREN and EDEN; John Stainer's GIDEON and Edward Elgar's DREAM OF GERONTIUS, LIGHT OF LIFE, THE APOSTLES, and THE KINGDOM. Among contemporary English composers, William Walton has written BELSHAZZAR'S FEAST; Frederick Delius THE MASS OF LIFE; and Gustav Holst a HYMN TO JESUS.

American composers have contributed a number of notable oratorios to the repertory. Among the best known are John Knowles Paine's ST. PETER; Horatio Parker's HORA NOVISSIMA and LEGEND OF ST. CHRISTOPHER; Edgar Stillman Kelley's PILGRIM'S PROGRESS; Charles Martin Loeffler's CANTICLE TO ST. FRANCIS; Harry Rowe Shelley's DEATH AND LIFE; and David Stanley Smith's RHAPSODY OF ST. BERNARD.

Twentieth-century composers continued the established traditions with such oratorios as Vincent d'Indy's LEGEND OF ST. CHRISTOPHER; Ermanno Wolf-Ferrari's LA VETA NUOVA, based on Dante's poem; and Pierné's CHILDREN'S CRUSADE.

Not many contemporary oratorios have as yet been made available on records. Consequently, to gain an idea of what the modern idiom in this form is like, one has, in most cases, to hear an actual performance. For a contrast between the old and the new, listen to the recorded excerpts from Honegger's oratorios: KING DAVID, *De mon coeur jaillit un cantique* (From My Heart There Sprang a Hymn); the *Penitential Psalm*; the Psalm, *I Was Conceived in Sin*; and the *Death of David*. This is powerful choral music, with a quality of primitivism, if you will, and an abundance of dissonances.

Chapter Nine

Music in the Theatre
Incidental Music: The Suite[1]

A S WE saw in our chapter on the opera, music has been used in connection with dramatic performances since ancient times. The theatre of the Greeks, of the Middle Ages, of Shakespeare and Molière and Calderon, all made extensive use of music. When the songs and dances become so important as to change the character of the play, we have the several varieties of operetta and comic opera. When the music remains in the background, that is, "incidental' to the play, we have one of the most delightful genres of the art—incidental music.

Incidental music may be played before the curtain goes up (*overture*); between the acts (*entr'acte* music); between two scenes (*interlude* or *intermezzo*); or during the course of a scene. It must rise out of the salient incidents in the play; must capture and project the mood. If it is used as an integral part of a dramatic scene, it must either heighten its emotion or underscore the feelings and actions of the characters. Just as in a song the high points of the poetry and of the music must coincide, so here the music becomes part of the forward-driving momentum of the scene and helps to carry it to its climax. Because it can be so effective, incidental music as a rule is used rather sparingly and is reserved, in most cases, for high points of the play.

Often the incidental music for a play is arranged by the composer as a *suite* for concert performance and in this form becomes far more popular than the play for which it was written. Thus, thousands of people who have never seen Ibsen's poetic drama, Peer Gynt, are familiar with Grieg's Peer Gynt Suite. In this sense, the word *suite* is used to indicate a group of movements of

---

[1] Essential listening for this chapter includes: *Valse Triste* by Sibelius, *Peer Gynt Suite* by Grieg, *Midsummer Night's Dream Suite* (Overture, Nocturne, Scherzo, and Wedding March) by Mendelssohn, and MacDowell's *Indian Suite*. Others, including Taylor's *Through the Looking Glass Suite*, are supplementary and optional.

114

instrumental music, often concert versions of theatre or ballet music, and therefore bound together by some literary thread. In the eighteenth century, as the reader may recall from the Bach suite that we heard in the chapter on music and dance, the word denoted a group of dances in contrasting moods and metres often in the same key, or in closely related keys.

"*Valse Triste*" *by Sibelius*

A fine example of the function of incidental music is offered by the ever-popular *Valse Triste*, which Sibelius wrote for Arvid Jarnefelt's romantic drama KUOLEMA (Death). The scene portrays a young man watching at the bedside of his dying mother. It is night, and he has fallen asleep. Suddenly a strange glow and the sound of distant music pervades the room. We hear the rhythm of a slow, mournful waltz. The mother rises from her bed. Her long white garment takes on the semblance of a ball dress. She moves amid a host of pale wraiths who sway silently to the rhythm and finally falls exhausted on her bed. The music breaks off. Presently she gathers her strength and goes back to the dance. The eerie music grows ever faster, reaches its climax. There is a knock at the door. The mother utters a dreadful cry; the guests vanish; Death stands on the threshold.

It is evident that in a scene such as this the music is not in the least incidental. Actually, the scene as it was imagined in the mind of the dramatist could not be carried out without the aid of the music. Nor, obviously, would any mournful waltz do. It must be a composition that not only catches the spirit of the fantasy but that—even more important—carries it in a steady intensification of emotion to the dread climax. In addition, the music must have the indefinable quality that makes good theatre; it must be vivid, forthright, not oversubtle; it must achieve its dramatic effect in a direct, concise manner. Notice how well Sibelius' piece satisfies not only the general requirements of the theatre music but also the specific needs of the scene for which it was written. The sorrowful waltz theme announced by stringed instruments in a low register is a haunting melody that seems to spring right out of the dramatic situation. The contrasting second theme, gliding downward from the treble in eighth notes, is lyrical and nostalgic. Then come the ghostly staccato chords in waltz rhythm that constitute the third theme. There is an effective crescendo and a steady quickening of the pulse as the music mounts in intensity. Now the music rushes forward in a kind of delirious agitation. Suddenly comes a dramatic pause—and then the final chords, strangely calm.

"Peer Gynt Suite" by Grieg

No less imaginative as mood-painting is Grieg's incidental music for PEER GYNT which he arranged in two concert suites, each containing four numbers. The SUITE NO. 1 has become quite popular. It opens with *Morning*, a serene picture of day settling over the Norwegian forest, done in Grieg's best lyrical manner. There is something cool and transparent about the music with its broadly flowing melody in six-eight time.

The second number is the dirge for the mother in the play, *Ase's Death*. The solemn chords and the heartfelt melody ascending in accents of grief communicate with proper simplicity the tone of elegiac music. The repetition of the repeated melodic figure grips one most thoroughly.

Next comes the seductive *Anitra's Dance* (performed in the play by the exotic beauty whom Peer meets on his travels). As with the *Valse Triste*, the music here is, strictly speaking, not incidental since it enters into the action of the play. The dance is in graceful three-four time. The use of muted strings, of the staccato figure in the accompaniment, and of the *pizzicato* (plucked strings) effect creates an atmosphere of subtle Oriental allure. Note particularly that when the original dance theme returns Grieg varies the effect by having the 'cellos sing a new, full-throated melody against it— in other words, a *countermelody*. The addition of a countermelody to a repeated theme is obviously a subtle and effective means by which a composer may vary his material.

The final number, *In the Hall of the Mountain King*, depicts the exciting scene when Peer, lost in the mountains, is surrounded by mischievous trolls and sprites who perform a grotesque dance around him. The piece presents an extraordinary combination of the three most striking devices for building a climax—*crescendo, accelerando*, and a steady rise in pitch. The dance opens at a fairly slow pace, softly, in the lowest register, with a bizarre staccato effect on the bassoons. From then on the simple motive is repeated again and again—somewhat in the manner of the ascending half of the *Ase's Death* pattern—each time louder, faster, and higher, building up steadily until all the sonorities of the orchestra are engaged in an overpowering climax at breakneck speed punctuated by the shattering exclamations of cymbals and drums. Here, too, the music is not incidental in any sense of the term, but captures the very essence of the scene as envisaged in the imagination of the poet-dramatist.

Suite from "Midsummer Night's Dream" by Mendelssohn

For a full century Mendelssohn's incidental music to MID-SUMMER NIGHT'S DREAM has been a favourite. The *Overture* was written in 1826, when the composer was seventeen, in the form of a piano duet. Seventeen years later, in 1843, King Frederick William IV of Prussia asked Mendelssohn to add the other numbers. Of the thirteen that he wrote, the *Overture, Nocturne, Scherzo,* and *Wedding March* are generally heard in the concert version. Shakespeare's fairy play called forth all the delicacy and grace, the polished craftsmanship and elfin lightness, so frequently associated with Mendelssohn's music.

The *Overture* ranks as one of his best works and is truly an amazing production for a boy of seventeen. Four mysterious chords in the woodwinds introduce us to the magic world of Oberon and Titania. The violins, in high register, announce the twittering staccato theme of the woodland sprites, which grows into a joyous outburst from the entire orchestra. A romantic legato motive floats for a moment before us, faintly suggesting the lovers in the play. This suave second theme offers a perfect contrast to the staccato opening theme. Then comes the jolly *Bergomasque Dance* from the fifth act of the play, with its great downward leap in the melody, a vivid musical picture of the sprawling movements of the uncouth peasant dancers. We hear a braying-like figure in the strings reminding us of Bottom, the immortal clown, who through magic spell receives the head of a donkey—and the adoration of Titania.

The themes are developed at some length with much fantasy and zest and then return in their original form. The mysterious chords of the opening return; finally the music floats away, higher and higher, into space.

The lovely *Nocturne* comes at the end of the third act, when sleep has descended upon the bewitched Titania and her doltish lover, Bottom. The serene melody for the horn is one of the famous passages written for that instrument. Here all the mystery, the remoteness, the intangible beauty of its tone are used by Mendelssohn to paint the dream-filled loveliness of the summer night. Too often, after success and fame had come to him, Mendelssohn allowed himself to substitute the perfection of form, which he mistakenly held up to himself as the classical ideal, for warmth and depth of feeling. Here, for once, he let himself recapture the romantic fervour of his youthful vision and articulated it in accents of unmistakable sincerity. (By *nocturne* we designate either a composition that describes the romantic beauty of the night––the word is derived from the latin *nox*, "night"—or a tender, lyrical outpouring of romantic feeling, a night song such as a lover might address to the object of his affections.)

The *Scherzo*, a favourite with concert and radio audiences, is a lacy bit of playfulness that serves as a prelude to the second act of the play. The opening vaguely resembles the first theme of the overture in its use of the violin staccato in high register. (Both themes, incidentally, are in the key of E minor.) The vigorous triple metre and the abrupt accents lend a bubbling energy to the theme in the middle section, a lusty dance tune in low register. Then the music returns to the first theme; little wisps of sound dart through the air and dissolve in a silvery mist. (*Scherzo*, from the Italian word meaning "a jest," is the title of a composition usually in rapid triple metre, often of a humorous or whimsical character, either a movement of a symphony or an independent concert piece.)

The suite is brought to a close by the *Wedding March*, which we spoke of in the chapter on music and ceremonial. Its opening chords, with their commingling of stateliness and joy, have become the universal processional at the end of the marriage ceremony. Detached from its original setting in a mythical Athenian court, this music has become a part of the personal experience of all mankind. There could, perhaps, be no greater tribute to any composer.

Edward MacDowell (1861-1908)

We have previously seen that suites may be made up of contrasting dance tunes, and in this chapter we have learned that suites may be an assembly of incidental music written for plays. Now we direct attention to suites that have no connection with the ballet or dramatic performance; instead, they were composed directly for the concert programme and have as their underlying element of unification a poem, a story, or a series of similar or parallel moods. A good example of the so-called concert suite, and also one of the finest examples of its kind of American genius, is MacDowell's INDIAN SUITE, where the unification is secured through the use of salient and characteristic American Indian melodies.

The composer of the universally popular WOODLAND SKETCHES, from which come *To a Wild Rose* and *To a Water Lily*, was born in New York City in 1861. After studying piano

Portrait of Edward MacDowell

with Teresa Carreño, the famous Venezuelan pianist and teacher, he entered the Paris Conservatoire at the age of fifteen, remaining there for three years. For five years after that he studied, played, and taught in the musical centres of Germany —Stuttgart, Wiesbaden, Darmstadt, and Frankfort—coming under the influence of the leading German Romanticists, notably his teacher Raff, and Liszt. He found the artistic atmosphere of Germany so congenial to his nature and the German musical world so appreciative of his talents that for a time he considered the possibility of settling there permanently. He married his pupil, Marion Nevins, in 1884. In 1887, he returned to America, settled in Boston, and appeared successfully as a concert pianist, introducing his two brilliant piano concertos, the second of which has remained a favourite both with virtuosi and their audiences. In 1896 he became the first professor of music at Columbia University, where he remained for eight years during which he fought unceasingly to have music recognized as a full-fledged member of the curriculum. Despite his zeal in the cause, the university authorities did not see eye to eye with him; and in 1904, after much vexation, he resigned his post. His pioneer efforts in this direction bore fruit later. For the remaining years of his life he devoted himself to composing and to conducting the Mendelssohn Glee Club, which he made into one of the best male choruses in the country. He died prematurely in 1908, the victim of a cruel and tragic illness.

MacDowell remains America's first great composer in the formal sense. His lovely melodies, such as the two we mentioned, have found wide popularity among the nation at large; his more ambitious works, especially his brilliant and colourful SECOND PIANO CONCERTO, have remained in the standard repertory. He fought steadfastly for the cause of music in America, seeking to bring it to independence and self-expression; he was the first American to command respect from the musical circles of Europe. Like his contemporary, Henry James, he sought to combine the best in the old tradition with the new. In many of his works, such as the INDIAN SUITE and WOODLAND SKETCHES, he turned to Indian themes for inspiration; although, unlike Dvořák, who was active in this country in the same decade as he, MacDowell was not greatly influenced by Negro themes. In MacDowell, as in so many of the nineteenth-century composers, the Romantic impulse fused with the nationalistic. Like Dvořák and Grieg, he sought to adapt the German Romantic tradition to the needs of his native land. Like them, he is "folksy" at times; but there is a vein of rich, tender lyricism in his work, of real poetic imagination and deep feeling. The titles of some of his compositions are revealing: *Forgotten Fairy Tales; Moon Pictures*, after Hans Christian Andersen; *Launcelot and Elaine; From an Old Garden; Six Idylls After Goethe; Six Poems After Heine; The Song of Roland; Sonata Tragica; Norse Sonata; Celtic Sonata; Fireside Tales; New England Idylls; Indian Suite*, and the *Woodland Sketches,* which contains such numbers as "Br'er Rabbit" and "From an Indian Lodge." To round out the picture of his nationalism, it is interesting to note that he made a practice of writing the tempo indications for his compositions in English instead of using the "allegros" and "adagios" of conventional musical usage—a sort of gesture of independence that some of his disciples have adhered to.

After his tragic death in 1908, his widow transferred his estate at Peterboro, New Hampshire, to the MacDowell Memorial Association for use as an artists' colony. Here every summer, writers, painters, and composers gather from all parts of the country; the name of the composer thus continues to be a symbol for the progress of the arts in America.

MacDowell's Suite No. 2 for Orchestra ("Indian") in E minor, Op. 48 [2]

THE SUITE is of five numbers: *Legend, Love Song, In War Time, Dirge,* and *Village Festival.* In the *Legend,* there is a melody of the Iroquois tribe and a Chippewa theme; the second number is built on a love song of the Iowa tribes; the third has a Dakota theme, as well as some features of an Iroquois scalp dance; the fourth is a Kiowa—a woman's song of mourning for her absent son; and the *Village Festival* includes a women's dance and a war song of the Iroquois tribe. The Suite is scored for piccolo, two flutes, two oboes, two clarinets, two bassoons, four horns, two trumpets, three trombones, bass tuba, a set of three kettledrums, a bass drum, cymbals, and strings.

Legend: Not fast; with much dignity and character. E minor, 2-2. This number is reported to have been inspired by Thomas Bailey Aldrich's Indian legend, "Miantowona." The composer, however, made no attempt to relate the incidents of the poem, but suggested, rather, the general mood and atmosphere.

Love Song: Not fast; tenderly, A major, 6-8. A lyrical melody introduced by the woodwinds is developed, with an answer from the strings that is followed by another melody, more determined in character, in the woodwinds.

In War Time: With rough vigour, almost savagely, D minor, 2-4. Two flutes, unaccompanied, announce the chief theme in unison. A secondary theme is sung by two clarinets, also in unison and unaccompanied. The material is worked out in a well-knit musical form with frequent changes of rhythm toward the end from 2-4 to 6-8 and back again.

Dirge: Dirgelike, mournfully, in G minor, 4-4. The lamentation is sung by muted violins in unison that are then reinforced by violas, while woodwinds and muted horn sustain the harmony rooted on the tonic note G. MacDowell directs that, to create the proper effect, one of the muted horns be played offstage.

Village Festival: Swift and light, in E major, 2-4. Several themes, all of them more or less related to those in the first movement, are developed in animated dance rhythms. The general mood of a tribal festival is captured with great felicity.

Violins II
pizz

ADDITIONAL SUGGESTIONS FOR LISTENING

Deems Taylor's Suite: "Through the Looking Glass"

More typical, perhaps, of the cosmopolitan East is Deems Taylor, composer, music critic, and author of books on music. In composition he is known for his incidental music for the BEGGAR ON HORSEBACK, his opera THE KING'S HENCHMAN, on a text by Edna St. Vincent Millay; his PETER IBBETSON, on a libretto adapted from the celebrated novel of du Maurier; and his ORCHESTRAL SUITE based on Lewis Carroll's sequel to *Alice in Wonderland*. Originally written for chamber orchestra, Taylor later revised the score for full orchestra. His own programme notes for the first performance of the suite offer the best introduction to the music:[3]

> The Suite needs no extended analysis. It is based on Lewis Carroll's immortal nonsense fairytale: *Through the Looking-Glass and What Alice Found There*, and the five pictures it presents will, if all goes well, be readily recognizable to lovers of the book. There are four movements, the first being subdivided into two connected parts.

I. (a) Dedication

Carroll precedes the tale with a charming poetical foreword, the first stanza of which the music aims to express. It runs:

> "Child of the pure unclouded brow
> And dreaming eyes of wonder!
> Though the time be fleet, and I and thou
> Are half a mile asunder,
> Thy loving smile will surely hail
> The love-gift of a fairy-tale."

A simple song theme, briefly developed, leads without pause to

(b) The Garden of Live Flowers

Shortly after Alice had entered the looking-glass country, she came to a lovely garden in which the flowers were talking:

"O Tiger-Lily," said Alice, addressing herself to one that was waving gracefully about in the wind, "I wish you could talk."

[3] From the programme notes of the New York Symphony Orchestra.

"We can talk," said the Tiger-Lily, "when there's anybody worth talking to."

"And can all the flowers talk?"

"As well as you can," said the Tiger-Lily, "and a great deal louder."

The music reflects the brisk chatter of the swaying, bright-coloured denizens of the garden.

II. *Jabberwocky*

This is the poem that so puzzled Alice, and which Humpty Dumpty finally explained to her:

" 'Twas brillig, and the slithy toves
  Did gyre and gimble in the wabe;
All mimsy were the borogoves
  And the mome raths outgrabe.

"Beware the Jabberwock, my son!
  The jaws that bite, the claws that catch!
Beware the Jubjub bird, and shun
  The fruminous Bandersnatch!

"He took his vorpal sword in hand;
  Long time the manxome foe he sought—
So rested he by the Tumtum tree,
  And stood awhile in thought.

"And, as in uffish thought he stood,
  The Jabberwock, with eyes of flame,
Came whiffling through the tulgey wood,
  And burbled as it came!

"One, two! One two! and through and through
  The vorpal blade went snicker-snack!
He left it dead, and with its head
  He went galumphing back.

"And hast thou slain the Jabberwock?
  Come to my arms, my beamish boy!
O frabjous day! Callooh! Callay!
  He chortled in his joy.

" 'Twas brillig, and the slithy toves
  Did gyre and gimble in the wabe;
All mimsy were the borogoves,
  And the mome raths outgrabe."

The theme of that fruitful beast, the Jabberwock, is first announced (*lento*) by the full orchestra. The clarinet then begins the tale, recounting how, on a "brillig" afternoon, the "slithy toves did gyre and gimble in the wabe." Muttered imprecations by the bassoon warn us to "beware the Jabberwock, my son." A miniature march signalizes the approach of our hero, taking "his vorpal sword in hand." Trouble starts among the trombones—the Jabberwock is upon us! The battle with the monster is recounted in a short and rather repellent fugue, the double basses bringing up the subject and the hero fighting back in the interludes. Finally, his vorpal blade (really a xylophone) goes snicker-snack, and the monster impersonated by the solo bassoon, dies a lingering and convulsive death. The hero returns, to the victorious strain of his own theme—"O frabjous day! Callooh! Callay!" The whole orchestra rejoices—the church bells are rung—alarms and excursions.

Conclusion. Once more the slithy toves perform their pleasing evolutions, undisturbed by the uneasy ghost of the late Jabberwock.

III. *Looking-Glass Insects*

The score contains this extract:

This was anything but a regular bee; in fact, it was an elephant —as Alice soon found out, though the idea quite took her breath away at first. . . .

The gnat (for that was the insect she had been talking to) was balancing itself on a twig just over her head, and fanning her with its wings. It certainly was a very large gnat: "About the size of a chicken," Alice thought.

"——then don't you like all insects?" the gnat went on, as quietly as if nothing had happened.

"I like them when they can talk," Alice said. "None of them ever talk, where I come from. . . ."

"Half-way up that bush, you'll see a Rocking-horse-fly, if you look. Look on the branch above your head, . . . and there you'll find a Snapdragon-fly. . . . Crawling at your feet, you may observe a Bread-and-butter-fly."

"And what does it live on?"

"Weak tea with cream in it."

"Supposing it couldn't find any?"

"Then it would die, of course."

"But that must happen very often," Alice remarked thoughtfully.

"It always happens," said the gnat.

Here we find the vociferous *diptera* that made such an impression upon Alice—the Bee-elephant, the Gnat, the Rocking-horse-fly, the Snapdragon-fly, and the Bread-and-butter-fly. There are several themes, but there is no use trying to decide which insect any one of them stands for.

IV. *The White Knight*

He was a toy Don Quixote, mild, chivalrous, ridiculous, and rather touching. He carried a mouse-trap on his saddle-bow, "because, if they *do* come, I don't choose to have them running about." He couldn't ride very well, but he was a gentle soul, with good intentions. There are two themes: the first a sort of instrumental prance, being the Knight's own conception of himself as a slashing, dare-devil fellow. The second is bland, mellifluous, a little sentimental—much more like the Knight as he really was. The theme starts off bravely, but falls out of the saddle before long, and has to give way to the second. The two alternate, in various guises, until the end, when the Knight rides off, with Alice waving her handkerchief—he thought it would encourage him if she did.

Music for the Cinema

In recent years a new field of musical composition has been made possible through the cinema. From very modest beginnings —for we are only a few decades away from the movie pianist and fiddler with their albums of set excerpts appropriate for storm scenes, deathbeds, "hurries," battles, love, Indians, and the like— a new type of incidental music has developed, with a technique and an idiom of its own.

The opportunity for cinema music came, naturally, with the development of sound pictures. At first the musical accompaniment consisted of excerpts from various musical works selected to fit the needs of the particular moving picture. But it soon became customary to write original scores for the better pictures. The studios, especially the artistically advanced ones in Germany and France during the twenties, soon began to engage the services of distinguished composers for these scores. Among the outstanding musical scores in the years before the war may be mentioned that of Karol Rathaus for Ufa's production of *The Brothers Karamazov*; Arthur Honegger's score for *Giono's Harvest*; William Walton's for

Shaw's *Major Barbara*; Sergei Prokofieff's for *Lieutenant Kije* and *Alexander Nevsky*; and Arthur Bliss's for H. G. Wells' fantastic movie, *Shape of Things to Come*.

Hollywood has adopted the practice of commissioning a special score for each movie; and in the past decade American cinema music has made great strides forward. Among notable musical scores in the past few years have been Max Steiner's atmospheric background music for Somerset Maugham's *The Letter*; Erich Korngold's, for *Marco Polo*; Aaron Copland's, for *Of Mice and Men*; Virgil Thomson's, for *The River;* and Hans Eisler's for *The Forgotten Village*. The reader may recall how effectively the approaching tragedy in *Of Mice and Men*—the scene in the stable before the murder—is proclaimed in the music through the insistent repetition of an ominous staccato figure deep in the bass; or how the mood of mystery and suspense in *The Letter* was intensified through the recurrence again and again throughout the picture of the sinister motive heard at the beginning. In *Major Barbara*, the heroine's emotional conflict, which constitutes the climax of the film, is projected completely through the stirring symphonic interlude of Walton as Barbara walks alone towards the river. Here the music takes on an even greater importance than it would have in a play. There is hardly any external action, or acting; we see only the heroine walking slowly away; the drama is an inner one and is conveyed almost exclusively through music.

Perhaps new and as yet unanticipated musical forms and styles may come from incidental and suite compositions, as well as briefer sequences, composed directly for the films. Only the future can tell.

Additional styles of the suite will be presented in the succeeding chapters.

K

Chapter Ten

Music and Ballet

THE spontaneous dances of the folk had their counterpart in the domain of art in the highly organized dance pageants that figured prominently in religious ceremonials and in the entertainments at the royal courts. In Greek tragedy, the chorus (from *choros*, a round dance) danced as it chanted. The ballet thus lent itself simultaneously to the needs of the theatre, the temple, and the palace entertainment, absorbing elements from each.

In our theatre the ballet figures in two ways: first, as a spectacular interlude in drama or opera; second, as an independent art form in which dramatic action and atmosphere are conveyed to the audience through dance pantomime. In either case, the music is of paramount importance both in furnishing an accompaniment for the actual dancing and in communicating and intensifying the mood. Ballet music as a rule combines the qualities of good dance music—melodious charm, strong rhythmic appeal, simplicity of form and content—with theatrical atmosphere, the dramatic *élan* of incidental music. It represents, in short, a fine fusion of the spirit of the dance with that of the theatre.

Much of the outstanding ballet music of the nineteenth century was written as part of operas, or incidental music to dramatic performances, and might or might not be an integral part of the dramatic plot and action of the moment. For instance, in an opera like Gounod's FAUST, the plot and action cease for the moment, and out of the wings from either side of the stage ballet dancers flutter on to the stage on the tips of their toes. They go through well-prepared graceful movements, singly and in ensembles, presenting the eye with a pleasing sight of charm in rhythmic motion and design—all this to music of a comparable character. Then the dancers disappear into the wings again, to reappear at a later time. Degas, the French painter, has caught the various moods and life of such ballet dancers in many of his paintings. Similar ballets are

Degas

Ballet Rehearsal on Stage

to be found in many French operas from the time of Lully, and before. A popular ballet of this type is Delibes' SYLVIA.[1]

As the ballet established itself as an independent art form, it employed music in conjunction with dance, pantomime, scenery, and costume to create a distinctive type of dramatic-musical entertainment. In some cases, ballets were arranged to music already in existence. Thus, Rimsky-Korsakoff's SCHEHEREZADE (Chapter XV) and Debussy's AFTERNOON OF A FAUN (Chapter XXVII) are two of the many famous orchestral compositions to which ballets were adapted. Often, however, the music was written specifically for the ballet. As with incidental music, the composers of these ballets frequently arranged the music into concert suites, some of which became very popular as independent compositions, preserving as they did their excitement and rhythmic verve even when removed from the glamour of the ballet theatre. Thus was established a continual interplay between music and ballet, with symphonic compositions moving into the ballet theatre, and ballet music becoming part of the symphonic repertory.

As to the relationship between the two arts, the reader may recall our discussion on musical architecture in Chapter V, where we pointed out that the qualities of symmetry and balance, which are space concepts in painting, sculpture, and architecture, become time concepts in music. The ballet affords a vivid example of the transformation from the one dimension to the other. The musical phrases that balance each other in time, in the music become the basis for movements that balance each other in space in the dance, producing a synchronization of the two dimensions.

To make a long story short, then, the new art form of the ballet was built upon a story with a well-defined dramatic plot, and the action, or pantomime, served as the basis of telling the story and of providing a proper and desirable vehicle for the dancers themselves in the medium of their own art. Of course, the costumes, stage settings, and, what concerns us most for the moment, the music, combined to provide the complete performance, the result being a dramatic stage performance through dancing, pantomime, and music—*sans* words of the drama and *sans* singing of the opera.

[1] Essential listening for this chapter includes: *Ritual Fire Dance* from EL AMOR BRUJO by Falla, PETROUCHKA by Stravinsky, SKYSCRAPERS by Carpenter, and the MOTHER GOOSE BALLET by Ravel. All other ballets mentioned in the text are to be considered supplementary and optional. If time does not permit complete performances of the required listening, select excerpts, or movements, from them accordingly.

Naturally, to enjoy such ballets to the full, one must know the story and the plot, the choreographic interpretation of these, as well as an understanding of the other arts that fuse into this art form. (Those who are especially interested in this subject will want to acquaint themselves with further information concerning the French, the Russian, and later-day ballet styles. Read John Martin on *The Dance*.)

There are many choices of this new ballet style that we might make for our first offering; but, for more or less arbitrary reasons, let us begin with EL AMOR BRUJO (Love the Magician), a "choreographic fantasy" in sixteen parts (with vocal parts also), by the eminent Spanish composer, Manuel de Falla (1876-   ). The story, based on Andalusian life, concerns a Gipsy girl whose dead lover is jealous of her friendliness with his successor. The ghost makes several attempts to break up the new affair, but is foiled by another Gipsy girl who is courageous enough to flirt with him and distract him from his plot. The thematic material, while original with Falla, is so true to the character and spirit of the people that it is often mistaken for folk music. The orchestral version for concert use was made by the composer after the first performance of the ballet in 1915, and it is frequently played in that form. Since the whole, sixteen scenes or movements, is too long for the nonce, let us hear number seven of the series, the *Ritual Fire Dance to Exorcise Evil Spirits*.

The scene is in a dark cavern in the centre of which the magic fire flickers, musically depicted by the mysterious *pizzicato* (plucking the strings rather than bowing them) in the stringed instruments of the orchestra. A weird incantation sweeps through the music over a strange seductive rhythmic foundation. Abrupt chords sounded by the full orchestra punctuate the ritual dance; but the inexorable rhythm never ceases. The dance grows steadily more abandoned; the theme is now repeated in a kind of fury; and a series of savage chords, suggestive of the wild figures leaping through the air, brings the music to a close. Notice how successfully the composer has projected the atmosphere of "black magic" and strange, fantastic shapes, and how adroitly he has used orchestral timbre, or instrumental tone colour, of the oboes, clarinets, 'cellos and double basses, and throbbing drums, to portray and intensify the dramatic action and to arouse the proper emotions. Of course we miss the "seeing" part of the performance.

Now let us listen to a much more complete ballet of the Russian School, provided in Igor Stravinsky's ballet-suite PETROUCHKA. But first, because the composer is an outstanding world figure in music of our own time, a brief biographical sketch.

Igor Stravinsky

Stravinsky, the son of a Russian opera singer, was born near St. Petersburg (Leningrad) in 1882 and now resides in the United States. Like Tchaikovsky and Sibelius, he prepared himself for a legal career. But his talent manifested itself so clearly that Rimsky-Korsakoff, whom he met when he was twenty-two, advised him to devote himself entirely to music, and it was under the Russian master that he received his first systematic training. The teacher's influence has always made itself felt in Stravinsky's brilliant orchestration and sensitivity to instrumental effects.

Stravinsky came to fame in the years before the outbreak of the first World War as one of the brilliant artists whom Serge Diaghileff grouped around him in the Ballet Russe. (For an interesting account of that eventful period, the reader is referred to Romola Nijinsky's biography of Nijinsky, the great dancer, and Haskell's book on Diaghileff.) THE FIREBIRD, performed by Diaghileff's Company in 1910, and PETROUCHKA, performed the following year, established Stravinsky as one of the most original spirits in the hectic pre-war scene. PETROUCHKA has remained the most popular of his works, and in brilliance of orchestration, dramatic power, verve, and melodic richness is generally considered his masterpiece. THE RITES OF SPRING, which appeared in 1913, created a furore in Paris by its brutal primitiveness, its strange rhythms and dissonances. For many years afterward, its performance in the musical centres of the world seldom failed to provoke violent demonstrations. Although the next twenty-five years saw a steady output of works—among them an opera, THE NIGHTINGALE, based on the fairy tale of Hans Christian Andersen; PULCINELLA, a ballet based on the music of the charming eighteenth-century master, Pergolese; a piano concerto in the style of Bach; as well as a number of compositions for chamber groups—the first three ballets still remain his most popular works and the ones most likely to be encountered at symphony concerts.

"*Petrouchka*"

PETROUCHKA was first performed during the famous season of the Diaghileff ballet at the Chatelet in 1911, with Nijinsky in the title role and Karsavina as the ballerina. A concert suite was arranged from the ballet by Serge Koussevitzky, conductor of the Boston Symphony Orchestra, in collaboration with the composer.

The action takes place at a carnival in a public square of St. Petersburg a century ago; the chief characters are a showman and the three puppets whom he exhibits, endowing them with human emotions in order to entertain his audience—the lovely Ballerina, the swashbuckling Moor, and the lovelorn clown, Petrouchka. The Showman blows his flute against the bustle of the carnival to attract customers to his puppet show. The puppets are brought to life; Petrouchka, ugly and the object of ridicule, falls hopelessly in love with the Ballerina, who prefers the Moor. After the puppet show is over the carnival continues; but behind the scene the sawdust tragedy plays itself out. At the height of the revelry Petrouchka is seen running across the stage of the puppet theatre wildly pursued by the Moor who with a stroke of the sword crushes the unfortunate clown's head. He dies as the crowd gathers about, horrified. The Showman appears and explains to the crowd that his puppets are but stuffed dolls incapable of real emotion. He succeeds in convincing them; they depart. But at the end the ghost of Petrouchka appears above the booth, terrifying them with a grimace. There are obviously things in the lives of his puppets which the Showman does not understand. He has been wrong in assuming that his puppets have no souls. . . .

The Suite for concert opens with the boisterous *Russian Dance* from the opening scene of the ballet, music electric with the bustle and animation of the carnival mood. The music is taut and angular; that is the dance that the three stuffed puppets perform for the delectation of the unfeeling crowd. Notice the sharply contrasting timbres; the development of the theme by an interesting variety of instruments; the vivid ever-shifting rhythms; above all, the overpowering gusto and virility of the music.

The second part centres about the appearance of the Ballerina, accompanied by a dainty piano solo. Next the music depicts the sufferings of the love-smitten clown, his helpless rage at being rejected, his forlorn cries.

A Scene from the Ballet "Petrouchka"

Stravinsky

The third part is a brilliant carnival scene, one of the most colourful tone pictures from the composer's hand. A motley procession surges past our eyes—gay peasants, rollicking children, hawkers and fakirs and barkers, their cries intermingled with the tinny sounds of carousels and hurdy-gurdies. There is much dancing and gaiety that is rapidly dissipated as the crowd scatters at the arrival of a peasant leading a trained bear.

The peasant pipes a tune; the bear walks on his hind legs to a ponderous accompaniment on the double basses. The spotlight soon switches to a rich merchant who amuses himself by throwing money to the crowd. Gipsies dance, snatching at the wind-tossed bank notes. Then coachmen and ostlers perform a vigorous dance marked by great stamping of boots to typical Russian rhythms.

The final scene depicts the masquerade at nightfall. Clowning motives in the bass herald the approach of the masqueraders. Disguised as buffoons, devils, pigs, and goats, the merrymakers frolic together in a mad whirl. It is on this note that the concert ends, omitting the personal tragedy of the puppet, who from being put through the outer semblance of human emotions so unexpectedly, developed a soul—and a capacity for suffering—of his own.

Of course, the next step is to see the ballet as well as to hear it, if you can. Now for a more abstract and symbolic ballet by our own native composer, John Alden Carpenter.

John Alden Carpenter

The ballet has been assiduously cultivated in America; several of our contemporary composers have produced highly successful scores. One of the outstanding among these is SKYSCRAPERS by John Alden Carpenter (1876-   ), which not only is a fine example of modern tendencies in the art of ballet, but also presents to us in a racy, thoroughly alive idiom, the dynamic tempo, the vitality and surging rhythms of modern American life.

Carpenter, a descendant of John Alden, stands in the forefront of American composers. His music, delightful, intelligent, and witty, has attained wide popularity with the general public. SKYSCRAPERS is his best-known work; it was first performed at the Metropolitan Opera House in 1926 with scenery and costumes by the noted stage designer, Robert Edmond Jones. Arranged as a concert suite it has found a sure place for itself on symphonic programmes.

"Skyscrapers"

The composer has built his music around the polarities of work and play, each, as he says, "with its own peculiar and distinctive rhythmic character." The fevered, restlessly pulsating rhythms of the work episodes alternate with the gay foxtrot and "Blues" rhythms of the play episodes. The ballet is divided into six scenes: 1. Symbols of Restlessness. 2. Abstraction of the Skyscraper; the Work that produces it; the Crowds passing it. 3. The transition from Work to Play. 4. An Amusement Park of the Coney Island type, and its varied, restless activities; a "flashback" to the idea of Work, and back again to Play. 5. The return from Play to Work. 6. Skyscrapers.

As in most ballet music, the rhythmic element predominates in this work; the rhythms of jazz, of foxtrot, of subways and motors and machines, of carousels and roller coasters—a brilliant and feverish conglomerate of the sounds and sights of the metropolis. The "symbols of restlessness" which permeate the first scenes; the blatant, hurdy-gurdy, "Coney Island" atmosphere of the fourth, with its hectic and synthetic gaiety; the *Dance of "Herself"* introduced by a muted trumpet; the *Dance of the Strutter*, the Negro scene which ushers in the *Blues*; *The Sandwich Man*, trudging along wearily between his gaudy placards; the factory whistle summoning the workers back to the shops, and the imposing chords at the end which drive relentlessly onward, symbolic of glittering skyscrapers thrusting against the sky—all these are interwoven in a score of compact brilliance that has humour and verve and a topical pointedness, capturing with rare felicity the drive and tension of American industrial life for which the skyscraper is so apt a symbol.

Note particularly the colourfulness of the orchestration: the use of the brass and complex piano parts in the "Symbols of Restlessness" scene; the woodwind and brass, in jagged rhythms, in the "Abstraction of the Skyscraper"; the happy-go-lucky dance tune on the banjo in the "Transition from Work to Play"; the muted trumpet and brass band effects in the "Amusement Park" episode; the crooning solo for English horn which introduces the "Negro

Scene"; the imaginative use of trumpets and horns in the "Sand-wich Man" scene; and the fierce power and glitter of the finale. Here is a wealth of melodic ideas, of striking harmonies that abound in pungent dissonances united with never-flagging rhythms in a composition of great excitement and forward drive.

For our last illustration, we have chosen Maurice Ravel's ever popular MA MÈRE L'OYE (Mother Goose) SUITE. (More of this composer and his impressionistic suite, DAPHNIS AND CHLOE, will be found in Chapter XXVIII, page 467.) These two ballets have been temporarily thrown out of proper perspective among the laymen by the abnormal popularity of Ravel's ballet BOLERO, a brilliant *tour de force* in the art of orchestration, an art and craft in which Ravel takes his rightful place beside the greatest in music history. One of the reasons we have chosen this particular work at this place is the value we can get in the way of appreciation of instrumental tone colour, or timbre, if we will but listen carefully. (See also Chapter XI.)

Maurice Ravel: "Mother Goose Ballet Suite"

The MOTHER GOOSE SUITE music, originally composed for piano duet in 1908, was later orchestrated by Ravel and, like Debussy's AFTERNOON OF A FAUN, achieved popularity as a ballet. An interesting characteristic of Ravel is the fact that, although he transcribed for orchestra several compositions originally written for piano, his sense of style was so acute that the orchestral versions do not in the least have that "made-over" feeling that so often attends transcriptions, but seem to have a personality of their own quite distinct from the original form of the piece.

The *Suite*, arranged from the ballet music, consists of five children's pieces. The *Pavane of the Sleeping Beauty* has a slow somnolent grace. A *pavane* is an old stately dance of Spanish origin; Ravel's other pavane, *For a Dead Princess*, widely popular in this country, has achieved the distinction (?) of inspiring a foxtrot. Note the effect of two solo flutes, later English horn and flute.

To the second number, *Hop o' My Thumb*, Ravel appended a quotation from Perrault, the great French writer of fairy tales: "He believed that he would easily find his path by means of his bread crumbs which he had scattered wherever he had passed; but he was very much surprised when he could not find a single crumb: the birds had come and eaten everything up." Note the effect of the oboe solo over the muted first and second violins. Can you notice also the frequent change of time?

Third is *Laideronnette, Empress of the Pagodas*. *Pagoda* once indicated not only the fanciful little tower but also the idol or image lodged in it. When the Princess Laideronnette, who had been cursed at birth with supreme ugliness, entered her bath, the pagodas and their ladies—grotesque little figures with movable heads—"began to sing and play on instruments; some had theorbos made of walnut shells, some had viols made of almond shells; for they were obliged to proportion the instruments to their figure." Note that the quick theme played by the solo flute resembles the nursery tune "Chop Sticks," or "Peter, Peter, Pumpkin Eater," which all of us have played in our youth on the black keys of the piano. Such a scale is called a *pentatonic* scale. Many Chinese melodies are in such a scale, thus Ravel was making a proper musical pun.

Next comes the *Conversations of Beauty and the Beast*. In the metre of a slow waltz, with a double bassoon representing the Beast, this number is one of the most popular of the suite. Since Beauty was able to see through the ugly exterior of the Beast to the kind heart and fine soul underneath, she was able to release him from his enchantment. "The Beast disappeared, and she saw at her feet only a prince more beautiful than Love. . . ."

The first of the following musical illustrations, for harp with clarinet solo, is used to depict the "Beauty"; the second, which is played by the contrabassoon and which sounds an octave lower than written, is a delightful characterization of the "Beast."

The Fairy Garden, which closes the suite, reveals to us the composer in an unusually poetic mood. In slow three-four time, the movement sums up the spirit of fairy-tale magic. Here Ravel weaves a spell no less potent than that of the fairies and magicians who people the tales on which his music is based. How the strings, played very softly, contribute just the right "atmosphere" for the fairy waltzlike theme!

ADDITIONAL SUGGESTIONS FOR LISTENING

Among the popular ballet suites and excerpts that figure on symphonic programmes and illustrate the nineteenth-century style in this genre are Tchaikovsky's SWAN LAKE, SLEEPING BEAUTY (also known as *Aurora's Wedding*); the charming excerpts from the ballets of the French composer, Léo Delibes (1836-1891), COPPÉLIA and SYLVIA; the ballet GAIETÉ PARISIENNE by the composer of *Tales of Hoffmann*, Jacques Offenbach (1819-1890); the *Bacchanale* from Glazounov's ballet THE SEASONS; and LES SYLPHIDES, the ballet arranged from the works of Chopin.

Other modern ballet suites that the reader will enjoy and that will give him an idea of some very delightful music of recent years are the popular ballets of Stravinsky, SACRÉ DU PRINTEMPS and THE FIREBIRD, to which we shall return when we discuss modern music; the gay music from THE INCREDIBLE FLUTIST, by the American composer, Walter Pison (1894-   ); Darius Milhaud's ballet LA CRÉATION DU MONDE

(The Creation of the World), an interesting example of the use of the American jazz idiom by a European composer; Ravel's BOLERO, which attained wide popularity in America as a concert piece, although it was originally written as a ballet for the dancer Ida Rubinstein; *Yablochko*, or *Russian Sailors' Dance*, from Reinhold Glière's ballet THE RED POPPY, which is lustily satirized by his younger compatriot Dmitri Shostakovitch (1906-   ) in the *Russian Dance* from the ballet THE GOLDEN AGE; and Aaron Copland's BILLY THE KID.

Chapter Eleven

Tone Colour in Music

The Orchestra

I. The Instruments of the Orchestra

NO DOUBT the listener's curiosity has been aroused from time to time up to this point as to what instrument was playing the theme at a particular moment. At least, it is hoped that such has been the case; in fact, during the analysis of Ravel's MOTHER GOOSE SUITE in the preceding chapter, we drew your attention to several instruments of the orchestra and we saw how the composer used the tone colour of such instruments to depict, characterize, or incite a certain emotional effect. The time has now come to look into such matters more objectively and with more detail than was before possible.

We often speak of the character of tone produced by an instrument as *timbre*. Each instrument and each type of human voice has its own quality of tone, its distinctive colour. The timbre of the violin differs from that of the bassoon; the soprano's tone quality is altogether different from that of the bass. Like the painter with his palette, the composer mixes his colours, blends or contrasts them as he sees fit. He must be as sensitive to timbre as the painter is to colour, and he must have the same capacity for picturing the subtlest shadings of colour in his imagination.

Timbre is a constituent element in every conceivable type of music. It is of prime importance in compositions for the various solo instruments—piano, violin, 'cello, organ, and the like. It is equally important in vocal music, whether solo as in the art song, or in ensemble and chorus as in opera and oratorio and in the blending of the various vocal timbres with the instrumental accompaniment. Above all, timbre enters as a predominant aesthetic consideration in the blending and contrasting of the different instrumental colours in the small ensemble, or chamber

music groups (see Chapter XXV), and in that mighty instrumental aggregate, the modern symphony orchestra.[1]

If the reader were taking a course in music of the sixteenth century, most of the works that he would study would be choral. Since
then, the instruments have forged ahead steadily, first to a position
of equality with the vocal branch, and finally to a point where the
symphony orchestra is the favourite instrument of our time—a
many-tongued, wonderfully sensitive instrument on which the
composer runs the gamut from a mysterious whisper to a tornado
of sound, suitable beyond compare, as we saw in some of the
modern ballets that we have just listened to, depicting the moods
and rhythms, the furious activity and dynamism, of twentieth-
century life.

In the history of music, this shifting of the spotlight from the
vocal to the instrumental branch is one of the most significant
changes of the past five hundred years. The instruments entered
the domain of serious music timidly, at first mainly furnishing the
accompaniment by doubling or duplicating the voice parts. The
next step came when the madrigals of the Renaissance began to
be performed occasionally by the instruments without the voices,
probably when no singers happened to be available. Naturally,
the composers of the period did not realize at once that instruments could manage an altogether different type of music from
that which the voice could carry. They thought of the instruments
as simply so many voices substituting for or duplicating the real
things, and often inscribed their madrigals, "apt for voyces or
viols."

The seventeenth century witnessed a steady development in the
mechanical and tonal aspects of instruments, as well as in playing
techniques. Throughout the century the instruments forged ahead
in importance. Little *interludes* were introduced into the *madrigals*
while the voices rested. Gradually these interludes took on a specifically instrumental character, independent of the vocal style.
With the development of the opera, a new phase began: Monteverde, as we saw, began to exploit the dramatic possibilities of the
instruments, their individual colour and personality. Instrumental interludes began to play an increasingly important role in the

---

[1] For pictures and more detailed descriptions of the instruments, see *Instruments
of the Modern Symphony Orchestra and Band*, new and revised edition by Edwin John
Stringham (New York: Carl Fischer, 1930), a useful and inexpensive book for the
general music lover.

opera. Most of all, it became fashionable to open the performance with a more or less ambitious overture, for instruments alone. These interludes took on a specifically instrumental character, independent of the vocal style. With the development of the opera, a new phase began: Monteverde, as we saw, began to exploit the dramatic possibilities of the instruments, their individual colour and personality. Instrumental interludes began to play an increasingly important role in the opera. Most of all, it became fashionable to open the performance with a more or less ambitious overture, for instruments alone. These interludes and overtures were loosely called *symphonias*, literally, a "sounding together" (from the Greek *syn*, "together," and *phonē*, "sound"). The path was thus opened for the emergence of what is, as far as many music lovers are concerned, the most important branch of the art—symphonic music.

The general composition of the orchestra as we know it was already fairly well established by the end of the eighteenth century. The Romantic movement in the nineteenth century, with its search for new effects, for picturesque tone colours and vivid description, naturally provided an enormous stimulus for expansion of orchestral resources, and for new developments in the art of instrumentation. Consequently, the past hundred years have witnessed a great growth in size of the orchestra, in the improvement of old instruments and the introduction of new, as well as in the artistic and technical standards of playing them. Whereas the orchestra of Mozart and Haydn usually contained about thirty-five players, our leading orchestras have well over a hundred expertly trained musicians, many of them artists on their instruments, who perform under the batons of gifted conductors the works of the masters of the past and the moderns alike with the greatest skill and artistic fidelity.[2]

The string choir

The modern symphony orchestra consists of four instrumental families or choirs: the string choir, the woodwind, the brass, and the percussion. The string group, considered the backbone of the orchestra, contains the four types of stringed instruments played

[2] The author urges that at this point you listen to Serge Prokofieff's delightful *Peter and the Wolf*, wherein the instruments of the orchestra are pointed out in a most effective manner.

L

with the bow: the violin, the viola, the 'cello, and the double bass. Each of these is based upon the acoustical law that by changing the length, thickness, and tension of the vibrating string we change the pitch of the tone. The player manipulates the bow with his right hand, setting the strings in vibration. With his left, he presses the strings at various points, producing different pitches. The strings have the great advantage, compared with a piano, for instance, of sustaining the tone as long as desired, modulating it the while (making it louder or softer).

It will be found helpful in studying the timbre of the various instruments to use the special records that illustrate the tone colour of each instrument separately. The sound should be associated with the description in our text and with the appearance of the instrument. However, the real appreciation of instrumental tone colour comes with repeated listening to the works of the masters, in the original orchestral environment.[3]

The violin is the "soprano" of the string choir. It is the foremost singer of lyrical melody; its legato possesses something of the warmth and expressiveness of the human voice. On the other hand, its agility in executing rapid notes makes it equally useful in intricate running passages. A number of special effects are possible on the violin: playing two notes at once, or "double stopping"; bouncing the bow on the strings (*saltando*); playing rapidly a number of staccato notes in one stroke of the bow (*spiccato*); plucking the strings (*pizzicato*); vibrating the left hand from the wrist as the finger presses against the string to produce that tremulous tone known as *vibrato*; playing with the wooden part of the bow to create a strange hollow tone (*col legno*); rapidly repeating the same note with brusque up-and-down strokes of the bow to achieve the *tremolo*, the favourite stand-by for producing effects of suspense, danger, fear and the like; sliding the left hand along the string while bowing with the right, which gives us the *glissando*; and pressing lightly at certain points of the string, which prevents the string from vibrating as a whole and brings into prominence the vibrations of its segments, thus producing those high-pitched, ethereal tones known as *harmonics*.

The four strings of the violin are tuned G.D.A.E, ranging from

<hr/>

[3] Essential listening for this chapter includes: *Peter and the Wolf* by Prokofieff, "Instruments of the Symphony Orchestra" records for string, woodwind, brass choirs and percussion, "Introduction and Allegro" for strings or "Serenade" for strings by Elgar, NUTCRACKER SUITE by Tchaikovsky, and selected solo and ensemble records.

the full-throated expressiveness of the G string to the brilliance of the upper register of the E.

Its effective range is approximately three and a half octaves, beginning from G below middle C. The modern symphony orchestra has two groups of violins, known as the first and second violins, with about sixteen players in each.

The viola is held and played like the violin, but it is larger in size and produces a deeper, more veiled tone. It is the "alto" of the string choir. It is pitched five tones lower than the violin; that is, it cannot sing as high as the violin, but it compensates by being able to go lower. If it lacks the brilliance of the violin, the viola possesses a subdued charm and dignity of its own, which in the lower register takes on a darkly brooding quality. The viola blends so well with the more brilliant violin or the richer-toned 'cello that for many years its own personality was subordinated to these two. But in the past century composers grew more and more appreciative of its lyrical possibilities. Its subtle colouring, now gently mournful, now coldly penetrating, has come to assume an important part in the orchestral palette. Its four strings are tuned C.G.D.A.; and since most of its music lies between the bass and treble clefs, for convenience it uses the alto (movable C) clef (middle C is on the middle line):

It is capable of all the technical effects of the violin; its effective range is slightly less—about three octaves, from the C below middle C. The symphony orchestra usually contains from ten to twelve viola players.

The 'cello (shortened name for *violoncello*) is a still larger instrument and is propped between the player's knees. Tuned an octave lower than the viola, it may be considered the "tenor" or "baritone" of the string quartet. Its strings are thicker and over twice as long as those of the violin; its tone is mellow and full-throated. Its capacity for poignant emotion and sustained song have led composers to entrust to the 'cello some of their loveliest melodies. It is capable of the special effects of the violin; is tuned C.G.D.A:

It has an effective range of over three and a half octaves, from C two octaves below middle C. There are usually eight to ten 'cellos in the modern symphony orchestra, which supply a warm, rich mass of tone to the string section.

The double bass, known also as the contrabass or string bass, is the lowest pitched and largest of the string family. It is about six feet high; the player either stands, or sits on a high stool. It was originally used mainly to duplicate the 'cello parts an octave lower—in other words, to double the bass; hence its name. Its deep, heavy tone is equally effective in portraying darkest gloom or gruff, heavy-handed humour; but it seldom functions as a solo instrument. Its principal task is to supply a firm base for the harmonic structure above it. Recently it has acquired a new importance in jazz bands, where it is played in "slapping" fashion to emphasize the beat, almost like a percussion instrument. The double bass is tuned E.A.D.G. and sounds an octave lower than written:

Its sounding range is slightly over three octaves, from E three octaves below middle C. There are eight to ten double-bass players in the symphony orchestra.

Between the brilliant colour of the violin, the soft "greys" of the viola, the rich glow of the 'cello and the powerful background of the double bass, the composer can look to the string section for an interesting assortment of tone colours and special tonal effects. When necessary, these instruments are muted by slipping a small contraption of metal, bone, or wood, called the mute (Italian, *sordino*), over the bridge. This lessens the sonority and produces a veiled, sensitive tone.

The harp, one of the oldest and most "romantic" of instruments, is a stringed instrument sounded by plucking. It was popular with the ancient Egyptians, Assyrians, Hebrews, and Greeks, and with the troubadours and minstrels of the Middle Ages. It was played by Alfred the Great; and, limned in gold on a field of green, it became the national emblem of Ireland.

The harp has a silvery, dreamlike tone that stands out among all the timbres of the orchestra. Beginners in composition are fascinated by its tone, and introduce it lavishly into their works; but masters of orchestral style know that its effectiveness depends upon sparing use. We will hear it used most effectively by Rimsky-Korsakoff to give the effect of Oriental languor in his SCHEHERE-ZADE. Debussy, Ravel, and other members of the Impressionist school (Chapter XXVIII) were very fond of the floating, silvery tones of the harp.

The range of the harp is five octaves. Its music is written like that for the piano. Chords on the harp are often "broken," that is to say, the tones are played in succession instead of simultaneously; whence is derived our name for a broken chord, *arpeggio* (from *arpa*, "harp"), an effect that appears frequently in piano music. The modern orchestra possesses one or two harps.

For our second listening project, hear the "String Choir" records from the available sets offered by the Columbia, Victor, or Decca companies, illustrating the various "Instruments of the Symphony Orchestra"; and for the third listening project, either hear the "Introduction and Allegro" for Strings, Opus 47, or the "Serenade" for Strings, Opus 28, by Edward Elgar.

The ranges of the instruments of the string choir and the harp are:

The woodwind choir

The woodwind section, with its haunting tone colours, is unquestionably one of the most fascinating and variegated parts of the orchestra. The members of this choir have sharply differentiated personalities that, whether in combination with one another or with the instruments of other choirs, contribute some of the most piquant colours of the modern orchestral palette. Since their timbre is so much more striking than that of most of the other instruments, the woodwinds have to be used with greater circumspection and sustained for shorter periods than the strings.

In the woodwinds, the tone is produced by a vibrating column of air within the tube: the shorter the air column, the more vibra-

Doodle-Sack Player   *Dürer*

tions per second and the higher the pitch. The air is set in motion by a single or double reed (except in the flute); and it is the resultant reediness of tone that lends to these instruments their distinctive individuality. Each of the four principal members of this group—flute, oboe, clarinet, and bassoon—has a related family instrument so similar to it in construction that the player can change from one to the other without too great difficulty. The flute is related to the piccolo; the oboe, to the English horn; the clarinet, to the bass clarinet (and saxophone); and the bassoon, to the double bassoon. While all these are wind instruments—that is to say, blown with the breath—a number of them are no longer made of wood; but this does not affect their being classified as woodwinds. The saxophone is included in this group because, even though it is made of brass, it is a single reed instrument and possesses other characteristics of the woodwind choir; clarinets, flutes, and even oboes are sometimes made of metal.

The flute is one of the most ancient of instruments, having been extensively cultivated in its earliest form among the Egyptians and the Greeks. It is the most brilliant member of the woodwinds, as well as the most agile; it can execute rapid passages with greater dexterity than any of them. It is not a reed instrument at all; the tone is produced by blowing across a hole in the side called *embouchure*, instead of into a mouthpiece at one end. The modern instrument is held horizontally. The flute has a liquid tone that in the upper registers takes on a birdlike lightness and brilliance, while in the lower there is a veiled, expressive quality. The flute is the "coloratura soprano" of the woodwinds, and is capable of legato melody as well as brilliant rapid passages.

The flute has a range of about three octaves, from middle C. The first octave has a veiled and fluid colour; the second is smooth and clear; the upper register is sharp and penetrating. Romantic and Impressionist composers were very fond of the flute. Ravel makes effective use of it in *La Flute Enchantée* (The Enchanted Flute) from his SCHEHEREZADE, as well as in the DAPHNIS AND CHLOE suite. Rimsky-Korsakoff uses it extensively in his SCHE-HEREZADE (Chapter XV); Tchaikovsky in his *Dance of the Toy Flutes* from the NUTCRACKER SUITE (see next section); and Debussy assigns to it the celebrated opening theme of THE AFTERNOON OF A FAUN (Chapter XXVIII). There are generally two or three flautists in the orchestra; one or two may double on the piccolo.

The piccolo (from *flauto piccolo*, the Italian for "little flute") is half as long as the flute and sounds an octave higher. Its range is about three octaves, in the lower register very brilliant, in the upper, shrill and piercing. Its tone heightens the colour of an orchestral climax, and it is much used for special effects, such as the whistling of the wind, the howling of a thunderstorm, and the like. The piccolo is used in military bands and in drum and fife bands. Its scintillating tone, suggesting the bizarre and even—as in Berlioz's DAMNATION OF FAUST—the infernal, has caused it to be nicknamed the "imp of the orchestra." It sounds an octave higher than written; therefore it is called a transposing instrument. One piccolo is used in the modern orchestra.

The oboe, a conical woodwind pipe terminating in a bell, is a double reed instrument and has a nasal, "pleading" tone that at times takes on a startlingly human quality. Possessing a certain lyrical, pastoral character, it is indispensable to the tone painters of pastoral scenes. In addition, its powers for expressing poignant emotion—whether grief, beseeching, or longing—made it one of the favourite instruments of the late Romantic and Impressionist composers. Saint-Saëns uses the oboe to represent the crowing of the cock in his DANSE MACABRE (Chapter XIII). Beethoven uses its mournful colouring in the *Funeral March* (second movement) of the "EROICA" SYMPHONY. Berlioz employs it to represent a shepherd in the "Pastoral Scene" of his SYMPHONIE FANTASTIQUE. The oboe may be considered the "lyric soprano" of the woodwinds. Its range extends two and a half octaves, from B flat below middle C. It is capable of brilliant and agile running passages, as well as of sustained melody.. There are generally two or three oboe players in the full symphony orchestra, one of whom doubles on the alto oboe, the English horn. (For example, see MOTHER GOOSE SUITE, page 137.)

The English horn is not very well named, since it is neither English nor a horn. Some historians derive its name from a corruption of *cor angle* (bent horn) which gradually became *cor anglais* (English horn)—a plausible explanation. It is one and a half times as large as the oboe, transposing its sound a fifth lower than written. It may be considered the alto of the woodwind choir; it substitutes for the penetrating reediness of the oboe a plaintive quality all its own, vaguely nostalgic, sorrowful yet resigned. Dvořák entrusts to the English horn the famous melody of the *Largo* of his NEW WORLD SYMPHONY (see Chapter XIX).

The clarinet is a cylindrical pipe generally of wood, two feet in length, with a narrow bell at one end. It has a single reed mouthpiece. Its smooth, liquid tone is more colourful than that of the oboe; it has something of the agility and brilliance of the flute. The clarinet is the "dramatic soprano" of the woodwind choir. It has a great range of volume of tone, running the gamut from a

mysterious whisper to the fullest sonority. Its lowest register has a
specially haunting quality, while its capacity for pure, clear song
in the upper register makes it most effective in lyrical passages.
The clarinet, along with the violin, is one of the most useful instruments of the orchestra. Its range extends for about three and
a half octaves, from the E below middle C. There are generally
three clarinetists in the modern symphony orchestra, of whom one
doubles on the bass clarinet. For examples of the instrument's
versatile powers, listen to the lyric theme of the Princess in the
third movement of Rimsky-Korsakoff's SCHEHEREZADE (Chapter
XV):

(note the smooth ascending and descending runs in the same
movement); the wonderfully liquid tone of the clarinets in the first
movement of Mozart's G-MINOR SYMPHONY (Chapter XXII); the
imitation of the call of the yellowhammer in Beethoven's SIXTH
SYMPHONY (*Pastoral*), and its use in combination with the horns
in the same work, to give the shepherd's call after the storm. The
clarinet has an extensive repertoire as a solo instrument. It is a
transposing instrument (the written note and the tone that is
produced from it are not the same); thus, the clarinet in B flat
sounds down one step from the written note in the key of C, and
the A clarinet sounds down a tone and a half.

The bass clarinet is, in structure, an enlarged clarinet that
sounds an octave below the B-flat clarinet. Its tone is deep and
full and encompasses a range of about three octaves. The lowest
tones are extremely rich and powerful, resembling certain pedal
stops on the organ. With its turned-up metal bell it might be mistaken for a saxophone, except that its body is made of wood. The
richness and sonority of its tone, especially in the low register,
lend themselves to solemnity and the ominous. In the second act
of LOHENGRIN, Wagner allots the sinister motive of "warning" to
the bass clarinet:

In Die Walküre, the bass clarinet carries the motive of Wotan's anger:

Wagner also gives it prominence in the tragic scene at the close of the second act of Tristan and Isolde, where King Mark discovers the lovers and gives vent to his grief in tones of great dignity and pathos. The bass clarinet is a transposing instrument. If it is written in the treble clef, it sounds down a ninth; if in the bass clef, a second down. The orchestra includes one bass clarinet.

The clarinet reed was adapted to conical brass tubes by the French instrument maker Adolphe Sax, for whom the saxophone was named. These instruments, which come in several varieties—soprano, alto, tenor, baritone, and bass—combine the liquid quality of the clarinet with the soft reediness of the English horn and the lyricism of the 'cello. They have become closely associated with American jazz music—witness their effective use by Carpenter in his Skyscrapers—and are effective both in sustained melody and in rapid, decorative passages. They did not enter the symphonic ensemble until modern times; although the reader may recall that Bizet assigned to the saxophone a passage of great beauty, the theme symbolizing "The Innocent," in the *Prelude* to L'Arlésienne. The French composers have always been partial to this liquid-voiced instrument. Debussy composed a Rhapsody for Saxophone and Orchestra; Saint-Saëns, Delibes, and Vincent D'Indy were fond of it. D'Indy has a quartet of saxophones in his opera Fervaal. The American composer Werner Janssen (1899-   ) used the instrument memorably in his symphonic poem New Year's Eve in New York. Gershwin, Ferde Grofé, and Arthur Shepard have written effective passages for it.

The bassoon is the "bass" of the woodwinds. Its pipe is a conical tube about eight feet in length, folded or doubled upon itself and joined together in a block of solid wood. Since its primitive form bore some resemblance to a bundle of sticks—the tube was originally six to nine feet long, bent several times—the Italians named this instrument *fagotto*, a faggot. The instrument is capable of a dry, hollow tone that in staccato produces a somewhat grotesque effect, as a result of which it has come to be called the "clown of the orchestra." (Notice this effect, in the next section, at the opening of the *Chinese Dance* of Tchaikovsky's NUTCRACKER SUITE, as well as the famous use of three bassoons to imitate the hopping of the broom in Dukas' SORCERER'S APPRENTICE, Chapter XIII.) At the same time, the bassoon is capable of lyric melody, of a sustained and expressive legato of solemn or passionate hue. It is nontransposing and sounds where written. The bassoon sings the serene, lyrical theme in the course of the second movement of Beethoven's FIFTH SYMPHONY (see Chapter XX).

The whimsical side of its versatile nature is expressed in the folk-songlike theme of the happy-go-lucky Kalendar Prince in Rimsky-Korsakoff's SCHEHEREZADE. (See Chapter XV.)

The bassoon has a range of about three and a half octaves. There are three bassoonists in the modern symphony orchestra, one of whom doubles on the contrabassoon.

The contrabassoon is the woodwind equivalent of the double bass. It is pitched an octave below the bassoon (sounds an octave lower than written) and can sound the deepest notes in the orchestral ensemble. It is a conical pipe of sixteen feet in length, doubled back upon itself four times and possessing a metal bell at its largest end. One is usually included in the modern orchestra. It is not often used as a solo instrument, its main function, like that of the double bass, being to furnish a foundation for the orchestral harmony. It figures also where a sepulchral or ominous colour is needed, or for special effects—growling, rumbling, and the like. Ravel, in the *Beauty and the Beast* section of his MOTHER GOOSE SUITE, used it to depict the Beast:

(Listen to the "Woodwind Choir" selections from the sets, "Instruments of the Symphony Orchestra," mentioned above.) The ranges and transpositions of the woodwind instruments are:

The brass choir

If the string choir provides the lyricism and the harmonic foundation for the symphonic web, and the woodwinds supply the subtle colour effects, it is the brass choir that furnishes the patches of blazing colour, the thunderous sonorities of conflict and triumph as also the sustained, organlike harmonies. In the instruments of this group—trumpet, French horn, trombone, and tuba—there is a cup-shaped mouthpiece against which the taut lips of the player act as a vibrating reed, and a series of valves to regulate the length of the column of air within the tube. For many years these instruments were able to produce only certain tones of the scale; the characteristic bugle calls, such as Taps and Reveille, are based upon these. As a result of a series of mechanical improvements throughout the nineteenth century, their limitations were overcome and they are now effective and useful members of the orchestral family. The brass instruments were very popular among the nations of antiquity, who made full use of their stirring, martial effects. Latin literature abounds in references to the *tibia* and *bucina*; and in the Old Testament story the walls of Jericho came tumbling down before them. In turn, the brasses may be stately, dignified, and organlike in sound, and they are often highly effective in melodic and lyrical passages.

The trumpet is the "brilliant soprano" of the brass choir. Its sharp, imperious tone is an indispensable element of all heroic climaxes, as we heard in the *Triumphal March* from AïDA. It is equally useful in sustaining sonority or in executing complicated passages. By introducing a mute, a pear-shaped device, its tone takes on another character. When the muted tone is forced, we get a snarling, defiant effect. When played softly, the muted trumpet produces a sensitive flutelike tone. Jazz-band trumpet players are developing a large assortment of mutes, each with its special effect. Muted trumpets imitate the tiny trumpets of the Guild of the Tailors in the last act of DIE MEISTERSINGER:

Muted trumpets are also used effectively by Tchaikovsky in the middle part of the *Dance of the Flutes* from the NUTCRACKER SUITE. (See next section of this chapter.) The range of the trumpet is approximately two and a half octaves. There are three or four trumpets in the modern orchestra.

The horn, generally called the French horn because of its extensive use at the hunts of the French kings, is the most important of the brass instruments and one of the most beautiful voices in the orchestral family. It should not be confused with the English horn, which is an alto oboe and a woodwind. The French horn, which may be considered the "alto" of the brass choir, is easily identified through its flaring bell and complicated coils of tubing. It combines effectively with strings or woodwinds as well as with brass. It is the noblest of the brass instruments; its lovely tone is extraordinarily poetic and expressive. When played loudly, it takes on a character of majestic sonority. Descended from the hunting horn (*cor-de-chasse, waldhorn, jagdhorn*), it has retained its woodland associations: no other instrument conveys so well the sense of spacious outdoors, of magical remoteness. Weber made use of this quality in the opening of his "OBERON" OVERTURE. We heard a lovely passage for horns in the *Nocturne* from the MIDSUMMER NIGHT'S DREAM music:

The range of the horn is three and a half octaves. The fact that there are four to eight French horns in the modern orchestra enables the composer to write four-part harmony completely within this timbre. The horn in F sounds down a fifth. One of the most effective devices in symphonic writing is to give the horns sustained, noble harmonies while the strings and woodwinds weave an intricate tonal web about them. Wagner makes unforgettable use of the horns in his *Valhalla* motif in the majestic final scene of DAS RHINEGOLD:

The tone of the horn may be "stopped" either with a mute or by inserting the hand in the bell of the instrument. The muted horn like the muted trumpet is capable of various effects. Forcing the tone gives a guttural, rasping quality. Played softly, the muted horn never fails to produce an effect of loveliness and remoteness. The snarling defiance produced by forcing the tone of the muted horn is well exemplified in the climax of the last movement of Tchaikovsky's SIXTH SYMPHONY, the *Pathétique:*

Among other outstanding horn passages may be mentioned the mischievous theme of Till in Richard Strauss' symphonic poem, THE MERRY PRANKS OF TILL EULENSPIEGEL (see Chapter XVIII);

and the triumphant call of Siegfried in GÖTTERDÄMMERUNG:

The trombone is a stately, nontransposing instrument that resembles the horn in its tone and the trumpet in brilliance and power. It is used for effects of solemn grandeur and great amplitude of tone. The trombone is the simplest of the brasses: instead of a complicated system of valves, it has a U-shaped sliding tube, because of which it is often called the slide trombone. This sliding tube lengthens or shortens the column of air in the tube, either lowering or raising the pitch. The trombone player must have a well-trained ear, for he himself determines the pitch of the tones by "sliding," and the slightest miscalculation brings dire results.

The pompous, rotund tone of the trombone is well exemplified in Wagner's "TANNHAUSER" OVERTURE, when the trombones take over the solemn *Chorus of the Pilgrims*:

Similarly, the theme of the "Compact" between Wotan and the Giants, in the second scene of DAS RHINEGOLD, is given to the trombones, which play the phrase in brilliant unison:

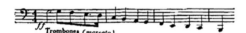

There are three or four trombones in the modern orchestra. The range of this instrument, which may be considered the "tenor" (or oft-times the "bass") of the brass choir, is two and a half octaves.

The tuba is an imposing-looking instrument (nontransposing), which fulfils the same function in the brass as the double bass in the strings and the contrabassoon in the woodwinds: it provides the harmonic foundation, combining with the other members of the choir more often than playing an independent part. It has a deep, heavy tone, and is a somewhat unwieldy instrument. Stravinsky makes it portray the Bear in his ballet PETROUCHKA; and Wagner appropriately uses it to depict the dragon in his SIEGFRIED:

The tuba has a range of two and a half or three octaves. The orchestra uses one tuba. (Listen to the "Brass Choir" selections from the sets, "Instruments of the Symphony Orchestra," mentioned above.) The ranges and transpositions of the instruments of the brass choir are:

(Consult a record catalogue for examples of Brass instrument solos.)

7 percussion group

This group, also known as the battery, includes the instruments that are sounded by being struck. These are the descendants of the drums and rattles of the jungle; most of them have no set pitch. Besides accentuating the rhythm, they heighten the sense of climax and add a number of very spicy colour effects to the other instruments. Like all seasoning, they have to be used sparingly.

Most important of this group are the kettledrums or tympani, huge copper "kettles" across which sheepskin or calfskin has been stretched. They are sounded by striking with sticks that have large felt ends. The tympani have definite pitch, which can be changed by controlling screws or foot pedals. They are used to build up the orchestral volume of sound, for dramatic suspense, for thunderous climaxes. Nothing portends so fully the sense of death or doom as a roll on the muffled drum. On the other hand, this instrument can be stirring and lively.

The snare or side drum is the ordinary small military drum; its crisp, rattling tone is almost invariably associated with martial effects. The bass drum, familiar through its use in the dance orchestra, provides the regular beat for the military march as well as special effects, such as thunder or artillery.

The rest of this group includes a wide assortment of instruments, such as the tambourine, associated with Gipsy and Spanish music; the various primitive or Oriental drums, used to give the atmosphere of exotic music; and the castanets, whose clacking sound is an indispensable part of the Spanish dance.

The cymbals are large, slightly cupped discs of brass which, when struck together, produce an intensely dramatic effect. They add greatly to the excitement of orchestral climaxes.

The triangle, a metal bar bent into the shape of a triangle, when struck with a small metal rod, produces a light, tinkling sound.

The gong is a large disk of hammered metal, generally brass, of Chinese origin. When fairly struck with a large felt-headed stick it gives forth an ominous, metallic sound; but when softly struck it gives a mysterious effect.

The xylophone (pronounced zī'lō-fōn) consists of a series of tuned wooden bars or slabs of various lengths that are struck with two wooden mallets. It has a hollow, clanking sound, and is used with excellent effect in Saint-Saëns' DANSE MACABRE (Dance of Death) to imitate the rattling of the bones of the skeletons as they dance on the tombstones. (See Chapter XIII.)

Chimes are tubular bells suspended from a metal frame and struck with a hammer. They reproduce the tolling of bells.

Glockenspiel, or orchestra bells, consist of a set of steel or aluminium horizontal bars arranged ladderlike in two parallel rows, sometimes operated from a keyboard, more often played with two wooden hammers. They add a bright bell-like quality to the orchestral fabric.

The celesta, invented by August Mustel of Paris in the last quarter of the nineteenth century, is described in detail in the next section, in connection with Tchaikovsky's NUTCRACKER SUITE, where it is used as a solo instrument for the first time in the *Dance of the Sugar Plum Fairy*. (See page 165.)

In addition to these percussion instruments, there is a varied assortment of whistles, rattles, wind machines, and similar noisemakers to create all the special effects that the intricate scores of a modern symphonic work may demand.

The piano is a stringed instrument in which the tone is produced by little hammers controlled by a keyboard. Technically, it is a percussion instrument. Pianists, however, vehemently disclaim any kinship with the family that includes the drum. We may sidestep the issue by listing the piano as a keyboard instrument, and let it go at that.

M

Since the piano can play both melody and accompaniment, it developed into a solo instrument (see Chapter XXVI), and as such has not been considered an integral part of the symphonic ensemble. Modern composers, however, are increasingly attracted by its percussive possibilities, which fit in with their prevailing moods, and are including it more and more often in their orchestral scores.

Arrangement of the orchestra

We may take the personnel of the Boston Symphony Orchestra as fairly representative of our great ensembles. There are 103 players: 63 strings, 16 woodwinds, 15 brass, 7 percussion, and 2 harps. Thus, the string choir amounts to about three-fifths of the total; the woodwinds and brass somewhat less than one-fifth each.

The strings contain 16 first and 16 second violins, 12 violas, 10 'cellos, and 9 double basses. The woodwinds contain 3 flutes, 1 doubling on piccolo; 2 oboes; 2 English horns; 3 clarinets, 1 doubling on bass clarinet; and 3 bassoons, 1 doubling on the contrabassoon. The brass has 6 French horns, 4 trumpets, 4 trombones and 1 tuba. The percussion has 2 kettledrums, or tympani; 3 in the battery, which includes the various small percussion instruments; and 1 celesta.

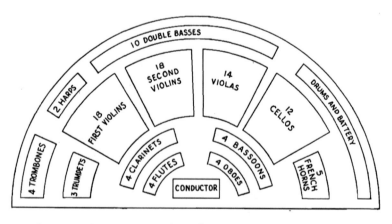

Symphony Orchestra seating plan of a novel and experimental nature as has been used by Leopold Stokowski.

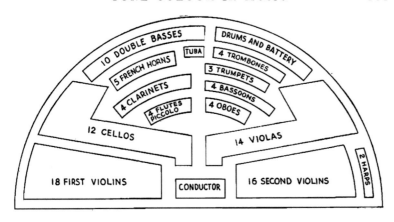

Symphony Orchestra seating plan of a conventional type generally used by Arturo Toscanini and many other conductors.

While each conductor varies the seating plan of his group to suit the acoustics of a hall or his personal taste, the general arrangement is more or less uniform. The orchestra is arranged in a huge semicircle about the conductor, who stands on a small platform or podium, directing with his baton. The various instruments are arranged in groups so as to blend properly.

Orchestration

Writing for a full orchestra is no mean art. The composer must not only create his melodies; he must hear them in his imagination in the particular timbre, or tone colour, of each single instrument or combination of instruments, selecting and blending his colours to achieve the exact shade he desires. He must know what theme will sound more effective on one group of instruments, and what on another. He must be familiar with the personality, with the technical peculiarities, of each instrument, and assign to it only what it can do best. These are but a few of the problems in orchestration, the art of writing for orchestra. The popular notion that composers create their music at the piano and then arrange it for orchestra is altogether inaccurate. Although they may use a piano to assist them, composers generally hear their themes, to begin with, in a certain timbre. In this respect they differ from many writers of jazz music, who merely pick out their tunes on the piano and leave the orchestration to the arranger who specializes in that technique. Art composers, on the other hand, consider their orchestration as much an expression of their creative personalities as the melody itself. Indeed, great composers have so distinctive a method of orchestrating that often an experienced listener will be able to recognize Beethoven, Wagner, or Tchaikovsky merely from the way the orchestra is handled.

Orchestral score

The actual writing out of the parts for the instruments is known as scoring; the parts are arranged one below the other in the score. In piano music there are but two staves, the treble and the bass. A modern orchestral score may employ thirty staves or more: what is happening at any one moment in the orchestra is indicated on all thirty staves at the same point clear down the page. The full page of such a score is consequently only one line, to be read straight across. The composer in effect has thirty threads stretching horizontally, which he interweaves into one marvellously intricate texture. If the student will examine the illustration on page 163, he will notice that in the score the various choirs are grouped together, the woodwinds on top, then, going down the page, the brass, percussion, and strings. Following an orchestral work from score is apt to be bewildering to the novice, since there seem to be so many lines to keep track of; but with a little practice one learns to keep up with the activities of the various choirs quite easily. Following from score then becomes a most revealing way of listening to a symphonic work.

II. The Orchestra in Action

The "Nutcracker Suite"

For a glimpse of the orchestra in action, we have chosen the perennially popular NUTCRACKER SUITE that Tchaikovsky arranged from his NUTCRACKER ballet. The music, written in 1891, only two years before his death when he was at the summit of his powers, reveals to us a master of delicate orchestral colours and nuances.

The scenario for the ballet was taken from the elder Dumas'
version of a fairy tale by E. T. A. Hoffmann, the writer of fantastic
stories who exercised so powerful an influence upon the composers
of the nineteenth century, particularly Schumann, Berlioz, and
Wagner, although he is known today chiefly through Offenbach's

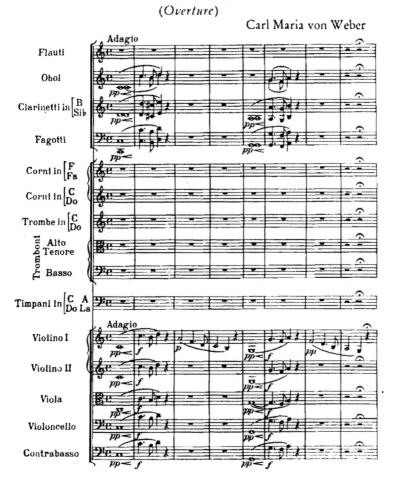

First page of Score of "Der Freischütz" Overture   Weber

TALES OF HOFFMANN. The ballet centres about a little girl, Marie, and the wonderful dream that comes to her on Christmas Eve after everybody else has gone to sleep. The toys and sweetmeats around the Christmas tree come to life; the plain old nutcracker she has received for her gift turns into a handsome young prince. Together they fly away to the court of the Sugar-Plum Fairy, where all the sweetmeats and the flowers come to dance for the happy young lovers.

1. *Miniature Overture.* Tchaikovsky omitted the bass instruments—'cellos, double bass and lower brass—from his little overture, thus achieving a light and graceful effect.

The second theme, by contrast, is a flowing melody of simple quarter notes played legato by the violins. The music works up to a scintillating climax for full orchestra, after which both themes are repeated from the beginning with an even longer climax at the end.

Notice that in order to achieve the effect of intensification upon which the climax is built, the music grows louder and faster, and mounts to the higher, more brilliant pitches. These are the three ways most frequently used to build an effective orchestral climax. It will be instructive to observe how the different composers use these ways.

The shrill pitches in high register evoke a sharper response from our nervous systems than do the low, mellow tones. For this reason, a climb to the upper register always produces an effect of intensification of emotion or brilliance of colour. Conversely, a descent to the low register gives the impression of slackening, of fading colour.

2. *March.* The march, with its brave opening flourish on trumpets, horns, and clarinets, is a gaily strutting affair. Here Tchaikovsky uses the rhythmic figure that occurs so frequently in trumpet and bugle calls, the triplet indicated by a small figure 3 over the eighth notes:

Clarinet

Violins

The dainty groups of notes that alternate with the flourish serve to remind us that this is a march for twirling ballerinas rather than for ordinary mortals.

The second theme is built on another of those pirouetting, staccato motives so dear to the heart of Tchaikovsky. Three flutes and a clarinet are echoed by violins and violas. Then the first theme returns in regular A-B-A form, with the strings and flutes providing new "sliding" effects in the accompaniment.

3. *Dance of the Sugar-Plum Fairy.* Nothing so well reveals Tchaikovsky's love of picturesque instrumental effects as his excitement at discovering the celesta, which he introduced into the orchestral family through this piece. He wrote enthusiastically to his publisher in June, 1891, after his return from America, that he planned to incorporate music for the new instrument—described as something between a piano and a glockenspiel, possessing a divinely beautiful tone—into his ballet. He instructed that it be ordered from Paris where he had discovered it and delivered in St. Petersburg in utmost secrecy, since he feared that Rimsky-Korsakoff and Glazounov might learn of it and, by using its effects before he himself should have a chance to do so, rob him of the glory of introducing it and detract from the sensation he expected to create.

The celesta, a member of the percussion group, consists of a series of small steel bars or plates set in vibration by hammers which are controlled by a keyboard like the piano. It has a range of four octaves above middle C. Its silvery, liquid tone captures perfectly the spirit of the Bountiful Fairy of Hoffmann's tale.

After a short pizzicato introduction on the strings, the transparent harmonics come floating gently downward:

Celesta

This is interspersed with guttural comments by the bass clarinet that give a truly bizarre effect. The brief middle section ends with a brilliant cadenza on the celesta. (A *cadenza* is a flowery passage interpolated in a composition in order to show off the technical resources of the solo instrument or performer. Notice that the rest of the orchestra is silent during the cadenza, so as to focus attention more upon the featured player.) The cadenza leads back to the opening phrase, now played an octave higher than before. We therefore have here another example of three-part, or A-B-A form. Strings sound in the background; the silvery fairy floats aloft for a brief space—and fades away.

4. *"Trepak"* (*Russian Dance*). The *Trepak* brings us the full orchestra in an outburst of furious activity. One can see the figures bobbing up and down, arms akimbo, heels flying, in a folk dance of vigorous accents:

A contrasting theme appears, the first returns, in a clear-cut A-B-A pattern. The orchestration is brilliant throughout. Tambourines add gaiety to the proceedings. Ever faster and louder, the dance mounts to the brilliant upper register, and ends on a note of wild abandon.

5. *Arab Dance.* This number summons up the languor and allure of the East. Muted violas and 'cellos introduce a droning figure in the bass that is reiterated with a kind of hypnotic insistence, alternating between piano and pianissimo. A tom-tom throbs dully in the distance. Against this sombre background two clarinets and an English horn intone the mysterious opening chords. The melody itself is sung by muted violins; there is but one theme, which rises and falls in a broad languid curve.

Presently an oboe lets out a long piercing wail in that nasal manner associated with Oriental song. The violas and 'cellos drone on and on; the tom-tom continues to weave its spell; the music fades away to the merest whisper, *ppppp*.

6. *Chinese Dance.* Flutes and piccolos running shrilly up the scale, forte, impart to the next dance its "Chinese" flavour. The strings answer, pizzicato, with a droll seriousness that reminds one of a Pooh-bah bobbing up and down. Throughout, the bassoons keep up a steady staccato beat deep in the bass.

If we compare the second theme with the first, we notice that it does everything Theme I does, but in the opposite direction. Where Theme I runs up the scale to a trill and then jumps down along the tones of the chord, Theme II runs down the scale to a trill and then jumps up along the scales of the chord; in other words, it is an inversion of Theme I:

This device, rather difficult to handle effectively, attests again to Tchaikovsky's mastery of the technical resources of his art.

After the inversion, the theme is heard in its original form, giving us an A-B-A pattern. The music works up in a steady crescendo to the climax, fortissimo; and comes to an abrupt end.

7. *Dance of the Toy Flutes.* Next comes one of Tchaikovsky's happiest inspirations. A brief "vamp till ready" introduction leads to the airy tune of staccato sixteenth notes played by three flutes, piano. This sparkling music captures the very spirit of the dance. After a fragment of legato melody sung by the English horn, the theme is repeated:

The middle section, in contrast to the opening, lies in a lower register and is given to the brass choir. Here we have a famous passage for muted trumpet, the theme of sixteenth notes rising and falling in a gentle swell. After this, we return to the melody of the flutes in a clear three-part, or ternary, form.

8. *Waltz of the Flowers.* The *Waltz of the Flowers* has taken its place beside Johann Strauss' *Blue Danube* and *Tales From the Vienna Woods* as one of the world's beloved waltzes. Here we have Tchaikovsky's gifts as a ballet composer—a feeling for beautiful melody, for flowing line and the sheer excitement of movement— at their best. The gracious opening theme of the horns, the gay second theme with its suggestion of swirling figures, the middle section, which veers to a tender melancholy—all breathe a gentle nostalgia. True, these flowers grew amidst red plush and crystal chandeliers, and the world out of which they stemmed never really was as we have pictured it. No matter—they bring us the gentle aroma of their period preserved for us by a master of sentiment.

The introduction contains an elaborate cadenza for the harp, built of arpeggios, or broken chords. The reader should distinguish, incidentally, between an arpeggio and a scale. A *scale* is a series of neighbouring tones. But an *arpeggio* is built of the tones of a chord, which do not necessarily lie next to each other. In a scale, therefore, we proceed stepwise, while in an arpeggio we jump along the tones of the chord.

After the final arpeggios of the cadenza fade in a gradual diminuendo, the French horns announce the suave waltz theme, softly, as from a distance:

With the second theme, the swaying waltz movement gathers momentum. Notice how the string choir alternates with the woodwinds in a kind of dialogue—a favourite device in orchestration. Presently the first theme returns, A-B-A, embroidered with a charming countermelody.

The middle section opens with a graceful theme played by the flute and oboe, with the violins gliding downward in a countermelody. Now a lyrical melody emerges deep down in the violas and 'cellos. In returning to the preceding theme, Tchaikovsky cleverly reverses his orchestration: the violins carry the melody, while flutes and oboes glide downward in the countermelody. The middle section is therefore also an A-B-A pattern.

The first section is repeated substantially as before and worked up to a brilliant climax. The movement is accelerated, the volume increased; the orchestra rises steadily into the bright upper register, *fff*, overflowing with animation and brilliant colour, bringing the ballet to a triumphant finale.

In form, the waltz presents us with an extended A-B-A structure in which each section is itself an A-B-A. This ingenious construction might be diagrammed as

$$
\begin{array}{ccc}
A & B & A \\
\cdot & \cdot & \cdot \\
\cdot & \cdot & \cdot \\
\cdot & \cdot & \cdot \\
aba & cdc & aba
\end{array}
$$

Notice how, throughout the suite, all the elements are combined—lilting melody, rich and vivid harmonies, compelling rhythms, simple, clear-cut structures, and imaginative orchestral colouring—into one unified effect.

For further introduction to the varied colour palettes of the orchestra, listen to Saint-Saëns' clever suite, the CARNIVAL OF THE ANIMALS, which contains, among other numbers of interest, the popular and lovely 'cello and harp composition, *The Swan*. These may be supplemented by playing over the commercially prepared record series, "Instruments of the Symphony Orchestra," and similar sets that are generally available. (Consult your record catalogue.) Get so you can "spot" any instrument of the orchestra as soon as it sounds. Perhaps you will become proficient enough to analyse several different instruments playing together—that is a real challenge to anyone, no matter how well educated musically he may be! Of course, the listener is urged to hear these instruments in the regular symphony concerts whenever possible—there is a wide difference in quality of sound between records, the radio, and the actual concert performance, even under the most favourable circumstances. (We have not included here an extended list of "Additional Suggestions for Listening," for most of the remainder of the text is an application of the ideas and principles enunciated in this chapter.)

Chapter Twelve

Classic and Romantic Elements in Art

OF THE several approaches an artist may choose to make toward his material, at least two or three seem more basic and elemental than the others. There is always the *Realistic*, or more or less exact imitation of nature, approach; but let us set that aside for a future chapter, leaving the two others for immediate discussion.

Thus, on the one hand, the artist may seek to give expression to the emotional experiences of mankind in their widest, most universal aspect. He will try to remain as objective as possible toward his material, fashioning it into the most polished, most enduring, shape. He will be concerned not only with what he says—the content—but also with the perfection of the manner of saying it—the form. If he is a composer, he will be deeply involved with developing tonal design and metamorphosis of germinal musical ideas as such to the utmost of their potentialities. Fundamentally, this creator is the artist-philosopher, whose duty it is to present rather than to question, to affirm rather than to rebel. He will exercise restraint, present emotion "recollected in tranquillity"; he will aim for the conventional (in the best sense of the word) rather than for striking effects. He will work within established traditions, bringing them to a higher level, rather than striking out into new paths. Chastity of style, harmony, or outline, simplicity, balance, and self-control—these will be foremost among his ideals. In short, such a creator will be a *Classicist*.

Let us ponder a bit over that term, "classical"; but first let us try to define it somewhat broadly and, if possible, so as to include as many of the fine arts as we can. The dictionary tells us that *classical* means "resembling, modelled after, or in the spirit of, the highest forms of ancient Roman or Greek art." Thus, one might deduce that any art created since that time which embraces or is influenced by a style or temper similar to that which prompted, or characterizes, those ancient art works, may be said to be "classical." (Be careful to distinguish between the words "classic" and "classical"—consult an unabridged dictionary. Also bear in mind that each art medium will have its own peculiarities and that, in music especially, there will be many unique values.)

The Parthenon from the north-west   *(From a photograph)*

We refer you now to the picture of our "National Capitol Building" at Washington, D.C., page 52. You will see that there are unmistakable evidences of ancient Greek and Roman influences in this product of the Classical Revival during colonial times. Compare the Capitol building with the *Parthenon*, considered by many to be "the most complete example of the Doric style in temple architecture ever built."[1] This celebrated old temple was built by Iktinos and Kallikrates from the years 447

[1] Read Chapters III and IV of *Art in the Western World* by David M. Robb and J. J. Garrison (New York: Harper and Brothers, 1942).

to 432 B.C.; it gives eloquent evidence to the highest degree of designing and building skill, and it is no wonder that it has been the marvel and inspiration of the entire western world for the past 2400 years—so much so that the building, though a mere ruin, may be considered the very symbol of perfection. Here, in a single edifice, are exemplified: the perfect consonance of purpose and design, the attractive severity of line and surface, the epitome and triumph of mathematical and formal perfection, a monument to impersonal and epochal expression, a model of quiet serenity and nobility without pomp and overindulgence of fancy; and there are also exemplified minutely calculated effects that never become ostentatious or conspicuous in themselves. Finally, one can see in the *Parthenon* the ideal achievement in the relationship between the separate parts and the whole. Such richness of virtues was destined to fire the ideals of beauty in man in all the fine arts through twenty-five centuries, and to serve him as a perpetual model for those attributes he has chosen to call the spirit or temper of "classicism."[2]

Now let us look at the reproduction of the classical painting, "Orpheus and Eurydice" (page 174), by the French artist, Nicolas Poussin (1594-1665), The subject matter, or literary content, of this story has served as the basis for more operas than has any other. It is a classical tale, in the exact sense, and it is "told" in such a way that moral, intellectual, and emotional elements are set forth with utmost clarity of means. There is in this picture the positive spirit of the ideal perfection, and the absence of excessive sensuality and flamboyance. Although the artist was not without influence from the early spirit of the *Baroque* (see page 428), he steadfastly held to the ideals of beauty as passed on by ancient cultures. He strove to create paintings that evidenced harmony, concord, and masterly control rather than turbulence, discord, and ecstatic emotional expression. His figures seem to be enlivened Greek statues—note the postures, as though they were arrested gestures during a dignified and graceful Greek dance. Poussin seeks to charm the appreciator, to mollify rather than to startle by novelty or shock by boldness of expression; all is polished perfection, as near as he could achieve the ideal.

---

[2] By the word "temper" we mean "The quality of mind with reference to the passions, emotion, or affections; nature or disposition of; medium; organization; form." See the *Standard Dictionary*. We also use the words "spirit," "tendency," "element," "character," throughout the text as closely akin in meaning.

Orpheus and Eurydice

In striving for such ideals, Poussin was not unlike Corneille and Racine in the theatre, wherein man asserted his mastery over himself and his mundane fate through the control of his emotions and actions by the intellect—really an ancient "classical" idea. So the paintings of Poussin reflect that same kind of control and mastery of one's emotional expressions by means of a well-ordered and meticulously executed plan or design. Nothing was left to chance or to momentary extemporization. He was consciously concerned with making everything he painted exemplary of the characteristic rather than of the transient incident, or exception, or personalized interpretation—a trait also marked in the aspects of conventionality that exist in "classical" music. We must observe, however, that though the emphasis is on the formal manner rather than free fancy, the latter is by no means absent; it remains a matter of control and degree of emphasis. One is reminded of some of the artistic ideals of the Renaissance. Internal units of design, as in the *Parthenon*, are subordinate but organically contributory to the whole. Here, in "Orpheus and Eurydice," are those qualities which have provoked the term "heroic landscape." It is unlike any scene one may have witnessed; rather, it is the ideal and perfect landscape for the setting of the picture.

On the other hand, the artist may seek to project his own personality into his art, to view the world about him through the lens of intense personal feeling. He will be proudly subjective and proclaim his very differentness from other men. He will revolt against the established order of things, a passionate rebel against all traditions and forms. He will stress feeling rather than reflection; content rather than form (though he will not abandon the latter, by any means); and he will hanker after what is strange and picturesque. Giving free rein to his imagination, he will prefer the bizarre and the particular to the serene and the universal. He will seem to lean toward mysticism and fervour rather than toward lucidity and discipline of the intellect; yet he will not be devoid of the latter. Technique and design will not be ends in themselves; instead, they will be the means for the projection of his individual, intensely emotional utterance. He will be novel, bold, and individual rather than characteristic and conventional. In short, such a creative artist would represent the *Romantic temper* in art; he would be a *Romanticist*.

Here again, it is best that we seek to define our terms as much

N

as possible. The dictionary tells us that the romantic is: "founded upon or influenced by what is extravagantly ideal; sentimental rather than rational; visionary; pertaining to or suggestive of the strange and fantastic; picturesque, imaginative, wild [*sic!*], fictitious, dreamy, . . ." Compare these attributes with those we have just discussed in "classicism." No doubt extended and varied experience in the appreciation of actual art works of both schools will prove to be better definers than our old and constant friend, the Dictionary.

At any rate, let us first consider the reproduction of the picture, "The Abduction of Rebecca" (see page 177), by another French painter, Ferdinand V. Eugene Delacroix (1798-1863). Here is action, drama, force, conflict, novelty, and what might well be called ordered disorder. The picture is a highly personalized expression in which a certain deliberate indefiniteness of line and form contrast strongly with the type of drawing we ordinarily see in classic realism. Delacroix has put into the picture novel and highly imaginative contents (plastic as well as literary); he has provided striking contrasts in design and composition, and he has used colour in a vivid and dynamically moving manner. Rather than trying to conform to an ideal or a convention (which is another way of saying general acceptance of an ideal), the painter has projected a very individualized picture, and he has expressed it in a manner and with the means that best suited his fancy at the moment. He is not moralizing; yet he is telling a story, and with it he is giving one a psychological insight into the characters of the drama in a most uncanny manner. Over all, the picture involves an extra-plastic art—literature. The exciting moment of the tale that he desires to depict is evidently of greater importance to him than the traditional classical perfection of details of line and form, or faithfulness to reality and regularity. Yet all these elements may be found in the picture, to a degree and well subordinated. Finally, the onlooker is a much more active "participant" in the picture than is the case with the Poussin work.

One is quite right in considering Delacroix the leader of the French Romantic "school"; by means of the high flights of his poetic imagination, one has a fleeting glimpse into the future, yes, even into our own day—and one might just as truthfully say the same of Poussin!

There are a number of common attributes in the two schools we

Abduction of Rebecca   *Delacroix*

have discussed, and a number that are opposite ends of the same pole; there are also a few that are unique in each instance, though these are very few indeed. The reader will do well to emulate the mystery-story teller by "enumerating at this point" the stylistic attributes that are peculiar to each type, those that are conflicting and, most important, those that differ largely through combinations and accents. Let us develop some of these ideas still further.

Nineteenth-century critics, sharing the love of their age for neat, water-tight classifications, used the labels *classic* and *romantic* with much assiduity; with the result that there emerged two concepts or styles that were then considered diametrically opposed to each other—the first rigidly excluding the second. Yet it takes little reflection to understand that each might be a complement of the other; that neither exists often in pure form; that, on the contrary, the classic and the romantic often co-exist; and that the differences between them are often due to the degree of emphasis of values rather than complete opposition of kind. Indeed, one is frequently impressed by the fact that both tempers are present in the same artist. There are strong Romantic elements in the works of such Classicists as Virgil, Corneille, David, and Haydn. Conversely, there are powerful Classical tendencies at work in the art of such Romanticists as Millet, Swinburne, or Brahms. The composer who is most often held up as the epitome of the Classical spirit, Mozart, wrote measures that, for sheer emotional expressiveness and imagination, have not their superior in all music; while such figures as Shelley or Chopin, who are with equal consistency represented as types of the Romantic artist, display in their finest work a purity of form, a mastery of technique and design, that bear comparison with the great figures of the Classical school.

Equally misleading is the practice of labelling a period either *Classic* or *Romantic*, and then forcing everything created within the period to fit the label. So often has the eighteenth century been marked off as the special province of the Classical spirit in art, and the nineteenth relegated to the Romantic, that the student is likely to get the impression that between 1799 and 1801 Classicism died and Romanticism came into being. The error will be avoided if we consider the two tendencies as signposts revealing general trends, with generous overlappings on both sides, rather than as rigid categories. Actually, the eighteenth century—the age that saw the culmination of Classical form in music in the symphony—

produced such utterly unclassical works as Rousseau's *Autobiography*, Hogarth's "Shrimp Girl," Mozart's *Abduction from the Seraglio*, the lyrics of Robert Burns, the poetry and drawings of William Blake. On the other hand, the qualities that we lump together under the general concept of Romanticism—the intensely subjective approach to life, the emphasis upon deep feeling, the revolt against arbitrarily imposed restraints, the preoccupation with the supernatural and the picturesque—being of the very essence of man's personality, have flourished in one form or another throughout all periods, and may be found, now stronger, now weaker, from the Psalms, Homer, and Sophocles, to Virgil and Catullus; from Dante and Petrarch to Michelangelo and Dürer; from Shakespeare and Rembrandt, Bach and Haydn, to Goethe, Schubert, Beethoven, and the moderns.

The point that emerges from all this analysis is that classifications in music, poetry, or painting cannot and should not be applied as rigidly as in botany, zoology, or chemistry. If used with circumspection, such labels as *Classic* and *Romantic* are most helpful in giving us insight into the nature of art and a better appreciation of the style of the artist and his relation to his epoch. But the concepts must always remain flexible, fluid, and dynamic; otherwise they will lead us to a static attitude that is alien to the nature of art. Such connotations should be aids rather than stumbling blocks, or they would be better left unused.

The distinction between Classical and Romantic has been connected with an exaggerated distinction between form and content. It has been pointed out again and again that the Classical artist subordinated content to form, while the Romantic artist subordinated form to content. Since, in discussing so abstract a matter as style in art, there is an habitual temptation to drive the point home by exaggerating the distinctions behind it, the stress on these combinations of form and content inevitably led to the notion that the Classical artist was all form and no emotion, while the Romantic artist was all emotion and no form. No art work can exist if it possesses only one of the elements. A work given form without feeling and inspiration is no more than a technical stunt and has neither life nor meaning. Witness the thousands of perfectly formed fugues, sonatas, and symphonies composed by well-meaning musicians who followed all the rules but had nothing vital to say, that have been relegated to the oblivion they so richly deserved. Conversely, unless the artist can channel his emotion and direct it into a communicable art form, his work will be an incoherent jumble of rapture and exclamation points.

As applied to Western European art, the terms *Classical* and *Romantic* generally refer to the two great art styles that prevailed in the second half of the eighteenth and the whole of the nineteenth century and that were separated by the gigantic social upheaval brought about by the French Revolution. It can readily be seen why the eighteenth century, dominated by an ultraconservative aristocracy, has come to be known in the history of human thought as the *Age of Reason*, and in the history of art as the *Age of Classicism*. The nobility of the old regime, that semifeudal agricultural aristocracy whose power was soon to be overthrown by the rising industrial and mercantile *bourgeoisie*, had brought the business of living to the level of a fine art. The accent was definitely on correct form rather than on deep feeling, on the manner rather than on the matter. Emotion was channelled within the confines of an exquisite art just as brooks were channelled within the balanced landscape of a formal garden. The artist working under the system of patronage had to satisfy the fastidious tastes of his noble benefactor. He did not lack either deep feeling or imaginative power. But within the prevailing social framework it was inevitable that he placed enormous emphasis on the chiselled line, the exquisite finish, the restrained manner, the serene and objective vision that have come to be associated with Classical art.

The nineteenth century, on the other hand, presented a completely different picture. The aristocracy had been supplanted in power by the *bourgeoisie*; the cult of personal freedom, of aggressive individualism, had taken hold of the new industrial society. The world-shaking slogan of the Revolution—Liberty, Equality, Fraternity—released forces that had been pent up for centuries; the artificialities and restraints of the old order were swept aside. Emancipated from his subservience to kings and courts, the artist now addressed an audience of his social equals. He could dare to be himself, to express his innermost feelings, to defy the stifling conventions. Intensity of feeling and picturesque effect were his natural idiom, as the classic style had been the natural idiom of his predecessor. The difference of expression did not mean that he was not as careful a craftsman, as great a master of technique, as the eighteenth-century artist. It meant simply that his interest in technique was subordinated, owing to the prevailing social pattern of the age, to the emotional and subjective, to the Romantic elements of artistic expression.

We may get a good insight into the relative values of the two idioms if we compare the didacticisms, the impersonality, the objective "sweet reasonableness" of a passage such as the closing lines of Pope's *Essay on Man*, written in the 1730's and characteristic of the Age of Reason—

> Submit: in this or any other sphere,
> Secure to be as blessed as thou canst bear;
> Safe in the hand of one disposing Power,
> Or in the natal or the mortal hour.
> All Nature is but Art unknown to thee;
> All chance, direction, which thou canst not see;
> All discord, harmony not understood;
> All partial evil, universal good;
> And spite of Pride, in erring Reason's spite,
> One truth is clear, *Whatever is, is right*—

with the passionate lyricism, the subjectivity and intense feeling of a poem such as Shelley's "Ode to the West Wind," which has so often been cited as the quintessence of the romantic attitude:

> Oh! lift me as a wave, a leaf, a cloud!
> I fall upon the thorns of life! I bleed!
> A heavy weight of hours has chained and bowed
> One too like thee—tameless, and swift, and proud. . . .

Or Heine's poignant:

> Out of my great, great sorrow
> I make my little songs. . . .

Or Byron's bitter:

> I have thought
> Too long and darkly, till my brain became,
> In its own eddy boiling and o'erwrought,
> A whirling gulf of phantasy and flame:
> And thus, untaught in youth my heart to tame,
> My springs of life were poisoned.

Or the no less significant hymn to the night in the love scene of Wagner's TRISTAN AND ISOLDE with its longing for oblivion:

> O sink down upon us, night of love,
> Let us now forget that we live,
> Take us up within your arms,
> Free us forever from the world!

Or Rousseau's defiant: "I am different from all the men I have
ever seen; if I am not better, at least I am different!" Here we
have the prevailing attitudes of the romantic artist. So, too, we
might compare the delicate landscapes with their nymphs and
shepherdesses of Watteau and Fragonard with the grand sweep
and melodrama of the canvases of Delacroix and Géricault; or the
exquisite finish of an early minuet by Haydn or Mozart with the
surge and thunder of a composition by Wagner or Tchaikovsky.

The Romantic Movement in Music[3]

We have drawn a distinction between the spirit, or temper, of
Classicism, and a contrasting spirit, or temper, of Romanticism as
concepts in art that are limited to no one century; and the Age of
Classicism and the Romantic Period as the epochs when the
qualities associated with either one or the other tendency appeared to predominate. For the music lover, the Romantic Movement is of particular interest, since practically nine-tenths of the
music we hear today was either inspired by it or came under its
influence. To begin with, the two masters who are most often
held out as perfect examples of the Classical style, Mozart and
Haydn, showed strong Romantic characteristics, especially in the
works written in the latter part of their careers. Mozart died in
1791, two years after the beginning of the French Revolution;
Haydn did some of his most important work in the following
decade.

Beethoven, Weber, and Schubert encompassed the transition
from the Classical style to the spirit of the new country. Mendelssohn, Chopin, and Schumann saw the full unfolding of the
Romantic Movement. Wagner, Liszt, Berlioz became the pro-
phets of mid-nineteenth-century Romanticism. Brahms, Tchaikovsky, Grieg, Dvořák, Smetana, César Franck, Moussorgsky,

[3] Essential listening for this chapter includes: *Minuet* from SYMPHONY IN E FLAT by
Mozart; *Liebestod* music from TRISTAN AND ISOLDE by Wagner; and the Overture-
Fantasy, ROMEO AND JULIET, by Tchaikovsky.

Rimsky-Korsakoff, Saint-Saëns, Massenet, Gounod, Bizet, Verdi, Puccini, Elgar, MacDowell—these composers are of the Romantic Movement. One need not extend the list to make it apparent that for all practical purposes the general public of today still lives, musically speaking, in the Romanticism of the nineteenth century. And even after the twilight of Romanticism, when the interlude known as post-Romanticism bridged the gap between the nineteenth and twentieth century, the outstanding men—Sibelius, Richard Strauss, Debussy, Ravel, Falla, and their compeers— still preserved in new guise many of the influences of nineteenth-century Romanticism.

In the following chapters, we shall study in detail a number of compositions that exemplify various characteristics of musical Romanticism. As an introduction, let us now listen to and compare an example of the Classical style such as the *Minuet* from Mozart's SYMPHONY IN E-FLAT MAJOR, with a piece of Romantic music such as the *Liebestod* from Wagner's TRISTAN AND ISOLDE. The choice of such extreme examples of the two styles will the more clearly demonstrate the differences between them.

Perhaps the first thing that strikes us, as we listen to the two compositions, is the fact that Wagner's orchestra is so much larger than Mozart's—a fact due to the tremendous increase in symphonic resources during the Romantic Period. From this increased size of orchestra there spring several other differences. Wagner's orchestral writing is much more involved than is Mozart's. Where Mozart's is a wonderful example of economy of means, Wagner piles on his effects with a lavish hand. Mozart relies in the main on his string section with an occasional touch of colour from the woodwinds and brasses. Wagner revels in the timbres of clarinet, oboe, flute, bassoon, and in the sonorities of the brass, and the sweep and power of the strings. The dynamic range in Wagner's music, the contrast between soft and loud, and the intensity of the climax, are naturally much greater in the Romantic master than in the Classical. The *Minuet* represents a simple and limpid texture; the *Liebestod*, on the other hand, is an elaborate tonal tapestry of great opulence and splendour. It should not be assumed that the characters of these two works mark all the works of Wagner and Mozart as being similarly differentiated.

In regard to form, the *Minuet* consists of regular phrases and periods and sections all stemming out of a clear-cut, four-measure structure. In contrast, Wagner's music sweeps forward with either no segmentation at all, or with sections that run together in a continuous movement. In Mozart, the qualities of symmetry, balance, and contrast are presented in a graceful, easily perceived architecture. In Wagner, there is a mighty flow of sound, as of a current that threatens to surge over its banks. Mozart's writing stays securely within the key; that is to say, it is predominantly diatonic. Whatever modulations there may be are carefully prepared and negotiated. Wagner modulates continually in a restless chromaticism charged with emotion. Mozart's harmony is in the main consonant; the discords are placed at strategic points and resolved almost immediately; the prevailing mood is one of well-being and satisfaction. Wagner's harmony, on the other hand, abounds in dissonance, in active tones left palpitating in suspension, in all the accents of despair and longing. Mozart is suave and urbane, restrained and rationally objective; his melody is crystal clear, his harmony transparent. Wagner is tragic, sensuous, and passionate. Mozart's is a music of pure beauty and delicate emotion, a song of sunlight and sensibility; Wagner's is a music of night, of ecstasy, of strange and hidden things.

Between these two extremes are innumerable shadings where one may find the characteristics of one style imperceptibly blending with those of the other. It is the combination of the many factors involved that produces the total stylistic effect. Through the detailed analysis of the compositions we shall examine in the next chapters, as well as of others that the reader might hear, it is hoped that he will gain an insight into the manner in which the composer manipulates and combines the various elements and concomitants of style, and will thus become sensitive to the subtle and distinctive quality of the great art styles in music—Classical and Romantic, Baroque, Impressionistic, post-Romantic and Contemporary, and the three basic and universal tempers of Classicism, Romanticism, and Realism.

Programme music

One of the most important developments in the Romantic Movement was that, under its influence, music moved closer to its sister arts, poetry and painting. Composers chose to tell stories, to paint scenes, and to convey general poetic ideas and moods.

Such literary and pictorial influences provided an enormous stimulus to the writing of programme music—music, that is, with a story or synopsis attached to it.

From the beginnings of the art, composers had often turned out musical imitations of birds, brooks, battles, and hunting scenes. It was in the nineteenth century, however, that the descriptive and narrative tendencies emerged to a position of general dominance in European music. For this reason, even though programme music in no sense originated in the nineteenth century, it has come to be considered one of the most characteristic developments of the Romantic Movement in music.

Programme music is to be distinguished from *absolute*, or *pure*, music in which the composer attached no specific literary or pictorial connotations to his themes, but worked them out in purely musical terms.[4] Thus, Beethoven's FIRST SYMPHONY or Mozart's SONATA IN A MAJOR are examples of absolute music; Liszt's *Faust* SYMPHONY, Tchaikovsky's *Overture-Fantasy* ROMEO AND JULIET are examples of programme music. The distinction between the two types is often a subtle one. Naturally, all music tells something to the listener. However, if the composer has given the listener no extramusical clue as to what he had in mind when he composed the music, no literary or pictorial association, actual or divined, we may consider it absolute or "pure" music. If, on the other hand, the composer indicates either through his title or through his remarks about the composition that he was influenced by or had in mind a definite literary, pictorial, or general poetic idea, we consider it programme music.

For many years a fierce controversy raged among musical aestheticians as to the respective merits of the two genres. The problem no longer seems as important as it once did. There is great absolute music as well as mediocre; there is great programme music as well as mediocre. The chances are that if a composer has something worth while to say, he will say it no matter which style he is writing in. It is fairly apparent that, programme or not, the music should be able to stand on its own feet as good music and to be appreciated as such. No programme, however fanciful or picturesque, can supply imagination or power if the music itself is

---

[4] See article "Absolute Music" in Grove's *Dictionary*. Our use here is largely based on that definition. This term, though general, is unsatisfactory and leaves much to be desired. The best discussion is "On the Elements of Expression in Music" by Donald N. Ferguson, University of Minnesota, 1944.

weak or dull. Certain composers, as Beethoven and Brahms, seemed to gravitate more naturally toward the absolute type; their musical imagination seemed to function best when unhampered by extramusical associations. On the other hand, some like Wagner, Liszt, and their disciple, Richard Strauss, appeared to need the stimulus of a literary or pictorial programme to spur them on to creation. Still others, like Tchaikovsky and Sibelius, have written copiously in both genres.

For our immediate and particular purpose, the programme has a definite value. The person who has thought all his life in terms of verbal language in which each word has a concrete meaning inevitably feels bewildered when confronted with a language that consistently avoids all specific connotations. "But what does it mean?" is his first reaction. By tackling programme music first, instead of absolute, we can reduce this bewilderment to a minimum. The pictorial and literary associations will assist the student through the initial period while he is still learning the vocabulary and the meaning of absolute musical expression. After that he will be free either to lean on the composer's story, or supply his own, or do without any at all.

If the enormously increased "programming" of music was the most striking characteristic of the art during the Romantic Movement, it will be found that the programme was generally of the kind that fitted in with the prevailing literary mood of the period. We shall discuss this problem at greater length in the chapter on Franz Liszt (see Chapter XVI). At this point we may observe that the Romantic composers were influenced by the same poets from whom the literary Romanticists drew their inspiration, chief among them such figures as Shakespeare and Goethe, Dante and Schiller.

In the chapter on the orchestra we pointed out the enormous strides made in the art of orchestration during the nineteenth century. We can now see why these strides were made. In their search for new emotional effects, for picturesqueness and atmosphere, for brilliant and exotic colouring, the Romantic composers turned in far greater degree than did their Classical predecessors to the element of tone colour as such. Certain general factors unquestionably helped: the mechanical improvements in instruments; the marked development of the orchestra in size and in the playing ability of its members; the general rise in the level of instrumental proficiency. In addition, there were important changes in the social conditions surrounding the making of music, such as the rise of a widespread middle class with an interest in the art, replacing the former patronage that had been limited to the nobility. With the rise of a music-hungry public, there came also the public concert as an important social institution, instead of the private musicales at the homes of the aristocracy that had characterized music-making in the eighteenth century. This public encouraged and was able to support orchestras much greater in size than those of the nobility; and the orchestra consequently forged ahead steadily in importance.

Yet, despite all these external encouragements, the central stimulus to the growth of the orchestral art lay in the very nature of the Romantic composer's attitude toward his art: in the exuberant emotionalism that demanded rich colour effects and new expressive devices; in the unprecedented interest in the feelings evoked by the distinctive timbres of the different instruments and by strange combinations untried until then. We may therefore consider tone colour—the reliance upon novel or picturesque orchestral effects—as the second outstanding characteristic of musical Romanticism; and we shall have frequent occasion to point out examples of it in the compositions we study.

Peter Ilyitch Tchaikovsky (1840-1893)

We begin our study of the Romantic style with a work by the composer who represents perhaps as fully as any other the spirit of late nineteenth-century Romanticism. Both in choice of subject and in spirit, the ROMEO AND JULIET OVERTURE fantasy exemplifies several important features of the programme music of its time.

Biography

Peter Ilyitch Tchaikovsky was born at Kamsko-Votinsk in 1840, the son of a government official. He gave no early signs of his future eminence in music and did not, in fact, undertake serious musical study until after he had graduated from the School of Jurisprudence in St. Petersburg. For two years longer, while working in the Ministry of Justice, he vacillated between an official and a musical career. At twenty-three, however, he made his decision, relinquished his post, and devoted himself rigorously to his studies in composition. In a letter to his sister he justified his choice, declaring that he must do the work for which he felt fitted. Whether he was to become a celebrated composer or merely a struggling teacher, his conscience would be clear and he would not grumble at his lot. In two years' time he completed his course at the Conservatoire of St. Petersburg and was awarded a silver medal for his setting of Schiller's "Ode to Joy."

For the next twelve years he occupied the post of professor of harmony at the newly founded Conservatoire at Moscow. The great pianist, conductor, and director of the Conservatoire, Nicholas Rubinstein, speedily recognized his pupil's gifts; he performed Tchaikovsky's works almost as soon as they were written. Slowly, doggedly, the young composer forged ahead. To this period of his life belongs the ROMEO AND JULIET OVERTURE, now one of the best beloved of his compositions, although it was hissed at Paris and Vienna when first performed; and the PIANO CONCERTO IN B-FLAT MINOR, which Rubinstein pronounced absolutely worthless and unplayable when he first saw it but which he later performed throughout Europe with the most brilliant success.

The Moscow period in Tchaikovsky's career came to an end in 1877 with his brief and unhappy marriage, followed by complete nervous collapse. The same year brought into his life Mme. Nadejda von Meck, the benefactress who for the next thirteen years supported him with a generous annuity, making it possible for him to give up his onerous duties at the Conservatoire and devote himself completely to composition. Their relationship forms one of the strangest chapters in musical biography. Although both lived in Moscow, they never met, carrying on their friendship through a series of intensely revealing letters. These, published in English by Mme. von Meck's grandniece and Catherine Drinker Bowen under the title of *Beloved Friend*, furnish an interesting sidelight on the composer's character and music.

From 1877 until his death in 1893 Tchaikovsky produced, in a steady stream, the works upon which his fame rests. Success did not come easily; but he was sustained by the devotion and encouragement of a little band of trusted friends and by the inner conviction that his music would ultimately come into its own. In the last years of his life he overcame his almost morbid fear of strangers sufficiently to undertake concert tours and popularize his works; and he had the satisfaction of seeing himself become a European figure. In 1891 he was invited to come to America to conduct the opening concert at Carnegie Hall. Two years later, at the Jubilee celebration at Cambridge University, he was honoured with the degree of Doctor of Music. He returned to Russia to finish his SIXTH SYMPHONY, the *Pathétique*, considered by many his greatest work; went to St. Petersburg to conduct it; fell ill with cholera a few days after the first performance; and died on November 6, 1893, at the age of 53.

If in his personal life Tchaikovsky was emotionally unstable, vacillating, hypersensitive and subject to severe spells of depression; if he could write: "To regret the past, to hope in the future, and never to be satisfied with the present—this is my life," in everything pertaining to his art he was the careful craftsman, the tireless and completely devoted worker for whom musical creation was the supreme function of living. A child of his age, only through music did he find the strength, the meaning, the sense of pattern that life itself denied to his overwrought temperament. The music written out of such compulsion is of necessity intensely subjective, sometimes to the point of morbidity; but it possesses a sincerity, an emotional exuberance, a richness of melody, and a brilliance of orchestral colouring that have endeared it to the broad masses of music lovers and made Tchaikovsky a century after his birth one of the most universally loved of composers. Nothing, surely, gives us so complete an insight into the intensely personal attitude of the man toward his art than the moving letter to Mme. von Meck in which he pays tribute to music:

You see, my dear friend, I am made up of contradictions, and I have reached a very mature age without resting upon anything positive, without having calmed my restless spirit either by religion or philosophy. Undoubtedly I should have gone mad but for music. Music is indeed the most beautiful of all Heaven's gifts to humanity wandering in the darkness. Alone it calms, enlightens, and stills our souls. It is not the straw to which the drowning man clings; but a true friend, refuge, and comforter, for whose sake life is worth living. Perhaps there will be no music in heaven. Well then, let us give our mortal life to it as long as it lasts.[5]

[5] Catherine Drinker Bowen and B. von Meck, *Beloved Friend*. (New York: Random House, 1937.)

Overture fantasy "Romeo and Juliet" (1869)

Tchaikovsky was twenty-nine years old when he wrote the ROMEO AND JULIET OVERTURE. This was, indeed, the first work in which his creative personality fully revealed itself. After three-quarters of a century, it still remains as one of the peaks of Romantic programme music—definitely conceived and built upon a literary story.

The Overture was dedicated to the composer Balakirev, the leader of the Russian nationalist school, who suggested the literary basis of the subject. Tchaikovsky seems to have had some trouble in getting started. Balakirev wrote him to keep trying:

First get enthusiastic over the scheme. Then arm yourself with galoshes and a walking-stick and go for a walk along the boulevards. Begin with the Nikitsky, let yourself be thoroughly saturated with your subject; and I am convinced that by the time you reach the Stretensky Boulevard some theme or episode will have come to you.[6]

The advice seems to have worked, for shortly afterward we find Balakirev writing:

I am delighted that the child of your fancy has quickened. God grant that it come to a happy birth. . . . Do send me what you have done so far, and I promise not to make any remarks—good or bad—until the thing is finished.[7]

When Tchaikovsky complied with this request, Balakirev wrote back:

As your overture is all but finished, and will soon be played, I will tell you what I think of it quite frankly. . . . The first subject does not please me at all . . . it has neither strength nor beauty, and does not sufficiently suggest the character of Friar Laurence. Here something like one of Liszt's chorales, in the old Catholic Church style, would be very appropriate. Your motive is of quite a different order, in the style of a quartet by Haydn, that genius of "burgher" music that induces a fierce thirst for beer.[8]

---

[6] M. I. Tchaikovsky, *Life and Letters of Peter Ilyitch Tchaikovsky.* (New York: Dodd, Mead and Company, 1924.)
[7] *Ibid.*
[8] *Ibid.* The three excerpts that follow are also from this work.

The famous Romeo theme—its lyric loveliness has survived even a popular fox-trot version—Balakirev considered "very pretty, although rather colourless." The Juliet theme he called "simply fascinating."

> I often play it, and could hug you for it. It has the sweetness of love, its tenderness, its longing. . . . I have only one thing to say against this theme: it does not sufficiently express a mystic, inward spiritual love, but rather a fantastic passionate glow which has hardly any nuance of Italian sentiment. Romeo and Juliet were not Persian lovers, they were Europeans.

The first performance took place in 1870 at a concert of the Moscow Musical Society. Unfortunately, Nicholas Rubinstein, who conducted, had just been involved in a lawsuit concerning his right to dismiss a student from the Conservatoire, and the entire musical world of Moscow was on hand to demonstrate its solidarity with him. A friend of Tchaikovsky's wrote:

> From the moment Rubinstein came on the platform until the end of the concert he received an extraordinary ovation. No one thought of the music; and I felt indignant that the first performance of "Romeo and Juliet" should have taken place under such conditions.

Tchaikovsky too was dispirited over the reception of his work:

> My overture "Romeo and Juliet" had hardly any success here, and has remained quite unnoticed. . . . After the concert a group of us went to a restaurant. During the whole evening no one said a word to me about the overture. And yet I longed so for appreciation and kindness.

Considering that it is now one of the works upon which his fame most securely rests, the overture made its way into the European repertory with unbelievable slowness. In 1878 Tchaikovsky wrote to Mme. von Meck: "My overture . . . has been played in every capital, but always without success. In Vienna and Paris it was hissed; a short time ago it met with no better reception in Dresden!" At the end of the letter he eloquently affirmed his deep inner faith in the ultimate victory of his work:

> If fame is destined for me, it will come with slow but sure steps. History convinces us that the success which is long delayed is often more

o

lasting than when it comes easily and at a bound. . . . An artist should
not be troubled by the indifference of his contemporaries. He should go
on working and say all that he has been predestined to say. He should
know that posterity alone can deliver a true and just verdict. . . . Perhaps I can accept my modest share of success with so little complaint
because my faith in the judgment of the future is unshakable. I have a
foretaste during my lifetime of the fame which will be meted out to
me when the history of Russian music comes to be written. For the
present I am satisfied with what I have already acquired. I have no
right to complain. I have met some people on my way through life
whose warm sympathy for my music more than compensates me for
the indifference, misunderstanding and ill-will of the others.[9]

The word *overture* (from the French *ouvrir*, "to open") originally
referred to an orchestral composition played as an introduction
to an opera, oratorio, ballet, or play, which generally prepared
the audience for what was to follow by presenting the principal
themes of the work. Being essentially a "curtain raiser," the conventional overture was spirited, swift-moving, and closed with a
rousing finale. Many overtures became so popular that they
began to be performed at concerts independently of the opera or
play for which they had been written. Some of them survived long
after the work itself had been forgotten. From this custom was
derived the second meaning of the word: a concert piece for
symphony orchestra built around a strongly dramatic or pictorial
theme and lending itself to brilliant and theatrical treatment.
Whether the overture is an introduction to an opera or an independent concert piece can generally be determined from the title.
Thus, *Overture* to TANNHÄUSER indicates the existence of an opera
by that name; while 1812 OVERTURE or ROMEO AND JULIET
OVERTURE refers to an independent concert piece built around a
respective theme.

ANALYSIS. The Overture opens in the pale twilight of a medieval
chorale symbolizing the good Friar Laurence. (A *chorale* is a
simple, hymnlike tune.) The churchly chords are played in simple
four-part harmony by two clarinets and two bassoons *andante
quasi moderato* (fairly slow, almost in moderate tempo), in quadruple metre:

[9] Catherine Drinker Bowen and B. von Meck, *Beloved Friend*. (New York: Random
House, 1937.)

The mysterious effect is enhanced by ethereal arpeggios on the harp. The chorale returns on the woodwinds with a running accompaniment in the strings. Gradually, with a *poco a poco accelerando* (faster little by little) and a steadily mounting crescendo, we are thrown into the fury and strife of the Feud theme, whose brusque, irregular accents aptly describe the ancient grudge and new mutiny of the Capulets and Montagues. The tempo is allegro; the theme is announced with the full orchestra in action, forte, and with those upward and downward sweeps on the violin that are so characteristic of Tchaikovsky's style:

A passage of mounting excitement through the running passages on the strings brings us the repetition of the Feud theme, this time fortissimo. Then the tumult dies; out of a tremulous background there emerges the love song of Romeo, with its broad lyric curve and poignant harmonies, sung by a solo English horn and muted violas, *mf, dolce* (sweetly) and *espressivo:*

This song is answered immediately by the Juliet theme on muted violins playing in four-part harmony. The strings are therefore divided—that is, they are not playing in unison. Lawrence Gilman remarks, "There are not many things in modern music more justly and beautifully expressive, more richly poetic, than the mood of the enraptured pair as they watch the coming of the dawn in Juliet's chamber."

The two themes are now repeated in a somewhat more developed form that closes the first section of the work.

In the middle section, the violins again take up their broad sweeps. The Feud theme is presented in an exciting development, with echoes of the Friar Laurence motive in the horns, as though warning of impending disaster. The mood of strife is built up through a gradual intensification until the entire orchestra is alive and seething. A broadly sweeping passage on the strings leads us into the third section, which recapitulates the thematic material of the first with important changes. The Feud theme is heard fortissimo, substantially as before. Then comes the Juliet music, *dolce espressivo* (sweetly expressive). And after that the Romeo theme is developed in one of those eloquent crescendos so dear to the heart of Tchaikovsky—wave upon wave of ingratiating sound, striving upward, accumulating, until the entire orchestra is surging forward in a mighty outpouring. The glow fades; stern outcroppings of the Feud theme carry us from the music of love to that which portends death. The epilogue is in a moderate pace, marked by the sombre chorale of the prologue, while celestial arpeggios on the harp are heard above the muffled drum that beats a dirge for the dead and eternally faithful lovers. The spirit and mood of the Shakespearean play is thus told in the art of music by a master, in the spirit of Romanticism.

Chapter Thirteen

The Symphonic Poem
Tone Painting, Narrative, and Mood

WE HAVE just listened to an extended orchestral composition one purpose of which was to project through music the moods, emotions, and story suggested by a literary theme—the ROMEO AND JULIET OVERTURE by Tchaikovsky based on the play by Shakespeare. In spite of the fact that this story served as the basis for the overture and prescribed the sequence of events to a great extent, the composer was careful to see that the musical work had a structure and organization of its own, aside from the dictates of the underlying drama; and, in several instances, where the sequence of events in the story were in conflict with what the composer considered desirable musical structure, the musical significance determined the issue. Thus, certain musical themes appeared, were contrasted and developed, and reappeared within a broadly traditional musical framework; and the composer gave these themes and the process of musical development an interest and importance in themselves. One can see here the workings of the classical as well as the romantic tempers.

The point becomes clear when we realize that in Shakespeare's play Friar Laurence appears in the middle of the play, while in the musical narrative the chorale symbolizing the Friar serves as prologue and epilogue. In short, the composer was guided by purely musical as well as literary considerations in the composition of his material—even if his themes possessed more or less precise symbolic literary connotations.

We now come to the most highly developed type of programme music—the symphonic poem or tone poem—in which the form is completely free and determined to a great extent by the literary or pictorial programme. Just as the symphony represents the highest level of organization in absolute music, the symphonic poem or tone poem is the most ambitious type of composition in programme music. The symphony was perfected by the masters of late eighteenth-century Classicism. Similarly, nineteenth-century Romanticism, with its strong admixture of literary and pictorial influences, turned enthusiastically to the symphonic poem.

A symphonic poem does through music what a poem does through words: it tells a story, paints a scene, describes or projects a mood, or presents a general poetic idea in musical symbols. The time was when the designation *symphonic poem* implied that the composition projected a story, and *tone poem* that it concerned itself principally with scene or mood; but now the two terms have become practically interchangeable. The symphonic poem has no fixed form, this being shaped in each case by the necessities of a particular programme, with the transformation in the musical themes paralleling and reflecting changes in the poetic or literary idea. Naturally, the programme in many cases clearly reveals the prevalent literary influences of the period. Thus, in the three tone poems that have been selected as an introduction to the form—Saint-Saëns' *Danse Macabre*, Moussorgsky's *Night on Bald Mountain*, and Paul Dukas' *Sorcerer's Apprentice*—we find in the music the same embodiment of the fantastic and the bizarre that played so prominent a part in the Romantic literature of the time.[1]

While we shall confine our immediate study to the three typical symphonic poems just mentioned, and though future pages of this book will present additional examples of this form, it might be well to mention here a comparatively rare occurrence in music—a symphonic poem inspired by a painting.[2] This is Sergei Rachmaninoff's *The Isle of the Dead*, after the painting of the same name (see page 197) by Arnold Böcklin (1827-1901). The poem was written in Paris, in 1909, where the composer first saw the painting. It is scored for a large orchestra and the work begins with a figure in the 'cellos suggestive of the quiet lapping of the water, then a softly intoned French horn theme is heard which serves well throughout the poem. A climax is reached and the "Chant of the Dead," *Dies Irae*, comes forth from the brasses. Gradually

[1] Essential listening for this chapter includes: *Danse Macabre* by Saint-Saëns, *Night on Bald Mountain* by Moussorgsky, and the *Sorcerer's Apprentice* by Dukas—in that order. Rachmaninoff's symphonic poem, "The Isle of the Dead," may be considered as suggested supplementary listening.

[2] A more recent example of such an inspiration is Paul Hindemith's *Mathis der Maler*, originally an opera inspired by the Isenheim alterpiece by Matthias Grünewald. The music is usually heard as a symphonic suite.

Isle of the Dead   *Böcklin*

This striking romantic picture sets forth moods of eternal peace, tranquillity, sorrow, and tragedy. The literary content is obvious; but equally forceful and not observable in the half-tone cut is the intensification of the forms conveyed through the contrasting colours of the black cypress trees, the towering red cliffs, the white mausoleums, and the stark figure standing in the boat. It is interesting to observe how the composer Rachmaninoff expressed the feelings aroused by the painter Böcklin.

the work calms down and a theme appears in the strings which is somewhat reminiscent, and a development, of the horn theme heard at the beginning. This theme is worked up to the real climax of the composition when the horn theme played in the beginning is loudly intoned by the brasses. Little by little the mood subsides; finally the symphonic poem closes with the material of the opening section being heard once more, and quiet reigns. (Rachmaninoff was born in Russia in 1873 and died in the United States in 1943. He is more generally known for his short piano pieces, songs, his four concerti for piano, and his three symphonies.)

Camille Saint-Saëns (1835-1921)

We pointed out earlier in this chapter that Romanticism was a middle-class art, as opposed to eighteenth-century Classicism, which was essentially aristocratic in nature. The middle class, however, was too firmly rooted in practical affairs to float indefinitely in the mists of the supernatural and the bizarre. Thus there developed within the framework of literary Romanticism, and side by side with the emotional excesses of a Hugo, a Byron, or a Poe, a tradition of Realism which ran down the century, from Balzac and Flaubert to Dickens, George Eliot, and Thackeray, culminating at the end of the century in the Naturalism of Zola, de Maupassant, Thomas Hardy, Ibsen, Chekhov, and the American school.

It need hardly be said that this tendency to capture all aspects of reality in literature made itself felt also in music. Liszt, Berlioz, and their contemporaries of the middle of the century based their programme music on highly symbolic and quite general literary or pictorial elements presented with a maximum of poetic suggestion. Throughout the last quarter of the century there was a steady movement in programme music toward Realism, culminating in the 1890's in the tone poems of Richard Strauss (Chapter XVIII) which, substituting literalness for suggestion, may be considered the musical counterpart of the tendency represented by Zola. The beginnings of this tendency may already be traced in a work such as Saint-Saëns' (pronounced săn'säns') *Danse Macabre* (Dance of Death), written in 1874, that combines the love of the macabre we have noticed in Romanticism with certain elements of satire and literalness that were to dominate the programme music of the end of the century. The symphonic poem of the Frenchman, Saint-Saëns, may therefore be considered as a kind of middle point between the tone-poem style of Liszt and that of Richard Strauss.

Biography

Camille Saint-Saëns, known to the American public mainly through the ever-popular *Danse Macabre*, the *Swan*, which the great Pavlova transformed into a famous dance, and the aria *My Heart at Thy Sweet Voice* from the Opera SAMSON AND DELILAH, began his long and supremely successful career as a wonder child. He composed at seven, gave his first piano recital at eleven, and won a prize in organ playing at the Paris Conservatoire at fourteen. His first symphony was performed when he was eighteen; at twenty-two he was appointed organist of the Madeleine, one of the most famous churches in Paris. He was thus spared much of the disappointment and bitterness that beset so many great musicians. Indeed, after the seventies his career was an almost uninterrupted succession of triumphs. He composed steadily in almost every branch of music and made brilliant concert tours as organist and pianist; his piano and violin concertos, his operas, symphonies, and tone poems were performed throughout Europe. He received the order of the Legion of Honour in 1868, was elected a member of the French Institute in 1881, and was given the honorary degree of Doctor of Music by Cambridge University in 1892. Witty, facile, and a tireless worker, he found time from his musical activity to dabble in literature, producing a volume of poetry, several farces, a number of essays on music and the theatre, and, curiously enough, some papers on scientific subjects.

Saint-Saëns' music is brilliant rather than moving, pleasant rather than profound. For this reason, a good part of his output is not bearing up too well under the test of time. A thorough craftsman and a master of orchestration, his melodies are facile, his ideas interestingly worked out. But he is definitely a product of his period, rather than one of the chosen few who stand above all limitations of time and place. He appeared at a time when the French nation was completely apathetic to its own living composers. He devoted himself tirelessly to the cause of French music and, through the *Société Nationale de Musique*, which he helped found, fought for recognition for the young composers of the new French school. The wave of nationalism that swept France as an aftermath of the Franco-Prussian War helped bring the movement to its ultimate success. When the influence of Wagner came to dominate the musical life of the Continent, Saint-Saëns stood up for the particular qualities—clarity, measure, poise—that his great contemporary, Anatole France, considered the essence of the Gallic spirit in art. He was in effect one of the most important influences in initiating and moulding the modern French symphonic school. His was, however, the peculiar fate of all reformers who outlive their period: he began as a flaming radical in music, became more and more conservative as he went along, and ended completely out of sympathy with the very developments that he himself had been instrumental in getting under way. The last of the great nineteenth-century composers, he survived in a world completely alien to that which he had so ably represented; his death in 1921 at the age of eighty-six marked the end of an era.

"*Danse Macabre*" (*Dance of Death*)

Death had been a popular theme in art during the Middle Ages and the Renaissance. Holbein's famous "*Dance of Death*" shows the grim figure playing a *strohfiedel*, the medieval ancestor of the xylophone, which Saint-Saëns used so effectively in this work to imitate the rattling of skeleton bones. The Age of Classicism, of the Enlightenment, naturally discouraged the use of such obviously melodramatic themes. But when Romanticism turned for inspiration to the Middle Ages—just as Classicism had turned to antiquity—death became again a motif in art. In their reaction from the reason and light of the eighteenth century, the early Romantics swung so far toward the Gothic that an almost morbid preoccupation with horror and strangeness soon became one of the mannerisms of the movement.

Danse Macabre was written in 1874 and first performed the following year. Saint-Saëns originally wrote it as a song, but since the melody turned out to be somewhat hard to sing, he used it as the basis for his orchestral piece. The poem that served as his inspiration seems rather crude and dated now, but it must be remembered that half a century is a long time for second-rate literature. Cazlis' poem has been translated as follows:

> Zig, zag, zig, Death in cadence
> Striking a tomb with his heel,
> Death at midnight plays a dance-tune
> On his violin.
>
> The winter wind blows, the night is sombre,
> Moans are heard in the linden trees;
> The white skeletons flit through the shadows,
> Shrouded shapes moving strangely.
>
> Zig, zag, zig, each one is frisking;
> The bones of the dancers rattle . . .
> But pst! suddenly the cock crows!
> They quit the dance, they run, they fly.

Around this rather obvious programme the brilliantly ironic Saint-Saëns, with a kind of grim relish, constructed a composition that shocked and startled his contemporaries, although its devices have become familiar through incessant repetition. The twelve strokes of the clock sounded on the harp and the mysterious plucked strings of 'cellos and bass violins set the scene. Death tunes his fiddle, with the E string lowered out of tune; the dance opens with an appropriately cheerless theme on the flutes leading to the waltz tune proper. The xylophone imitates the clanking of skeleton bones, while chill chromatic scales suggest the howling of the night wind. (*Chromatic scales* are scales that ascend or descend in half steps—that is, they include the sharps and flats. They belong to no particular key, and present twelve semitones, or half steps, within the octave. They are much used in "picture music" for storms, howling of the wind, and so forth.)

chromatic scales:

After a brief lyrical interlude in the violins, as though two spectres had met who remembered each other from happier days, the chromatic scales return, the dance grows ever faster, louder, more abandoned. Suddenly the horns announce the glimmer of dawn; the oboe imitates the crowing of the cock. Death packs his fiddle; the spectres unwillingly trudge back to their graves; the ghostly revel is over.

When *Danse Macabre* was first performed in London in 1879, the critic of the *Daily News* threw up his hands, calling it "horrible, hideous, and disgusting," and an example of the "intense and coarse realism that is entering into much of the musical composition (so-called) of the day." Saint-Saëns enjoyed the outcry; but his music aged more rapidly than either he or his critics suspected. What was so shocking to the 1870's has become fairly tame to the audiences of the twentieth century.[3]

ANALYSIS. The two main themes out of which the composition is built offer an excellent contrast to each other. The first consists of rapid eighth notes, staccato, in brusque rhythmic patterns:

The second is a flowing, legato, waltz theme, consisting of half and quarter notes, all held together by a *slur*. (This word indicates the curved line covering the notes as a sign that they are to "melt" into each other in legato fashion.) The melody is presented with a kind of ironic warmth by all the strings in unison:

[3] The work is one of a series—Berlioz' SYMPHONIE FANTASTIQUE, Liszt's DANCE OF DEATH and MEPHISTO WALTZ, Gounod's FAUST and Boito's MEPHISTOPHELES—in

Besides the numerous variations in which the two principal themes are presented, we hear also, well on in the composition, a travesty of the *Dies Irae*, the medieval, impressive *Hymn to the Dead*:[4]

"Dies Irae"

The orchestration is expertly done, making use of all the colours and contrasts of the various choirs and instrumental combinations. Notice how, when Saint-Saëns begins to build toward his climax, we hear the opening notes of Theme I bandied about in quick succession by trombones, horns, oboes, clarinets, and flutes, each imitating the other. As the music mounts in intensity in the final section, the brilliant voices of flute and piccolo are added to the ensemble. Noteworthy, too, is the effect of rattling bones on the xylophone; the mysterious horns, as though from a distance, signalling the coming of dawn; and the oboe announcing cockcrow. A violin shudders as the wraiths flit away. We hear a last fleet echo of the opening theme, and two chords plucked furtively on the strings (pizzicato) brings the piece to a close.

The form of *Danse Macabre*, like its orchestration, bespeaks the master craftsman. There are three sections: the first, in the nature of an introduction, includes the striking of the clock and Death tuning his violin; the second consists of the dance proper, in which the two main themes of the waltz are worked out; the third is a sort of *postlude*, which recalls some ideas of the first section. We shall meet this device again and again in symphonic literature; the final measures, reminding the listener of the opening, help

which the "diabolism" so dear to the Romantic poets and novelists found musical expression. From the horror stories of Mrs. Radcliffe to the fantastic tales of E. T. A. Hoffmann, from the "Ancient Mariner" and "Christabel" and "Kubla Khan" to the tales of Poe, the visions of De Quincey, and the novels of Victor Hugo, the love of the supernatural, the strange, and the picturesquely macabre constituted one of the strongest motifs in literary Romanticism.

[4] The traditional chant is as follows:

Di · es i · rae, di · es il · la, Sol · vet sae · clum in fa · vil · la. Etc.

unify the entire musical structure. (This restatement-after-contrast is a basic form in all the fine arts, and the minor arts as well.)

Rhythmically the music is compelling, particularly in the swaying triple metre of the waltz theme. The tempo is clear-cut. The piece begins in moderate waltz time—*mouvement modéré de valse.* (As a nationalist, Saint-Saëns used French indications instead of the conventional Italian.) As the dance gets under way and approaches the climax there is a steady speeding up (accelerando). With the coming of dawn we return to Tempo I, known as *Tempo Primo,* or the first tempo. Thus, sections one and three, the prelude-postlude frame, are in identical tempo.

Equally simple is the dynamic design in *Danse Macabre.* The music opens *ppp* (pianissimo) the merest whisper; proceeds gradually to pianissimo and piano. The second theme enters forte, works up to fortissimo, and finally, at the climax, *fff* (fortississimo). With the return to Tempo I, the gradation of the opening is reversed: *p* leads to *pp,* and the music dies away *ppp.* We see here how both tempo and dynamics help to bring out the structural element of the prelude-postlude form—another instance of how the diverse elements of music supplement one another in producing the total effect.

Modest Moussorgsky (*1839-1881*)

Biography

Modest Moussorgsky was born in Russia (Pskov) in 1839, of a family of landowners. Like many sons of the gentry he was prepared for a military career and became an officer in one of the fashionable Guards regiments. Like Tchaikovsky and Rimsky-Korsakoff, he began as a musical dilettante. Like them, too, he came under the influence of Mily Balakirev, the leader of the Russian national school. It was only then that he decided to devote himself to a musical career. He resigned his commission when he was nineteen and embarked upon a musical career rich in achievement yet darkened by the shadow of great hopes left unfulfilled. Moussorgsky aimed at naturalism in music, at uncompromising honesty as he himself felt it, and at simplicity. He was profoundly interested in the nationalistic folk arts, especially folk songs. Technique as such was, for him, a species of artifice. Consequently, he never became as dexterous or as polished in musical composition as either Tchaikovsky or Rimsky-Korsakoff. On the other hand, he submitted much less than they to the traditional influences, Italian, German, and French; he stands today as one of the most indigenous of the Russian nationalist composers, his nationalism reaching its peak in his historical music drama, BORIS GODOUNOV.

Moussorgsky's life became a continual struggle against poverty and lack of appreciation on the part of the musical public of his time. He held an ill-paid government post; his personality, although most attractive and endowed with charm, was not strong enough to withstand the continual disappointments and strain to which he was subject. He sought refuge in drink and drugs, which ended by sapping his powers for sustained creative effort. He was able to finish small pieces—the wonderful songs, and the piano compositions of which the best known is the suite of sketches, PICTURES AT AN EXHIBITION. But most of his large works, operatic and orchestral, were either abandoned midway or left unfinished at his death. The manuscripts that he left were completed by his musical friends, chief among them Rimsky-Korsakoff. These include the comic opera THE FAIR AT SOROTCHINSK, the opera KHOVANTCHINA, the orchestral fantasy NIGHT ON BALD MOUNTAIN, and BORIS GODOUNOV, the historical opera.

"Night on Bald Mountain"

In 1860, when he was twenty-one, Moussorgsky wrote to Balakirev of "a most interesting work" he had been commissioned to do: music for the first act of THE BALD MOUNTAIN, to be based on Megden's drama, *The Witch*. It was to describe a gathering of the witches as they practised some of the mysterious rites of their craft, a pageant of sorcerers, and in the finale a dance in tribute to Satan. Moussorgsky was hopeful about the composition: he considered the libretto unusually good and announced that he had already conceived some of its themes.

As in the case of Tchaikovsky's ROMEO AND JULIET, Balakirev does not seem to have shared his protégé's enthusiasm. Two years later Moussorgsky wrote to his mentor concerning the work that he was not to be shaken in his belief that his music was entirely satisfactory. He felt that the music was a genuine expression of the story it conveyed, "without tricks or pretensions," and that he had discharged the task set him to the best of his ability. He remained adamant in his determination not to alter the plan or its development, but consented to change the percussion, which he admitted he had misused. He rewrote the fantasy in 1867, and intended on two occasions to introduce it into a dramatic work: once into a fairy opera MLADA, of which he, Rimsky-Korsakoff, Alexander Borodin, and César Cui were each to write portions, and in which the symphonic poem was to serve as background for a fantastic scene, "The Sacrifice to the Black Goat on Bald Mountain." The scheme fell through because of financial reasons, and again in 1877, when he intended to introduce it as an interlude in his unfinished opera THE FAIR AT SOROTCHINSK.

The score was revised by Rimsky-Korsakoff, after Moussorgsky's death, and received its first performance in 1886 when Rimsky-Korsakoff conducted it with great success. It was the first work that earned for the composer the popular acclaim that had been denied him during his lifetime.

Rimsky-Korsakoff appended Moussorgsky's programme note to the score:

Subterranean sounds of supernatural voices. Appearance of the spirits of darkness, followed by that of Satan himself. Glorification of Satan and celebration of the Black Mass. The Sabbath Revels. At the height of the orgies the bell of the village church, sounding in the distance, disperses the spirits of darkness. Daybreak.

ANALYSIS. The tone poem opens *allegro feroce* (fast and fierce), with a turbulent figure in the strings against which trombones, tuba, and bassoons thunder the Satanic theme:

The dance that ushers in the "glorification of Satan" is saturated with the Russian folk idiom and appears in strongly marked rhythms in the oboes and clarinets, presenting an effective contrast to the opening theme:

After the movement has somewhat slackened, the *allegro feroce* of the opening returns, the brass weaving its theme against rapid chromatic passages in woodwinds and strings. A new dance theme appears, at first in fairly slow tempo, but gradually working up to a frenzied climax.

Clarinet- Bassoon

At the height of the festivities the bell tolls mournfully six times. Strings and harp tranquilly announce the coming of dawn in a coda suffused with poetic feeling.

The music has verve and gusto, permeated by a supernatural aspect. Like the ROMEO AND JULIET OVERTURE, it is the work of a young and ardent imagination, projected with such sincerity of feeling and richness of fantasy that it needs no further intermediary between the composer and his listener.

Paul Dukas (1865-1935)

THE SORCERER'S APPRENTICE was written in 1897, almost a quarter century after *Danse Macabre*, in what has come to be known as the post-Romantic era. This was the transitional period from the nineteenth century to our own, when the great Romantic tradition had given way to a *fin de siècle* spirit—the Mauve Decade, as Beer aptly called it, the period of Oscar Wilde and the *Yellow Book*, of Whistler and Aubrey Beardsley. The rich emotionalism of the ROMEO AND JULIET OVERTURE, the demonic imaginativeness of NIGHT ON BALD MOUNTAIN or *Danse Macabre* were retreating before the sophistication and the objectivity that characterize the modern temper; we are already in the atmosphere of the Straussian tone poem. From a purely technical standpoint, the experiments of Berlioz, Liszt, and Wagner in orchestral writing had opened to their followers a new world of dazzling colour effects. It was out of this combination of influences that a number of exciting orchestral works, of which Dukas' joyous orchestral scherzo is typical, came into being.

P

Biography

Paul Dukas (pronounced dü-kăhs′) was one of the most distinguished French composers of his time. Born in Paris in 1865, he entered the Conservatoire at the age of seventeen and soon displayed a talent for composition. His first symphony was performed in 1896. The following year, when he was thirty-two, he wrote L'APPRENTI SORCIER (The Sorcerer's Apprentice), which has remained his most popular work. His operatic setting of Maeterlinck's ARIANE AND BLUEBEARD also won much acclaim. He was not only a versatile musician but also won distinction as teacher, editor, musical critic, and essayist. He was a member of the Legion of Honour, professor of orchestration at the Conservatoire, and holder of an official post in the ministry of fine arts.

"The Sorcerer's Apprentice"

The programme upon which Dukas based his composition concerns the sorcerer's apprentice who could start a magic spell but could not stop it. The theme had been popular for centuries—*The Golem* and *Frankenstein* are two famous variants—and may be traced back to the Roman poet Lucian. In Goethe's version the young apprentice has repeatedly watched his master utter a charm over a broomstick, whereupon the stick sprouted hands and feet and carried out the magician's bidding. One day, after his master goes out, the apprentice utters the charm and orders the broomstick to fetch water for his bath. When he tries to stop the stick he realizes to his horror that he has forgotten the formula for removing the spell. The stick continues to haul the water; the apprentice falls into panic. He seizes an axe and splits the stick in half, whereupon two sticks proceed to fetch water. Just as the mounting flood threatens to engulf the luckless boy, the sorcerer returns, pronounces the formula, and with a brusque command sends the broom back to its corner. The apprentice has learned his lesson.

ANALYSIS. The introduction is in a lento movement (*lento* means slow, like *adagio*). The atmosphere of enchantment is established at the outset by the violas and 'cellos playing *harmonics*. These, the reader will recall, are the flutelike tones in the very highest register produced by touching the finger lightly to the string at certain

Mickey Mouse as the Sorcerer's Apprentice   *From "Fantasia"*

points, causing it to vibrate in small segments, to produce an effect of delicacy and charm.

The theme of the magic spell is chanted piano by the muted violins, a plaintive melody in high register descending gradually in a series of little leaps:

The woodwinds and brass answer brilliantly with the choppy, staccato theme of the broom. (See ensuing example.)

Notice the interesting contrast between the two themes out of which the composition is woven: the first in high register, languidly legato, played by the strings; the second in low register, brusque and staccato, given to woodwinds and brass.

Presently the apprentice utters the fatal formula. There is an ominous silence. Then the uncanny business begins, allegro and piano, with three bassoons and a contrabassoon keeping up a curiously hopping rhythm in the deepest register.

The music works steadily into a mood of feverish activity. The theme of the magic formula returns fleetingly, now plaintive, now with gleeful malice; the broom theme is tossed about among clarinets, bassoons, horns, and trumpets, while the rest of the orchestra weaves a shimmering background of chromatic scales. The mounting consternation of the would-be wizard is portrayed with brilliant drollery; horns and trumpets fortissimo blare out his frantic cries for help. The movement climbs steadily to the point where he splits the broom in two. There is a breathless pause —and then the cursed activity begins anew, with bassoons and contrabassoon as at the beginning. The movement mounts in a steady crescendo to the final climax: the Sorcerer, announced by thunderous blasts in the brass, returns and puts an end to the spell. We hear again the magical chords of the introduction as the apprentice comes to, a sadder and wiser man. A final blast of the orchestra sends the broom back to its corner.

The work reveals Dukas as a composer of brilliant imagination and wit, a master of orchestration and colour. From the moment when the broomstick begins its activity there is a rhythmic pulsation that sweeps the listener along with a kind of relentless energy. The metre, as the signature indicates, is $\frac{9}{8}$, a compound of triple metre; the student will have no difficulty in feeling the triple beat as soon as the movement gets under way. In general, the composition is more sophisticated and modern than *Danse Macabre*. The melodic line is jagged and brusque; the harmonies rich and complicated; the orchestration remarkably varied.

Dukas called his piece an "Orchestral Scherzo." Like Mendelssohn's "Scherzo" from the *Midsummer Night's Dream* music, Dukas' piece is strongly rhythmic and movemented; but where Mendelssohn's "Scherzo" is delicate and elfin, Dukas' is gaily boisterous. The structure is simple. There is the unifying prelude-postlude formation that we noticed in *Danse Macabre* in the Magic

Spell theme. The movement itself falls into two parts: from the point where the broom begins until the moment when the apprentice splits it in two, and from then on until the return of the sorcerer. The dynamic scheme fits this structure: prelude and postlude generally pianissimo (interspersed with outbursts of furious energy when the broom theme is introduced); while in the two halves of the work itself there is a steady crescendo from the pianissimo of the three bassoons to the full orchestral outburst at each climax. The tempo outline fits this scheme. The introduction is lento, the action proper allegro with a steady accelerando to the climax, and the postlude is marked *Tempo I*, the same as the introduction.

The composition is largely built on the broom theme. The contrasting material includes the enchantment theme and a playful subsidiary theme that flits through the body of the work. But Dukas has relied for the necessary variety not so much on diverse thematic material as on the richness of his orchestral palette. Thematically, this piece is much less diversified than some of the others we have listened to; yet because of the brilliant handling of the orchestra, it sustains the interest of the listener throughout. Notice that Dukas, like Moussorgsky and Saint-Saëns, has used chromatic scales throughout the work to create a feeling of agitation and climax. It is evident that the chromatic-scale passage was a staple device in nineteenth-century programme music. We shall encounter it again and again in symphonic climaxes.

Chapter Fourteen

❦❧❦❧❦❧❦❧❦❧❦❧❦❧❦❧❦❧❦❧❦❧

Nationalism in Music

O F THE utmost significance to musical Romanticism was the upsurge of nationalism that manifested itself throughout Europe during the nineteenth century. Napoleon's dream of a subjugated continent crumbled before the outburst of patriotism that demanded Spain for the Spaniards, Holland for the Dutch, Italy for the Italians. Both among the small nations struggling for their liberty and the large states bent on fulfilling their expansionist ambitions, nationalism became an ideal worth fighting and dying for. This sentiment fitted in excellently with the prevailing mood of the Romantic movement. Romanticism had taken over the abstract Rousseauesque notion of a "return to nature"; nationalism transformed this into a return to the natural beauties of one's own homeland. Romanticism had encouraged an interest in the humble joys and sorrows of the common folk; nationalism shifted this interest toward an enthusiasm for the folklore and folkways of one's own people. Thus the Romantic artist became a nationalist artist.

Nationalism and the Arts

In literature, painting, and music we have the rise of strongly nationalist schools out of which emerged some of the most memorable work of the period. The legends of the national hero furnished inspiration to such dissimilar works as the Arthurian poems of Tennyson, the historical novels of Walter Scott and Dumas, the SIEGFRIED cycle of Wagner, the poetry of Pushkin in Russia, of Robert Burns in Scotland, of Mieczkewitz in Poland. David, in his epic canvases, aimed to perpetuate the glory of Napoleon; Constable and Turner celebrated the English landscape; the Barbizon painters did the same for France. National folklore inspired the FREISCHÜTZ of Weber, the fairy tales of Grimm, Andrew Lang, and Hans Christian Andersen. At a time when music was turning more and more to picturesque effects, to colour and atmosphere, the folk tunes and dances of the various racial stocks became an inexhaustible treasure-house upon which composers could draw to their hearts' content. Idiomatic melodies and characteristic rhythms united with the powerful emotional associations evoked by a patriotic programme to open up a rich new

Midnight Ride of Paul Revere   *Grant Wood*

field to music. Grieg became the musical voice of Norway; Tchaikovsky, Rimsky-Korsakoff, and Moussorgsky, of Russia; Weber and Wagner, of Germany; Liszt, of Hungary; Chopin, of Poland; Dvořák and Smetana, of Bohemia; Albeniz, of Spain; Elgar, of England; MacDowell, of America; Debussy and Ravel, of France; Sibelius, of Finland.

A composer could use his gifts to glorify the national heritage in various ways. He could utilize folk-song and folk-dance idioms of his people, as Dvořák did in the *Slavonic Dances*, Chopin in the *Polonaises* and *Mazurkas*, Liszt in the *Hungarian Rhapsodies*. He could weave his music around the life of a national hero or king, as Wagner did in the music dramas based on the life of Siegfried, or Moussorgsky in his BORIS GODUNOFF. He could glorify the scenic beauties, the rivers and forests of his native land, as Johann Strauss did in his *Blue Danube* and *Tales from the Vienna Woods*, Smetana in *The Moldau*, Respighi in *The Pines of Rome*, and our own Stephen Foster in such songs as *Swanee River* and *My Old Kentucky Home*. He could use an historic event that had great emotional significance to his countrymen, generally one in which his nation had been victorious, as Tchaikovsky did in the OVERTURE 1812. Or he could set his music to the work of a native poet, as Grieg did with Ibsen's *Peer Gynt*, Debussy with the poetry of Verlaine, Tchaikovsky with the dramas of Pushkin. Most nationalist composers used several of these methods and thereby communicated to their audiences the essence of the spirit of their country.

As the century wore on, the struggle for freedom on the part of the oppressed nations became ever more bitter. Music, because of its intensely emotional appeal, became a weapon of first importance. Auber's *Masaniello*, with its stirring choruses in praise of liberty, became the rallying cry of an awakening Italy against the Austrian yoke. Later, when the operas of Verdi became popular, the frenzied shouts of "Viva Verdi" that greeted his works took on the nature of a political demonstration against the Austrians: the letters of Verdi's name happened to correspond with the initials of the nationalist slogan *Vittorio Emanuele Re d'Italia* (Victor Emanuel King of Italy). So too, when Finland was struggling to liberate itself from Czarist rule, Sibelius' FINLANDIA touched off such demonstrations on the part of Finnish patriots that the Czarist officials forbade its performance. In the tragic upheavals of our own time, music has again taken on this political role.

As our essential listening for this chapter, let us hear THE MOLDAU by Smetana, the OVERTURE 1812 by Tchaikovsky, and FINLANDIA by Sibelius. A number of suggested and supplementary projects may be found at the close of the chapter.

Bedrich Smetana (1824-1884)

Biography

Bedrich Smetana (sme'tà-nà), the founder of the Czech nationalist school, was born in 1824 in Litomyschl, Bohemia. His father was a brewer and was passionately fond of music. Like Saint-Saëns and Dukas, Smetana displayed marked musical gifts at an early age: he improvised on the violin at the age of five, and made frequent public appearances as a pianist during his adolescence. Finally, after overcoming the opposition of his family he went to Prague to study composition.

Weathering all sorts of privations—at times he practically starved—he eventually became music master in the family of Count Thun. The revolution of 1848 aroused his national consciousness as a Czech. In the next years Liszt, then at the height of his fame, became interested in him and helped him to establish a school of music. From then on his career was a slow progress to recognition and fame. He moved to Gothenburg, Sweden, where he became conductor of the new Philharmonic Society. Smetana returned to his home in Prague after the death of his wife. On his journey back from Sweden to his homeland, he stopped at Weimar to visit his benefactor, Liszt, and came strongly under the influence of the latter's symphonic poems.

Several years were spent in concert tours over the Continent before Smetana settled permanently in Prague. Here he became the leading figure in the nascent movement for a Czech national music, as composer, conductor, teacher, music critic, and writer. The production of his masterpiece, the gay folk opera THE BARTERED BRIDE, was followed by a number of successful musical-dramatic works, all strongly nationalistic, either based on the Bohemian folk idiom or on national legends. Of these, LIBUSSA, THE TWO WIDOWS, and THE KISS are best known.

In 1874, after his health had broken down under the strain of overwork, Smetana suddenly became completely deaf. It was in this final period that the composer wrote some of his greatest works—the autobiographical string quartet AUS MEINEN (From My Life) 1876, and the warmly romantic, patriotic symphonic cycle of six tone poems, MÁ VLAST (My Country), of which *Vltava (The Moldau)* 1874, has become popular throughout the musical world. In 1883 Smetana suffered a complete mental breakdown and died a year later in an asylum at the age of sixty.

"*The Moldau*" (*1874*)

Of the six symphonic poems that make up the cycle MÁ VLAST the description of the River Moldau is the second. The first, *Vyšehrad*, concerns the castle of popular Czech legend, its former glory conjured up by the bard Lumir. The third, *Šárka*, portrays a legendary warrior queen of Czechoslovakia who, to satisfy her hatred against men, entertains the knight Ctirad and his followers at a banquet and, after having plied them with drink, murders them. The fourth is the famous *From the Fields and Groves of Bohemia*, an idyllic pastoral poem of serene beauty. The fifth, *Tábor*, is a fantasy on an old chorale that was sung by the followers of John Huss. The sixth, *Blanik*, describes the mountain known to Czech folklore. When foreign oppressors come, the heroes, who have been hiding in the mountain, drive out the invader and restore Bohemia to her freedom.

The Moldau is one of the most successful pieces of descriptive music in the symphonic repertoire. Smetana appended the following note to the score:

Two springs gush forth in the shade of the Bohemian forest, the one warm and spouting, the other cold and tranquil. Their ripples, gaily flowing over rocky beds, unite and glisten in the morning sun. The forest brook, rushing on, becomes the River Vlatava (Moldau), which hurrying through Bohemia's valleys, grows into a mighty stream. It flows through dense woods, where the joyous noise of the hunt and the tones of the hunter's horns resound nearer and nearer. It flows through verdant meadows and lowlands where a wedding feast is celebrated with song and dancing. At night the wood nymphs and water sprites revel in its glistening waves, which reflect many fortresses and castles— witnesses of the past splendour of chivalry and the vanished martial fame of bygone days. At the Rapids of St. John the stream speeds on, winding its way over cataracts and cutting a channel with its foaming waters through the rocky chasm into the broad river bed in which it flows on in majestic calm toward Prague, welcomed by time-honoured Vyšehrad (the famous Bohemian castle, citadel of the ancient kings). Then it disappears in the far distance from the poet's gaze.

Smetana heard this music, which was destined to become his most popular symphonic composition, only in his imagination, for it was written in 1874, after total deafness had descended upon him.

ANALYSIS. The music opens *allegro commodo non agitato* (fast, at an easy pace, not agitated) in E minor, with a flowing sextuple metre, a rippling figure in the flutes portraying the two springs. Presently, against the rippling figure now taken by the strings the broad lyrical melody of the river emerges, played by first violins, oboes, and bassoons, a theme of great tenderness and simplicity in a minor key. Notice here, as well as in the folk-dance theme later, the regular four-measure phrase structure:

After a spacious development, the melody returns. But by raising the G to a G-sharp—that is, by using the raised third step of the scale—Smetana shifts the tune from minor to major in an extraordinarily effective transformation:

Hunting calls sound on the horns and woodwinds, at first remote, but soon approaching in a steady crescendo while the music grows more boisterous. With the next section, "Peasant Wedding," we modulate to G major. A rustic folk dance appears, abounding in gay little groups of sixteenth notes, played by strings and woodwinds:

The tune swells to a fortissimo and dies away. In the next section, "The Moon Rises—Dance of the Nymphs," we hear soft harmonies on the flutes, clarinets, and harp. The magical atmosphere of the forest permeates this section with the horns, trombones, and tuba intoning stately harmonies, as from afar, in the rhythm of a solemn march. At the section marked "The Rapids of St. John" we return to *Tempo I*, the music quickening in the original rippling figure with an upward gliding on the strings. The principal theme is heard much as before, first in the minor, then with a broad development, finally in the major. The music takes on majesty and power as "The Moldau broadens out" with the solemn motive of Vyšehrad—the historic castle—intoned triumphantly, like a hymn of praise, by brass and woodwinds against a rich orchestral background. The climax passes; the music dies down to a gentle rippling, and flows farther and farther away.

Here is heartfelt lyricism, imaginative orchestration, fantasy, and rare pictorial power blended in a work of universal appeal that well deserves its popularity.

"Overture Solennelle 1812," Op. 49 (1880), by Peter Ilyitch Tchaikovsky

In a letter from Italy to Mme. von Meck, Tchaikovsky writes:

Why is it that the simple Russian landscape, a walk in summer through Russian fields and forest or on the steppes at evening, can affect me so that I have lain on the ground numb, overcome by a wave of love for nature, by the indescribably sweet and intoxicating atmosphere that drifted over me from the forest, the steppe, the little river, the faraway village, the modest little church—in short, all that makes the poor Russian landscape?[1]

Although there were strong foreign elements in his work—he worshipped Mozart and admired Italian opera, French ballet, and German song—he considered his music Russian to the core. In response to a question of Mme. von Meck he writes (the reference to "our symphony" is to the *Fourth* which he dedicated to her):

As to the Russian element in my compositions, it is true that I often begin to write with the intention of using one or another popular song. Sometimes (as in the *Finale* of our symphony) this happens of itself, quite unexpectedly. As to the Russian element in general in my music —the relation to the popular song in melody and harmony—I grew

---

[1] Catherine Drinker Bowen and B. von Meck, *Beloved Friend*. (New York: Random House, 1937.)

up in a peaceful spot, saturated from earliest childhood with the miraculous beauty of Russian spirit. In short, I am a Russian through and
through.[2]

This intense nationalism increased as he grew famous and
began to be recognized as the foremost representative of Russian
music. It was further reinforced by the personal attention and
friendship that, in the last two decades of his life, members of the
Imperial family bestowed upon him. In the light of all this it is
not difficult to understand why the 1812 OVERTURE became one
of Tchaikovsky's most popular and most overplayed works. For
the average Russian, the year 1812 had an almost mystical significance: Napoleon's invasion had been thrown back, not by armies
or strategic victories, but by the Russian winter. It was literally
as if the country itself had arisen to hurl back the enemy.

The work was written at the request of Nicholas Rubinstein for
the Moscow Exhibition of Arts and Industries, at which it was
first performed, with booming cannons and other stirring effects,
on August 20, 1882. Tchaikovsky was given the choice of three
themes, of which he picked: "Solemn Overture on the Dedication
of the Church of the Saviour in Moscow." Conceived along the
broad outdoor lines proper to an exhibition, the *Overture* uses all
kinds of effects designed to capture the popular fancy.

This composition offers the music listener a lucid example of
how the composer's mind works and how he handles his themes.
In this case, the insight we get is particularly clear because one
of the principal themes in the development of the *Overture* is the
opening phrase of the *Marseillaise*, which symbolizes the approach
and later the retreat of the French army. Because of its familiarity,
the listener can easily follow it as the composer tosses the theme
about from one choir to the next, combines it with other thematic
material, presents it with all kinds of changes in timbre, dynamics,
tempo, and register. By following these transformations carefully
we gain an insight into one of the most important elements of
symphonic style—the handling and developing of the basic
musical ideas, the themes out of which a large musical form is
constructed.

ANALYSIS. Tchaikovsky's *Overture* opens with a solemn chorale
in E-flat major that seems to be invoking divine aid in the face of

[2] *Ibid.*

approaching calamity. Marked *largo*, the chorale is in simple four-part harmony; violas and 'cellos, playing mezzo-forte, *mf*, bring out the rich colouring of the solemn chords:

After a climax of great dignity and breadth, an oboe sings a plaintive tune. The strings sweep upward ominously; the mood becomes one of impending disaster. After a gradual crescendo and accelerando, which works up to *fff*, we hear the rattle of military drums; woodwinds and horns announce the second theme of the introduction, the famous Cavalry theme, in a martial andante, mezzo-forte:

With this, the introduction may be said to end and the movement proper to begin. The Strife theme, a grim motive of strife and anger, is played by the strings, allegro and forte, with abrupt runs and fierce accents and those upward and downward sweeps on the strings that we have already pointed out as an unmistakable characteristic of Tchaikovsky's orchestral style. There is a resemblance here to the Feud theme in the ROMEO AND JULIET OVERTURE.

Notice the change of key. The tumult mounts; we hear the opening strains of the *Marseillaise* played by trumpets and taken up by cornets, as if announcing the approach of the enemy, while vigorous upward scale passages on the strings and woodwinds provide a turbulent accompaniment. After working up to a stirring *fff* climax, the movement subsides; the second theme of the exposition emerges, a broad lyrical melody rising from the violins and violas in a broad sustained curve, a song of hope and love for the homeland, in F-sharp major:

A Cossack dance follows. Based upon one of those Russian folk tunes Tchaikovsky so loved, it is played piano by flute and English horn with tambourine accompaniment in a plaintive minor key:

The development brings us echoes of the Strife theme ingeniously combined with snatches of the *Marseillaise* bandied about among the brass and woodwind instruments. The music gradually gains momentum and surges forward with irresistible force to the point where the Strife theme re-enters *fff*. The first part is recapitulated in a somewhat abridged form, the Hope theme followed by the Cossack dance, more or less as we heard them before. An imposing transitional passage, based on a downward movement in the strings, leads to the grandiose coda, which is fashioned from the material of the introduction, giving us the prelude-postlude formation as a frame for the Overture. The chorale, largo as in the introduction, is now transformed into a mighty paean of thanksgiving accompanied by pealing bells and booming percussion, while woodwinds and strings execute the characteristic upward and downward sweeps. The Cavalry theme follows, *ffff*, allegro vivace, and is repeated as a countermelody, while the lower brass and string instruments blare out the national anthem, *God Save the Czar.* Meanwhile, the *Marseillaise* has completely faded from the scene, overpowered, retreating to oblivion as booming cannon and pealing bells bring the work to a triumphant close.

Jean Sibelius—a Finnish Tone Poet

Biography

Jean Sibelius, universally recognized as one of the greatest of present-day composers, was born in Finland on December 8, 1865, the son of a well-known physician. Like Tchaikovsky, he studied law. But with him, too, the urge to compose soon proved too strong to resist. He gave up all thoughts of a legal career and entered the Conservatoire at Helsingfors, continuing his musical studies in Berlin and Vienna. Returning to Finland at the age of twenty-eight, he soon won such recognition as a national composer that in 1897 the state offered him a life grant, on which he was able to retire and devote himself entirely to composing. Since then, except for short trips abroad, he has lived in his native land, turning out the works that have spread his fame throughout the world. Just as the career of Haydn has gone down in the history of music as a singularly happy illustration of princely patronage at its best, so that of Sibelius will be remembered as a shining example of what an enlightened government can do to protect and encourage its creative artists.

Throughout his career nationalism has played a fundamental part in Sibelius' music. Springing as he did from a national minority under the yoke of Czarist oppression, his music could not but reflect the intense patriotism, the pride, the sufferings, and the aspirations of his people. So saturated is his music with the spirit of his race that it is commonly assumed that he makes extensive use of folk-song material. That such is not the case Sibelius himself has pointed out. In a letter to Rosa Newmarch he claimed the themes so often described as folk tunes as entirely his own, declaring that the thematic material employed in FINLANDIA and EN SAGA were his own invention. The fact that he had to make this explanation shows how completely he has succeeded in capturing the musical idiom of the folk.

Sibelius' music reflects not only the spirit of his people but also their natural setting—the hard soil, the wintry skies and grey horizons, the swirling snows and lonely Arctic nights of the Northland, as well as the more cheerful days of the brief season of sunshine and warmth. Actually, the affinity of Sibelius with soil and forest is in the great "back-to-nature" tradition of the early Romanticists. (See Chapter XXIX for more about Sibelius.)

"*Finlandia*" (*1899*)

FINLANDIA, the work by which Sibelius is best known to the general public, was composed in 1899. This was two years after the composition of Dukas' SORCERER's APPRENTICE. But there was nothing of the *fin de siècle* sophistication about it. The year was one of smouldering resentment against the oppressive measures that the Russian government had just introduced, aimed at throttling the Finnish press. The nationalist party decided to carry on a campaign for the press fund, culminating in a gala performance at Helsingfors of a series of "Tableaux from the Past" with music by Sibelius. The music for the final tableau—"Finland Awakes" —after revision became the tone poem that the world now knows as FINLANDIA. Karl Ekmann, Sibelius' biographer, states that this work was of greater value to the nationalist cause than were hundreds of pamphlets and newspaper articles. The work soon came to be considered so inflammatory by the Czarist authorities that its performance was forbidden in Finland; in other parts of the empire it was not allowed to be played under any name that indicated its patriotic character. Sibelius tells that when he conducted it in Riga in the summer of 1904 he had to programme it under the politically harmless title of *Impromptu*.

After Finland gained her independence by the Treaty of Versailles, the tone poem became a kind of national symbol for the jubilant little republic. To the famous melody of the chorale have been set innumerable hymns and poems throughout the world, and in Finland it has become a national anthem.

ANALYSIS. The composition opens andante, in duple metre, with grim, snarling chords of defiance given out in the low register of the brasses, forte. The woodwinds and strings answer with a short, prayerful passage. A vigorous clarion call proclaimed by trumpets and trombones, like a summons to action, opens the allegro moderato (moderately fast) section. The orchestra leaps into activity, allegro. Over a persistent accompanying figure, reiterated by 'cellos and double basses, the woodwinds and violins sing a joyously defiant melody in quadruple metre, *ff*. Notice the regular

Q

formation: two four-measure periods with a semicadence in the middle and a cadence at the end:

The music works up to an exultant fortissimo climax, then suddenly subsides. There emerges the celebrated chorale, pianissimo, intoned first by the woodwinds, then in unison by 'cellos and violins: a serene, broadly flowing melody, expressing calm inner faith in the justice of the cause and in its ultimate victory:

Notice that the melody consists of three regular eight-measure periods.

The themes of conflict and defiance return and are developed with great vigour, after which, in a kind of brief coda, the wind instruments proclaim the opening of the chorale, fortissimo, bringing the work to a triumphant close.

The form of FINLANDIA is rather free. The sections follow each other—andante, allegro moderato, allegro—in accordance with the idea that the music is seeking to convey—that is, in accordance with the programme rather than with any strict musical form.

Like everything else Sibelius has written, FINLANDIA reveals what Gerald Abraham has aptly called his "granite" manner of orchestration, "the fine harsh bleakness of his harmonies, . . . his marvellous exploitation of the darker colours and lower registers of the orchestra."[3] When a friend of Sibelius spoke to the composer

[3] Gerald Abraham, *One Hundred Years of Music* (New York: Alfred A. Knopf, Inc., 1938.) Quoted by permission.

of his first impression of Finland, "low, reddish granite rocks emerging from the pale blue sea," Sibelius replied: "Yes, and when we see those granite rocks we know why we are able to treat the orchestra as we do." In the same vein Paul Rosenfeld has spoken of the "wet greys and blacks" of Sibelius' instrumentation: "The works are full of the gnawing of bassoons and the bleakness of the English horn, full of shattering trombones and screaming violins, full of the sinister rolling of drums, the menacing reverberation of cymbals, the icy glittering of harps."[4]

If we compare FINLANDIA with the Tchaikovsky work, we are struck first of all by Sibelius' economy of means. Here are none of the transitions, repetitions, interludes, and postludes that abound in the 1812 OVERTURE. The composer has his say; when he has had it, he closes. Sibelius' terseness seems to belong to a method diametrically opposite to that of the Russian master of tone. Where Tchaikovsky spins out, expands, and reiterates, Sibelius pares away mercilessly until nothing is left but the bare essentials, achieving thereby a compact texture of great intensity and power. It is this concision that in Sibelius' best scores gives the same impression as one has when reading a paragraph by a master of prose style—that not a single word could be omitted without marring the total effect.

In general, Sibelius' piece avoids the bombast and obviousness of Tchaikovsky's. It is less theatrical and more deeply felt. Sibelius at the beginning of his career was strongly influenced by that Russian master of tone. But he learned from the older man not only what to do, but also—what is often much more important— what to leave undone.

Although written in the same decade as SORCERER'S APPRENTICE, FINLANDIA belongs much more to the earlier Romantic tradition. This may be accounted for partly by the fact that the nationalist mood out of which Sibelius' first works stemmed definitely derived from an earlier decade, from the heyday of Smetana, Tchaikovsky, Dvořák, Grieg, and the other great nationalists rather than from the post-Romantic and more modern trends of the end of the century. Partly, too, the answer lies in Sibelius' creative personality. Although the greater part of his career fell in the twentieth century, he has never been considered one of the

[4] Paul Rosenfeld, *Musical Portraits: Interpretations of Twenty Modern Composers.* (New York: Harcourt Brace and Co., Inc., 1920.) Quoted by permission.

"moderns," and he has been influenced by the contemporary scene far less than the other important composers of our time. In a very real sense his music is a continuation of nineteenth-century Romanticism. This very timelessness, according to his admirers, gives his work a quality that lifts it far above the fads and fancies of the moment.

ADDITIONAL SUGGESTIONS FOR LISTENING

THE SWAN OF TUONELA and PAHJOLA'S DAUGHTER by Sibelius; IBERIA by Albeniz; NORWEGIAN DANCES by Grieg; *Overture* to THE BARTERED BRIDE by Smetana; HARY JANOS SUITE by Kodály; RUSSIAN EASTER OVERTURE by Rimsky-Korsakoff; THE ENCHANTED LAKE by Liadov; HENRY THE EIGHTH DANCES by Edward German; GRAND CANON SUITE by Ferde Grofe; ROMANIAN RHAPSODY No. 1, by Enesco; THE SANTE FE TRAIL by Harl McDonald—this will serve as a good beginning for your own list of nationalistic music; and we wish to stress as much as we possibly can the enjoyment to be derived from making such "discoveries" for yourselves. Throughout this book we shall only suggest a beginning, never a comprehensive list, or anything near that; for such a practice would be contrary to our real purpose, which is to stimulate the listener to develop himself. The listener should have at his elbow a first-rate, up-to-date phonograph record catalogue—and leisure time to "shop" by actually hearing before he buys. The personality of the music lover is shown just as much by the record library he builds as by the friends he keeps.

Chapter Fifteen

Exoticism in Music
Rimsky-Korsakoff

THE glamour of the East has intrigued the European imagination ever since the Crusades and the travels of Marco Polo. The Romantic movement, with its love of the strange and the picturesque, naturally stimulated this interest in the exotic.[1] In literature of the nineteenth century we have Fitzgerald's adaptation of the *Rubáiyát* of Omar Khayyám, Burton's translation of the *Arabian Nights*, and a whole series of works laid in the East, from Scott's *Talisman* to the tales of Kipling, Rider Haggard, Pierre Loti, and Joseph Conrad. In painting, besides the oriental scenes of such great colourists as Delacroix, Géricault, Turner, Decamps and Fromentin, Bakst and Roerich, we have throughout the century a crop of highly romanticized scenes of Tunis and Morocco with all the proper accoutrements of turbans, minarets, and camels. Music—as we have seen from Tchaikovsky's *Arab Dance*—lent itself pre-eminently to this kind of picturesqueness, especially in a period when composers were becoming increasingly preoccupied with atmosphere, orchestration, and piquant tone colours. Thus we have Saint-Saëns turning for inspiration to the Orient in his ALGERIAN SUITE and SAMSON AND DELILAH; Felicien David doing the same in his tone poem THE DESERT. Massanet's THAÏS, Verdi's AÏDA, and Puccini's MADAME BUTTERFLY, César Cui's *Orientale*, Borodin's *In the Steppes of Central Asia*, Rimsky-Korsakoff's *Song of India*, and *Hymn to the Sun* from SADKO are but a few well-known items in a list that could include many of the Romantic composers. It was inevitable that the Russian composers should play a leading part in spreading the influence of the East, springing as they did from an empire that was Asiatic as well as European. Of all the works inspired by

---

[1] The reader should carefully discriminate between *exoticism* and the use of the *exotic* in art. There is a wide difference of meaning in the two expressions.

The Girl in the Purple Robe   *Matisse*

This painting by the French artist Henri Matisse (born in 1869) is an excellent example of exoticism in European art. Here, in the decorative values of composition, internal designs, and arabesques, together with the bold use of colour and the forceful resultant rhythms, concords, and dissonances, are inescapable evidences of influences from the Near and Far East. To those who are attuned, there is a strange and fascinating modern "music" in the painting of Matisse, as there is "painting" in the music of Rimsky-Korsakoff and others.

exoticism, Rimsky-Korsakoff's Symphonic Suite SCHEHEREZADE, after *A Thousand and One Nights*, has become one of the most firmly established works of its kind.

Nicholas Rimsky-Korsakoff (1844-1908)

Biography

Rimsky-Korsakoff was one of the most brilliant members of the Russian nationalist school. Like Tchaikovsky and Sibelius, he did not start out with a musical career in view. Rather, his well-to-do family intended that he should become a naval officer, and thus he studied at the Naval College in St. Petersburg for six years until he was eighteen. He also studied the 'cello and piano in dilettante fashion and learned enough to entertain his friends with the popular arias from Italian opera. At seventeen, however, he made the acquaintance of Balakirev, the leader of the new Russian nationalist school, who played so important a part in the conception of Tchaikovsky's ROMEO AND JULIET. The friendship that developed with Balakirev marked a turning point in Rimsky-Korsakoff's life. He decided to devote himself to music seriously and began to study under Balakirev. In the meantime, his course at the Naval Academy came to an end, and he was assigned to a practice cruise around the world. Despite his duties on board ship, he worked on a symphony throughout the three years of the cruise, sending the work, movement by movement, to Balakirev for correction. Balakirev conducted the symphony in St. Petersburg in 1865 when Rimsky-Korsakoff returned from the cruise; the work met with a hearty reception. The audience was astonished to see a young naval officer step forward to acknowledge the applause.

The squadron to which Rimsky-Korsakoff was assigned went to America in 1863. The composer writes, "During the whole of our stay in the United States the Americans were engaged in their Civil War. . . . We followed the course of events with deep interest, though we kept exclusively within the Northern territory."[2]

[2] Nicholas Rimsky-Korsakoff, *My Musical Life*. (New York: Alfred A. Knopf, Inc., 1923.)

Back in St. Petersburg, Rimsky-Korsakoff made rapid strides in his art. In 1871 he was appointed professor of composition and instrumentation at the St. Petersburg Conservatory. Two years later he retired from the navy in order to devote himself wholly to composition. At the wish of the Grand Duke Constantine he became inspector of naval bands, a post in which he exerted a strong influence on musical standards throughout Russia. He succeeded Balakirev as director of the Free School of Music in St. Petersburg and conducted the concerts of the Russian Symphony Society, at which many important works of the new Russian school received their first performance. He soon became the most important composer of the "Five," as they came to be known in the musical world: the group of composers in St. Petersburg who devoted all their energies toward creating a Russian national school. Besides Rimsky-Korsakoff, the group included Mily Balakirev, the leader (1837-1910), and the latter's three disciples— César Cui (1835-1918), known in this country mainly through his popular violin piece *Orientale*; Alexander Borodin (1833-1887), whose *Polovtzian Dances* from the opera PRINCE IGOR are a favourite with concert and ballet audiences; and Modest Moussorgsky (1839-1881). Tchaikovsky considered the "Five" as amateurs, himself as a professional composer.

The "Five," whose activities centred about St. Petersburg, believed in and practised "art for Russia's sake." Revolting against what they considered the strangling influence of Western European musical culture, they preached that genius, inspiration, and a return to the riches of the national heritage were infinitely more valuable to the composer than the technical and harmonic disciplines of the traditional European conservatory training.

The most conscientious and self-critical of the group, Rimsky-Korsakoff recognized early that there might be some truth in Tchaikovsky's charges, and that his self-education in music had possibly not prepared him thoroughly enough for his task as a composer. Despite the fact that he was already professor of composition at the Conservatory, with several important symphonic works and an opera to his credit, he put himself through a severe course in theoretical exercises—a rare example of self-discipline on the part of an artist who had already "arrived" in his field. As a result of this continual striving he developed his genius to its full powers, became a painstaking craftsman, and was the only one of the "Five" to leave a deep imprint on the technical development of European music, especially in orchestration.

With never-failing generosity Rimsky-Korsakoff placed his brilliant technical gifts, particularly his mastery of the art of instrumentation, at the disposal of his fellow composers. He orchestrated THE STONE GUEST, which Alexander Dargomijsky (1813-1869) had tried to finish on his deathbed, as well as parts of Borodin's PRINCE IGOR and Moussorgsky's operas BORIS GODOU-NOV and KHOVANTSCHINA. Throughout a long and successful career he laboured unceasingly to raise the standards of musical taste in Russia, while through his classes at the Conservatoire— among his pupils were Stravinsky and Respighi—he exerted a direct personal influence on the rising generation of composers.

Both as musician and man Rimsky-Korsakoff was singularly free from the melancholy, the moody introspection and morbidity that literary legend has attached to the artistic temperament in general and the Slavic artist in particular. It might perhaps be wise to attempt here to puncture the popularly accepted fiction of the great genius in his garret, unkempt and unbalanced, consuming himself in fiery torturings of the soul. Of the distinguished composers whose careers we have examined thus far—Saint-Saëns, Dukas, Smetana, Moussorgsky, Tchaikovsky, Sibelius, and Rimsky-Korsakoff—all but one received due public acclaim and official recognition during their lifetimes.

"Scheherezade Suite" (1888)

The sea, which plays so important a part in the SCHEHEREZADE SUITE, fascinated Rimsky-Korsakoff from his childhood. During his naval cruise, he came again under its spell; was impressed with the glowing colours of the tropical ocean and the tropical skies. In SCHEHEREZADE, probably his most famous work, this love for the sea united with his love of exotic atmosphere, his dazzling use of orchestral colour, and the bent of his imagination toward folklore and fairy tale to produce a work that captured completely the imagination and splendour of the Arabian Nights. From a purely technical standpoint, the work has come to be considered a veritable textbook for the aspiring young composer. The score reveals with salient eloquence the possibilities of the modern symphony orchestra for poetry, lyricism, humour, colour, and pictorial opulence. Its influence on the younger composers at the turn of the century was incalculable.

The score, published in 1889, was titled *Scheherezade—After a Thousand and One Nights—Symphonic Suite for Orchestra, Op. 35.* The use of the term *symphonic suite* was the composer's way of indicating that he had built his work on a larger scale and with greater emphasis on the orchestral element than was the case with the ordinary suite. (*Op.* is the abbreviation of *opus*, the Latin for "work." Followed by a number, it indicates the order either of composition or publication of the particular piece among the composer's works. When a composer has written many works of the same type, as Beethoven's sonatas or Chopin's waltzes, the opus number is helpful in identifying a particular work.)

The score carried the following prefatory note:

The Sultan Schahriar, convinced of the faithlessness of women, had resolved to put to death each of his wives, after the wedding night. But the Sultana Scheherezade saved her life by diverting him with tales which she told him a thousand and one nights. Conquered by curiosity, the Sultan postponed from one day to the next the execution of his wife, and in the end renounced completely his bloody vow.

Many wonders were narrated to Schahriar by the Sultana Scheherezade. For her tales the Sultana borrowed from the poets—their verses, from the songs of the folk—the words; and she fitted them together in many tales and adventures.

ANALYSIS. The composition is scored for piccolo, two flutes, two oboes (one interchangeable with English horn), two clarinets, two bassoons, four horns, two trumpets, three trombones, bass tuba, kettle drums, snare-drum, bass drum, tambourine, cymbals, triangle, tom-tom, harp, and strings.

The Sea and the Ship of Sinbad.[3] We hear first the theme of the grim Sultan announced fortissimo by most of the orchestra and pitched in a low register:

After some mysterious chords and a pause, a solo violin soars

---

[3] The titles for the different movements were suggested by the composer himself.

high above the arpeggios of the harp, lento and espressivo (slow and expressive)—the tender Oriental theme of the Sultana.

The introduction over, we are ready for the wonderful sea voyage. The entire movement is built out of two melodic figures, of which the first is repeated over and over but with ever-changing colours—now the reediness of the oboe fused with the warmer tints of the viola; now the distant fogginess of horns pitted against the shimmering clarinets and violins; and now the entire orchestra rising in a surge of storm and thunder while the gentle roll of the accompaniment persists throughout, weaving its hypnotic spell over the listener and painting in tones a magnificent picture of the sea. Above all, Rimsky-Korsakoff succeeded in capturing the wonder and unreality of the fairy tale, the feeling of "a painted ship upon a painted ocean." There never was such a ship, there never was such a sea—save in the dreams of poets, whether of words, or pigments, or tones.

The introduction is marked *largo e maestoso* (broad and majestic), the movement proper is *allegro non troppo* (not too fast), and is in six-four time, a fine example of the use of sextuple metre to achieve a sense of spaciousness and a gently rolling effect. The Ship theme is in reality the Sultan theme shifted into six-four time and provided with a rolling accompaniment, as though the Sultan listening to the tale were in fancy projecting himself on to Sinbad's ship:

It is a regular four-measure phrase, legato, noteworthy for the trill in the third measure. The two staccato notes in the last measure are repeated pizzicato, like an afterthought, by the rest of the orchestra, making a fifth measure—a charmingly irregular formation.

This theme, worked up in a *crescendo poco a poco* (gradually louder), alternates with the Calm-of-the Sea theme, one of Rimsky-

Korsakoff's happiest inspirations—a series of chords played by clarinets and bassoon, later by flutes and clarinet:

Notice that the phrase consists of a two-measure motive repeated an octave higher. Notice also the contrast between these two themes—the Ship theme in low register with irregular rhythm formations, the Calm theme ascending to the upper register in a perfectly regular rhythm. Such contrasts are most valuable in securing variety and balance. Equally noteworthy is the contrast between the two themes of the introduction: the Sultan theme in low register announced by full orchestra, grim and brusque, in a regular four-measure phrase of which the last two notes are repeated; the Sultana theme in high register played by solo violin in a highly ornamented arabesque, a cadenza-like passage that in its freedom of form and rhythm suggests an improvisation.

The movement as a whole is free in form. Unity is achieved through the constant reiteration of the Ship theme, a reiteration that assists materially in projecting the mood of the Oriental storyteller. Variety is achieved mainly through the wonderful interplay of the different instrumental colours. Now an oboe solo plays a counter-melody to the Ship theme echoed by a clarinet, now the solo violin interposes with the Narrator (Scheherezade) theme, acting as a unifying thread to the movement. Now the Calm-of-the-Sea theme is given over to the violins, while clarinet and flute descend in broadly curving countermelody. Theme A (Ship) is finally built up on a surging crescendo to a fortissimo climax, after which the whole movement is repeated with interesting changes in instrumentation and dies away tranquillo (tranquilly), dolce (sweetly) and pianissimo.

As for the other elements—the lyrical melodic line, the sensuous harmonies, the subtle modulations from one key to the next, the steady beat of the sextuple metre, and the brilliant interplay of instrumental timbres, all fuse in one composite and unified effect. The dynamic scheme is fairly simple: forte (Sultan) and piano (Sultana) in the introduction; thereafter a piano built up to a fortissimo, repeated, and dying away in a gentle diminuendo.

Notice particularly the satisfying effect of the prolonged final cadence.

The Tale of the Prince Kalender. The second movement recounts the tale of the Prince Kalender. The Kalenders were a Persian sect of wandering beggar-dervishes. There are three who figure in the story of "The Porter and the Three Ladies of Bagdad," all by a coincidence disguised as princes. Rimsky-Korsakoff was careful not to specify which one he had in mind; nor, truth to tell, does it matter much. A whimsical folk tune on the bassoon hits off perfectly the happy-go-lucky quality of the wandering beggar. The melody is repeated, each time a little faster, as the Kalender gets off on his adventure. He plods along amiably until—has he come to one of those enchanted castles in which doors open mysteriously, luring the unwary wanderer from one room to the next? Perhaps he succumbs to temptation and slips an emerald into his pocket, or—worse still—catches a glimpse of something he should not have seen. Abruptly the mood changes: a trumpet call sounds closer; the violins shudder ominously; a grim march emerges. We do not know what sentence is decreed for the luckless beggar, but that it is one of those terrible punishments that abound in the *Arabian Nights* there can be no doubt. But now we hear again the happy-go-lucky theme of the opening as he picks himself up and continues on his way.

The movement is introduced by the unifying Scheherezade theme on the solo violin, *lento* and *espressivo* (slowly and expressively), developed into a more elaborate cadenza than at the opening as though, having survived the first night, the Sultana had greater confidence in her storytelling powers. Actually, Rimsky-Korsakoff is here following one of the fundamental laws of musical aesthetics: when a theme is frequently repeated, it should be varied or elaborated now and then to sustain interest.

After the introduction, the movement proper is *andantino* (somewhat slowly; faster than *andante*) and *cappricioso* (capriciously). The bassoon announces the whimsical theme of the Kalender Prince, which opens with a grace note. (This term indicates a note of little or no value used before a note of regular value; thus an ornament or "grace" note.) The Kalender Prince theme contains "grace" notes in the second and third measures as well, providing a wonderful balance within the phrase—and simulating one of the characteristics of Oriental music.

Bassoon

The melody is marked *dolce ed espressivo* (sweet and expressively), is in ⅜ metre, and in a plaintive minor mode.

The phrase is irregular, consisting of five measures. Notice the cadence effect obtained through the long note in the last measure. Throughout the movement Rimsky-Korsakoff eschews the regular four-measure structure. This irregularity, like the grace notes, contributes to the whimsical quality of the tale.

The theme is repeated several times in succession, each time in a higher register and *piu animato* (a little more animated) by the oboe, strings, and woodwinds. This continuous accelerando and climb in pitch is a wonderful buildup to the eventful middle section. The ominous trumpet call announced by trombones and tuba is echoed by muted trumpets. Notice the effective way in which the various brass instruments imitate each other. Tremolos on first and second violins complete the atmosphere of suspense. (A *tremolo*, the reader may recall, is a repetition of a note on a string instrument produced by moving the bow back and forth rapidly, giving a shuddering, scintillating, or trembling sound.)

The tempo changes to *allegro molto* (very fast). Just before the entire orchestra leaps into action we hear the unifying theme of the Narrator spun out into an elaborate cadenza on the clarinet, as if the wily Sultana were tantalizing her audience before getting to the nub of the story. The grim march is played by full orchestra in a clear-cut quadruple metre. A somewhat sorrowful cadenza on the bassoon, derived from material of the Kalender theme, leads us back to the reappearance of the first theme where the luckless dervish proceeds on his journey.

The structure is a clear-cut basic ternary, or ABA, with the first and third sections balancing each other. The movement is unified within by the repetitions of the Kalender theme and united to the first movement by the reappearances of the Sultana theme. The clarion call and march of the middle section offer an effective contrast to the Kalender theme; particularly noteworthy is the use of special effects—tremolo, harmonics, and pizzicato—in the middle part.

The melodic line of the first section is notable for its plaintive, folk-tale flavour. In the middle section, by contrast, the melodies are brusque and vigorous. The harmonies support this contrast: in the first part, restful; in the middle section, pungent harmonic effects, abrupt contrasts, a sense of activity and suspense. The rhythmic pattern, too, contributes its part: in the opening, a flowing triple metre, gracefully nonchalant; in the middle, brusque irregular rhythms, frequent changes in tempo and metre, action and excitement. Timbre is used in the same way: in the beginning, mild strings and woodwind colours blending imperceptibly; in the middle, the sharp colours of the brasses pitted against each other, shrill harmonics, and full tonal masses in the march. We see, therefore, that all four elements—melody, harmony, rhythm, and timbre—combine to bolster up the structural contrast of the A-B-A form.

The Young Prince and the Young Princess. Again the composer has left no clue as to which prince and princess he had in mind; but that they were young and beautiful and very much in love there can be no doubt. We encounter here nothing of the narrative style that abounded in the Kalender movement. This is a mood of romantic sentiment with all the proper accoutrements. First, the young prince serenades his beloved in a lyrical melody. Then, the princess dances for her love to the muffled beat of the tambourine; and then we hear again the serenade of the prince.

First and second violins announce the melody of the Prince's serenade in a flowing sextuple metre, piano:

Here Rimsky-Korsakoff returns to the regular four-bar structure. Notice the longer notes that create the pause at the cadence. The tempo is *andantino quasi allegretto* (a subtle tempo somewhere between andantino and allegretto). When the theme is repeated, flutes and clarinets swoop up and down in broadly curving arabesques.

The graceful dance of the princess, which begins *ppp grazioso* (gracefully) with a clarinet solo, is a regular two-phrase period (symmetry of structure is essential in a dance tune) accompanied throughout by the muffled beat of the tambourine:

After the symmetrical periods of the dance we return to the love song, *dolce ed cantabile* (sweet and in singing style). As it gets under way, the unifying Narrator theme (Scheherezade) breaks in *lento* and *espressivo* in the familiar violin solo and harp accompaniment, but this time still more elaborate than before. This continual adding of ornament to each repetition of the theme is in line with the aesthetic principle we pointed out a few pages back and serves to keep the theme always fresh and interesting. Besides, it is a good trick of simulating native Oriental music.

The cadenza is cleverly transformed into an accompaniment for the serenade of the prince. The flutes and clarinets now combine in languorous runs as the movement draws to a close. There is a last outburst of romantic fervour; then the music floats up in a delicate final cadence. This is the lyrical movement of the suite. The basic structure is a simple ABA; the ⁶⁄₈ metre makes for a broad flowing movement. The melody is smooth and gentle; the harmonies are consonant. Incidentally, notice the balance of movements: the first pictorial; the second an exciting narrative; the third lyrical; and the fourth the brilliant, vivacious, event-packed narrative of the Sultana.

Festival at Bagdad—the Ship is Sunk. The final movement is divided into two parts. First is the *Festival at Bagdad*, a whirl of colour and movement that seems to capture the pulse-beat of the ancient city at the height of its splendour under the great Haroun-al-Raschid. The exciting mood and scene of the festive day are set. Swept along by a rhythmic force that never falters, the familiar themes—the Sultan, the Kalender, the young Princess—turn up for a moment and disappear. The riotous carnival gathers momentum; the dance works up to a climax. Suddenly we are transported back to the vessel of Sinbad. The doomed ship draws closer

to the magnetic mountain on top of which stands the figure of the
bronze warrior. The sea heaves and threatens; storm winds blow
up on the rushing chromatic scales; the ship is swept headlong on
great, surging billows of sound. Now within the magnetic pull of
the mountain the nails and iron bolts fly out, the wooden planks
fall apart with a great thud as the warrior lifts his trumpet and
pronounces the motive of doom. There is a last growl as the
wreckage sinks; and a great calm descends upon the sea.

We hear the violin cadenza of Scheherezade for the last time—
her task is done. The theme of the Sultan which opened the work
returns at the close, strangely soft and tender: the misanthropic
Schahriar has been won over at last by the wit of the fascinating
Sultana.

The movement opens *allegro molto* and *fortissimo*, with a snatch
of wild dance music based on the Sultan theme followed by the
unifying Narrator theme in its most elaborate version. The dance
proper is announced by flutes and taken up by the violins, *vivo*
(lively). In order to get a maximum of accent, the composer needs
the shortest possible measure. The music is therefore in a vigorous
duple rhythm—a regular four-measure formation of four phrases,
or two periods. See how unmistakably the composer turns to
regular four-measure structure as soon as he has a dance pattern
in mind. How Oriental this seems!

(Note the multiple time signature $\frac{2}{8}$ ($\frac{6}{16}$-$\frac{3}{8}$) by which means the
composer has tried to indicate varying metres and rhythm that
appear in the course of the melody. See if you can distinguish
which is which as they appear.)

A *vivace* or *allegro* movement is most appropriate at the end of a
work in several movements in order to pitch the finale in a mood

of gaiety or triumph. This pattern prevails in many suites and symphonies.

Throughout the nineteenth century, composers were concerned with attaining unity not only within the separate movements of their longer works such as symphonies and suites, but also between the movements. They began more and more to introduce in one movement themes and ideas already heard in a previous one, thus knitting their movements together more closely in a cycle. This type of compositional technique is known as *cyclical* and has become very popular with composers.[4] Thus far Rimsky-Korsakoff has unified his movements by the Narrator, or Scheherezade, theme running like a thread through all of them. In the final movement he further strengthens the bond by bringing back the themes of the Sultan, the Kalender Prince, and the young Princess. We have here an excellent example of the achievement of continuity in programme music through the use of the cyclical structure and musical themes attached to definite characters.

The music works up through a crescendo and accelerando to the higher and more brilliant register in a slowly accumulating climax, *fff*. Tonal masses are hurled against each other in clashing dissonance, woodwinds against brass, then against strings; but the timbre, like the melody and harmony, is here subordinated to the wild, relentless rhythm of the dance. As the climax is reached, there is an abrupt pause and the movement shifts to *allegro con troppo, maestoso* (not too fast, majestic). We now return to the $\frac{6}{4}$ metre of the first movement with the Ship theme thundered forth by trombones and tuba against a seething orchestral background. Fierce chromatic scales are whipped up to a *fff* as the ship goes

---

[4] We pointed out in our discussion of form that the repetition of a theme solves the composer's problem of achieving unity in his work. As compositions grow more and more extended, there are likely to be quite a number of restatements of the original theme. To ward off the ever-present danger of monotony, composers have developed a fairly elaborate technique of varying their themes, thus achieving a kind of variety even within the unifying element.

A theme may be varied, as in Tchaikovsky's NUTCRACKER SUITE, by changes in the orchestration. The rhythm may be changed: an example is the free, cadenzalike Scheherezade theme that is shifted into a sextuple metre when it reappears in the course of the first movement. The chords in the accompaniment may be different, as was the case when the Kalender Prince theme reappeared after the middle section. The melody itself may be elaborated or ornamented, as we saw in each reappearance of the Scheherezade theme. To sum up: the composer may keep the same melody with different timbre, rhythm, or harmony; or he may vary the melody itself; or he may use several of these changes in every possible combination. How many different ways did you hear in the work just studied?

down. A final "growl"; then, *pp*, dolce, we hear for the last time the Calm of the Sea, the Sultana themes soaring aloft over the orchestra in Tempo I, and the Sultan theme rising in a slow curve to the benign final cadence.

ADDITIONAL SUGGESTIONS FOR LISTENING

For Additional Suggestions for Listening see opening paragraph. It will be quite easy and very enjoyable for you to extend this list to your own pleasure. Be sure you list the CAUCASIAN SKETCHES by Ippolitov-Ivanov. Remember to include some "moderns."

⊚⟲⌒⟲⌒⟲⌒⟲⌒⟲⌒⟲⌒⟲⌒⟲⌒⟲⌒⟲⌒⟲⌒⟲⌒⟲⌒⟲⌒⟲⌒⟲⊚

Chapter Sixteen

The Symphonic Poem
Franz Liszt

NO ONE sums up so well the prevailing moods of mid-nineteenth-century Romanticism—the emotional exuberance and theatricalism that found their perfect literary expression first in Byron then in Victor Hugo—as the composer of the *Liebestraume* and many *Hungarian Rhapsodies*. He was born when the Romantic movement had just got under way, and his career stretched clear across the century almost until the nineties, by which time it had exhausted itself and made way for newer modes of expression. For over half a century his star shone with extraordinary brilliance over the horizon of musical Europe. And when it set, one of the most colourful periods in the history of the art had come to a close.

Franz Liszt (1811-1886)

Biography

Franz Liszt was born in Hungary on October 22, 1811, the son of a steward on the estate of Prince Esterhazy. His father gave him his first lessons in piano playing. At the age of nine he appeared in public with such success that some Hungarian noblemen granted him a subsidy. The great master Czerny was Liszt's piano teacher. At eleven he played in Vienna where, it should be noted, Beethoven recognized his genius publicly; at twelve, in Paris where, ironically enough, the Conservatoire refused to admit the boy who was to become the greatest pianist of the age on the ground that he was a foreigner. Throughout the first phase of his career he made Paris his home and became the "fashionable" virtuoso. Here, too, he drew close to the literary leaders of French Romanticism—Victor Hugo, Lamartine, George Sand, Alfred de Musset —who exercised considerable influence on his artistic development. In 1834 he met the novelist Countess d'Agoult, known in the literary world as Daniel Stern. One of their daughters, Cosima, became the wife of Richard Wagner and, after Wagner's death, the organizing genius behind the Wagnerian festivals at Bayreuth.

Liszt concertized all over Europe for years and firmly established his reputation as a great, perhaps the greatest, pianist of all time. The emotional power and dazzling virtuosity of his playing have become a legend. Endowed with an electric personality, striking appearance, and a marvellous sensitivity to his audience, he captured the imagination of Europe much as Byron had done a generation earlier. Yet in 1847, at the height of his triumph, he gave up his public career as a pianist in order to develop himself as a composer and conductor. He was made the court conductor of the Grand Duke of Weimar; composed steadily; and became the champion of the "New Music," devoting himself to furthering the works of then unknown composers, especially Wagner, with an unselfishness and singleness of purpose which have few parallels in music. From the Weimar period, too, dates his friendship with the Princess Caroline Wittgenstein. Their home, the "Altenberg," became a centre of artistic activity where the enormous musical and social influence of Liszt and the Princess were constantly exerted on behalf of all that was new and progressive in art. Some of the key events of the new movement—the production of Wagner's LOHENGRIN, TANNHÄUSER and THE FLYING DUTCHMAN, of Berlioz' BENVENUTO CELLINI, of Schumann's GENOVEVA and music to Byron's MANFRED—took place under Liszt's direction at Weimar, the city where half a century before Goethe and Schiller had been instrumental in ushering in the reign of literary Romanticism.

In the last years of his life, Liszt divided his time between Weimar, Budapest, and Rome. In Budapest, his countrymen acclaimed the composer of the fiery *Hungarian Rhapsodies* in transports of patriotic fervour. At Weimar, aspiring young pianists came to him from all over the world to be instructed in the mysteries of his art, the majority of them unfortunately carrying away a style of piano-playing that retained all the acrobatics and bombast of the master but little of his poetry or fire. In Rome, the brilliant man of the world, the former radical, who in his youth had welcomed the Revolution of 1830 and indulged in atheistic tracts, fell more and more under the sway of the religious mysticism in his nature and ended by becoming an Abbé in the church. He joined the Order of St. Francis, wore priestly garb, and composed religious works—the MASS FOR GRAN CATHEDRAL, the LEGEND OF ST. ELIZABETH, and the CHRISTUS—which contain some of his finest music. He died on July 31, 1886, appropriately enough at the Wagner festival in Bayreuth where the "Music of the Future" of his old comrade-in-arms for which he had laboured so well was finally entering upon its hour of victory.

Liszt belongs to the most colourful era of the Romantic movement. His literary counterparts are Byron and Hugo; among painters, Delacroix, Géricault and Turner stand closest to him in their theatricalism, colourfulness, and grand manner. If some of his music seems oversentimental to us, the tendency of his age must be remembered. Precisely because he so perfectly expressed the prevailing tastes and ideals of his own period he was bound to suffer an eclipse as soon as the pendulum had swung the other way. As is usual in such cases, the reaction against Liszt's ostentatious expression of emotionalism went a little too far. He was unquestionably one of the most gifted of the Romanticists, a pioneer in exploiting new forms, a daring experimenter in compositional technique, harmonic invention, and creation of new orchestral effects. His ideas were borrowed not only by Wagner but to some degree by a large number of the composers in the second half of the century; and evidences of this borrowing are heard everywhere, even today!

For a time, musical criticism was excessively hostile to his music and everything he represented; but recent writers are evaluating his contribution more justly. Paul Bekker, one of the most discerning of modern critics, says of him:

Liszt was one of the great practical organizers of public musical activity. He thought of the artist as a sort of prophet—and he saw himself as one—who passes through the stage of virtuoso and champion of everything new and good, to become the high priest, the mediator between God and man. This was the course Liszt's own life took.[1]

[1] Paul Bekker, *The Story of Music.* (New York: N. W. Norton and Company, Inc., 1927.)

Although programme music received a great impetus fairly early in the Romantic Period—Beethoven wrote his *Pastoral* SIXTH SYMPHONY and his dramatic overtures in the first quarter of the nineteenth century—it was not until some decades later that there emerged the musical form that summed up most completely and remained most closely associated with the storytelling tendencies of Romantic music—the *Symphonic Poem*. It was Liszt who first used this somewhat romantic term to describe a musical composition, and he it was who played the decisive part in its development, with the result that he has come to be known in histories of music as the "father of the symphonic poem."

The characteristic most frequently associated with the Lisztian tone poem is the principle of *theme transformation*, which Liszt used to unify and integrate his work. Liszt transformed and varied his themes in rhythm, harmony, timbre, tempo, and general style to mirror the development or changes in the poetic thought. He applied the principle with great ingenuity and effectiveness and through its use secured a solidity of structure and unity of mood that the symphonic poem did not always achieve in the hands of his disciples. We shall have occasion to point out some interesting theme transformation in LES PRÉLUDES.

The literary idols of the Romantic composers and painters, as we have seen, were Shakespeare, Goethe, Schiller, Dante, Petrarch. Their more immediate inspiration stemmed from Hugo, Byron, Walter Scott, Heine, and the imaginative E. T. A. Hoffmann (whose influence we noticed in the NUTCRACKER SUITE). The return to the spirit of the Middle Ages found expression in the Catholic revival of Lamartine and Chateaubriand (paralleled in England by Cardinal Newman and the Oxford movement). The pessimism of Schopenhauer and the all-embracing humanism that Goethe passed on to his disciples were no less important, while in the background stood the towering figure of Jean Jacques Rousseau with his doctrine of "the natural man" and the "return to nature."

We can see some of these influences at work in examining the titles of Liszt's symphonic poems: FUNERAL HYMN FOR A HERO, intended as the first movement of a revolutionary symphony, an intention never carried out as the young composer's radicalism subsided; TASSO: *Lament and Triumph*, depicting the tragic career of the great poet, his hopeless love for Beatrice d'Este, and the triumph of his work after his death (both Byron and Goethe had treated the subject); LES PRÉLUDES, after the mystical Lamartine's POETIC MEDITATIONS; HUNGARIA, on a patriotic theme; WHAT ONE HEARS ON THE MOUNTAIN, dedicated to nature and solitude; MAZEPPA, dealing with the hero whose adventures had inspired Hugo, Byron, and Pushkin; PROMETHEUS, on the theme that had kindled the imagination of Shelley; FESTIVAL PIECE, to commemorate the fiftieth anniversary of the first production of Schiller's *Huldigung der Künste*; ORPHEUS, conceived during the rehearsals of Gluck's ORFÉO at Weimar; THE BATTLE OF THE HUNS, a return to the setting of the Dark Ages, inspired by Kaulbach's celebrated painting; THE IDEAL, after Schiller's poem; HAMLET, an attempt to unravel in music the riddle of Shakespeare's hero; FROM THE CRADLE TO THE GRAVE, consisting of three parts: *The Cradle, The Struggle for Life,* and *At the Grave, Cradle of a Future Life.* In addition, there are the two programme symphonies, the first based on Dante's *Divine Comedy,* containing an "Inferno," "Purgatory," and "Magnificat"; and the second his masterpiece, the *Faust* SYMPHONY, after Goethe, giving three magnificent tone pictures of Faust, Marguerite, and Mephistopheles. We have in these titles a veritable catalogue of the literary influences in music during the Romantic Period.[2]

"Les Préludes" (*1854*)

For Liszt, the programme was merely a point of departure, a symbol to be translated into musical terms. The music suggested the symbol with all the pomp and grandeur of which tone was capable, but it seldom imitated or gave a too literal interpretation of the symbol. Nothing better illustrates this attitude than the fact that the programme of LES PRÉLUDES was attached to the tone poem after the music was written. Almost a decade before he had written the music for a choral work, THE FOUR ELEMENTS (Earth, Winds, Waves, Stars), which he laid aside, discouraged by the stupidity of the words. He then made an orchestral version, but, still dissatisfied, discarded this also. In 1854, needing a new work for a benefit concert at Weimar, he recast the abandoned sketch in its present form and looked about for an appropriate poetic

---

[2] Works of Liszt that we have mentioned, aside from LES PRÉLUDES, might well serve as supplementary listening for the chapter on Liszt.

motto. Struck by one of Lamartine's poems, he lifted the title, wrote a programme of his own that bears some resemblance to what Lamartine actually said, and attached this to his work with the subtitle "After One of Lamartine's Poetic Meditations." Thus, music that had begun by representing earth, winds, waves, and stars ended by symbolizing love, human aspirations, nature, and immortality. Liszt then, even though he was sufficiently a Romanticist to want literary associations for his music, at the same time was musician enough to realize that these associations must of necessity be vague and that the music must present general emotional moods such as exaltation, triumph, grief, or defeat rather than the concrete details of a story.

The programme that Liszt wrote for LES PRÉLUDES reads as follows:

What is life but a series of preludes to that unknown song whose initial solemn note is tolled by Death? The enchanted dawn of every life is love; but where is the destiny on whose first delicious joys some storm does not break?—a storm whose deadly blast disperses youth's illusions, whose fatal bolt consumes its altar. And what soul thus cruelly bruised, when the tempest rolls away, seeks not to rest its memories in the pleasant calm of rural life? Yet man allows himself not long to taste the kindly quiet which first attracted him to Nature's lap; but when the trumpet gives the signal he hastens to danger's post, whatever be the fight which draws him to its lists; that in the struggle he may once more regain full knowledge of himself and all his strength.

We have here a number of elements characteristic of literary Romanticism: the religious mysticism and "intimations of immortality"; the idealization of love; the conception of life as a struggle against destiny, cruel and disillusioning; the longing for solitude and healing in nature's lap; and the glorious return to the battle. Liszt follows his programme rather loosely, treating it as a motto rather than a restriction.

ANALYSIS. Although LES PRÉLUDES is written in a single continuous movement, close inspection will reveal that it is a work of a number of episodes (some eight or nine) grouped into four contrasting sections which may be said to correspond roughly to the separate movements of a complete symphony—a sort of telescoping condensation. Then, too, most of the work is constructed out of the metamorphosis of a simple "germinal motive" which is heard in the third measure of the Introduction and which bears close observation throughout the entire symphonic poem:[3]

What we have chosen to call Part I opens with an introduction presenting the grave Questioning motive as part of the first theme, played by the strings. Note the ominous opening pizzicato (plucked) tones and, in the third measure, the "germinal motive" marked with an "a"—, played with the bow (*arco*):

This phrase is repeated several times, with slight changes, until the movement proper begins (*Andante maestoso*—with majestic movement), with the theme sounded loudly in the trombones, 'cellos, and basses. As we have indicated, it is formed out of the "germinal motive" marked with an "a".

The strings frame this theme in an arpeggiated (broken-chord-wise), undulated figure not unlike a wave.

Presently another theme is woven out of the germinal motive and played by the second violins, violas, and 'cellos, with a rippling figure in the first violins the while, and the basses pizzicato:

This idea is developed for some twenty measures, when the

---

[3] This musical idea seems to have some inherent universal significance, for one can find one similar to it in a number of widely separated periods, among which are: Bach's C-sharp minor Fugue (No. 4) of the *Well-tempered Clavichord*, the *Muss es sein* string quartet, Op. 135, of Beethoven, the *D-minor Symphony* of César Franck, the *Freischütz Overture* of Weber, the "Fate" motif in Wagner's *Die Walküre*, and so forth. See footnote in Chapter XXIII, page 362.

lyrical second theme proper appears in the French horns and
muted violas, each divided into three parts. Though the theme is
not without its trite sentimentality, it is, nevertheless, a very clever
development of the germinal motive as indicated:

Liszt builds this up to a forceful and passionate climax through
the use of the full orchestra, only to calm it down suddenly into a
sort of brief dialogue between the strings and woodwinds (note
the ethereal close with the sustained chord held by the woodwinds,
delicately punctuated by harmonics on the harp—like tiny bells).

Immediately Part II, not without its parallel to a scherzo movement, appears when the tempo suddenly hastens (*allegro ma non
troppo*—fast, but not too much so). Here is a storm scene, *par excellence*, with all the chromatic trappings and sound-effect "tricks"
that all too often accompany such scenes in the cinema. Of course
it was a remarkable bit of writing when Liszt composed it—too
frequent imitation has, however, deprived the idea of its freshness.

There will be little difficulty in visualizing a tremendous wind and
storm. In due time, quiet prevails and the idea set forth in Mus.
Ill. 4, page 248, reappears in the woodwinds.

Part III, which follows the storm scene, might well be considered to parallel a usual romantic and lyrical Slow Movement
of the symphony. Marked *Allegretto pastorale* (fairly lively and in a
rustic spirit), this main theme of the section is played, *in extensio*,
by the first clarinet, but not until it has been anticipated in part
by the solo French horn, and then the solo oboe.

It is a lovely theme that still brings with it the sprightliness and
freshness of spring; and it still causes one to marvel at Liszt's com-

positional sensitiveness, for it is to be noted that the theme is not beholden to the germinal motive. The theme is tossed about between the strings and woodwinds in a frolicsome manner. Eventually a forceful climax evolves in which the theme of Mus. Ill. 1, page 249, is prominently set forth; the key changes markedly, the pulse quickens, and the brasses play bits of anticipatory fanfares—something very important is about to happen!

Part IV, parallel to the final in a symphony, is ushered in by scale passages, lively passes between the first and second violins, while the French horns and trumpets play the martial theme "A" and the trombones interrupt with the idea "B"—which was first heard in Mus. Ill. 3, page 248. The tempo is *allegro marziale animato* (in a lively and animated martial tempo).

A complex tonal picture ensues, with the bass drums, snare drums, and cymbals adding to the volume of sound; the tempo broadens to a more majestic pace, with the trombones and strings returning to the ideas that came immediately after the introduction—serving to bring about a feeling of formal unity and coherence. Thus the symphonic poem, LES PRÉLUDES, closes in a lustily proclaimed victorious spirit, and one wonders, nevertheless, just what victory does this final section celebrate? What do you think?

SUGGESTED SUPPLEMENTARY LISTENING

Additional works of Liszt have been mentioned throughout the earlier part of the chapter.

Chapter Seventeen

❦❧❦❧❦❧❦❧❦❧❦❧❦❧❦❧❦❧❦❧❦❧❧

Richard Wagner
The Leit Motif Technique

NO PICTURE of the orchestral idiom of the nineteenth
century would be complete without a consideration of the
career and achievement of Liszt's friend, Richard Wagner
(1813-1883). Technically, Wagner was an opera composer, and his
main reforms, as he thought of them, were carried out in the realm
of dramatic music. Actually, he was one of the century's great masters of orchestral writing, whose innovations in harmony and instrumentation, as well as intensity of emotional pitch, exerted incalculable influence on the whole domain of Romantic music.
Indeed, it is hardly an exaggeration to say that Wagner's music
shaped the entire course of orchestral writing in the second half
of the century, both through the composers who considered themselves his disciples, like Richard Strauss, Anton Bruckner, and
Gustav Mahler, and those who, like Debussy, sought to shake off
his influence by striking out into new paths. In any case, Wagnerism represents the very culmination of Romanticism, a brilliant, impassioned style of overwhelming—sometimes almost
brutal—power, of dazzling orchestral colour and virtuosity, so
distinctive that some historians of nineteenth-century art use it as
a landmark. In our own time, too, although his music dramas still
hold the centre of the operatic stage, his greatest influence is in the
concert hall where symphonic excerpts from the operas, to all
intents and purposes great tone poems, are among the staples of
the orchestral repertoire.

Biography

The career of this volcanic iconoclast makes one of the most
colourful sagas in the story of music. His life, like Liszt's, stretches
well across the nineteenth century. He was born in Leipzig in

251

1813, two years after his great friend, and died in 1883, three years before him. As a youth, Wagner was attracted principally to literature, particularly the Greek classics. At fourteen, having discovered Shakespeare, he wrote a grand tragedy in the course of the early acts of which forty-two characters died; a number of them had to return as ghosts to keep the fifth act going. Hearing Beethoven's symphonies—the effect upon him was overwhelming—he forthwith decided that what his tragedy needed was precisely such music as this. In order to compose it he borrowed a textbook on harmony and ploughed through it; but somehow the "system" described in the text could not be made to work. A few lessons from an organist named Müller disappointed him: he thought his teacher a dry pedant, and Müller considered his pupil pigheaded and eccentric. The boy's interest now turned back to literature. He fell under the spell of E. T. A. Hoffmann, the author who exercised such an extraordinary influence on Schumann, Weber, and other Romantic composers; and in Hoffmann's tales he came across some of the material that he later used in his operas. When he was seventeen, he managed to get an overture performed at a concert. It was, he admits in his autobiography, the high peak of his absurdities. The excesses of the drummer, who was directed to play a beat *fortissimo* every four bars, amazed the audience, which grew impatient and finally dismissed the work as a joke.

At the University of Leipzig, Wagner studied composition with Theodor Weinlig for about six months, this being practically all the formal musical training he ever had. Thereafter he buried himself in the scores of his idol, Beethoven. Leaving the University at twenty, he spent the next six years knocking about the third-rate opera houses that dotted provincial Germany, acquiring through practical experience as chorus master, stage director, and conductor that intimate knowledge of the stage that is one of the prime requisites for the successful opera composer. At Königsberg he married an actress of his company, Minna Planer—he was then twenty-three—and got an engagement as conductor at Riga. Growing dissatisfied with the rut into which he had drifted, he turned his eyes, as all ambitious young artists then did, toward Paris. He completed the first two acts of his grand opera RIENZI; *Last of the Tribunes,* based on the novel by Bulwer-Lytton, and set out with his wife to seek his fortune in the French capital. During the voyage through the North Sea the legend of THE FLYING

DUTCHMAN which he had come across in a story by Heine took possession of his mind. Thus the seed was planted for his first truly important work.

His life in Paris was a bitter disappointment, a grinding struggle with poverty, a futile knocking at doors that remained closed. Despite the letter of introduction given him by Meyerbeer, at that time the virtual ruler of grand opera, the young man was unable to gain a foothold anywhere. To support himself and his wife he was reduced to hack work, "arranging rubbish for various instruments—the cornet among them"; he wrote vaudeville airs, and at one time tried to get a job as a chorus man. "The conductor who tested my capabilities discovered that I could not sing at all, and pronounced me a hopeless case all around." Despite all obstacles, he finished RIENZI, which he dispatched to the Dresden Opera House, and set to work on the libretto of THE FLYING DUTCHMAN. (He had a distinctive literary gift and wrote the poems of all his operas.) In dire straits, he tried to write for a living and turned out some articles on music that were published in the Parisian journals. Just when the outlook was gloomiest, the news came that RIENZI had been accepted for performance at Dresden. He shook the dust of Paris from his feet and set out for his native land. With tears in his eyes, he tells us, he beheld the Rhine "and swore eternal fidelity to the German fatherland."

RIENZI scored a sensational success. Almost overnight the twenty-eight-year-old composer found himself lifted from obscurity to the position of *Kapellmeister* (conductor and general music director) to the King of Saxony. He now had everything a composer could wish for—security, a theatre under his direction, an enthusiastic audience. He needed only to continue to turn out works in the conventional grand-opera manner. But his integrity as an artist would not permit him to do this. He had a vision of music drama more lofty than anything that had been done up till then and he was determined to force this vision upon the world. The audiences that had applauded the flamboyant RIENZI were totally unprepared for the stark simplicity and intensity of THE FLYING DUTCHMAN. They were repelled by the tragic ending of TANNHÄUSER and were puzzled by Wagner's new type of melody. When it came to LOHENGRIN, the second work that Wagner completed during his seven years at Dresden, the bureaucrats in charge of the royal opera did not care to continue what they

considered a dangerous experiment and refused to produce the work.

Wagner realized that he could not give the public what it wanted and it would not accept what he could give it. It was borne in upon him that he would never be able to rescue operatic music from the triviality and vulgarity into which it had fallen. His projected reform for the theatres of Saxony fell on the deaf ears of the conservative ministers who expected him to supply the court with conventional pleasantries. His restless intellect led him further in his search for the original evil. He saw that in order to reform the theatre, which was but a reflection of the social scene, he would have to reform the social scene itself and its basic determinant, the state. It was futile for an artist to seek to change his little corner of the universe, since what he really had to change was society as a whole. This line of reasoning led Wagner straight into the revolutionary camp and he had to flee.

With the years of political exile which he spent in Switzerland began the mature period of his creative career. He decided that the only way to create an audience for the "art work of the future" was to take up his pen to propagandize for and to explain his theories. For five years he wrote no music, turning out his chief literary works—*Art and Revolution* (1849), *The Art Work of the Future* (1850), and *Opera and Drama* (1851), besides a host of shorter essays on related subjects. Having thus cleared his mind for action, he "attempted" to put his principles into practice in the fully developed music dramas—he coined this term to distinguish his works from the conventional opera—of his maturity. How widely his practices veered from his theories is, by now, quite common knowledge.

The remaining three decades of his life he devoted, with a singleness of aim that has few parallels in the story of art, to imposing his will and his vision upon the world. How he forged ahead in a Europe that at the onset understood neither his music nor his ideas, and how he finally got the world to listen, to understand, and to worship, is one of the most incredible success stories of the nineteenth century. We get an insight into the lack of understanding he had to face at this period from the following description by Gasperini of Wagner's interview with the director of the Théâtre Lyrique in Paris where he had gone in the hope of getting TANN-HÄUSER performed:

One evening, arriving at Carvalho's house, I heard an extraordinary noise! Wagner was at the piano, struggling with the finale of the second act of TANNHÄUSER. He sang, he shouted, he performed all kinds of contortions; he played with his hands, his wrists, his elbows. M. Carvalho remained impassive, waiting with a patience worthy of antiquity for the bedlam to subside. The score finished, Carvalho stammered a few polite words, turned and fled.

Fortunately, Wagner did not have to conduct the struggle completely alone. Liszt was a staunch friend who did more perhaps than any other to launch the "music of the future." Other disciples included Hans von Bülow, the great pianist and conductor, and the fiery young Nietzsche, for whom the master's music was—for a time—the revelation of a new world. Liszt produced LOHENGRIN at Weimar; other productions of THE FLYING DUTCHMAN and TANNHÄUSER followed throughout Germany. Wagner was unable to hear these, for he was still forbidden to enter his homeland. Gradually the movement for Wagner's pardon gained strength. Through the intercession of Princess Metternich, the ban of exile was finally withdrawn and Wagner returned to Germany after an absence of eleven years. He plunged at once into the composition of his one comic masterpiece, THE MASTER SINGERS OF NÜREMBERG. Despite all this, the darkest period of his life now approached. Having completed the first two dramas of the RING OF THE NIBELUNG, he faced the realization that Europe contained neither a theatre nor singers capable of presenting them. His efforts to get TRISTAN AND ISOLDE produced fell through. He was estranged from his wife; his romantic friendship with Mathilde Wesendonck, who had played an important part in the inspiration of TRISTAN, ended in an unhappy separation. At last his power of resistance was broken. He thought of suicide, and finally decided to give up his public career.

And then the "miracle" happened. The throne of Bavaria fell to the eighteen-year-old Ludwig II, who had been an enthusiastic devotee of Wagner ever since he had heard LOHENGRIN. One of the first acts of the young King was to invite Wagner to come to Bavaria to finish his work. Thus opened the final and triumphant chapter in Wagner's life. He closes his autobiography at this point: "I was never again to feel the weight of everyday hardships of existence under the protection of my exalted friend."

He settled at the capital, Munich, where in 1865 TRISTAN was

s

produced under his supervision, von Bülow conducting. He now completed DIE MEISTERSINGER (*The Master Singers of Nüremberg*), twenty-two years after his first sketch of the poem. After an interruption of nine years, he returned to the RING and finished the poem and music of the fourth and final drama, GÖTTERDÄMMERUNG (The Twilight of the Gods). Now he was joined by Liszt's daughter Cosima, one of the most extraordinary women of her time, who brought Wagner the understanding he needed, together with an unflagging will and energy equal to his own in building the Wagnerian Festival Theatre at Bayreuth. The lifelong friendship between Liszt and Wagner received its first wrench at this domestic drama, for Cosima was the wife of Wagner's disciple von Bülow, and her decision occasioned a scandal that Wagner's enemies were only too eager to exploit. In 1870, after all legal obstacles had been swept away, they were married. There followed the crowning act of Wagner's life—the building of the theatre at Bayreuth, made possible by the contributions of Wagner societies throughout the world. In 1876 the first Bayreuth Festival was given, with the four dramas of the RING OF THE NIBELUNG (DAS RHEINGOLD, DIE WALKÜRE, SIEGFRIED, and GÖTTERDÄMMERUNG) performed in their entirety for the first time twenty-eight years after Wagner had begun to work on the librettos. Bayreuth now became the Mecca of all the adherents of the "music of the future"; the festivals, given every four years, later annually, became the focal point from which Wagner's music and ideas emanated all over the world. Every technical detail, from the seating plan of the theatre to the singing and coaching of the performers, was superintended by Wagner himself and represented the final realization of his notions of musical-dramatic art. Here his last work, PARSIFAL, was first produced (1882). A year later he died in Venice at seventy and was laid to rest in Bayreuth. Ernest Newman sums his life up well in his *Wagner as Man and Artist*:

He lived, indeed, to see himself victor everywhere, in possession of everything for which he had struggled his whole feverish life through. He completed and saw upon the stage every one of the great works he had planned. He found the one woman in the world who was fitted to share his throne with him when alive and to govern his kingdom after his death with something of his own overbearing, inconsiderate strength. He achieved the miracle of building in a tiny Bavarian town a theatre to which, for more than a generation after his death, musicians would still flock from all the ends of the earth.[1]

In his attempt to make the orchestra express all the emotional experience of his characters—love, passion, hate, despair, revenge—as well as the pictorial and scenic aspects of the myths upon which he built his dramas—storm, flame, the magic of the forest, the wonder of the rainbow, the shimmering of the Rhine—Wagner made his richest contribution to the symphonic idiom of the Romantic movement. Through the use of new orchestral combinations, particularly in the brass and woodwinds, through new harmonic progressions and the use of a restlessly chromatic and contrapuntal idiom that modulated ceaselessly from one key to the next, he immeasurably extended the capacities of the art for emotional expression and tone painting. His daring chordal combinations and their uses paved the way for a new concept of harmony. His writing became the basis of most subsequent developments in the final decades of the nineteenth century; and his influence carried over into the twentieth, even to this day.

Another contribution that Wagner made to music was the tremendous development and perfection of the use of leading motives, more exactly known as *leit motifs*. He is not here credited with the invention of this technique, for it was known long before; but he did perfect its use almost to the point of exhaustion of its possibilities. Since this technique is such a characteristic and large part of Wagner's style of composition, it is well to inquire into it, and we shall use the TANNHÄUSER OVERTURE as a typical example; but, first, we should acquire a better concept of the *leit motif* itself. Such a motif is a characteristic theme or musical figure that the composer attaches to a person (such as to Venus or Sirens), to a thing (such as a Sword or Holy Grail), to a condition (such as Love or Hate), or even to an abstract idea (such as Glorification of Venus or Love's Ban). Thus, whenever these ideas are pertinent to the moment in the storytelling, the appropriate motif, or motifs, will be performed. Obviously, if the listener is in possession of the composer's intentions and connotations pertaining to the motifs, a running communication and narration are quite feasible—and the extent to which Wagner made this communication intelligible

---

[1] Ernest Newman, *Wagner as Man and Artist*. (New York: Alfred A. Knopf, Inc., 1924.)

without loss of musicality is one of the wonders of this many-sided genius.[2] But more of this when we analyse TANNHÄUSER.

Overture to "Tannhäuser"

The Overture to TANNHÄUSER when heard in the opera house provides an appropriate introduction to the drama. When heard—as is much more often the case—apart from the opera, it is an exciting symphonic poem built around the inner conflict within the hero of the drama. As with much programme music, knowledge of the drama is an aid to the fullest appreciation of the score.

The knight Tannhäuser is torn between his love for Elisabeth, who represents all that is best in his nature, and the pagan goddess Venus. Surfeited with the goddess' sensuous rites and revels, he tears himself away from her and returns to the world of mortals. The second act centres about the "Tournament of Song" in Wartburg, the Thuringian castle of Elisabeth's uncle, in which each of the knightly minstrels sings in praise of love. When his turn comes, Tannhäuser, under the spell of the goddess, mocks the spiritual conception of love and sings the *Hymn to Venus*, a passionate dithyramb on the pleasures of voluptuous love. Finally realizing the depravity of his soul, he undertakes a pilgrimage to Rome to do penance. But the Pope, shocked at the enormity of his sins, tells him there is as much chance for his soul to win salvation as for his withered pilgrim's staff to sprout leaves. Tannhäuser, returning home in deepest despair, is on the verge of giving himself over to Venus and eternal perdition; but the faith of Elisabeth, who dies with a prayer for him on her lips, recalls him to his better self and saves him. As he falls dead on her bier, the pilgrims returning from Rome bring news of a miracle: Tannhäuser's staff has sprouted leaves, and the sinner has won salvation through the steadfast love and sacrifice of Elisabeth.

[2] While it must be admitted that a *knowledge* of the "leit motifs," together with the *recognition* of them as they appear in the performance, enhances the enjoyment (and in the opera itself they are quite indispensable), it is to Wagner's everlasting credit that the music, when performed as concert music, is fully capable of standing on its own feet, so to speak; and often the difference of enjoyment between the intimate *knowing* and the *not-knowing* of the motifs is in kind rather than degree. However, "The Perfect Wagnerite" (read G. B. Shaw's book by that name) will know all the "leit motifs" as well as "The Perfect Baseball Fan" knows the rules of the game and the men who play it. It is interesting to differentiate between the "leit motif" of Wagner and the "germinal motive" as we found it in use in Liszt's *Les Préludes*.

ANALYSIS. The Overture to the opera delineates, in condensed form, the central conflict of the action that is to follow, and we shall name the leit motifs as they appear in the Overture so that their narrative function can be more clearly apprehended. First we hear the stately hymn, the *Pilgrims' Chorus*, called the "Salvation by Grace" motive (in the old Breitkopf and Härtel edition that is serving as a source book). This hymn is played softly at the beginning as though heard from afar, and it increases in volume as it approaches, in a slow and majestic pace (*andante maestoso*). It is played, at the onset, by two clarinets, two horns, and two bassoons (fagottos).

Gradually more instruments are added until the full orchestra bursts forth with a new motif called "The Pulse of Life," or "Unfettered Passions." This is a descending sixteenth note figure that appears in the first and second violins, while the trombones and tuba blare out the melody, "Salvation by Grace," just heard. (The descending figure in the violins should be noted carefully as it assumes a most important part in the composition of the Overture.)

This motif goes on for some time, working itself up to a fortissimo climax which eventually dies down to a small volume of tone, when the "Pilgrims' Chorus" theme is heard as though it were far in the distance. (Observe how Wagner has thus provided a well-balanced section.) Notice that for the hymnlike effect Wagner has adhered to the regular, square-cut, four-measure phrase so common in actual hymns.

Suddenly, and in complete contrast, a theme appears like a whisper in the violas, amidst the tremolo figure in the violins; all is hushed, and still, and quietly subdued, suggesting the enchanted background against which the nymphs and bacchantes of Venus' train disport themselves. In fact, this theme is known as the "Venusberg" motif, or one of the nine [*sic*] "Bacchanale" motifs.

No sooner has this wisp of a suggestion passed by when another Bacchanale motif is heard, very softly in the strings and woodwinds, only to give way to the seductive Sirens motif heard in the flutes, oboes, and clarinets, with the strings playing a harplike arpeggio.

Soon the "Venusberg" theme is heard again, this time played at first by the clarinet and then tossed to the bassoons and violas, to be joined at last by the oboes. The dance becomes louder and more impassioned, and presently a new motif is heard in the first and second violins, with a rumbling and most exciting chromatic figure in the 'cellos. The new theme, in the violins, is merely another Bacchanale motif as follows:

This last motif is worked up to a loud, fortissimo, climax, where still another motif bursts forth. This time it is in the strings and woodwinds, and it is called the "Glorification of Venus" motif:

It is obviously a theme of mock majesty, of pomp and circumstance, and it is worked up to a mighty volume of tone by the full orchestra; whereupon, with a sudden drop of dynamics to a mere *piano*, the Venusberg theme appears in the violas with the Siren motif in the woodwinds. The music becomes softer and softer, and almost ethereal, as the strings put on their mutes (*sordini*) and softly trill as though the scene were in an enchanted forest. A note of melancholy, of nostalgia, now is injected into the carefree orgy of the Bacchanale by a sombre melody played by the solo clarinet.

This melody is called the "Love's Ban" motif. It is promptly dispelled by the intrusion of the Venusberg motif; and still another Bacchanale motif is heard, until the full orchestra awakens into new life as though from a dream. All is alive with renewed vigour and agitation, as the Glorification of Venus motif blares forth with all its pomp and power. Without lessening, the Siren motif returns, this time played by the full orchestra, and one realizes that, finally, here is the real climax of the Overture.[3] The Venusberg and Unfettered Passions motifs assume prime importance in the scheme of the composition. Gradually the volume of tone subsides, the strings continue with the Unfettered Passions motif, while beneath is heard the *Pilgrims' Hymn*. An appropriate and brilliant coda is appended for the close in the concert version, providing a subject for much debate among musicians of today as of previous years. Perhaps you would like to discuss the appropriateness of the close provided for the concert version. Have you noticed the counterpoint in this work?

ADDITIONAL SUGGESTIONS FOR LISTENING

We have previously mentioned, among other works in the chapter on religious music, the *Preludes* to LOHENGRIN and PARSIFAL. For other examples of Wagner's symphonic style, listen to the *Prelude* to DIE MEISTERSINGER and to the famous excerpts from the four dramas that

[3] In the so-called "Paris Edition," which Wagner reluctantly made in 1861 to meet the demands of the Paris Opera authorities, he greatly changed the second act and added the "Bacchanale" in Act I. It is at this last point in the programme that the curtain rises, revealing the Venusberg scene with the ballet in progress; of course the music continues without interruption into the opera and the ballet.

constitute the Ring of the Nibelung. From Das Rheingold (the first of the cycle), hear the *Prelude* describing the River Rhine, and the final scene, the *Entrance of the Gods into Valhalla*.

From Die Walk"re (The Valkyrie) listen to the stirring *Ride of the Valkyries* and the *Farewell of Wotan*, culminating in the "Magic Fire" scene. The "Ride" is built upon a clarion figure repeated over and over with a kind of brutal insistence, while headlong chromatic scales and a luminous orchestral background suggest the neighing of the steeds as the Valkyrie hurtle through the storm. In the "Magic Fire" scene that closes the opera, Wotan takes leave of his favourite daughter Brünnhilde. Because she has disobeyed him, Brünnhilde must lose her power as goddess and know all the sorrows of a mortal woman. But Wotan consents to ring her about with a wall of fire so that only the hero may pass through and claim her as his bride. The warrior maiden lies down on the magic rock, clad in her armour, and falls asleep as Wotan summons the god of fire, Loki, to wrap the rock in flame. Lifting his spear, Wotan proclaims that only he who knows no fear may pass through the fire. As he does so he sings the theme of Siegfried who will claim the sleeping goddess in the next opera. The curtain falls upon one of the most poetic scenes on the lyric stage.

The magic of the forest is captured in the *Forest Murmurs* from Siegfried, when, as the hero lies dreaming in the woods after having killed the dragon, the forest whispers to him of his godlike ancestry and a bird tells him of the sleeping beauty who awaits him on the burning height.

From Götterdämmerung listen to Siegfried's "*Rhine Journey*" which proclaims the joyously defiant clarion call of young Siegfried; and from the final act of the opera the "Death Music" for the betrayed hero, one of the mightiest laments in all music.

To round out the suggestions for additional Wagner works, listen to the *Good-Friday Spell* from his last work, Parsifal; and to Siegfried's "Funeral March," which has been called the "greatest threnody in all music" (Gilman), and rightly so for, with the aid of leit motifs borrowed from all the dramas of which Siegfried was a part, the life story of Wagner's hero is told in symbolic detail; and be sure to include that delightful chamber-orchestra work written as a Serenade for Cosima, Siegfried Idyll. From here it will not be difficult for the music lover to make up his own list of "musts."

Chapter Eighteen

Richard Strauss

Realism in Music

IT WAS inevitable, once a musical form had been evolved that was expressly designed to project the message of poetry or painting by means of music, that composers should begin to experiment to achieve an even more graphic style in the depiction of programmatic values. During the decades after Liszt, the symphonic poem moved steadily closer to realism. This shift was undoubtedly accelerated by the tendency toward realism that made itself so strongly felt in the sister arts, especially in literature and painting, throughout the second half of the century. One need but mention the naturalism of Zola who dominated the literary scene in France, of Hardy in England, of Howells and Crane in America, and the romantic realism of such painters as Courbet, Manet, and Millet. All these artists were deeply concerned with drawing their art closer to life, with transplanting the elements of reality with the closest possible fidelity into the art work.

As to composers, those who came after Liszt fell into two camps as far as their handling of the tone poem was concerned. On the one hand were composers like Tchaikovsky and Dukas, who continued in their essentially Romantic attitude toward the programme, making the music suggest the symbol rather than attempting to give a literal tonal imitation of it. On the other hand were realists like Saint-Saëns who, in his *Dance of Death*, gave a graphic representation of the rattle of the skeletons' bones, the howling of the winter wind over the cemetery, the striking of the witching hour, and similar details. This tendency was brought to its high state of development by Richard Strauss, the great naturalist in tone, who adapted Liszt's romantic conception to the more sophisticated temper of our own time and brought the symphonic poem to a stage of realism that Liszt had never foreseen.

Portrait of Georg Gisze   *Holbein*

Elsewhere Romanticism, Classicism, and Impressionism have been discussed and illustrated. Here we have an excellent example of Realism, wherein the hand of the artist tries faithfully to set forth what the eye beholds. Before the advent of photography the sole means of duplicating or simulating objectivity was through man's skill in art. Since then, man has been freed from many of the responsibilities in the direction of portraying reality. With such a knowledge, one cannot but admire the truth and uncanny skill of Holbein's perception and draughtsmanship.

Biography

Born in 1864, a year before Sibelius, Strauss blazed a cometlike path across the musical sky of the 1890's. By this time Liszt and Wagner, the high priests of Romanticism, were dead. Their successors—Saint-Saëns, Tchaikovsky, Rimsky-Korsakoff, Dvořák, Grieg—were middle-aged men entering on the final phase of their careers. They had brought the movement to its final stage; the time was ripe for a new departure. It was in this *fin de siècle* atmosphere that the young Richard Strauss wrote his witty, brilliantly original tone poems, startling and scandalizing his contemporaries, in effect ushering in the "Modern Period."

Strauss was born in Munich amidst a combination of circumstances well-nigh ideal for a future composer. His father was the leading horn player of the Munich Opera orchestra, a thorough musician who saw to it that Richard's musical training was in the strictest classical tradition. His mother came from a wealthy brewing family, so that the budding composer was spared the searing effects of poverty and insecurity. He showed his talent early: at the age of six he composed a polka and a Christmas song. By the time he entered the University of Munich at eighteen he already had had a number of compositions published and performed. Unlike Tchaikovsky and Sibelius, Strauss did not wait until his graduation to decide on a musical career. He left the university at the end of his first year and thenceforth devoted himself to composition.

His early works—a symphony, sonatas, concertos, and quartets in the conventional style—gave no hint of the future *enfant terrible* of programme music. When he was nineteen he met Alexander Ritter, nephew of Wagner and one of the most fervent apostles of the "music of the future," as the new style of Wagner and Liszt was called. The young man was forthwith converted to the programmatic approach—and found his medium. To Ritter he attributed his understanding of Liszt and Wagner and the moulding of his style into the poetic and expressive qualities characteristic of the "music of the future."

Strauss soon became the leader of the "Expressionist" composers, as they were then known. Their motto was: music for expression; their goal: to make music express life. Their uncompromising realism went far beyond the tentative, often naïve efforts of Saint-

Saëns and his generation. They believed that there was no facet
of human experience, whether abstract philosophical speculation,
psychological analysis, biting satire, or raw comedy, that music
could not be made to express. If the result was sometimes harshly
dissonant, that too was an expression of reality: since life was at
times discordant and ugly, why couldn't art be?

From his twenty-third year when he wrote DON JUAN, considered by many his masterpiece, Strauss turned out a series of
tone poems and operas that made him easily the most important
composer of the early 1900's, that seemed for a time to herald the
dawn of a new era in music, and that captured the mood of
Europe before the First World War—the fevered restlessness, the
hectic gaiety, the romantic nostalgia, the wit, the disillusion, the
weariness, the need of strong stimulants—as few artists and certainly no other composer succeeded in doing. Using a gigantic
orchestra, which he handled in masterly fashion—his scores are
of a complexity far beyond anything Wagner or Liszt had dreamed
of—the young iconoclast set out to express things in music that no
one had ever before attempted. Whether it was the jabbering of
the market women in TILL EULENSPIEGEL, the bleating sheep and
whirring windmills in DON QUIXOTE, the battle music in A HERO'S
LIFE, or the inner turmoil in Don Juan's soul, there was no situation, no subtlety of characterization or quirk of plot that Strauss
did not feel supremely able to depict in tones. On the one hand, he
aimed to develop the descriptive powers of his art to such an
extent that it would be possible "to describe a teaspoon in music"
(although there might be some question whether this was worth
doing). On the other hand, he was able to say of his THUS SPAKE
ZARATHUSTRA, with a courage that would have abashed a more
hardened philosopher, that he intended it as a musical expression of the development of the human race from its origin to
Nietzsche's Superman.

We may well understand the bewilderment of the musicians of
the old school. After hearing THUS SPAKE ZARATHUSTRA, Sir
George Grove, the venerable author of the great musical dictionary, wrote: "What can have happened to drag down music from
the high level of beauty, interest, sense, force, grace, coherence,
and any other good quality which it rises to in Beethoven . . .
down to the low level of ugliness and want of interest that we had
in Strauss' absurd farrago? *Noise* and *effect* seem to be so much the

aim now,"[1] Nothing so well illustrates the forward march of history as the fact that Grove held up as the high representative of "beauty, interest, sense" and all the other good qualities Beethoven, who less than a century before had shocked and startled his contemporaries with a new conception of beauty in music.

As for Strauss himself, he not only was not crushed by the opposition, he seemed positively to thrive on it. His early works breathed an amazing vitality and zest, scorching humour, buoyancy and exuberance—the lusty defiance of a young giant with supreme confidence in his power. To the tone poems we have already mentioned may be added MACBETH and DEATH AND TRANSFIGURATION, the latter somewhat more in the poetic tradition of Liszt, and his three principal operas—SALOME (1905), an extraordinarily effective setting of Oscar Wilde's one-act play; ELEKTRA (1909), a powerful one-act music drama centring about the heroine of Greek tragedy; and DER ROSENKAVALIER, or CAVALIER OF THE ROSE (1911), a comedy in the eighteenth-century manner combining Mozartian grace, the Viennese waltz, and the piquant harmonies of the modern idiom.

In all these works Strauss managed in an astonishing way to fuse his Romantic heritage with the idiom of a more modern age. He will go down in the history of music as one of the first great composers of the post-Romantic era. For, although he stemmed from Romanticism—his use of strikingly dramatic plots, his reliance upon theatrical effects of orchestration, and his luscious melodies are all in the great Romantic tradition—there is an element of intellectuality in his work, of sophistication and objectivity that stamps him as a post-Romantic, a child of the twentieth century. Strauss has been called the prose artist of music, the one who substituted the tone of the modern realistic novel with its psychological probings, its devotion to detail, its objectivity for the poetic drama of the earlier epoch. In short, Strauss achieved in music what the "naturalistic" writers of the end of the century—Zola, de Maupassant, Chekhov—achieved in literature. Through his wonderful sense of musical characterization, his bold imagination, the sweep and power of his style, he was able to describe, to analyse, to satirize, to conjure up the details of a scene with a vividness never before achieved. DON JUAN, TILL EULEN-

---

[1] Sir George Grove, *Dictionary of Music and Musicians*. (New York: The Macmillan Company, 1927.)

SPIEGEL, DON QUIXOTE—these are no mere symbols for vague, generalized poetic moods as the protagonists of the earlier tone poems had been. These are fully realized, distinctive individuals hit off with deep insight and psychological acumen, projected with merciless clarity, with an incisiveness and completeness little short of the phenomenal.

The Merry Pranks of Till Eulenspiegel (1895)

Of all Strauss' works, the brilliant portrayal of the medieval rogue, Till Eulenspiegel, has attained the widest popularity. Strauss was thirty-one when he wrote it. He had already written MACBETH, DON JUAN, DEATH AND TRANSFIGURATION, and the opera GUNTRAM. Whether because he was smarting from the reluctance of his fellow musicians to respond to his art or because his genius for comedy was coming to maturity, Strauss now turned his gifts to sarcasm and impudent waywardness. In more than one spot the mocking laughter of the vagabond-rogue seems but to echo his own. As we listen to the startling leaps of flutes and oboes, the bold curve of the melodic line, the novel harmonies and orchestral effects, it is difficult to believe that this music was written but four years after the NUTCRACKER SUITE and two years before FINLANDIA.

The young composer chose a fit symbol, for Till is one of the eternal rebels, the scoffers, who fail to fit into the accepted social patterns. He is related to François Villon and Gil Blas, to Puck and Robin Hood, to Rabelais' lusty Pantagruel and Anatole France's equally lusty Tournebroche. In German folklore he occupies a position analogous to that of Huckleberry Finn and the Katzenjammer Kids in America.

Historically, Till Eulenspiegel—the name, literally translated Till Owl-Glass, is derived from an old German proverb to the effect that "Man sees his own faults as little as an owl recognizes his ugliness in looking into a mirror"—came into German literature through a collection of folk tales and anecdotes about his doings written by Thomas Mürner (1475-1530) toward the end of the fifteenth century. It was a period of vast social change. The feudal system was breaking up under the rise of the guilds and burgesses; the semi-independent barons were being subdued by the centralized monarchy of the modern European state; the new humanism was raising its head against medieval scholasticism; the scene was being laid for the deepest upheaval of all—the revolt against the Church of Rome, the Reformation. In English literature we have a stirring expression of the period in *Piers the Plowman*, in Malory's *Death of Arthur*, and in the works of Chaucer. Mürner, in open revolt against the clergy, told the life of Till as a satire against the smug monks, the domineering lords, and the grasping bourgeois. He pictured Till as continually outsmarting the victims of his wit, dying peacefully in bed after a long and eventful career, and at the very last playing a joke on his heirs by refusing to lie still in his grave. By the end of the nineteenth century, as Strauss knew, society was much more effectively organized to deal with such spirits. His "Till" accordingly pays on the gallows for his daring.

Unlike LES PRÉLUDES and FINLANDIA, in which the music gives a vague suggestion of a vague programme, the music of TILL EULENSPIEGEL depicts the adventures of the rogue in the most literal, realistic terms. Consequently, a knowledge of the programme is much more important for a proper appreciation of this music than is the case with Liszt's or Sibelius's tone poems. Here the listener cannot substitute for the programme of the composer whatever image happens to strike his fancy, for the music at any given moment is depicting a concrete detail of the story. If less leeway is given to the imagination of the hearer, there is compensation in following the cleverness and rich fancy with which the composer has transcribed the images of the everyday world into the world of tone. The programme was derived by Strauss' closest friends from the markings of the principal themes in Strauss' own copy of the score; the music falls into several distinct episodes.

ANALYSIS. "*Once upon a time there lived a wag.*" Violins announce a tender "dipping" theme, piano, setting a mood of long ago and projecting the essential lovableness of the rogue:

"*Named Till Eulenspiegel.*" The staccato Mischief theme symbolizing the wayward side of Till's nature is announced by the horn, piano, in $\frac{6}{8}$ time—a wonderful little etching in tone of the charming scapegrace who has never learned how to stay out of trouble. Notice the subtle shift of accent in the melody whereby the little figure marked "A" begins each time on another beat in the measure.

Like all truly great orchestrators, Strauss hears his themes not as abstract melodic patterns but always in the tone colour of a particular instrument. This theme is fundamentally a horn theme; it is literally moulded to the personality and technical peculiarities of the instrument that announced it. It reveals the secrets of Strauss' brilliance in orchestration—he always makes the instruments do what is specially fitted for them. These two themes and their ingenious transformations will reappear throughout the work. In his use of theme transformation Strauss, a faithful disciple of Liszt, carried the device to even greater lengths than the master.

"Off for new pranks." Repeated in quick succession by various instruments in a rapid crescendo, the Mischief theme is built up into a brilliant climax in which it is proclaimed by the entire orchestra, fortissimo. The scene is set for Till's first escapade. The tender Till theme with its characteristic "dip" is now transformed into roguishness on the clarinet, speeded up into a most flippant rhythm:

"Till in the market place." We hear the click of hoofbeats as Till approaches the market place. The two themes leap about maliciously. He catches sight of the women who sit gossiping in front of their stalls. Till's fertile brain hatches a plan. He sidles closer on his horse; looks about him innocently; suddenly jumps his horse right into the middle of the crowd. There is a terrific din and confusion: fishwives scream, pots and pans clatter, geese cackle—all of which gives Strauss an opportunity to indulge in one of those orgies of orchestral "noise" of which, as a realist, he was so fond.

"*Till and the priests*." The scene shifts. We hear a simple legato melody in the style of the German chorale on clarinets and bassoons:

Violas Clarinets Bassoons (as they sound)

Coming as he did at the end of the century, Strauss completely emancipated himself from the regular four-measure-phrase structure. Yet, notice that here when he wishes to give the effect of a hymn he reverts to the regular phrase pattern.

"*Disguised as a pastor, he drips with unction and morals.*" Till seems to be taking part in one of those theological disputations that formed one of the favourite pastimes of the Middle Ages. But a clarinet sliding precariously down the "dip" of the Till theme reminds us that despite his clerical garb "out of his big toe there peeps the rogue." The priests suddenly realize that Till is mocking them. Little shuddering triplets seem to warn that the scoffer will come to no good end. The first Till theme returns, insouciantly: he isn't afraid—as yet.

"*Till in love.*" A long glissando on the violin tells us that Till is now deep down "in the dumps," a victim of the tender passion. (A *glissando* is a wailing, gliding sound made by passing the fingers in a smooth, unbroken manner over the keys or strings—a common humorous effect used in the cinema.) The present glissando goes from the topmost E flat to the G below middle C—the lowest string on the violin.[2] In this romantic episode, Strauss has had his opportunity of poking fun at the emotional extravagances of the Romantic composers. The Till themes languish, grow sick with longing, now light up with ardour. A lovely romanza (built, as a romanza should be, on the regular four-measure-phrase pattern) emerges as the impassioned swain serenades his beloved. But the lady says *no*, which only whets the suitor's ardour. The Till theme, on brass and strings, becomes agitated. He storms and fumes and threatens to depart; but the fair one remains adamant.

At this point Strauss transforms the whimsical "dip" theme into one of anger by augmenting the time values of the notes—that is, playing them as dotted quarters instead of eighth notes. This kind

[2] For those who can read the score, the glissando is twelve measures before Figure 15.

T

of transformation is called *rhythmic augmentation.* Compare this
version with Mus. Ill. 1, page 269:[3]

The opposite of augmenting a theme would be to diminish the
note values, speed it up, as it were. This process is known as
diminution. We had an example of this when the Till theme reappeared in sixteenth notes on the flutes before the market episode.

Having been rejected in love, his theme is flung out angrily by
the entire orchestra as poor Till storms away. A moment later, we
hear again the mischievous, carefree undulation on the clarinets,
and we are aware that Till is off on his next adventure.

"*Till and the Philistines.*" A persistent, plodding rhythm in the
darkest register of the winds announces the advent of the profes-
sors and pedants, the pompous mediocrities and "stuffed shirts"—
in short, the pillars of society against whom the artist—especially
when he is still young and unsuccessful—is in perpetual revolt. A
brilliant orchestral colloquy follows, with the sparkling Till theme
hurled in defiance against the plodding, nagging chords of the
Philistines. The opposing tonal masses seem to represent personalities and viewpoints that can never come together.

"*Till's self-questioning: should he reform?*" A delightful street song,
with something very naïve and childlike about it (quite like a
polka), ushers in the next episode:

(Note that this is at Figure 26 in the printed score—Aibl
Edition.) Notice that here, too, in order to give the effect of veri-
similitude, Strauss uses the folk-songlike regularity in the four-
measure-phrase structure. As Till watches the contented folk
about him, there steals into his heart that sense of loneliness that
comes sooner or later to all who refuse to submit to the accepted

[3] *One measure after Figure* 19.

order of things. A wave of tenderness passes over the orchestra as Till catches a glimpse of what life might really be if he would only mend his ways. The woodwinds utter a searching question (not unlike the questioning theme in LES PRÉLUDES, with an appropriate rising inflection): should he not try to reform? Just as he is about to succumb, we hear the ascending horn theme of "Mischief" followed by the whimsical "dip" motive, both slowly gathering strength, becoming louder and louder as the realization sweeps over Till that he can never change, that he must remain true to the fundamental character of his nature. Till he is and Till he must remain, come what may!—the orchestra bursts forth in triumph; the Mischief theme, originally played in staccato eighth notes, is now heard in a rhythmic augmentation played by the four French horns and two trombones (at Figure 31 in the printed score and here transposed into the concert key for convenience):

The music breaks forth presently with a joyous, furious dance. The two themes shown in Mus. Ill. 2, page 270, and Mus. Ill. 1, page 273, are developed in intricate orchestral tone patterns and tossed about cleverly from one instrument to another. "Now," thinks Till, "I can really be myself"—or words to that effect.

"*The judgment of Till: his sad end.*" But those who dare to defy society must pay the price. At the height of the festive mood, the brasses proclaim the opening measures of the chorale—the warning of the priests is about to come true. A long drum-roll announces the convening of the court of justice: the culprit has been arrested and brought to trial. Menacing and ponderous chords, *ff*, in the low, dark registers of the brasses, low woodwinds and strings over a roll in the drums, announce the ministers of the law. Unabashed, the irrepressible Till greets them with his defiant theme on the clarinet as though he were mocking them: he is confident that he will wiggle out of this fix as he has out of so many others. The drums roll again; but Till is still cocky. As the court proceeds he loses his composure; the judge obviously means business. The clarinets indicate that Till has become panicky; we hear again the shuddering little triplets from the episode with the priests. Lower strings and brasses pronounce sentence: Till is to be hanged by the neck until dead. There is a savage snarl in tubas and contrabassoons as the trap door is swung. Clarinets and flutes whine piteously. "There he swings; he gasps for air . . . the mortal part of Till is no more." (The hanging of Till is an outstanding example of stark and brutal realism.)

Epilogue. A long pause. And then we hear again the opening measures of the tone poem. "Once upon a time there was a wag named Till—and now you have heard his story." It is a gallant farewell to Till, a passage drenched in nostalgia and dreams. Perhaps he wasn't so bad after all. . . . There is a final outburst of roguery just at the end. Till is dead—but his spirit lives on!

Strauss called his work "a rondo in the old roguish manner." He had a somewhat mischievous intent in labelling his completely programmatic and realistic tone poem with a term reserved for one of the most "abstract" forms of so-called pure music. Increasingly the charge was levelled at the programme composers that their music possessed no inherent musical structure, that it derived all its organization from the literary programme. Strauss took up the challenge by showing his critics that his piece had a musical form, and a quite intricate one at that, at the same time that it told a highly complicated story. Strauss proved his point in more than brilliant fashion. Yet it must be remembered that any tone poem that tells the adventures of a central character can often be adapted to rondo form, if for no other reason than that the theme of the central character will reappear quite naturally after each of the episodes. If this be a rondo, it is certainly one such as the eighteenth-century masters of that form never conceived.

So firmly has the work established itself in the affections of present-day audiences that it is difficult to understand the reactions it aroused only a generation ago.

ADDITIONAL SUGGESTIONS FOR LISTENING

Among the works of Richard Strauss mentioned in the text of this chapter, we suggest that the reader listen to any or all of these Symphonic Poems: DON JUAN, DON QUIXOTE, DEATH AND TRANSFIGURATION, HELDENLEBEN (A Hero's Life) and THUS SPAKE ZARATHUSTRA. It will not be difficult to add to this list, if the reader is eager to hear more of this composer's works.

It will be a splendid challenge to the listener, at this point, to review and compare the character and use of the "germinal motive" of Liszt, the "leit motif" of Wagner, and the realistic "descriptive theme" of Richard Strauss.

Chapter Nineteen

The Sonata and the Symphony
A Romantic Symphonist: Antonín Dvořák

W E HAVE, up to this point, occupied ourselves largely with various kinds of programmatic music, or music that had extra-musical values—the symphonic poem, opera, and music drama, oratorio, suite, ballet, the different kinds of songs, and so forth. We now come to the domain of so-called *absolute* music in which the composer does not necessarily rely on extra-musical associations, either literary or pictorial; in other words, where the "story" of the music is the music itself, and the action consists of the working out of musical themes to their fullest possibilities, as the composer sees them.[1]

Since in *absolute* music, as we here use the word, there is no external literary plot to hold the music together, the form naturally plays a most important part in supplying cohesion and clarity. We may therefore expect to find that the flowering of absolute music is bound up with the emergence of extensive musical forms. Of these, unquestionably the most important is the *sonata* (from *sonare*, to sound, indicating a piece to be sounded as distinct from *cantata*, a piece to be sung). The sonata is an extended musical composition in several contrasting movements, generally three or four, of which the first usually is designed in the sonata-allegro form. It is well to emphasize the word "usually." For just as every novel presents another version of the basic formula of development, climax, and denouement, so here there are so many variations of the form of the sonata as a whole, so many exceptions to rule, that only the most generalized picture of the entire structure can be drawn. Actually, in our study of the sonata we shall aim principally at understanding the basic aesthetic principles that underlie it rather than the technical details of which these are but a manifestation.

---

[1] See article "Absolute Music" in Grove's *Dictionary of Music and Musicians* for more detailed explanation of the term.

The Sonata

The sonata, as signifying a work of several movements, is a form used for all the instruments. There are solo sonatas for piano, for violin, 'cello, organ, and the like, or for any two instruments. If three instruments are involved, we speak of a trio sonata; if four, of a quartet. Quintets, sextets, septets, octets—all refer to the same form, the difference in title merely indicating the number of instruments used. Naturally, the more instruments the greater the opportunity for interplay and contrast among them and the more extended and elaborate the basic form becomes. If the form as a whole is used for solo instrument and orchestra, we have a concerto; thus, we speak of Beethoven's *Piano Concerto*, or Mendelssohn's *Violin Concerto*. And if the form is written for full orchestra, we have one of the noblest and most ambitious types of composition in music: the symphony.[2]

The rise of the sonata was intimately bound up with two of the most important developments in the history of Western European music: the shift in emphasis from vocal to instrumental forms, and the establishment of our major-minor system of keys. We have had occasion to touch on both. It took a long time to realize that instruments could play an independent part in music instead of being merely an adjunct of vocal or dance music. The interludes inserted in the madrigals and operas, the overtures that preceded the performance of vocal works, gradually gave rise to a distinctive instrumental style independent of the older vocal style.

Throughout the seventeenth century instrumental music was emancipating itself from bondage to the voice. The technique of playing rose steadily. The organ, the violin, the harpsichord, and the clavichord came into prominence. Composers faced a new aesthetic problem. As long as they set their music to a text, whether religious, dramatic, or poetic, the meaning of the words furnished a skeleton upon which they could drape their musical inspiration. But in attempting to write for instruments alone they had to organize their musical thinking without any assistance from verbal

[2] When we speak of a *sonata*, we refer to an entire work of several movements; but when we use the term *sonata form*, we refer to a specific first-movement, or *sonata-allegro*, structure consisting of three sections: exposition, development, and reprise. For a fuller description and history of the sonata than we can give here, see articles "Sonata" and "Symphony" in Grove's *Dictionary*, Thompson's *International Cyclopaedia of Music*, Hadow's *Sonata Form*, or any standard reference in music.

association or dramatic plot: they had, in other words, to learn to think along purely musical lines. At first they clung for support to the popular dance rhythms of the day and developed the *suite*, a group of fairly short movements based on popular dances in various rhythms and tempos but all in the same key. As they grew more confident of their ability to think along purely musical lines, they branched off into the more extensive form of the *sonata*.

At the same time that instrumental modes of thought were shaking the supremacy of the vocal style, the new major and minor system of keys was supplanting the modes or scales that had been the foundation of medieval church music. The two tendencies amalgamated in the sonata. Not only did this form represent a more highly organized attempt than had ever been made before to think in terms of pure music by presenting and developing themes that had a distinct personality of their own, but in an even deeper sense the sonata became a drama of contrasting tonalities in which the action shifted from the home-key centre, the tonic, to surrounding tonalities, mainly the dominant, and then triumphantly fought its way back to the original key. The plan of the sonata came to be based upon the new awareness of keys and their relationships, upon what were then daring experiments in modulation and transposition. Throughout the eighteenth century composers experimented with this new drama of keys and themes. Their experiments bore fruit, in the second half of the century, in a magnificent flowering of the Classic sonata form, which reached its peak in the art of the two masters, Haydn and Mozart. Inside of two centuries music had evolved a new language and a new technique, the sheer perfection of which still dazzles us.

The first movement of a typical nineteenth-century sonata is generally allegro. This is, as a rule, the most important of the movements as regards structure, wealth of thematic material, and ingenuity of development. The second movement, for contrast, is andante or adagio in tempo, and cantabile; this is the most lyrical and melodic movement of the set. The third movement, often a minuet, or scherzo vivace in character, is the dance movement, strongly rhythmical and sprightly. The fourth movement, like the first, is elaborate and structurally of impressive dimensions. In the Classical symphony it is generally a rondo—an allegro molto or a vivace built on a dance pattern. In the nineteenth century, the fourth movement more often became a triumphal climax in which the struggle and aspiration of earlier movements were brought to their resolution. Sometimes composers reviewed in the final movement the themes of the previous movements, thus unifying their work most effectively. (Of course it is to be understood that the foregoing is intended only as suggestive generalities, for there are actually no hard and fixed rules.)

We have, then, in the typical sonata, a sequence of four movements, of which the first and fourth are fast and intricate; the second slow and lyrical; the third lively, strongly rhythmic, and dancelike. Sometimes composers switch the second and third movements about; in his *Pathétique Symphony*, Tchaikovsky transposes the slow movement as the Finale.[3] In the celebrated *Moonlight Sonata*, Beethoven began with an adagio and followed it with a minuet and a presto.

We may at this point differentiate between the sonata and the suite of the eighteenth century, which also had several movements. The suite movements were each based on the persistence of a uniform dance rhythm. They were all in the same key. They therefore exhibited none of the dramatic contrast of key and theme, of theme development and organization, which was the very basis of the sonata. In short, the movements of the suite did not aim at that impression of organic unity, of architectural organization, of diversity of mood and material, which distinguished the sonata.

The Symphony

We have, so far, referred to the sonata as being played by a solo instrument, or by several such instruments grouped into a small chamber ensemble; but we now come to the use of the form in a composition to be played by the large number of instruments comprising the modern symphony orchestra—and we appropriately refer to the form thus used also as a *symphony*. Therefore, in a general way, we may think of a symphony as a sonata performed by an orchestra. Of course we realize that countless qualifications and exceptions might be made to such a generality, and we shall

---

[3] The author has always considered this a mechanical rather than a compositional transposition and the third movement to be, in reality, the *Finale proper*, from a compositional standpoint. Witness audience reactions.

soon experience some of the conformities as well as exceptions as we go along in our study. For the present, the general definition is adequate and provocative.

Of course it is to be expected that this larger playing organization, the orchestra, should enrich the structure of the sonata, and the form, in turn, bind together the many different instruments and players that might otherwise seem to be antagonistic to each other or even to fall apart—the form unifies the performing medium. The inherent musical possibilities of the different instruments making up the orchestra, separately and in innumerable combinations, gave a new life and value to the sonata form. Composers were not slow in realizing these possibilities, and their imaginations were awakened as if by magic; they gave free rein to their inventiveness and experimented with new ideas and effects. Out of this has emerged the modern symphony—both the form and the performing medium. Composers dreamed of new vistas and made them come true; and they are still dreaming and experimenting with this seemingly inexhaustible combination of idea and reality—the sonata form and the symphony orchestra.

Boston Symphony Orchestra   *Sergei Koussevitzky, conductor*

We thus have an extraordinary growth in the power and sweep of the nineteenth-century symphony that spread like wildfire over the entire musical world. The symphony became the most important form in music—the equivalent in the tonal art of the fully developed novel of Tolstoy, Thackeray, or Balzac. Just as in the great novel, we have in the symphony the sense of an intensely concentrated emotional experience; the satisfaction of realizing the perfection of the minute parts in their relationship to the nobility and sweeping power of the grand structure; and, withal, the feeling of having actually lived with the varicoloured and vitalized themes for a space of time, and of having watched them grow, develop and pass on, as we do with the leading characters in a great novel.

And all these desiderata can be accomplished with or without extra-musical implications. Truly a great and noble instrument had come into the hands of the composer, and the rich symphonic literature that is our heritage stands as eloquent evidence to the justification of the efforts and circumstances that brought both the large symphonic form and the large symphonic orchestra to their present high state of perfection.[4] The years have shown, and continue to show, the adaptability of both form and medium to the highly diversified individual needs of our great composers, not the least among these being the symphonic poet of the common folk—Antonin Dvořák (dvôr'zhäk).

Antonin Dvořák (1841-1904) and His Symphony "From the New World"

We begin our listening study with the perennially popular *From the New World* SYMPHONY IN E MINOR, Op. 95, of Antonin Dvořák. This has a special interest for Americans since it was written while the composer was living in that country, and it presents some of his impressions of the New World. By far the most generally accepted of his works in this form, the vigorous rhythms and lovely melodies of this symphony have won for it a high place in the affections of

---

[4] It would be traditional to stop here for an inquiry into the technical details of the sonata-symphony form and to use them as a basis of intellection; but, as has been our philosophy and practice, we shall do so—if at all then necessary—only after we have enjoyed to the full the uniqueness of the listening experience.

the public, and it is today, half a century after it was written, one of the most widely and frequently played compositions in symphonic literature.

Biography

The composer of the universally beloved *Humoresque* and *Songs My Mother Taught Me* was born in 1841, a year after Tchaikovsky, near Prague. His father, a village butcher and innkeeper, could do little for the boy, whose musical gifts were evident from childhood. Local musicians who believed in Antonin's talents helped him through the period when poverty threatened to put an end to his musical aspirations. But when he reached the age of sixteen, he was able to get to Prague where he pursued his musical education in earnest.

For more than ten years, during which he supported himself by playing viola in the orchestra of the Czech National Theatre in Prague and by giving private lessons, only a few of his intimate friends knew anything about his attempts at composition. Gradually, though, his works made headway and began to attract the attention of the musical world. His first great success came in 1873, when he was thirty-two, with his HYMNUS, a work for voices and orchestra infused with intense devotion to his fatherland, which was under Hapsburg dominion. From then on he espoused the cause of Czech nationalism, turned to the folk songs, dances, and legends of his beloved Bohemia and, under the influence of his older contemporary, Smetana, became one of the leading figures of the Czech nationalist school. The songs and dances of the Gipsy fiddlers who had passed through his father's tavern, the songs and dances of the village folk among whom he had grown up, formed the chief source of his inspiration.

Enabled by his success to devote himself exclusively to composition, he produced a series of works that spread his fame and the cause of Czech music throughout the world. Among the works directly inspired by his nationalism may be mentioned the MORAVIAN DUETS, the popular SLAVONIC DANCES, the three SLAVONIC RHAPSODIES for orchestra, the dramatic overture HUSITSKA, dedicated to the national ideal of religious freedom as symbolized by the martyr Jan Huss and the Hussite movement, the oratorio LUDMILLA, and the folk operas, RUSALKA, KING AND COLLIER,

THE CUNNING PEASANT, THE PIGHEADED PEASANT, all set to the works of Czech nationalist poets and suffused with the folklore and folkways of Bohemia.

Like Tchaikovsky and Sibelius, Dvořák was not only a nationalist. Besides the programme works directly inspired by his love of country, he wrote much in the "absolute" forms, carrying on the great tradition of Beethoven and Schubert, Schumann and Mendelssohn. His symphonies, trios, quartets, and quintet, while adapting the hallowed Classical forms to his needs as a Romantic and a nationalist, nevertheless show an impressive command of musical structure and an ability to think in the classical spirit, or temper. In this domain he was influenced and encouraged by Brahms, who became his staunch friend.

Toward the end of the century, Dvořák was recognized as one of the ranking composers of his time. In 1891, at the tercentenary celebration of Cambridge University, he was among the musicians—Tchaikovsky was another—who were given the honorary degree of Doctor of Music. He was made professor of composition at the Prague Conservatoire, elected to the Czech Academy of Art and Science, and decorated by the Austrian government. In 1892—a year after Tchaikovsky's visit to America—he was invited to go to New York and direct the National Conservatory of Music. He was enthusiastically welcomed there and remained for three years, achieving great success as teacher, conductor of his own works, and composer. He travelled through the country, responding to its vastness, its great cities, its sense of power and promise. His summers he spent in the simple, intimate atmosphere of the Czech colony at Spillville, Iowa, where he could almost fancy himself back in his native land.

Despite his great success in America, his homesickness grew apace. In 1895 he returned to Europe. His joy at the prospect of homecoming found expression in a series of short piano pieces, the *Humoresques*, of which the seventh has become a most popular gem. After his return he took up his post at the Prague Conservatoire, becoming director of the school in 1901. In the final period of his career he devoted himself exclusively to symphonic poems and operas based on legendary material. His best work along these lines, the poetic opera RUSALKA, belongs to these years. His death in 1904 at the age of sixty-three was mourned by the entire Czech nation as well as by music lovers all over the world.

He was a master of warm, spontaneous melody, of poetic and lyrical moods. His peasant stock and his love for the folk came out in his vigorous rhythms and his strongly accented musical speech. He was one of the masters of orchestration, achieving magical effects with the subtlest of means, especially in his works for smaller instrumental combinations. A poet of nature, he was steeped in the music of the rivers and prairies of his fatherland. There is a warmth and freshness of feeling about his music, a verve and manliness, a tenderness and a humanity that have endeared him to the multitude.

"*Symphony in E Minor*" (*From the New World*), *Op. 95*

The most famous of Dvořák's orchestral works was completed in 1893 in the Bohemian colony at Spillville, Iowa, where the homesick composer had gone to be as close as possible to the language and customs of his native land. It aroused a violent controversy when it was first performed: did it really capture the spirit of the New World, or was it, despite the Negro and Indian flavour of some of its themes, a work fundamentally Czech in character and outlook? The issue no longer seems as crucial as it once did. There can be no question that Dvořák, a great nationalist composer acting as teacher and guide to the younger generation of American musicians, gave much thought to the establishment of an American school and the development of a musical idiom that would express the spirit and strivings of the new continent. Music in America at that time was largely in the hands of men who had been trained abroad in the traditions of German Romanticism and who simply transplanted those traditions to another soil. Edward MacDowell, the first American composer to make an impression on the world scene, was still a young man. Stephen Foster's songs, in the true folk style, had been thus far the only real attempt to discover a distinctively American vein. Dvořák naturally felt that his students ought to do the same thing that he and Smetana had done in Bohemia, that Tchaikovsky and Rimsky-Korsakoff had done in Russia: they should turn to the indigenous rhythms and melodies of the folk. In attempting to portray in music his impressions of the New World and the emotions that it aroused in him Dvořák is said to have turned, in parts of the Symphony, to the inspiration of the Negro and Indian musical idiom, though the composer himself denied the contention. At the same time he was a European writing in the musical language that was natural for him. It would therefore be erroneous to regard the Symphony as American music. Rather it presents the impressions of a gifted and sensitive visitor, just as does the *Italian Caprice* of Tchaikovsky, or the *Spanish Caprice* of Rimsky-Korsakoff.

In any case, the *New World* SYMPHONY reveals Dvořák's gifts—spontaneous melody, vigorous rhythms, colourful orchestration, firm grasp of form, and a natural flow of ideas—at their best. Note how Dvořák obtains a feeling of unity and coherence between the several movements of the Symphony by restating themes that had appeared in previous movements—a species of "cyclical" treatment. See if you can discover the reappearances of such themes. The structure and form of the Symphony, as a whole and in parts, is very orthodox and "classical."

ANALYSIS. FIRST MOVEMENT: *Adagio—allegro molto. E minor. $\frac{2}{4}$ time.* The slow introduction gives a sense of mystery and spaciousness, beginning pianissimo and bearing traces of Indian song. The opening phrase of the 'cellos is answered by flutes and oboes. The music seems to draw nearer and nearer in a great swell and plunges us into the brusqueness and vigour of the movement proper, allegro molto.

The principal theme is announced by the horns in E minor, *mf* (*mezzo forte*), a bold arpeggio ascending and descending along the tones of the chord in the syncopated rhythm that already at that time impressed Dvořák as characteristic of the American musical idiom. (*Syncopation* means that the accent falls not on the strong beat of the measure, where we normally expect it, but on the weak beat, the "offbeat", producing an effect of waywardness and irregularity that adds a pleasant "snap" to the rhythmic effect. Thus, in the theme below we have in the second and fourth measures an unaccented eighth note falling on the principal beat of the measure, the "one," while the accented quarter note is shifted to the offbeat. This effect, characteristic of the shuffling dance steps of the Negroes of the South, became one of the most distinctive features of American dance music.)

The vigorous syncopation is retained as the theme is unfolded, first *ff* by the strings in unison, then *fff* by the entire orchestra. A short bridge, which modulates to G minor, leads to the first part of the second theme, announced by flutes and oboes, pianissimo, that has all the poignance of a Bohemian folk tune.

The naïve character of this melody is accentuated by the regular phrase structure. Shifted into the major mode, it is ingeniously transformed into a typical frontier song and has been used as accompaniment for countless Western scenes in the movies. Notice the engaging syncopation of the rhythm and the F natural in the last measure.

The second part (or real second theme) follows and, for reasons of comparison, the original *Swing Low* melody is shown below it.

Notice the regularity of phrase structure, the effect of the syncopation in the second and sixth measures, and the major mode. with the fortissimo repetition of this theme we come to the double bar, whereupon the entire section is repeated.

In the next section the themes are developed, or worked out. Fragments of the *Swing Low* melody are tossed about among the various choirs. The ascending-descending arpeggio figure of the first theme is hurled forth intermittently by the bass instruments. The themes take on new life from these startling juxtapositions; the music modulates frequently, shifting us from one tonality to another. After a fortissimo climax, a gradual retransition leads us back to the home tonality of E minor, where we hear the first theme as we heard it originally.

From then on we hear the three themes substantially as they appeared in the first section. For reasons that we shall soon consider, they are not in the same key as they were in the first section of the movement; they have been shifted bodily, or transposed, to other keys. But the melodies themselves are unchanged.

The third theme is followed by a coda marked by impetuously descending chromatic scale passages. The first theme, boomed forth triumphantly at the end by strings and trombones, leads into the stirring final cadence.

We therefore see that the *first-movement form* consists of three sections. In the first the themes are presented, or exposed; hence this section is known as the *exposition*. In the second, the development, the themes are developed or worked out. In the third, the *recapitulation*, or *reprise*, the themes are repeated or reviewed as at first. An introduction may often open the movement and a coda (a tailpiece) usually brings it to a close.

At this point the reader will quite naturally see a resemblance between the *sonata-allegro*, or *first-movement*, *form* and *ternary*, or *A-B-A*, *form*.[5] While the first-movement form contains three sections, of which the first and third are similar, the structural principle is not quite the same as in A-B-A form. In the latter we have unity in the two "A" sections and contrast in the "B." In first-movement form, the exposition (the "A") contains a contrast within itself, since two or more themes and keys are presented. The development (the "B"), although it contains contrast and variety, nevertheless uses the same basic thematic material as the first section presented in a new guise. The third section, the recapitulation, restores the themes in their original form to the home key. We have here the same basic effect of unity, contrast, and variety as in the simple A-B-A form, but this is achieved in a far more intricate design. These two forms satisfy a similar fundamental human desire for balance and symmetry. If the first-movement form had for its object merely the presentation of a succession of pleasant melodies, it would not differ substantially from the suite, or any of the lighter forms, such as Salon music. But because it presents these melodies of a more serious vein in an intricate, highly co-ordinated key organization, the first-movement form takes its place as one of the most ingenious and significant structural forms in music. Here key and modulation become the very determinants of form, and they do this, as we shall see, efficiently and subtly.

[5] The terms *first-movement form* and *sonata-allegro form* are here used interchangeably.

SECOND MOVEMENT: Largo, D-flat major. $\frac{4}{4}$ *Three-part, or song, form.* Mysterious chords, *ppp*, on bassoons and brass instruments usher in as a solo on the English horn one of the most famous melodies in symphonic literature.

The reedy, yearning quality of the instrument brings out to the full its poignant wistfulness. Here the son of a Bohemian village merchant has caught a world-wide feeling and has expressed it eloquently. It has been said that Dvořák was thinking of "Hiawatha's Wooing," but there is little substantiation. Set to the words of "Going Home," the melody has become widely popular with singing groups.

After the unfolding of the melody, which is based on a three-phrase pattern, we are shifted from the serene major mode into a dark, sombre minor, pianissimo, in a passage of brooding tenderness. It argues well for the universal quality of music that while for some this part has the flavour of a Bohemian lullaby, for others it might have the awesome beauty of a night on the prairie or a connotation closer to the individual listener's fancy.

Now the oboes and flutes begin to trill in what might conceivably be a nature scene.

Violins follow suit; the tempo quickens; the whole orchestra becomes tremulous with excitement. When it subsides we return to *Tempo I*; the *Going Home* melody is sung by the English horn; the movement flows on for a little while and then dissolves in a pianissimo chord for double basses.

U

THIRD MOVEMENT: Scherzo. Molto vivace. ¾ time. E minor. Minuet and trio (A-B-A)form.[6] In the "Scherzo" Dvořák forgets all about the New World and lets himself be swept away in a wave of nostalgia for the folk dances of his native land. A strumming accompaniment on violins and 'cellos introduces the first theme, its gaiety subtly overcast, as so often happens in Slav dances, by the minor mode. (The student may have noticed from the heading that we are now back in the E-minor tonality of the first movement.) An abrupt, twitching rhythm imparts a curious zest to the theme, which is piped staccato in high register by flutes and oboes:

As in many folk dances, the structure here is based on the regular four-measure phrase. The melodic imitation in this passage is interesting to follow.

After a repetition of this section we are brought into a suave major mode, *poco sostenuto* (a little sustained), where a gracefully swaying, almost languid dance is intoned by flutes and oboes against a string accompaniment. The asymmetrical formation—a three-measure phrase answered by one of five phrases—lends an elusive charm to the movement (Goetschius calls this the first Trio):

The melody is brought back in the bass, sung in mellow tones by bassoons and 'cellos, while the chords of the accompaniment soar

[6] According to the eminent American theorist, Percy Goetschius, this is a song-form with *Two* Trios; according to an equally eminent English theorist and programme annotator, Donald Tovey, the Scherzo is a simple song-form with *One* Trio, Mus. Ill. 2, page 288, being considered merely an interlude. Others describe the form as a Minuet and Trio with *Two* themes each.

high ahove. Then, *a tempo* (in the prevailing time), we return to the bı ttle staccato of the opening theme. Presently, in what Goetschius calls the *second* Trio and what many others call the *one* Trio proper, the strings play a bell-like reiteration over which the woodwinds play a motive not unlike a trumpet call.

The *Da Capo Scherzo* (repeat the scherzo from the beginning) rounds off the contrast with the "Trio." In the coda the reminiscence of the first movement suddenly returns, but this time it materializes into a full-fledged appearance, *fff*, of the ascending-and-descending arpeggio theme. As it fades, the rhythm of the opening of the Scherzo flits past, *ppp*, and a fortissimo final chord brings the movement to an abrupt close.

FOURTH MOVEMENT: Allegro con fuoco (fast, with fire). E minor. $\frac{4}{4}$ time. First-movement, or sonata-allegro form. Out of a tempestuous introduction emerges a marching song given out fortissimo by horns and trombones. Even the minor mode cannot dim the sense of power and promise, the high determination and courage that breathe through this music.[7]

(Note that the D natural at the mark N.B. shows the underlying scale structure to be the Aeolian Mode, an old Church "scale.") The theme is repeated with heightened colour by violins and woodwinds in high register. The music broadens into a torrent of triplets that courses onward, sweeping everything before it. There

---

[7] Dr. Sigmund Spaeth, in his book *A Guide to Great Orchestral Music* (New York: Random House, 1943), suggests that the opening theme of the final movement might have been influenced by an American folk song, "Peter Gray," and, further, that the final gay theme resembles "Yankee Doodle."

is a terrific energy and exultance about this transitional passage that leads to the second theme.

The mood changes to one of reverie. The second theme, given to the solo clarinet, unfolds in broad curves of melody to a climax on the strings (note the frequent interruptions by the 'cellos):

We are plunged into a popular fortissimo melody, each of whose phrases ends with three detached descending notes. This third (or closing) theme is sung by flutes and violins:

Expansive and joyous, it is a song for vast multitudes. The three descending notes at the end are repeated in the bass by 'cellos and basses and then blossom out as the opening of the familiar tune "Three Blind Mice" bandied about by the orchestra with humour and imagination. Now deep down amidst the bass strings, now high up on the woodwinds, this distinctive descending motive persists in imitative style against an intricate countermelody and finally disappears, imitated by a number of instruments at various registers in a continuous downward curve.

The development section is a rich mosaic of the three themes, the connective material, plus reminiscences of previously heard themes. The March theme on the horns, sounding mysteriously as from a distance, is pitted against fragments of the "Three Blind Mice" theme. Familiar melodies heard in new rhythmic patterns are interspersed among the energetic triplets that lent such verve to the exposition. Echoes of the "Going Home" theme from the *Largo* wreathe about the March theme like a pale memory. The syncopated arpeggio of the opening theme of the Symphony suddenly spurts upward in a surge of excitement, ever more pressing, until the March theme appears fortissimo against downward chromatic scales. The music veers toward the home key of E minor.

In the recapitulation, Dvořák touches upon the thematic material of the exposition. The March theme appears in E minor, strangely subdued. The dreaming second theme rises to a sonorous curve as before, but its orchestral colouring is altered. The popular song (third theme) has a plaintiveness about it. The recapitulation is in the nature of a brief review, preparing the way for the electrifying coda. The ascending-and-descending arpeggio of the opening movement gives way to a fortissimo entrance of the March theme. From a headlong climax we are thrust into the opening chords of the *Largo*, while the strings produce an upward thrust of great billows of sound. An abrupt diminuendo and a fragment of the "Going Home" theme sweep past in startling juxtaposition to the twitching opening rhythm of the *Scherzo*. It is as though all the themes we watched grow and expand in the earlier movements were hurrying past for a brief summation before the close. A last solemn announcement of the March theme, and we are swept into the final broad cadence on an E major—instead of minor—chord, an ending called, *Tierce de Picardie*.

Schematic Outline of a Symphony as a Whole

The first movement, or sonata-allegro, form

The first movement is often the most important of the entire work. It carries, in the sonata-allegro form, the fundamental principles of musical structure—unity and variety—to their utmost realization. Just as in the novel the action consists of the psychological and emotional interaction between several clearly defined personalities and the working out of their destiny in relation to one another, so here we are presented with two well-defined themes or groups of themes in contrasting character and tonalities, the action consisting in exploring their possibilities as independent entities and in working out their relationship—their "struggle"—with each other.

Since the first movement of the sonata was generally allegro, the first-movement form came to be known as *sonata-allegro form*. The term is not entirely satisfactory, since it is easy to confuse *sonata-allegro,* which refers specifically to the first movement, with *sonata,* which covers the three or four movements of the entire work. For this reason, many theorists in this country prefer to use *first-movement form,* which is not a good term either, since the form is sometimes used also for other movements, notably the fourth; but it is the best nomenclature we have.

We have seen that the first-movement form consists of an exposition, a development, and a recapitulation, which work out the contrast or "conflict" between two groups of themes in contrasting keys. Let us now see how this theme and key organization is worked out.

The exposition. The function of the exposition is to present the two themes or groups of themes out of which the movement is to be constructed. The first theme or group of themes is placed in the home, or tonic, key; the second theme or group of themes is in a foreign key. (In the typical Classical symphony, the second theme was generally in the key of the dominant—the key, that is, whose tonic was a fifth above—when the first theme was in the major. If the first theme was in the minor, the second theme was in the relative major; that is, the major key whose signature is the same as that of the minor. Thus, if the first theme was in C major, the second was in G major. If the first was in A minor, the second was in C major.)

A few words of advice to the listener: Listen intently to the themes in the exposition, over and over again, until they are memorized and can be readily recalled at will, either for enjoyment in themselves or for the added pleasure of making comparisons with what the composer might be doing with the theme, or themes, at the moment—so necessary in the development section. Again—memorize the themes and carefully watch their adventures throughout the movement, or symphony as a whole. If you will do this very simple thing, your enjoyment will be more certain.

In the first-movement form, the contrast in character between first and second theme may be reinforced by a contrast in dynamics (such as first theme *f,* second *p*); in register (first theme high, second low); in tempo (first theme fast, second slow); in rhythm (first theme vigorous and strongly accented, second languid); in phrase structure (first theme regular, second irregular); in tone quality (first theme legato, second staccato); in timbre (first theme given to strings, second to woodwinds or brass); above all in mode, by far the most effective contrast of all (first theme major, second minor). It is apparent that a striking combination of these contrasting elements will produce a complete emotional and psychological opposition between the two themes. Thus, in Beethoven's FIFTH SYMPHONY the first theme is brusque, passionate, choppy, in a sombre minor—"masculine" and commanding (in C minor):

The second is serenely lyrical, tender, legato, in major—"femininely" yielding (in E-flat major, the relative major key):

Similarly, in Tchaikovsky's FIFTH SYMPHONY, the first theme is staccato, rhythmically abrupt, in minor mode, intoned by the woodwinds (in E minor):

The second is legato, molto cantabile ed espressivo, flowing, in major, sung by the strings (in B minor—an unusual relative key):

In musical texts the first theme is generally referred to as the principal theme; the second, as the subordinate. This terminology is somewhat misleading, since it implies that the first is more important than the other, whereas what is meant is simply that the first is in the tonic, or home, key, and the second in the foreign key. Many theorists are therefore abandoning these terms and speaking of the first, second, and third themes.

Between the first and second themes or groups of themes comes a transition, or bridge, whose function it is to lead us from the home key to the foreign key. This bridge plays a most important part in the design, since its function is to carry us through the modulation from the tonality of the first theme to that of the second theme. Besides the first theme, bridge, and second theme, the exposition may contain an introduction, generally slow, before the composer plunges into the allegro of the movement proper, and a coda or codetta to round out the exposition of the themes. The introduction, which precedes the first theme, will be in the home key. The coda or codetta, which follows the second theme, will be in a foreign key, the same as the second theme. The composer sometimes employs a third, or closing, theme in the exposition, often in the home key.

The development. In the exposition, the composer makes use of his ability to create memorable themes; in the development, he exhibits his ingenuity in working them out: he displays his mastery over the technical resources of his art. He may take a snatch of his principal theme and combine it with a few bars of the subordinate theme, exhibiting both in an altogether new light. Or strains of his slow introduction may be used with various combinations of either of his themes. The development explores the latent possibilities of thematic material; reveals it in an altogether new light. The development is the most strictly intellectual part of the first movement. It is easy to understand how "intellectual" composers like Beethoven and Brahms brought this section to the highest level of importance and achieved some amazing effects in the manipulation of their thematic material.

The exposition, as we have seen, is built around two tonalities, or key centres, the tonic of the principal theme and the foreign key of the subordinate theme. But the development, which must give the listener the sense of leading him on to ever-fresh vistas, avoids the stabilizing effect of a definitely established tonality. In other words, just as it shifts constantly from scraps of one theme to those of another, so it shifts from one tonality to the next, this freedom of modulation contributing to the continual piquancy and interest of its progressions. It does, however, avoid the home key, which is saved for the "return" in the next section.

When the composer has had his say in the working out of his themes he gets ready for the return to the tonality and mood of his principal theme. Here he makes use of a rather elaborate retransition that brings us to the threshold of the home key.

The recapitulation, or reprise. The main point about the recapitulation is that it must resemble rather closely the exposition, with all the principal themes back in the original key, so that, after all the complexity of the development, we get here the definite impression of a return home, a feeling of satisfactory balance and unity. The recapitulation therefore re-exposes the first theme in the tonic key. When we come to the bridge, however, the composer abandons the plan of the exposition for a very good reason. In the exposition, the bridge and second theme modulated to a foreign key because the whole movement was ahead. Now, however, we are too close to the end of the movement to be able to leave the home tonality with impunity. The composer therefore presents the melody of the second theme as formerly—but he shifts it from the former foreign tonality into the home tonality; in other words, he transposes it to the key of the first theme. After this comes the closing theme and then the coda, which affirms as emphatically as possible the cadence chords of the home key in what is often a most stirring finale to the movement. The recapitulation is therefore either entirely in the tonic key or as close to it as possible.

We say "or as close to it as possible" because when the first theme is in the major and the second theme in the minor, or vice versa, the second theme often cannot be exactly transposed in the recapitulation to the key of the first. What the composer then does is to shift the second theme, if it is in minor mode, to that minor key that is closest in relationship to the major key of the first theme, though composers often do change the modes to conform to the first theme. Usually a section called a *coda* brings the movement to a close.

The following diagram will aid the student in visualizing the entire structure (bear in mind that this is merely a general pattern):

FIRST-MOVEMENT, OR SONATA-ALLEGRO, FORM

Slow Introduction (optional)

Exposition	*Development*	*Recapitulation*
1. Principal theme Tonic key	modulates freely	1. Principal theme Tonic key
Bridge, or transition, modulating to	avoids home key	Bridge remains in or close to home key

Exposition	*Development*	*Recapitulation*
2. Subordinate theme foreign key (dominant) or relative major	presents the thematic material of exposition in new combinations and transformations. Leads back, via transition to—	2. Subordinate theme transposed to tonic key
(Possible third, or closing theme) often in tonic key Codetta, ending in foreign key to— ("double bar and repeat" here in Classical form)		(all other themes in tonic key) Coda, reaffirming tonic key for Final and closing cadence.

The second movement

If the first movement is a highly involved part of the symphony, exhibiting a deep intellectual grasp of the material, the second movement, by contrast, is the more simple, lyrical, songlike section. Here the composer abandons the complexities of formal structure for melody pure and simple, of a pensive, serene, often of a melancholy character. This is the usual slow movement of the symphony, marked *andante*, *adagio*, or if very broad, as in Dvořák's NEW WORLD SYMPHONY, *largo*. The form frequently used is the simple, two-part (binary) or three-part (ternary) song—that is, either an A-B or A-B-A structure. The theme-and-variation form is also favoured by composers; examples are to be found in the second movements of Haydn's SURPRISE SYMPHONY and Beethoven's FIFTH SYMPHONY. The mood of the slow movement is intensely lyrical, intimate, personal, in contrast to the loftiness and more abstract character of the first movement. If the latter were stormy and agitated, in the andante all is tenderness and serenity. Schubert, Schumann, Beethoven, Brahms—all have revealed their deep humanity in the andantes and adagios of their symphonies and sonatas. Sometimes sonata-form, sonatina, and other forms are used in the slow movement.

It must be emphasized again that in this description only the typical outline, one might even say the stereotyped outline, of the form of the sonata is being presented. The reader must guard against the notion that there is anything fixed or rigid about

musical form. Actually, the form springs out of what the composer
has to say and the materials with which he says it. At the beginning of his career the composer will tend to shape his material on
the accepted moulds of the masters before him. But as he grows in
maturity he grows also in freedom and changes the accepted forms
or alters them to suit his own needs. Form, in this sense, is a fluid,
ever-shifting essential in art, and any attempt to regard it as fixed
or inflexible must lead to a basic misconception of its real value
and function. So here the composer is free to do in the second
movement, or the third, what he feels necessary in order to express
his conception. What the technical analyst of form can state is
merely that at a certain period a number of composers seem to have
preferred some forms to others.

The third movement

The third movement, in contrast to the lyrical slow movement,
is the dance movement of the sonata; in it one or more marked
rhythmic patterns predominate. The mood is often vivace; the
tempo is usually a lively allegro. In the Classical sonata the
minuet was the dance preferred for this movement, capturing the
courtly grace of the eighteenth century. Beethoven substituted the
scherzo (from the Italian word meaning a "jest")—a rapid, lilting
movement in triple metre like the minuet, but faster, jollier, more
vivacious. Sometimes it even had an overtone of grimness, as at
some cosmic jest that only an ironic Destiny would have conceived. Actually, even some of the Haydn minuets, at the end of
the eighteenth century, absorbed an extraordinary folk flavour.
With the Beethovenian scherzo, however, the third movement
was forever emancipated from the formal elegance of the minuet
form and became in the hands of the Romantic composers a
remarkably flexible medium for the most varied moods of the
dance.

In form, the Classical third movement consists of a minuet and
trio (so called because in the early eighteenth century the trio
section was generally played by three instruments. As often happens in music, the name has persisted long after the practice has
become obsolete). After the trio, the minuet is repeated. Instead of
writing it out again, composers would generally indicate the
repetition by putting down *minuet da capo* (the minuet to be played

from the beginning). The minuet-and-trio form is therefore a species of A-B-A structure. The minuet and/or the trio sometimes contain two tunes each, arranged in a simple pattern so that each section is really a small three-part form. In metre, the minuet, like our modern waltz, is in triple time. In mood, the trio is somewhat less sprightly than the minuet itself—more legato and sustained.

The scherzo keeps the general outline as well as the metre of its predecessor, but it goes at a much faster pace. Sometimes it is in duple metre. Its outstanding contribution to the entire work is a mood of boisterous, headlong gaiety communicated through incisive, compelling rhythms. Of course, composers are free to use other basic forms for this movement. For example, Tchaikovsky in his FIFTH SYMPHONY uses a waltz for the third movement; in his SIXTH SYMPHONY, a melody in $\frac{5}{4}$ time!

The fourth movement

Since the second and third movements are comparatively simple in form, the composer often uses an ambitious structural form for the final movement. In the Classical sonata, the rondo, gay, light, and good-humoured, was preferred. This form, we saw, came from an old French dance form, the rondeau, in which the opening tune comes back again and again; as in ABACA, or ABACADA (see page 4). The rondo leaves the audience in a good humour; it reached its greatest popularity in an epoch when optimism was a prevailing mood in art. Sometimes a theme and variation form were used, also the sonatina, a miniature variant of the sonata-allegro form, in which the development section was either absent or present only in a rudimentary state. Less often the sonata-allegro form was used.

As the Romantic composers began to experiment with the sonata, good humour at the end gave way more and more to a mood of exaltation, of triumph, of dramatic achievement. Thus, the complex sonata-allegro form came to be frequently used in the finale, balancing the first movement; in the symphony, the final movement often became an impassioned hymn of victory. Beethoven's FIFTH and NINTH, Tchaikovsky's FIFTH, Dvořák's NEW WORLD, the symphonies of Brahms, César Franck, and Sibelius all exhibit this quality of a sort of victory at the end. As often as not, the final movement contains references to themes heard in earlier movements—a kind of farewell review, in which case we speak of the work as *cyclical* in treatment. In any case the fourth movement generally ends with an imposing finale that does double duty in providing *a fitting ending not only for this particular movement but for the work as a whole.* We may now diagram the entire symphony as follows, but merely as a hypothetical and conventionalized case for immediate and practical reasons:

First Movement:

> Sonata-allegro form.
> Tempo: allegro.
> Intricate structure. Seriousness of mood. "Absolute" style.
> Presents principal themes of the work.
> "Intellectual" handling of material.
> Thematic development and architectonic treatment predominant features.

Second Movement:

> Simple binary or ternary song form.
> Theme and variation or sonatina form sometimes used.
> Tempo: andante, adagio, largo, cantabile, and so forth.
> Emotional, lyrical, personal, melodic. Songlike character predominates.
> Intimacy of mood.
> Emotional content predominant. Simplicity of structure.
> Sonatina form sometimes used.

Third Movement:

> Minuet and trio form (Minuet repeated after trio, da capo, A-B-A).
> Tempo: vivace, allegro vivace, and so forth.
> Rhythmic, lively, graceful. Dance character predominant.
> After Beethoven supplanted by scherzo.
> Vigorous, very fast. Simple structure.
> Both minuet and scherzo in triple metre, usually.
> Novel dance forms sometimes used.

Fourth Movement:

> Rondo form most popular in Classical sonata.
> Theme and variation; sonatina form sometimes used.
> Sonata-allegro form favoured by Romantic composers.

Tempo: allegro molto, allegro con brio, allegro con fuoco, and so forth.

Triumphal in mood. Imposing coda or finale.

Sometimes contains references to themes heard in previous movements—cyclical form; and effective device for unifying the work.

Climactic drive and cumulative aspects predominant. *Provides fitting climax for work as a whole.*

Chapter Twenty

Beethoven

Classicism and Romanticism in Ideal Balance

Ludwig van Beethoven (1770-1827)

BETWEEN the Classical spirit of the late eighteenth century and the Romantic upheaval of the early nineteenth stands Ludwig van Beethoven, heir of the old and harbinger of the new, one of the most arresting figures in the whole realm of art. He was in his early twenties when the slogan "Liberty, Equality, Fraternity" lit a flame in the heart of modern man.[1] He was barely thirty when the armies of General Bonaparte, who was then still the symbol of the new order, swept over Europe. Beethoven, therefore, as Edward Carpenter has well said, stands as the prophet of a new era launched by the nineteenth century—a forerunner of Shelley and Whitman in poetry, Turner and Millet in painting. He it was who became the spokesman of the new Romanticism, who brought into music the pathos, the sense of man's struggle with destiny and of his ultimate triumph, the passion, and the surging emotion of the new era. Like Bach and Wagner, Shakespeare and Goethe, he towers above his age, giving expression to its profoundest stirrings and leading it into new paths of self-realization.

Biography

Ludwig van Beethoven was born in Bonn, the famous university town near Cologne, December 16, 1770. Both his father and grandfather were musicians in the court band of the Elector of Cologne. He learned to play the violin and clavier from his father, and the organ from the court organist. His gifts revealed themselves early in his childhood. At eight he appeared in concert; at

---

[1] See also Chapter XII.

ten he began to compose. He was organist of the chapel at eleven and conducted the opera band at rehearsals when he was twelve. The first important event in his life was his first visit to Vienna when he was seventeen. Mozart, hearing him improvise on a theme, remarked, "Pay attention to him; he will make a noise in the world some day."

He continued in the Elector's service until he was twenty-two, playing viola in the opera band and, like Wagner after him, acquiring the technical foundation of his art through practical experience. In 1792, when Haydn passed through Bonn on his way back from London, Beethoven submitted a cantata to him that won the master's warm praise. The Elector now decided to send the young genius to Vienna to study at his expense. In November Beethoven left his birthplace, never to return to it.

He took lessons in strict counterpoint from Haydn, but the two men were too different temperamentally ever to achieve a truly cordial relationship. Becoming dissatisfied with the progress he was making—Haydn was probably much too occupied with his own affairs to pay more than perfunctory attention to his pupil—Beethoven transferred his study to the celebrated theoretician Albrechtsberger. The old master (Haydn) does not seem to have been impressed by his pupil. He told an inquirer, "He has learnt nothing, and will never do anything in decent style."

His playing, especially his improvising, which has become something of a legend, rapidly spread his fame among the music-loving aristocracy of Vienna. Prince Lichnowsky, Prince Lobkowitz, and Count Fries were among the circle of noblemen who soon became his fervent admirers. From the innumerable anecdotes that have come down to us there is no question that they had to put up with quite a bit from the temperament of the young genius. For Beethoven, in his dealings with his noble patrons, was the very opposite of the easy-going, at times even subservient Haydn. Morbidly sensitive, abrupt of manner, of a proud and fiery nature, he was the symbol of that new republicanism that was even then threatening to engulf the old regime. Indeed, he was the first great composer to fit into the nineteenth-century Romantic pattern of the "temperamental genius." In a previous age his defiance would have been unthinkable; now the courts and princes not only did not resent what they considered his eccentricities but accepted them, in nineteenth-century fashion, as a concomitant of his

Birthplace of Ludwig van Beethoven at Bonn
(on the uppermost floor)

v

genius. Once when he was playing a duet with Ries at the home of Count Browne, and a young nobleman at the other end of the room persisted in talking to a lady, Beethoven suddenly lifted Ries's fingers from the keys and announced loudly, "I play no longer for such swine!" Nor could the entreaties of his audience induce him to touch another note or allow Ries to do so. He once fancied himself slighted at a party at Prince Lichnowsky's. Leaving in a huff, he wrote the Prince a note: "There have been princes before you and there will be after—but there is only one Beethoven!" With Beethoven the artist unquestionably comes into a new social status. Whereas Mozart's revolt, as we shall see, turned out to be premature and was crushed, Beethoven, aided both by a stronger personality and the new spirit of the times, was able to sweep all before him.

This "natural man," in a Rousseauesque sense, in revolt emotionally and intellectually against all that was conventional and artificial, was manifestly the one best fitted to become the voice of the new Romanticism and to lead the art of music away from its eighteenth-century heritage. He could not improve greatly the formal elegance or the exquisiteness of design to which Haydn and Mozart had brought it; but he could widen its boundaries, deepen its emotional capacities to a degree undreamt of until then, smash the rules, and bring music into tune with the needs and emotions of the new age. This most likely he would have done in any case, since the time was ready for it. But the intensity with which he did it, the specifically Beethovenian pathos that he introduced into his art, were indubitably heightened by one of those soul-shattering experiences that, if they do not break a man, leave him changed for the rest of his days. On the threshold of a brilliant career, just as he was beginning to try his wings in music, he found himself going deaf. The disaster seemed to portend the certain end of his career as a composer: he had no way of knowing that he would create his greatest works by hearing them only in imagination. Even more, the deafness was threatening to cut away all normal contact with his fellows. The victim of a physical defect always tends to magnify its effect out of all correct proportion. Given Beethoven's morbid sensitivity, his emotional insecurity, his self-consciousness socially, we may well understand why he reacted as he did.

In a profoundly touching letter to his brothers, written from

Heiligenstadt, the suburb of Vienna where he spent the summer of 1802, he lamented the loneliness that his deafness imposed upon him. He shrank from any normal social relations, dreading to admit an infirmity in the one sense in which he felt he should be more perfect than others. He had gone to Heiligenstadt still hoping that the malady might be arrested. Now he gave up all hope; his thoughts dwelt on escape through death. Throughout the long lonely walks of that summer there raged within the thirty-two-year-old artist the crucial battle between what Carlyle so well described as the nay-saying and the yea-saying. And when he emerged, the will to live, to struggle and to create, had triumphed over the will to die. In the valley of shadow he had come to realize that life could not be for him as for other men—that only through his art could he hope to make up for all that reality itself would forever deny him—that out of the very renunciation he must build a new universe for himself. By a stupendous effort of will he lifted himself above despair, above illness, above frustration, into the Olympian sunlight of immortal things. For the twenty-five years of life that remained to him—a period of supreme achievement—there was to ring through his music the strength, the courage, the heart-warming affirmation of life possible only to one who had known the worst and conquered it. From the bitter knowledge, he extracted that sense of man struggling with fate that so inflamed the imagination of the nineteenth century; that wonderful awareness of the pathetic element in life; that intensity of emotion and high ethos that set his music apart from the music of other men. "He who truly understands my music," he remarked to Bettina von Arnim, "must thereby go free of all the misery which others bear about with them."

More and more as he withdrew into himself he left his generation behind. His final piano sonatas and quartets were a century ahead of their time. When the violinist Radicati, puzzled by the *Rasoumowsky Quartets*, said to him, "But surely you do not consider these works to be music," Beethoven retorted, "Oh, they are not for you—but for a later age." The familiar picture has come down to us of the short, stocky man striding hatless through the fields, his shaggy hair tossing in the wind, crying out and waving his arms as he stopped now and then to make a notation in his sketch book. In the fields and woods on the outskirts of Vienna, alone with Nature, his great works were sketched and resketched, erased and rewritten, and by an incredibly slow process advanced toward their ultimate shape. In his personal life Beethoven might be slovenly, absent-minded, impatient; in all matters pertaining to his work he was supremely meticulous, infinitely patient, one of the most hard-working and fastidious artists who ever lived. His method of composition was the very opposite of Mozart's spontaneous flow. After months, sometimes years of pondering, after page upon page of rewriting, recasting, and hewing away, the work took shape, emerged in its final perfection. The opening chords of the *Eroica* were rewritten literally scores of times; the themes of the FIFTH SYMPHONY appear in his sketch books seven years before it was finished. If Mozart's music gives us the impression of having "leaped into being full-formed like Athena from the brain of Jove," Beethoven's music is of the slow "growth of the soil."

Because of the lack of adequate documentation, it is difficult to gauge the exact cause and nature of Beethoven's deafness. The malady seems to have appeared in its incipient stages as early as his twenty-eighth year. By the time he was thirty-two, as we know from the Heiligenstadt Testament, he could no longer hear the songs of the birds. In 1815 he was still able to take an active part in the rehearsals of his opera FIDELIO; for a few years afterward he still insisted on conducting his own works. But the musicians would only pretend to be following him. As affecting as the aged Haydn's farewell public appearance at the performance of the CREATION is Beethoven's at the first performance of his last and greatest symphony, the NINTH, in 1824. Although the choir and orchestra were instructed to watch his direction, they paid no attention to his beating of the time. At the close of the "Scherzo" there was a burst of tremendous applause. Beethoven fumbled with his score, deaf to the acclaim until one of the singers pointed to the audience. Then he turned and bowed, and there was not a dry eye in the theatre.

The three years that were still left him witnessed the production of the final string quartets, those magnificent works in which he completely transcended the limits of the early nineteenth century and struck out new paths for the later age. Yet, having reached the most mature and exalted period of his life, the master was strangely humble. "It seems to me as though I had just begun to write!"

We have a last vivid glimpse of the composer visiting his brother and the latter's wife in the autumn of 1826, just before his final illness, deaf, untidy, unpresentable, ignoring every household rule. After a quarrel with his relatives, Beethoven abruptly decided to return to Vienna. Refusing to wait until a suitable carriage could be procured, he made the trip back in an open chaise. The cold, damp weather caused a cold in his stomach; an inflammation of the lungs supervened, soon complicated by dropsy. He was in bed for several months, without any inkling that death was near. Toward the end of March, 1827, his condition took a sudden turn for the worse; the truth dawned upon him. "*Plaudite amici, comoedia finita est!*" (Applaud friends, the comedy is over) he muttered to his companions. It had been something even more than a divine comedy—a deeply human one. His last gesture was typically Beethovenian. A sudden storm and clap of thunder roused the dying man. He shook his clenched fist and fell back dead.

Unlike his predecessor Mozart, he had made a deep impression on the Viennese; his funeral was his most triumphant public appearance. The schools were closed, the crowd was enormous. Soldiers cleared the way for the cortège; it took an hour and a half for the short trip from his house to the church. Mozart's REQUIEM was performed, as it had been at Haydn's funeral. One of the chief mourners was Franz Schubert. The following year, dead at thirty-one, he was to be laid to rest near Beethoven. Thus their paths cross—Mozart, Haydn, Beethoven, Schubert—the four great names of the Viennese school that confer upon the city of music a lustre that cannot fade.

Of the four, Beethoven has come to be looked upon as the greatest in actual achievement. Like Wagner in the following generation, he left the imprint of his mighty personality upon his age. He seemed single-handedly to have changed the course of music and to have opened up new vistas for the musicians who were to follow. He ushered in the era of distinctive personalities— Wagner, Liszt, Chopin, Schumann, Brahms, Tchaikovsky—each of whom was to add an intensely personal accent to a universal language, to pour the innermost griefs and longings of the soul into what had hitherto been a somewhat impersonal art in several respects.

The achievement of Beethoven

Like Haydn and Mozart, Beethoven was a versatile composer who was at home in every form: his songs and cantatas, his oratorio THE MOUNT OF OLIVES, his SOLEMN MASS, his solitary opera FIDELIO, his incidental music to Goethe's EGMONT, and his concert overtures are all landmarks in their respective fields. But his gift was pre-eminently in the realm of absolute instrumental music, and his contribution greatest to the various manifestations of the sonata form—the solo piano sonata, the duo for violin and piano, the chamber music combinations, trio, quartet, quintet, sextet, septet, octet, with special emphasis on the string quartet, the piano as well as the violin concerto, and, last and greatest, the symphony. Before turning to a detailed examination of the most famous and popular of all symphonies, his FIFTH, it may be well to summarize, however briefly, the achievements that are specifically associated with his name.

The first-movement, or sonata-allegro, form Beethoven immeasurably enlarged and enriched both from the standpoint of structure and of emotional content. He increased the size and complexity of the development until it became perhaps the single most important section of the movement, a truly intellectual working out of all the implications of the thematic material of the exposition, as well as of new material specially introduced here in a mood of free fantasy. So, too, he introduced a new freedom in the key relationships between principal and subordinate themes and a new daring in modulation, as well as a greater flexibility in the employment of subsidiary themes. As for the coda, which had previously been mainly a rounding off of the movement, he transformed it almost into an independent chapter as rich in emotional content and imaginative fire as the movement itself. Above all, he created in his greatest first movements—such as those of the THIRD, FIFTH, and NINTH SYMPHONIES, the APPASSIONATA SONATA, the SERIOSO QUARTET—the mood of titanic struggle, of tragic grandeur, of the Hero pitted against Fate that is the essence of the Romantic symphony.

In Beethoven's hands, the slow movement was deepened from an atmosphere of gently reflective lyricism to one of intense pathos and deeply personal utterance. The Beethovenian adagio in the sonatas, the quartets, and the symphonies, is a passionate outpouring of the soul, the first expression of the exalted lyricism of the great slow movements of nineteenth-century music. Indeed, Beethoven's slow movements are unsurpassed, perhaps unequalled, in all music.

The third movement of the Classical symphony had been the dainty, aristocratic minuet; but this dance was hardly congenial to the mood and spirit of the new age. Although Haydn, as we have seen, had already reached out toward a dance more democratic in spirit, it was Beethoven who achieved such an effect by making the third movement of the symphony into a scherzo—that fast, boisterous outburst of Homeric laughter, of folk fancy and peasant humour. As Schauffler points out, Beethoven did not invent the scherzo. Haydn first gave the minuet a new tempo; but Beethoven broadened, deepened, and elevated it, and made it into one of his most brilliant creations.

As a necessary adjunct of his dramatic power, Beethoven used nuance to a far greater degree than had his predecessors—pianissimo whispers gradually swelling to shattering crescendos; these, further dramatized by sudden pianissimos again. His scores abound in these violent, dramatic contrasts to a far greater degree than do those of Haydn or Mozart. What is most important, they were *an integral part of his composition,* and he was much more careful than they in writing down the symbols indicating the exact effects he desired. Building on the experiments of both Haydn and Mozart, Beethoven made great advances in the techniques of handling the orchestra. His tonal effects—notably in the use of the different choirs for colour and contrasts, in the achievement of orchestral sonorities, in the freer and more effective writing for the horns, the woodwinds, the violas, the double basses, the kettle-drums—were definite steps forward. In his effort to knit the various movements of his works into a more cohesive whole, he developed the procedure of quoting in one movement a theme, or themes, that had been employed in a previous movement—the cyclical treatment that became one of the most popular devices of the nineteenth-century composers. (The word "cyclical" is also used to mean that form of melodic treatment in which the material unwinds and evolves out of its very self. See César Franck, page 412.) In Beethoven we find the ideal balance of Romantic and Classic tempers.

The Fifth Symphony in C minor

The most popular of all symphonies affords us a good insight into the master's style. We know from the sketchbooks that some of the motives of this symphony germinated in Beethoven's mind as early as 1800. It was finished in the summer of 1807, together with the *Pastoral*, the SIXTH. At the first performance the following year, the two symphonies were numbered the other way around. The announcement of the concert throws an interesting sidelight on the musical conditions of the time:

On Thursday the 22nd of December (1808) Ludwig van Beethoven will have the honour to give a musical academy in the . . . Theatre An der Wien. All the pieces are of his composition, are entirely new, and not yet heard in public . . . First Part: 1. A symphony entitled: "A Recollection of Country Life", in F major (No. 5). [*Sic!*] 2. Aria. 3. Hymn with Latin text, composed in the Church style with chorus and solos. 4. Pianoforte Concerto played by himself.

Second Part. 1. Grand Symphony in C minor (No. 6). [*Sic!*] 2. Holy, with Latin text, composed in Church style . . . 3. Fantasia for pianoforte which culminates in the gradual entrance of the whole orchestra and at the end with the introduction of choruses as a finale. Boxes and reserved seats may be had in the Krugerstrasse No. 1074, first floor— beginning at half past six o'clock.

The programme was more than twice too long, the theatre cold, the audience scanty; orchestra and chorus, which had not undergone a single full rehearsal, broke down in one of the numbers, so that Beethoven jumped from his seat, calling out loudly and angrily, "Stop! That will not do! Badly played! Again!" One has but to think of the disciplined, highly co-ordinated orchestras of today to realize how far standards of performance have risen in the past century and under what handicaps some of our most treasured compositions were first given to the world. The Symphony struck Reichardt, a leading critic of the day, as "much worked out and very long." It was neither the first nor the last time in the history of music that the judgment of posterity has upset that of contemporaries.

The symphony, scored for two flutes, two oboes, two clarinets, two bassoons, two horns, two trumpets, kettledrums, and the usual complement of strings, is in four movements; in the last, piccolo, double bassoon, and three trombones are added.

In this work we find in unmistakable fashion the essentials of the

Beethovenian mood—the fiercely impassioned presentation of man pitted against fate in the first movement; the ideal serenity and faith of the second; the profound humanity and self-searching, alternating with outbursts of boisterous humour, even mystery, of the scherzo; and the flaming victory, the triumphant affirmation of the finale. Here, in its most eloquent tones, can be traced the drama that held the imagination of Europe throughout the early Romantic period, whether with Bonaparte at Austerlitz or with Byron at Mussolonghi.

ANALYSIS. *FIRST MOVEMENT: Allegro con brio (fast, with spirit). C minor. $\frac{2}{4}$ time. Sonata-allegro form.* Nothing could be simpler yet more powerful than the opening motif consisting of three notes, the first repeated three times, that has come to be associated in popular imagination with "Fate knocking on the door" (be sure to follow this motive throughout the Symphony):

Out of this motif, announced fortissimo by clarinets and strings, the whole movement grows with the inevitableness of the plant germinating from the seed. We are plunged at once into the maelstrom, the germ theme appearing again and again among the various choirs with an overpowering intensity and force. There is a fierce concentration and conciseness about the music; the modulation from first to second theme is accomplished virtually through two chords. And what a wealth of psychological contrast between the two themes! The first theme is gruff, masculine, commanding, in an impassioned minor; the second theme is tender, lyrical, legato, in a serene major—a brief song on violins and clarinets that is swept away in the passionate onrush of the movement.

Notice the regular phrase structure, so grateful after the impetuosity that has preceded it. Even while this theme is being played, we hear deep in the accompaniment the tapping rhythm of the opening theme. There is a brief closing theme:

ff Closing Theme (Violin)

After achieving a powerful climax, the brief exposition is repeated.

The development section grows with the same inevitability out of the original kernel. The rhythm is translated into groups of massively repeated chords. Then begins an intricate orchestral dialogue amongst the various choirs. The material is worked out with a relentless logic, each step seeming to lead in an unalterable sequence to the next. The music surges forward with a fierce momentum, leading back gradually, inexorably, to the C-minor tonality.

Just after the return, there is a brief letup in a poignantly sad solo on the oboe, like an improvisation. Then the recapitulation sweeps the listener straight on toward the towering coda. The second theme remains in the major mode but is transposed to the key of C. As soon as its plaintive measures fade, the Coda introduces a new surging theme; the music proceeds unwaveringly toward the massive final cadence in C minor. Grim defiance, demonic energy, brooding tenderness, sustaining hope—all are here, fused together in the fiery crucible of genius. The movement is a miracle of making so much out of so little.

SECOND MOVEMENT: Andante con moto (fairly slow, with motion). ⅜ *time. Theme and variation form.*[2] The second movement is basically in one of the Classical forms, the theme and variation; yet the original treatment of this form is unique in the literature. The first theme, announced dolce and piano by viola and 'cello, is a serene, broadly flowing melody. The major mode here sounds doubly restful after the sombre minor that came before.

---

[2] Goetschius calls this movement a "First Rondo-form " *i.e.*, a main theme, a subordinate theme, and a return to the main theme. The present author believes it to be a most subtle and intricate hybrid, or combination, structure of ternary and variations forms. However, the important concern is with the beauty of the movement.

This theme gives way to one of those soaring melodies filled with hope and an inner sense of power that must have been in Beethoven's mind when he made the remark to Bettina von Arnim about the healing power of his music.

The slow triple metre gives an effect of great dignity and breadth. The regularity of the phrases, the care with which the cadences are marked, above all the beautiful curve of the melodic line in both themes, add to the sense of spaciousness and freedom.

The variations serve not so much to show off the composer's ingenuity as to explore to the full the emotional possibilities of the thematic material. The first theme is presented again in a steadily flowing succession of sixteenth notes that retain the contours of the original. The second melody then returns, borne aloft by oboes and brass against a more elaborate accompaniment in thirty-second notes. The first theme is further elaborated into a running succession of thirty-second notes on the violas and 'cellos, repeated pianissimo by the violins against a pizzicato accompaniment on the lower string instruments and then as a running bass melody on 'cellos and double basses against loud chords in the rest of the orchestra. Now the upward-sweeping second theme is sounded forth by the full orchestra, reaching a triumphal climax and leading to the fortissimo statement of the first theme by first and second violins. The coda has an interestingly rhythmic accompaniment and works up to a powerful final cadence.

THIRD MOVEMENT: Scherzo, Allegro. C minor. ¾ time. Minuet and trio form.[3] The third movement begins pianissimo in the sombre

---

[3] This movement is sometimes described as a "Song-form with Trio."

tonality of the first. A mysterious phrase emerges from the deep register of the 'cellos and bass violins, answered by the violins:

Suddenly the horns announce a theme bearing a striking resemblance in rhythm to the Fate motif of the opening:

The two themes alternate, the Fate rhythm this time proclaimed triumphantly by woodwinds and brass. A new melody, a tender dance, sounds awhile before giving way to the ineluctable Fate rhythm.

The middle portion of the scherzo, corresponding to the Trio of the minuet, opens with 'cellos and double basses scampering through a rapidly running figure that reminded Berlioz of the "gambols of a frolicsome elephant."

The figure is ingeniously imitated, each time in a higher register, by violas and bassoons, second violins, finally first violins assisted by flutes and oboes. Note the frolicsome humour in the second part of the Trio section, where three starts have to be made by the 'cellos and basses ere they are on their way—as though they had made mistakes in this difficult, fast music.

The Trio subsides into the mysterious pianissimo of the opening; the first part is repeated. We hear as from afar the mysterious tapping of the Fate rhythm. Then begins the unforgettable transition string passage to the fourth movement, with kettledrums keeping up a steady beat, *ppp*, until, like a sudden blaze of light, the full orchestra leaps into the exultant C-major theme of the allegro.

FOURTH MOVEMENT: Allegro. C-major. $\frac{4}{4}$ *time. Sonata-allegro form.* Nowhere do we see more clearly the contrasting emotional colouring of major and minor than in the C-major chord that introduces the marchlike first theme of the final movement.

This is music of triumph, of irresistible power, of exultation and of glory! One is reminded of the observation of the biographer, Theodore Baker, when he said, in part, "Beethoven's loftiest originality, and that whence the differences in formal construction naturally flowed, is the intensity and fervour of subjective emotion which pervades his works. It is this mood of profound subjectivity, of individual, powerful soul-expression which, most of all, differentiates Beethoven's music from that of Bach, or Haydn, or Mozart, and which opens the era of 'romantic' composition."[4]

The second theme is fashioned broadly on the tones of the C-major chord, in that respect resembling the first; but it is more subdued in that it flows much more smoothly and is more reflective. It is announced by the woodwinds,

and after working up into a fortissimo climax, leads straight into the third theme, which is built on a vigorous triplet figure. A phrase on the violins is answered by one on the woodwinds:

[4] Theodore Baker, *Biographical Dictionary of Musicians*. (New York: G. Schirmer, Inc., 1940.)

Stormy scale passages lead to the codetta and the double bar at which the exposition is repeated.[5]

If in the sonata-allegro structure of the first movement Beethoven pared to the bone, he allowed himself ample room in this movement. The development is one of those highly intricate and extended working-out sections so closely associated with Beethoven. The ascending triplet figure is inverted; the thematic material of the exposition is intertwined in a rich mosaic of imitations from one choir to another. New material springs out of the old with that same "germinating" inevitability that we noticed in the first movement. The crescendos are spacious, the climaxes sustained and cumulative, the modulations swift and bold. At the very summit of development, Beethoven, by a daring stroke of imagination, plunges us into the insistent Fate rhythm of the opening of the scherzo, a final reminiscence before the close. The tapping figure broadens out thunderously as we swing back into the marchlike C major of the first theme. After recapitulating the thematic material of the exposition with some interesting transpositions that hover about the C-major tonality, we come to the final surprise of this amazing movement; for as Beethoven approaches his coda there is a gradual accelerando, increasing in momentum until the movement is more than twice the original speed. The listener is swept headlong into a breath-taking presto. Like a torrent finally reaching the sea, the music broadens into the final C-major cadence, with the tonic chord repeated again and again. One can see the stocky little Titan with the beetling brows shake his fist, defiant and individual to the end.

ADDITIONAL SUGGESTIONS FOR LISTENING

Besides the FIFTH SYMPHONY, the THIRD (*Eroica*), the SIXTH (*Pastorale*), the SEVENTH and the NINTH SYMPHONIES figure regularly in concert and radio programmes. The reader should have no special difficulty in familiarizing himself with them, and it is hoped that he will hear Beethoven's works in the fields of opera, chamber music, concerti (both for piano and violin), solo and duo sonatas, choral music, that are far too many to be listed here. See Grove's *Dictionary of Music and Musicians* and other reference works about Beethoven.

[5] There is no uniformity of practice nowadays pertaining to the repetition of the exposition in works written before our time.

Chapter Twenty-One

Brahms

The Classical Romanticist[1]

I T WAS not without justification that von Bülow made his now famous epigram, "The three B's—Bach, Beethoven, and Brahms." Schumann, in an article which created quite a disturbance at the time, called Brahms the true successor to Beethoven. Whether such comparisons are fully justified or not, they do indicate that Brahms occupies a lofty position among the great musical geniuses of all time. His works are found in the field of song, chorus, chamber music, concertos for various instruments, solo and duo sonatas, trios, and a number of orchestral works, including four symphonies; but he wrote no opera. We have mentioned Beethoven as being the link between the Classical and Romantic periods in Germany; and we can consider Brahms, coming at the peak of the period, as still another span to the same bridge between the two great stylistic tempers that pervade the music of history—classicism and romanticism. Brahms, like Beethoven, was great enough to embrace both to a superior degree.

Johannes Brahms (1833-1897)

We stated in our discussion of the Romantic and Classic tempers in art that the two may exist side by side, not only within the same period, but even in the works of the same composer. Nowhere is this point better exemplified than in the music of Johannes

---

[1] This chapter may be transposed to a position at the end of the Symphony Unit (after Haydn), or immediately after Mozart, if achievement levels indicate the advisability of such a postponement. The author suggests the following priority order as an aid in reducing the unit further to meet time allowance: 1-Dvořák, 1-Beethoven, 2-Mozart, 3-Brahms, and 4-Haydn. Eliminate in reverse order. Obviously the number and sequence of symphonies in this unit have been carefully determined and verified in practice by the author; thus the unit is to be preserved and studied as indicated in the text.

Brahms. In the fervour of his emotion, in brooding introspection and passionate lyricism, he is one of the foremost romantics. Yet, in an age dominated by the theatricalism of the Wagnerian music drama, by the flamboyant programme idiom of Liszt and Berlioz, Brahms adhered steadfastly to the great symphonic tradition of the past, a serene Olympian figure, the last in the long line of

Portrait of Johannes Brahms

great German masters whose supreme achievement was the perfection of organic structure, the development of germinal forms in so-called "absolute" music. Yet, we reiterate, Brahms was an ardent and sincere romanticist at heart.

Biography

Brahms was born in Hamburg in 1833, the son of a double-bass player in the theatre orchestra there. His mother had a profound influence on his development. Both in his youth and manhood, Brahms remained extremely attached to her, and her death in

1865, when the composer was thirty-two, is said to have inspired one of the most touching elegies in all music, the GERMAN REQUIEM.[2]

Brahms displayed his musical gifts from early childhood. He received a sound musical education, both in piano and theory, and made a public appearance as a pianist at the age of fifteen. The following year he appeared as a composer, playing a *Fantasy on a Favourite Waltz*. After a few years of diligent study, mostly with the teacher Marxsen, he became, at the age of twenty, the accompanist to the Gipsy violinist, Eduard Reményi. On their tour through North Germany he met the great violinist Joseph Joachim, who became a lifelong friend and played a notable part in Brahms' career. (The superb VIOLIN CONCERTO IN D, Op. 77, was dedicated to Joachim.) Joachim, who soon realized that Brahms' true gift lay in creative writing rather than in performance, gave him a letter of introduction to Schumann who was living at Düsseldorf. His meeting with Schumann was a key event in the young composer's career. The older man, in a famous article in the *Neue Zeitschrift für Musik*, entitled "*Neue Bahnen*" (New Paths), hailed the twenty-year-old Brahms as a genius, focusing on him the attention of all musical Europe—and history has proved how right Schumann was.

From then on, the history of Brahms' life is the history of his works. His personal existence was uneventful, compared with the stormy careers of Wagner and Liszt, for example. With external difficulties mitigated to a large extent, he was free to devote himself to the creation of the works that soon stamped him as one of the foremost composers of his time. From 1854 to 1858 he was concert director at the court of the Prince of Lippe-Detmold, a post that he resigned in order to give all his time to composing. He lived for a time in Hamburg and in Switzerland; but after 1862 he settled in Vienna, which remained the centre of his activities until his death. Here he was for a year the conductor of the Singakademie, producing the choral works of Bach, Beethoven, Schumann, and others, after which he held no post that entailed regular duties. Save for occasional concert appearances and holiday tours, the last three decades of his life were devoted to composing. He remained a bachelor, a burly, jovial figure in the

---

[2] There are good reasons for doubting the accuracy of this statement; but the spirit underlying it is worthy of preservation.

W

musical life of Vienna, surrounded by a wide circle of admirers
and friends. He was inclined to be forbidding and caustic with
strangers and had very little patience with sham and social airs;
but underneath the gruff exterior was a nature bubbling over
with kindliness and affection. Among the most cherished of his
friends was Schumann's widow, Clara (née Wieck), one of the
leading pianists of her time, who became a most sensitive inter-
preter of his works and played an important role in the criticism
of them before they were offered to the world. (The *F-minor Piano
Sonata* was dedicated to her.) It was at Mme. Schumann's funeral
that he caught a chill that is believed to have hastened his end.
He died at the age of sixty-four and was buried not far from
Beethoven and Schubert.

It was inevitable, in an age when music had turned toward such
strong literary and pictorial influences, when all the riches of
orchestral colouring, all the fascination of the bizarre and the
picturesque engaged the adherents of the "new music," that the
music of composers such as Brahms and César Franck should
become a rallying point for all who desired the art to maintain its
great traditions. The divergence between the two schools of
thought was dramatized by the acrimonious debates between the
"Brahmins" and the "Wagnerites" that lent so much excitement
to the artistic scene of the late nineteenth century. Seen from the
perspective of a half a century, the conflict does not seem to matter
so much today, since we have accepted both masters into our
musical heritage, taking from each what he alone has to offer.
Yet the reader should note that it is not altogether correct to regard the issue between the two factions merely as a difference
between classic and romantic ideals. Brahms is fundamentally one
of the most romantic among composers. It is merely that he represents a different type of Romanticism from that of the extreme
Romantics such as Wagner and Liszt who would have less to do
with the spirit of Classicism than Brahms. Because he poured the
impassioned content of his speech into the hallowed moulds of the
great Classicists, because his imagination perceived the particular,
the personal, in its most universal and general aspect, because for
him texture was often more important than colour, workmanship
more vital than bizarreness, because of the serenity of his vision,
the loftiness of his utterance, his unfailing mastery of his material
in the most absolute sense, his unflagging devotion to what he

considered eternal in art, Brahms may be considered—like Beethoven—a Classical Romanticist. Wagner was convinced that the music drama was the logical continuation of the choral *Finale* of the NINTH SYMPHONY. On their side, the conductor von Bülow and other adherents of Brahms called his FIRST SYMPHONY the TENTH. It is curious and illuminating that the two diametrically opposed tendencies within the late Romantic Movement should both have claimed a common source. Posterity, the ultimate judge in almost all such disputes, seems at this writing to favour Brahms rather than Wagner as the true inheritor of the mantle of Beethoven.

Except for opera and symphonic poem, which he never attempted—he once remarked to the critic Hanslick that it would be as difficult for him to write an opera as to marry, but that after the first experience he would probably try a second—Brahms essayed and enriched all the forms of music. He ranks with Schubert and Schumann as one of the masters of the German lied, infusing his songs with a wealth of poetic suggestion and tragic intensity. (See Chapter VI.) We have seen that, where melody was concerned, Brahms could be extraordinarily close to the spirit of the folk. In his choral works, as Fuller-Maitland points out in his excellent article in Grove's *Dictionary of Music*, Brahms "touched a point of sublimity that had not been reached since Beethoven." Most famous among these are the GERMAN REQUIEM, the TRIUMPHLIED, written in 1871 to celebrate the German victory over France, the beautiful SHICKSALSLIED (Song of Fate); and the RHAPSODIE for alto solo and male chorus. His chamber music—sextets, quintets, quartets, trios, and duo sonatas—and his piano music are among the finest in the literature of their respective forms. But his supreme achievements, as far as the musical public at large is concerned, are the orchestral works: four symphonies, two overtures, the SERENADE, two piano concertos, the violin concerto, the double concerto for violin and cello, and the brilliant and masterful (both in composition and orchestration) THEME AND VARIATION ON A THEME BY HAYDN, for symphony orchestra.

Brahms was past forty when he approached the composition of his first symphony, but he was already the master of a distinctive style and in the full maturity of his gifts. Consequently, he had no apprenticeship period in the symphonic form: his FIRST SYMPHONY IN C MINOR is one of the greatest "firsts" ever written. The symphonic idiom of Brahms is noteworthy for its simple diatonic melodies that achieve a quality of the highest lyricism, together with that sense of inevitability that characterizes only the greatest art. Brahms' symphonic works are also distinguished by spacious harmonies, rich and intricate rhythmic changes and combinations —in which he follows in the footsteps of Schumann—strange, subtle chord progressions so individual that they can be instantly recognized by the experienced music lover as being from the pen of Brahms, and for a remarkably complex interweaving of the inner voices in a splendid polyphonic texture—he was an unquestioned master of counterpoint. The slow movements have an atmosphere of brooding, of tenderness and ardent lyricism breaking through the reserve of a deeply introspective spirit, of nobility and strength that is in the Beethovenian tradition, yet is completely Brahmsian. But what truly distinguishes him from the romantic symphonists of his time is the spacious, plastic architecture in which this music is made manifest, the epic dimensions of the form, the technical mastery of the material. Here we find incisive themes germinating, developing with the inexorable power that is the hallmark of true symphonic style. The symphonic movement evolves and grows out of the themes, the simple motives reveal undreamt-of possibilities, all explored and unified within the logic of a well-wrought and inevitably correct structure —a splendid illustration of the working of the classical temper in a romantic spirit and mood.

At this point, we desire to draw the listener's attention to a technical device of Brahms that is especially noticeable in the FIRST and SECOND SYMPHONIES. He introduces a germ motive which is quite distinct from the themes proper and which he develops individually; sometimes, as often happens in the FIRST SYMPHONY, he does so with greater attention to the germ motive than to the organic themes themselves. Then, too, he uses this germ motive in several movements or even throughout the entire work, not unlike the Fate motive in Beethoven's FIFTH SYMPHONY, as a cyclical or unifying factor—and sometimes as a compositional foil for the organic theme sounding at the time. This technique is clearly seen in Brahm's SECOND SYMPHONY. The germ motive, in its initial and native state, is heard at the onset of the symphony and is marked "a" in Mus. Ill. 1, page 324. Thus the listener has a more involved problem than heretofore in that he is to be concerned consciously with the observation of the development of the regular themes of the movement *plus* the appearances and development of the germ motive—though we hasten to add that this is not as difficult as it appears in print. (After hearing Brahms' symphony, compare the character and function of this germ motive with the germinal motive of Liszt, the leit motif of Wagner, the descriptive motive-theme of Strauss, and the Fate motive of Beethoven. An interesting and enlightening discussion may be made on this point; and try to introduce the concepts of romanticism and classicism into the discussion.)

Symphony No. 2 in D major (1877)

For an introduction to the symphonic style of Brahms, let us consider the SECOND SYMPHONY. The FIRST has tragic and Olympian grandeur. The THIRD, abounding in wonderful melody, is one of the most poetic of symphonic works. The FOURTH is more melancholy, with luminous flights of fancy and a final movement based on one of the favourite forms of the Baroque Period, the *passacaglia* (see page 446), that is one of the most extraordinary feats of musical architecture in the literature. But for warmth and geniality and simple songfulness, for surging rhythms and brilliant climaxes, the SECOND takes precedence. (We are here reminded of a Toscanini story. It is well known that Brahms is one of his favourite composers. He was once asked which of the four symphonies was his favourite, and he replied, "The one upon which I am working at the moment.") Here, in the SECOND SYMPHONY, Brahms is in a most personal mood; and thus this work affords a fine beginning for anyone to become acquainted with the Brahms symphonies. Its complexity will also prove to be a real challenge to listening skills accumulated at this point in our study.

ANALYSIS. *FIRST MOVEMENT: Allegro non troppo.* ¾ *time. Sonata-allegro form.* The first part of the first theme is announced in a mood of reverie by the horns against a sombre background of 'cellos and double basses. Observe how the motive marked "A" appears throughout the movement, both in its original form and in many changes.

A broadly curving melody in the violins, in the nature of an interlude, is the second part of the principal theme, and

leads to the lyrical second theme on the 'cellos—a fine example of Brahmsian song that serves as main contrast to the first theme:

Two subsidiary themes are added to the basic material, strongly irregular in rhythm: the first, *ben marcato* (well marked), with broad leaps and vigorous accents, presented by flutes and oboes:

the second, played by bassoons and double basses, answered by flutes and oboes, has the sprawling, ungainly contours of which Brahms was so fond in his transitional material and drives forward with great propulsion:

The different melodic strands are intertwined in a complex tonal fabric with the two basic themes reappearing in all sorts of ingenious variations. The movement reaches its peak in the resurgence of the first theme and gradually subsides into a mood of joyous placidity.

SECOND MOVEMENT: Adagio non troppo: A-B-A (or first rondo) form. In this slow movement, we glimpse the restrained feeling, the tenderness and shy sensitivity that, for the admirers of Brahms, are among his greatest charms. Not all the reserve of the intricate polyphonic texture can hide the passion of this outpouring; yet the prevailing quality is one of manly feeling, the sensitivity that is filled with compassion. There are a number of simple, though very beautiful, themes. The opening song of the 'cellos is intertwined with a contrasting countermelody in the bassoons:

The main theme is presented with oboes imitating the horns against a plaintive countermelody:

The second melodic idea presents the woodwinds in a syncopated melody, dolce, against the pizzicato of the 'cellos:

Like the slow movements of the other three symphonies, this is one of the intensely human and ingratiating songs of Brahms.

THIRD MOVEMENT: Allegretto grazioso: Minuet and trio form.[3] Instead of the Beethovenian scherzo, Brahms gives us, in the third movement, a mood whimsical and tender. Oboes announce a simple theme, allegretto grazioso (quasi andantino)—lightly and

[3] According to Goetschius, the eminent American authority, there are two trios in this movement.

gracefully, in a pace somewhat faster than andante—the grace note on the third beat giving just a hint of waywardness that is almost wistful:

How charmingly this theme savours of the graceful, classical minuet, of the time of powdered wigs, even to the frequently accented third beat!

The metre changes suddenly to ¾; the tempo becomes presto. One scarcely recognizes the wistful tune of the opening measures in this bubbling, staccato variation with brusque accents off the beat. But if you compare the two melodies, you will discover how artfully the second is derived from the first. (This is an excellent example of rhythmic diminution. An interesting observation might be made here in respect to style and form. These two paces, one slow and graceful and the other lively and vivacious, alternate with each other throughout the movement, as though Brahms had telescoped a regular minuet movement with that of a scherzo. Watch for this effect.) This mastery of formal structure along with the mastery of thematic development is characteristic of Brahms and is among the attributes that place him so high among the great composers of all time. The lively (B) theme follows:

Flutes and oboes announce a new theme, strongly accented and impetuous:

Presently this theme, too, is altered in tempo and metre, retaining only its general contour as it is played by the woodwinds:

The movement returns in the end to the wistfulness of the open-ing theme, as though the presto interlude had been like something glimpsed but not fully realized until it had passed by.

FOURTH MOVEMENT: Allegro con spirito: sonata-allegro form.
This movement, to be played lively and spirited, is a joyous, head-long finale that has in it something of the rondos of the classical era, although in a more full-bodied, "earthier" form. The first theme is a proud and vigorous statement, even though the strings announce it sotto voce (almost whisperlike):

The second theme out of which the movement is built is one of those diatonic tunes that seem quite simple when we first hear them, but that, containing within themselves the miraculous life-giving element, achieve when they reveal themselves in their full splendour an effect that is quite magnificent:

Two subsidiary themes now follow: the first a pleasant interlude with descending bass:

the second one that is marked by the brusque rhythmic figure that we met in another context—the "Scotch Snap":

This completes the principal organic material.
    The development section reveals not a few instances of the

genius of Brahms in transforming a theme and his mastery of contrapuntal technique. It would lead us too far afield and into too
deep waters for the present to attempt to discover all such points
of interest; but repeated hearings will eventually reveal these virtues to those with sufficient interest.

The reprise, or recapitulation, is regular save for a few additional contrapuntal evidences of Brahms' craft, and we draw the
attention of the listener to an interesting version of the second
subject as it appears in the trombones, which, though quite
solemn, blossoms forth presently into a glorious triumph. The
mood brightens and sweeps forward in a resistless torrent, growing
in power and abandon until it achieves a momentum of triumphant
energy with vigorous chords hurling forth syncopated
accents with all their power and the sonorous brasses joining in a
climax of frenzied acclamation at the end.

ADDITIONAL SUGGESTIONS FOR LISTENING

This is no place to list all, or even many, of the romantic symphonies
one might hear in recordings. Rather we suggest only a few, leaving
others to be discovered by the listener. Of course the works of Brahms
mentioned in the foregoing text should serve as a basis for any list.
Appropriate articles should be read in such reference works as the
Oxford Companion to Music (Percy A. Scholes), the *International Cyclopedia
of Music and Musicians* (Oscar Thompson), Grove's *Dictionary of Music
and Musicians*. These and a number of more or less popular histories of
music will give ample sources for good lists—but remember to use a
good up-to-date gramophone record catalogue. However, for our immediate purpose, we suggest (besides the Brahms works already mentioned) Schubert's *Unfinished* as well as his SYMPHONY IN C MAJOR; the
FOURTH, FIFTH, and SIXTH SYMPHONIES of Tchaikovsky; SYMPHONY IN
D MINOR by César Franck; the *Italian* and *Scotch* SYMPHONIES of Mendelssohn; the *Spring* and *Rhenish* SYMPHONIES of Schumann; the SECOND
SYMPHONY IN E MINOR by Rachmaninoff; the FIRST, SECOND, FOURTH,
and FIFTH SYMPHONIES of Sibelius; the SYMPHONY FANTASTIQUE of
Berlioz, the *London* SYMPHONY of Vaughan Williams— but you will have
infinitely more enjoyment and satisfaction in completing your own list.

Chapter Twenty-Two

The Classical Symphony

Two Viennese Masters — Mozart and Haydn

JUST as we viewed the symphonic poem and the programme overture against the background of nineteenth-century Romanticism, so must we approach the first great masters of the symphony against the background of eighteenth-century Classicism. We saw that in the case of Romanticism the general social and cultural upheaval following in the train of the French Revolution had the most direct repercussions in the arts. So here, the social background of the feudal-aristocratic *ancien régime* exercised no less powerful an influence upon the artist. The whole weight of this influence, as we pointed out in an earlier chapter, tended in the direction of the Classical spirit.[1]

The fact that eighteenth-century art functioned in great measure under the system of patronage meant that the artist of the time was in much closer contact with his audience and much more susceptible to its immediate demands and influence than was the nineteenth-century artist, who worked for the open market. In this sense, art in the eighteenth century may be said to have reflected its social milieu much more faithfully than that of the nineteenth. To begin with, Classical art had before it the ideal of aristocratic formalism that animated the society out of which it sprang. It took over the sane objectivity upon which the "Age of Reason" prided itself; it looked upon unrestrained or too ostentatious expression of feeling as being not quite in good taste. It expressed deep feeling, but always with exquisite sensibility and restraint rather than outspoken torrential passion. Emotion here was sane and refined, contained within beauty of line and perfection of form. This was a healthy, optimistic art, moulded and balanced, impregnated with the ideal of moderation of the antique world, good-humoured and lovable, and achieving, at its greatest,

[1] See Chapter XII.

a serene loveliness, a limpid upwelling of true emotion, an exquisite finish, such as have never been equalled before or since.

Within this eighteenth-century style, we have to distinguish between the Rococo and the Classical. The Rococo was the overdainty, overelaborate, and overprecious manner in architecture, painting, furniture, decoration, sculpture, and music that summed up the main trends in art at the middle of the century, especially in France. In the plastic arts this spirit expressed itself in the fragile grace of Dresden china, in the nymphs and shepherdesses of Boucher and Fragonard, the delicate fountains and groves of Watteau. In architecture, we have the elegant palaces of the Rococo style, surrounded by formal gardens and furnished with all the ornaments—from crystal chandeliers to smiling Cupids and dainty screens—that gave a proper background for powdered wig and crinoline. The musical counterpart of the popular idea of the Rococo is to be found not in the major works of Haydn and Mozart—as is all too often stated—but in the cheerful, highly ornate rondos and allegros of a host of composers who came before them, such as Domenico Scarlatti (1685-1757), François Couperin (1668-1733), Johann Stamitz (1717-1757), Luigi Boccherini (1743-1805), Claude Daquin (1694-1772), and Karl Phillipp Emanuel Bach (1714-1788).

An appropriate reproduction of a painting by Jean Honoré Fragonard (1732-1806), "The Pursuit," from the Frick Collection of New York, may be seen on page 331. Here we have an example of the daintiness, the graceful and fanciful style that was so characteristic of this painter. There is in this work a "prettiness" and exquisiteness that could have found expression only at that time; a style that has been called "opera scenery." However, Fragonard was a master of his craft, and, according to the authors of *Art in the Western World*, his work is marked with "cosmopolitan wit and sophistication" and carefully wrought frivolity of unquestioned beauty and charm. It will not be difficult to compare this type of painting with analogous musical styles.

The Classical spirit, on the other hand, came into the art of music in the latter half of the century. This spirit had set the prevailing tone in literature for a century—from the drama of Racine and Corneille to the poetry of Pope and Thomson, Goldsmith and Gray, and the stately prose of Dr. Johnson, Edmund Burke, Gibbon, and Voltaire. In painting, the spirit that had animated the

The Pursuit   *Fragonard*

masters of the Renaissance—Raphael, Michelangelo, Verocchio, da Vinci—was due for a revival in the second half of the century through the neo-classicism of Poussin, Reynolds, Gainsborough, David, and Ingres. In music, the Classical spirit reached its peak in the works of Mozart and Haydn. Although these men, as we shall soon see, inherited the traditions of the Rococo and shared some of its characteristics, they deepened the content and emotional scope of music far beyond its former confines. They brought to music the sustained line, the vaulting patterns of the great Classical painters of the Renaissance. They did some of their most significant work in the final decade of the century, on the very threshold of Romanticism. To see Mozart and Haydn as the musical embodiment of the Rococo is to miss the essence of their genius and their achievement. True, they worked within the conventions of their time, just as Shakespeare or Raphael worked within the conventions of theirs. And there is unquestionably a side of both Haydn and Mozart that fits well into the notion of the courtier in powdered peruke and silk breeches amidst the Venetian lace and gilt snuffboxes of the Rococo palaces. But that is only one side—and the least important. They are, above all else, the two masters who brought the truly great Classical style of the late eighteenth century to its perfection and left for the nineteenth century, and for all time, an ever-inspiring revelation of absolute beauty in music.

Wolfgang Amadeus Mozart (1756-1791)

The reader may recall that in our discussion of Romanticism we warned against the danger of drawing too rigid distinctions in art, of "compartmentalizing" periods and styles and individual creators. We tried especially to show how closely interrelated and universal in time and place were the Classical and Romantic tempers, and how erroneous it was to draw a rigid and inflexible boundary between them. Nowhere is this warning more in order than in regard to the composer we now approach. One of the supreme figures in the history of the art of music, Mozart is also one of the most consistently misrepresented. If he had been no more than the polished master of the "Gallant style" of the late eighteenth century, he would have gone the way of dozens of his

Pietà   *Michelangelo*

forgotten contemporaries. It is precisely because what he produced is so distinctive, so completely above the limitations of any one time and place, that he occupies a special niche in the story of music. Mozart expressed the spirit of his age, but in a far greater degree he transcended it. Into the conventional moulds of his time, he poured the quintessence of eternal art. One has but to look beneath the outward grace and mannerisms of the period to see revealed in his full stature the luminous inner spirit, the creator of unfading beauty, the artistic companion of Raphael and Keats in many ways.

Like Beethoven, Mozart came between the close of one great epoch and the beginning of another. His works are not only the culmination of what had gone before, but also a harbinger of a new era. There is indeed something strangely prophetic in the music of Mozart. The opening theme of the G Minor Symphony is as romantic as the "Ode to the West Wind"; the serenity and exquisite formalism of the old intermingles with the passionate lyricism of the new. It is this that constitutes the fascinating duality of the Mozartian style. In him, the two elements meet in perfect fusion, strengthening and balancing each other. The classic serenity is humanized by heart-piercing emotion, and this, in turn, is purified by classic repose and restraint. Nothing better illustrates this duality in Mozart than the fascination which this so-called arch-classicist had upon the most romantic artists. Chopin is reported to have murmured on his deathbed, "Play Mozart in memory of me—and I will hear you." Marié Henri Beyle (Stendhal), who carried the banner of literary Romanticism in *Chartreuse de Parme* and *Rouge et Noir*, as well as in a number of works on musical subjects, wrote for the epitaph on his tombstone: "This soul adored Cimarosa, Mozart, and Shakespeare." Tchaikovsky, one of the most romantic of the Romantics, wrote to Mme. von Meck: "I not only like Mozart, I idolize him. To me the most beautiful opera ever written is Don Giovanni. No one else has ever known how to interpret so exquisitely in music the sense of resigned and inconsolable sorrow [*sic!*]. . . . It is thanks to Mozart that I have devoted my life to music."[2] If one were to choose the five greatest works in almost any form—opera, symphony, string quartet, and so on—a work by Mozart would most certainly be among those five in any or all the forms.

[2] Catherine Drinker Bowen and B. von Meck, *Beloved Friend.*

Biography

Wolfgang Amadeus Mozart was born in Salzburg, January 27, 1756, the son of Leopold Mozart, a musician who gained more than local fame as a composer, teacher, and vice-Kapellmeister to the Archbishop of Salzburg. Wolfgang's genius manifested itself from earliest childhood: indeed, he is the most extraordinary example of musical precocity in all history. He picked out tunes on the harpsichord at the age of three; and he composed at four. At six he appeared in concerts with his sister, who was some years his senior. Their father took the two prodigies on a tour over Europe; they played at the Austrian, French, English, and Dutch courts, arousing the greatest enthusiasm everywhere. Thus, Mozart's career opened under the most brilliant auspices. By the time he was twelve he had already written his first cantata, ten symphonies, an Italian opera, and the charming German operetta BASTIEN AND BASTIENNE (1768). The following year, a tour spread his name through Italy, then the world centre of music, where he amazed his audiences with his organ playing and his powers of improvisation. At Rome the boy caused a sensation when, after one hearing of Allegri's fairly long and very involved *Miserere* at the Sistine Chapel, he wrote down the entire work, note for note, from memory—an almost incredible feat!

The remainder of his brief career presents a fantastic pattern of ups and downs, of disappointments dotted with flashes of success; through it all he carried on with lightning speed and fluency the creation of his great works. The system of patronage was still all-powerful: a composer, painter, or poet depended for his livelihood not on his earnings but on the whims and vagaries of princely patrons—public concerts and public support through purchase of publications had not yet come into practice. Ironically enough, Mozart, who so often has been held up as the very incarnation of the classical spirit, was the first composer to revolt against the system of patronage; just as, some decades earlier, Dr. Johnson had been the first man of letters to defy it. Mozart refused to put up with the indignities that his patron, the Archbishop of Salzburg, heaped upon him as a matter of course.

Unfortunately, while the old regime with its system of patronage was beginning to crack, it was still too powerful to be defied. Haydn gracefully submitted and got through life peacefully.

x

Beethoven brushed it aside— but that was two decades later. Mozart came a generation too soon—and was crushed.

Having broken with his patron, he decided to try his fortune in Vienna. Everything depended on his obtaining a permanent appointment at the court. Had he been able to find a patron as appreciative of his genius as Prince Esterhazy was of Haydn's, there is no doubt that his life would have taken an altogether different turn. But despite the fact that both the Empress Maria Theresa and her son, Joseph II, were aware of his gifts, they never gave him more than passing recognition. Why the greatest musician of his time should have had to go begging for a permanent post when all about him mediocrities were established in comfortable sinecures is one of those mysteries that leave one aghast at the caprices of chance. Actually, Mozart had none of the suavity of the courtier when his artistic integrity was at stake. When the Emperor Joseph II remarked to him that his opera THE ABDUCTION FROM THE SERAGLIO (1782) seemed to have "much too many notes," the composer replied frankly: "Exactly as many notes as are necessary, Your Majesty." So too, when the King of Prussia, who was very proud of his orchestra, asked him what he thought of it, Mozart answered, "It contains great virtuosi, but if the gentlemen would play together they would make a better effect."

Lacking the mainstay of economic security, Mozart was doubly exposed to all the emotional instabilities of his temperament; one moment he was in high spirits, the next in deepest dejection. Amidst all the worries and distractions of a hectic life, the divine music continued to pour forth, but at an ever greater cost to its creator. His marriage with Constanze Weber, a pretty, thoughtless girl who seemed to combine in herself all the qualities necessary to make for him the least suitable wife, only added to his difficulties. Extravagance, debts, and illness followed in a constant cycle, aggravating the lack of a deep emotional relationship which might have given him the balance and strength he so desperately needed. Most tragic of all was the lack of understanding and appreciation he so often had to face as an artist from those who played the most decisive parts in his life. Against this dismal and discouraging background was produced some of the most consistently pleasant and sunny music the world has known and enjoyed.

The last years of his life were brightened by the enormous

success of his comic opera THE MARRIAGE OF FIGARO (1786) and of his dramatic masterpiece DON GIOVANNI (1787). In both of these he at last had a librettist worthy of him—the Italian poet-adventurer, Lorenzo da Ponte, a colourful character who ended his chequered career in the United States. Among other things da Ponte was the first Professor of Italian at Columbia College; he lies buried somewhere in downtown New York, like Mozart himself, in an unmarked grave. DON GIOVANNI was written for Prague where Mozart had his greatest triumph and where he spent the happiest weeks of his life. He composed it while sitting among his friends, enjoying the friendly chatter about him, taking his turn at a game of bowls, and then returning to put down another few lines of the matchless score. Like so many of his works, it was written in its finished form at the first attempt without revision or correction, for it had been thoroughly worked out, down to the last detail, in his head.

Within little more than six weeks in 1788, Mozart produced his three last and greatest symphonies, those in E flat, in G minor (the one we shall study presently), and the one in C (the "Jupiter"). During the three years that were left him there flowed from his pen a steady output of great works. But the struggle against discouragement was becoming ever more unequal; he was, as he put it, "always hovering between hope and anxiety." In the final year of his life, despite a continual turn for the worse in his physical and mental condition, he produced a number of his finest concertos, chamber music of all kinds, his greatest choral work, the REQUIEM MASS, and the opera THE MAGIC FLUTE (1791). This wonderfully gay fairy opera was written in the spell of dejection when he returned home, empty-handed, from the coronation of the Emperor Leopold II in Prague (his CORONATION CONCERTO and the opera THE CLEMENCY OF TITUS (1791) were written for this occasion). The opera was written for Schikaneder, the impresario of a little theatre on the outskirts of Vienna, who told Mozart that he could, "to a certain point, consult the taste of connoisseurs and your own glory," but must have "a particular regard to that class of persons who are not judges of good music . . ." In this manner was born one of the first, if not the first, German romantic operas that paved the way for Weber and Wagner.

Mozart survived the première of THE MAGIC FLUTE by only

two months, working feverishly all the while on his REQUIEM MASS. The writing of this work forms the final and strangest chapter of his career. He had received a visit from a stranger who had commissioned him to write a "Mass for the Dead" for his master who desired to remain unknown. Mozart accepted the order; but the mystery surrounding the whole matter made a strange impression on him. Actually, it was nothing more than a "ghosting" job for a Count Walsegg, who wished to pass himself off as a composer and needed a Mass in memory of his wife. As Mozart was starting out for the coronation in Prague, the mysterious stranger reappeared, asking what had become of the REQUIEM MASS. Profoundly disturbed, Mozart promised to have it ready as soon as he returned. In his highly unsettled state of mind, the summons of the stranger gave him the notion, which grew into a fixed idea as he proceeded, that he was writing his own requiem—and that he might not live to finish it. He redoubled his efforts, working against time on what was to remain as his choral masterpiece, and one of the greatest of all requiems—and he did leave it slightly incomplete; it was finished by his pupil, Franz Süssmayer, who also completed the opera, THE CLEMENCY OF TITUS.

Now, when it was too late, bright prospects opened before him. He learned that a number of Hungarian nobles had formed a fund to provide him with an annuity and that in Amsterdam a subscription fund had been started to commission new works from him. Night after night, in the illness of the final month, he would follow in his imagination the performance of his MAGIC FLUTE at Schikaneder's theatre, looking at his watch and going over the arias as the time for them arrived. He died of what is commonly held to have been a malignant typhus fever,[3] on December 5, 1791, a month before his thirty-sixth birthday.

He was given a pauper's funeral. A violent storm was raging; the half dozen friends who had come to the service followed to the city gates and then forsook him and turned back. No memorial marked his last resting place; the site was soon forgotten and has not since been discovered. But his monument is truly "more lasting than bronze": an art which for sheer refinement of feeling,

---

[3] Some authorities considered his death due to a general collapse from overwork and irregular living. According to Dr. J. Barrant, and quoted by W. J. Turner in his authoritative biography (Knopf, 1938), Mozart died of Bright's disease.

exquisiteness of line, and transparency of texture has never been equalled. It is a music of pure song, of fresh and sunlit things, of early morning and never-fading youth—a song dedicated to the eternal ideal of pure and perfect beauty in art.

Symphony in G minor, No. 40

The SYMPHONY IN G MINOR—about which Schubert said, "You can hear the angels singing through it!"—is one of the three last symphonies written with incredible speed in the summer of 1788. Finished on July 25, it seems to have taken little over ten days to compose. It is, for many music lovers, Mozart's most personal utterance: one of the few works in which the serenity of the artist has been pierced through by the torment and despair of the man; and it is one of the best examples of Mozart's deliberate dramatic expressions in instrumental music.

ANALYSIS. *FIRST MOVEMENT: Allegro molto. G minor. Alla breve tempo. Sonata-allegro.* The Symphony opens, after a brief, restless pulsation, with a clearly Romantic theme; a song of tenderness and grief purified in the flame of a proud and luminous spirit. (*Alla breve tempo* means that the pace is doubled up—twice as fast as usual.) The first theme is announced by the first and second violins, piano, and the theme successfully establishes the sombre colouring of the minor mood:

Notice the graceful regularity of the structure, built in four-measure phrases. The Classical period is, understandably enough, the period of maximum observance of the four-measure phrase and the careful layout of related tonalities.

A bridge of formal design modulates to the key of the second theme (B flat). Gentle, sustained, and legato, this theme offers a striking contrast to the opening melody. It is in major where the first was in minor; in a high register where the first was not; it is "pleading-like" whereas the first was most assertive; it is shared by strings and woodwinds, quite different in rhythmical outline from, and in a more lyrical mood than, the first theme. It is also characteristically Mozartian in its chromatic composition. Like the first theme, it is in regular four-measure structure.

The *Codetta* (a brief closing section) is composed of a figure in which an active, suspended tone descends in a poignant downward resolution, "as a sigh," and intertwined with the principal figure from the first theme. Vigorous scale passages complete the exposition, which ends in a double-bar and a sign that the entire exposition section should be repeated. This was a common procedure during the Classical Period, and even into the nineteenth century, though nowadays there is a variance in the observation of this repeat. The listener should be on the watch to see whether or not the repeat takes place.

The Development Section is fashioned out of the opening figure of the first theme, bandied about amongst the various instruments, and then presented in ever-new combination of instrumental colour, with intricate countermelody woven about it, and the harmony, the while, modulating from key to key. Having exploited its possibilities to the full, the composer launches on a long passage of coming back to the original tonality, which gives a certain sense of satisfactory balance. At the end, the liquid tones of the clarinets complete the retransition and return us to the G-minor tonality of the first theme in its original state.

The Recapitulation, or Reprise (the restatement of the material of the Exposition), pursues the same course as the Exposition up to the bridge passage to the second theme. Now Mozart does something extremely interesting. If he were to keep the melody of the second theme *exactly* as he presented it in the exposition, he would have to lead the music into the major mode. That would be out of the question, so he not only transposes the second theme into a key closer to the tonic, but he actually shifts it from the major into the minor mode, and thus remains in the G-minor tonality and modality. The Codetta, with its poignant, sighing resolutions of the active tones to the more inactive ones (the tones of the tonic chord are the ultimate "rest" tones, and of these, the tonic, or key-tone, is of absolute "rest"), is shifted to G minor; and the scale and chordal passages leading to the final cadence make a vigorous affirmation of the "home tonality."

SECOND MOVEMENT: Andante. E-flat major. ⁸⁄₈ time. Sonata-allegro form. As though fearful of having been too self-revealing in his first movement, Mozart retreats in the second to the bejewelled graces of the Rococo style. Tender, sparkling, and graceful, the music withal avoids the tone of deep personal feeling that the nineteenth-century composers infused into their slow movements. The use of the first-movement form for the slow movement is not usual.

The first theme, announced piano, is taken up and fugually imitated in turn by viola, second violin, and first violin. Here follows the principal theme:

The much more graceful second theme, played by the strings, is as follows:

There is something ineffably Viennese in the graceful intervallic "dip" of the violins at the beginning of the second phrase of the first theme. In the delicate little clusters of thirty-second notes with which the principal theme is ornamented upon its return, and in the lacy lines of the movement as a whole, one glimpses more than anywhere else in the symphony the gallantry and formality of the eighteenth-century style and manner. The structure is based on regular eight-measure periods with courtly cadences at the close of each. Noteworthy are the wonderful interweaving of melodies with constant imitations of the theme on the part of different instruments and the subdued colouring in which the movement as a whole is pitched. There is no coda.

THIRD MOVEMENT: Minuetto. Allegretto. G minor. ³⁄₄ time. Minuet and trio form. The third movement brings us back to the sombre G-minor tonality of the first movement. We hear a proud, stately dance that is more staid and serious than light and care-free. The vigorous, assertive theme, sprinkled with syncopations, is announced by the strings and woodwinds. Its structural irregularity—a six-measure phrase answered by one of eight measures—lends it something of waywardness.

The Trio section is in a contrasting G major, and it is much more suave and serene than the first theme—notice how the "question" of the strings is "answered" by the woodwinds:

The peculiar six- and eight-measure formation that was observed in the Minuet proper is retained. After brief colloquy between the lower strings—'cellos and double basses—and upper woodwinds, the Trio works up to a subtle climax. Then comes the direction, *menuetto da capo*, which means that the Minuet proper is repeated from the beginning and the final close comes just before the Trio.

FOURTH MOVEMENT: Allegro assai. G minor. Alla breve. Sonata-allegro form. In the last movement, we have one of those remarkable coincidences in music. The principal theme, with its upward sweep of the outline along a chordal formation, is similar to the main theme of the Scherzo movement of Beethoven's FIFTH SYMPHONY. (See page 314.) Likewise, the movement illustrates the subtle effect of the minor mode upon themes and rhythms that might well be considered to embody the spirit of the dance. There is to be found throughout the movement quite a play between the woodwinds and the strings, as though in dialogue, and frequent alternate moments of exquisiteness and compelling power—contrasted in a most dramatic manner and, of course, revealing the expression of *both* the heart and the intellect of the composer. The tempo is very lively (allegro assai) and in double-quick time (alla breve).

The first theme is given to the strings and played softly and crisply (piano and staccato). It is regular in formation, with the cadences holding forth at the appointed places.

The second theme is a perfect foil for the first. The principal theme ascends in a chord line while the second opens with sustained tones and moves in a much less vigorous manner—in a lyrical way, in fact. Then, too, the second theme is quite chromatic as we have, by now, come to expect in Mozart's subsidiary themes. Again, to point out essential differences between the two themes, the first is in a minor mode while the second is in a major; the first is restless and impetuous, while the second is suave and smooth; the first is to be played staccato, crisply and detached, while the second is to be played in a legato manner with the tones slurred, well joined together. The second theme is played by the first violins:

The Development Section opens with a curiously whimsical and even humorous version of the principal motive—the arpeggio up the tones of the chord. This is worked out into ingenious imitations amongst the different instruments. (Try to follow it closely in its development.)

In the Recapitulation Section, Mozart repeats his device of the first movement and shifts the second theme into G minor, thus not only transposing it (putting it into another key) but also changing its mode. The entire section is predominantly G minor, leading straight into the brief but vigorous affirmation of the "home" tonality by the final cadence. There is no coda.

Franz Joseph Haydn (1732-1809)

The career of Franz Joseph Haydn presents a strong contrast to that of Mozart. He adapted himself to the system of patronage and was fortunate enough to find in the Esterhazy princes of Austria understanding, generous, and magnanimous patrons who, throughout the thirty years of his supremely successful career, gave him every opportunity to develop his powers. Largely because of their wealth and generosity, and the way in which these were dispensed, Haydn was able to exercise and develop his genius to its utmost—to the everlasting enjoyment of mankind.

Biography

Haydn was born in 1732 at Rohrau, in Lower Austria, the son of a master wheelwright, and showed his musical gifts in early childhood. "Almighty God, to whom I render thanks for all his unnumbered mercies, gave me such facility in music that by the time I was six I stood up like a man and sang masses in the church choir, and could play a little on the clavier and the violin." He was given a chance to become chorister at the celebrated St. Stephen's Church in Vienna, where he sang until his voice began to break. Thrown then upon his own resources, he took whatever pupils he could find, and devoted himself to the study of composition. At twenty he wrote the music for a comic opera, THE NEW CROOKED DEVIL, which attained a certain popularity. The next few years he spent in teaching, accompanying, above all in learning the essentials of the musician's craft. He had no regular training; but through his own industry he acquired an independent style that marked all his works with originality.

A serious impetus to his composition dates from 1755 when he was invited to Weinzerl, the country home of a nobleman who was a patron of music. Adapting himself to the musical resources at hand—a few string and wind players—he turned out his first symphony and his first string quartet, the two forms in the development of which he was to play so important a role. But the turning point in his career came in 1761 when, at the age of twenty-nine, he was appointed Kapellmeister to Prince Paul Esterhazy at Eisenstadt. Thus began one of the most notable relationships between prince and artist in the history of music, an example of the patronage system at its best. For almost thirty years Haydn lived on the magnificent Esterhazy estate, freed from all care and devoting himself wholeheartedly to his art. He had a complete orchestra and a body of singers at his disposal, and turned out a steady stream of symphonies, operas for the Court theatre, cantatas, choral works for the Chapel, and chamber music, constantly experimenting and refining his work until he became one of the two great masters of the Classical Period.

During the lifetime of Prince Nicholas Esterhazy, designated "the Magnificent"—his establishment at Esterhazy rivalled Versailles—Haydn steadfastly refused all invitations elsewhere. In 1790, however, after the Prince's death, he took up the proposal of the impresario Salomon and went to England, composing the *Salomon Symphonies*—six in number—especially for the occasion and conducting them himself at the pianoforte. The visit was a sensational success; as a result, he made another two years later. He was fêted by the royal family and the nobility and received the degree of Doctor of Music from Oxford.[4] He was often at the house of the Prince of Wales, where the King's three sons took the 'cello, viola, and violin parts in the orchestra; but Haydn had some trouble in collecting his pay! He finally sent in a bill for 100 guineas; Parliament eventually discharged the debt. The London concerts not only assured him additional financial reserves but also spread his name more than ever throughout Europe. He himself often said that not until he had been in England did he become really famous in Germany. (How similar to the case of Edward MacDowell!)

Of special interest to students of English literature are his two oratorios, THE CREATION, based upon Milton's "Paradise Lost," and THE SEASONS from James Thomson's celebrated poem of that name. The oratorio, as we saw in Chapter VIII, had become enormously popular in England during the lifetime of Handel, who dominated English music throughout the first half of the

---

[4] The so-called OXFORD SYMPHONY, written for Paris in 1788, and first performed in London in 1791, was so named in recognition of the honour that had been accorded him by Oxford University (1791).

eighteenth century—and for centuries later, as a matter of fact, along certain lines of composition and instruction. During his visit to England, Haydn became thoroughly acquainted with Handel's music and, upon the suggestion of his manager, Salomon, essayed the form in which the great German had so distinguished himself. The nobility of Milton's subject found a ready response in the deeply religious Haydn. "Never was I so pious as when composing THE CREATION. I knelt down every day and prayed God to strengthen me for my work." The oratorio made an extraordinary impression; the audience at the first performance was deeply moved. As for Haydn himself, he wrote, "One moment I was as cold as ice, the next I seemed on fire. More than once I was afraid I should have a stroke." THE CREATION spread rapidly all over Europe, equalled in popularity only by Handel's masterpiece, THE MESSIAH. From the final years of the century, too, dates Haydn's most famous song, *God Save the Emperor*, which became the national anthem of Hapsburg Austria, as well as, in a later setting, *Deutschland über Alles*. It was the one outstanding occasion in modern times when a great composer gave his country its chief patriotic song. The hymn was a favourite of Haydn's; he introduced a set of masterly variations on it in the Slow Movement of his "EMPEROR" STRING QUARTET.

The last years of his life were spent in seclusion: his long, arduous career had sapped his strength. An intimate circle of friends and distinguished visitors lightened his struggle with the infirmities of old age. He appeared for the last time in public at a performance of THE CREATION at the University of Vienna in 1808 when he was seventy-six. He was carried into the hall in his armchair. Salieri conducted. As the words "And there was light" rang out, Haydn, greatly moved, lifted his arm and exclaimed, "It came from there!" As the work proceeded, his excitement rose and it was thought wiser to take him from the hall. The audience flocked to do him honour; Beethoven kissed his hand and forehead. At the door, he raised his hands as if in blessing. The occasion recalls the triumphal entry of the aged Voltaire into Paris.

His final illness came while the armies of Napoleon were bombarding Vienna. Five days before the end he called his servants around him and, having been carried to the piano, played the *Emperor's Hymn* three times. He died on May 31, 1809, and was buried in a suburban churchyard outside the battle lines. The

French invaders joined with his own countrymen in paying tribute to his greatness. When Mozart's REQUIEM MASS was performed in his honour, French officers of high rank joined the mourners and ordered a French guard of honour around his catafalque. In 1820, his remains were transferred to the parish church at Eisenstadt on the Esterhazy estates, where he had spent the greater part of his creative life.

In the matter of compositional style, Haydn was the last of the eighteenth-century masters. Both by temperament and achievement, he was part and parcel of the so-called Classical Age. "Papa Haydn" he was called affectionately by his younger contemporaries. Nothing could better sum up the geniality that characterized the man and the artist. His is a solid, forthright kind of music that has all the beauty of health and lucidity, of perfect balance and measure; in his rondos and allegros, he transports us to a sunny world where we smile in spite of ourselves—there is nothing in all music quite like the final rondo movements of his symphonies, with their outspoken life, vitality, and thoroughgoing good humour, and it is not without possibility that these will serve the symphony composers in the not too distant future as a worthy model to be emulated. Haydn was a most methodical and painstaking worker, in spite of the seeming spontaneity of his works; he was utterly unlike the romantic concept of the artist that came to be popularly accepted in the nineteenth century. He composed slowly, mulling over the themes deliberately before he wrote them down. His melodies were simple and flowing; his taste was impeccable; his imagination of inexhaustible fecundity. He was completely devoted to his art; indeed, he had toward it the almost religious attitude of Bach, Handel, and the older masters. He inscribed his scores "*In Nomine Domini*" (In God's Name) at the beginning, and "*Laus Deo*" (Praise Be to God) at the close. His genius he regarded as a gift from on high, to be put only to the loftiest uses.

Haydn has been called the father of the symphony and of the string quartet, and the composer who determined the make-up of the modern symphony orchestra. While these assertions are not exactly true, there can be no question that he, like Mozart, played a decisive part in the history of instrumental forms and in establishing the basic character of our modern orchestra; and we owe them both more than can be told in the matters of compositional and instrumentation techniques. It was Haydn who helped to perfect the sonata-allegro form about which we have written so much.[5] It was he, too, who laid down many of the basic principles of writing for string quartet as well as for the orchestra.

Every composer is indebted to the preliminary work done by a number of pioneers who precede him, many of whom may be forgotten later. In this sense, Haydn built upon the work of those who had come before him, bringing their work to a still higher level of artistic expression and passing that on to those who succeeded him. At the same time, he was unquestionably original and daring and had the type of mind that was congenial to large, clearly evolved structures. He laid much stress on the architectural values of his art. In his string quartets, which contain some of his most significant music, he transcended the gaiety and impersonality that have been held up as the two main characteristics of the Rococo age; the slow movements are exquisitely felt, personal songs projecting all the moods of wistful tenderness associated with a later age—and one must say that Haydn exhibited many traits of the romantic temper, as well as not a few of the realistic temper. His long life summarized his heritage and his time. Other masters may stir us more poignantly, but no one else gives us such a sense of well-being, of placidity, and kindliness, and good, solid contentment. All these are excellently set forth in the symphony we are about to study.

Symphony No. 6 in G Minor ("Surprise")

The SURPRISE SYMPHONY is one of the set of six that Haydn wrote for the concerts that his manager arranged on the occasion of his first visit to London in 1791 (the year of Mozart's death). The "Surprise" designation comes from the sudden orchestral crash that occurs at the end of the pianissimo theme of the slow movement (see page 350). The symphony is scored for two flutes, two oboes, two bassoons, two horns, two trumpets, tympani, and strings. (The Classical instrumentation was usually marked with

---

[5] The reader who is interested in pursuing the historical aspects of the subjects just discussed should note the contributions to the sonata-allegro form made by G. Sammartini (1701-1775), B. Galuppi (1706-1785), F. Gossec (1734-1829), and especially K. P. E. Bach (1714-1788) and Johann Stamitz (1717-1757). Both Haydn and Mozart owed a great deal to Stamitz in the perfection of the form as well as the performing medium of the symphony.

pairs of wind instruments, a practice that was changed to three
and then four of a kind in the Romantic Era and our own time.)

ANALYSIS. *FIRST MOVEMENT: Adagio cantabile—vivace assai.
G major.* $\frac{3}{4}$ - $\frac{6}{8}$ *time. Sonata-allegro form.* The SURPRISE SYMPHONY
opens, as the two tempo directions indicate, with a slow introduc-
tion (adagio cantabile— very slowly and in a singing style) that
presents a lyrical woodwind passage answered by the strings.
After a slowly gathering crescendo, we are plunged into the vivace
assai (very quick) tempo of the first movement proper, with the
violins announcing one of those sprightly tunes resembling a folk
dance; note the original and surprising effect of the principal
theme beginning in a foreign key (a minor) and reaching the
tonic key at its conclusion—quite a daring thing to do!

This theme is developed and extended, but reappears some
eighteen measures later.

The movement bustles along in a breezy manner with those running passages of sixteenth notes of which the composers of the
eighteenth century were so fond. The second theme, built on such
a running figure, at least in part, offers an effective contrast to the
first.

The following closing theme and codetta round out the exposition, sustaining the mood of buoyant good humour.

Now the listener has an opportunity to see what the composer
can do with the themes he has set forth in the exposition, and it is

hoped that the main themes are well in mind for that exercise. However, the development section of this movement is short but quite ingenious. It contains a number of modulations that Haydn's contemporaries must have found most daring. Even in brevity Haydn has plenty to say!

The recapitulation presents the three themes heard in the exposition, with the second and closing themes transposed, according to the conventions, to the key of the tonic. Throughout the entire movement, the music bubbles along with unflagging rhythmic vitality and with a cheerfulness that even the most rabid devotee of Romanticism could not resist. Note the important coda. Notice, too, the regular layout of the music. As in the Mozart works, we are dealing with one who has a great respect for regularity and perfection of form, based largely on the supremacy of the four-measure phrase.

SECOND MOVEMENT: Andante. G major. ¾ time. Theme and variations form. The well-known staccato theme of the second movement is a very simple one, quite folklike in its general character. It is played by the strings, piano, and consists of two rather sedate and very regular periods, each of which begins in C major and modulates into G major. The surprise comes with the sudden "crash" chord at the end of the second period, in the midst of a quiet, pianissimo passage.

Then Haydn makes a series of variations upon this theme, and in them he shows his inventiveness in a very happy manner. In the first variation, the melody is embroidered with a delectable countermelody. In the second, the melody undergoes a change of mode into the minor. The third is a variation in rhythm; the sedate eighth notes are transformed into bouncing sixteenths. Next we hear the melody against a new countermelody in the woodwinds. Now the melody is played loudly, fortissimo, by woodwinds and brass against a staccato triplet figure accompaniment in the strings. A rhythmic and melodic variant of the theme works up to a climax, after which we get our last echo of the tune, fading away, pianissimo, with a subtle change of harmony at the end to freshen up the final cadence—and a fine, though daring, stroke of genius it is, too!

THIRD MOVEMENT: Menuetto: Allegro molto. G major. ¾ time. Minuet and trio form. The minuet is a rollicking movement, filled with good, even rough, humour. There is nothing even remotely stiff or aristocratic about it. The opening theme might well have been a popular, peasant, wooden-shoe dance tune:

The trio section has a much more flowing and running theme, though one cannot help noticing the wide "jumps" in the melody that remind one of the joyful clicking of the wooden shoes.

A bluff humour pervades the music, and after the trio, the minuet is repeated, da capo. Here, as in the previous movement, the utmost regularity of phrase and period structure and the utmost simplicity of orchestration prevail—content and means combine in impeccable taste.

FOURTH MOVEMENT: Allegro molto. G major. ⅔. Rondo form. The finale is a typical Haydn rondo with its gay and frolicsome spirit; the violins scamper as fast as they can through the mazes of an irresistible dance. The thumping laughter of the minuet is replaced by a subtler vivacity. The first theme is announced by the

Y

first violins. (Watch for the reappearance of this theme as it alternates with the contrasting episodes, and see if you can sketch out
a schematic A-B-A-C-A- . . . outline for the movement as you
listen.)

This rollicking theme is matched in gaiety and wit by the second,
which has an accompaniment that remotely suggests some modern
"ragtime."

The two themes alternate, sweeping the listener along at a headlong pace and leaving him—which is more than can be said for
most dances at that speed—strangely refreshed. For the approach
to the final cadence we have those bustling runs in sixteenth notes
again, and the symphony ends, fortissimo, on a gay and brilliant
affirmation of the G-major tonality. Haydn's finales have a "go"
and sparkle that are quite distinctive in music.

ADDITIONAL SUGGESTIONS FOR LISTENING

The past few years have witnessed a remarkable upsurge of interest
in the two classical masters of the symphony we have just discussed.
Their works are heard more and more frequently in concert programmes and over the radio. The student will do well to take advantage of the opportunities that exist to familiarize himself with the principal symphonic works of these masters—and to create additional
opportunities by means of the gramophone. Of Mozart, the JUPITER
SYMPHONY, the SYMPHONY IN E-FLAT MAJOR, and the delightful serenade, *Ein Kleine Nachtmusik* (see page 388 for its presentation) are most
often played. In addition, one hears, now and then, broadcasts from
the Metropolitan Opera Company of Mozart's DON GIOVANNI and
THE MARRIAGE OF FIGARO. Of Haydn's symphonies, the most frequently heard are those called, respectively, OXFORD, PARIS, CLOCK,
and DRUM-ROLL. The listener will find a good representation of these
masters in an up-to-date record catalogue, and choices may be made
to suit one's desires.

Review of Salient Characteristics of the Classical Temper

Now that we have just heard two outstanding examples of the classical symphony, it might be well to enumerate some of the salient characteristics as revealed by these two works. Of course, we should always bear in mind that we ought not be too dogmatic about these distinctions; rather, we should consider them as broad aids to our thinking, and general in scope. Also it should be borne in mind, as we stated in a previous chapter, that though many of these characteristics may also be discovered in the Romantic temper, what is often called "Classical" is due to *emphasis* of certain basic items and various *combinations* of these. With little change of wording, the following might well apply to the other fine arts, but more especially to literature and painting. (The order or sequence of items has no significance of precedence.)

1. Most striking, perhaps, is the regularity and polished perfection of structure, the sense of symmetry and balance, that come from a structure rooted in the four-measure phrase and two-phrase period; also the intellectual rather than unfettered emotional expression and the obvious concern with logical development of ideas.

2. Almost as marked is the spaciousness of the layout in regard to tonality, the definite establishment of one key, the leisurely modulations to the next, and the care with which the cadence feeling is driven home. At the final cadences the dominant, or active, harmony of the key resolves again and again to the tonic chord, giving a sense of completeness and key-feeling that, in our modern days of speeded-up awareness of key, seems more than ample.

3. The orchestration is relatively simple and transparent compared with that of today. The strings play by far the most important part; the woodwinds and brasses, in pairs, are used largely for reinforcement during climaxes or in solo or ensemble passages not unlike chamber music uses. Of course the orchestra is much smaller than in the nineteenth century; the whole scale of values is much more limited and, on the whole, much more subtle than those of today.

4. The climaxes are naturally much less grandiose, the contrasts much less violent than in a typical Romantic work. The

allegros are likely to be faster, lighter, and gayer; the *andantes* not quite so slow or heavy. Of course there is individuality in the music of the Classical temper, but there is not an ostentatious display of it for its own effect—the Classicist would rather charm and please than startle and disturb his listeners, in spite of what we have just heard in the Haydn SURPRISE SYMPHONY.

5. The emotional values fit in with the purely musical ones. The prevailing mood is one of grace and merriment instead of grandeur or pathos. The music is urbane and suave, tender and dreamy, rather than "deep" and disturbed. There is much less dependence on atmosphere and picturesqueness. Perfection is a vital ideal, and reason and intellect are emphasized more than capricious emotional expression; emotion there is a-plenty, to be sure, but it is more likely to be held in check, controlled, and never allowed to run away with the musical ideas or musical logic.

6. The melody is simple, songlike, spontaneous, and flows naturally. The harmony is appropriately light and uncomplicated. Tempo and dynamics do not change so often or so violently within the movement as they do in the "high" romantic music.

7. The form as a whole is more clearly articulated and of relatively smaller dimensions. The form fits the content. There is about it a great sense of flexibility; it follows the conventional pattern without any strain or stiffness. The Classical composer was a master of form, of purely musical design and the organic development of musical ideas and figures.

8. The music is of what is so often called—rightly or wrongly—a "pure" or "absolute" genre. The music tells its message without the assistance of a programme, without literary, extramusical, or pictorial connotations. It develops musical figures and ideas as such; the classicist is intent on "working out" a musical figure or design to its logical and ultimate conclusion.

9. Above all, the Classical composer looks upon the world with a serene objectivity instead of through the highly strung, often exaggerated subjectivity of the Romantic. He conceives his prime function to be the writing of beautiful music. In a sense, he subordinates his personality to the music, whereas the Romantic sometimes subordinates the music to his personality. The Classicist practises constraint and reserve, and worships the ideals of conventionality in the very best sense of the word; he would rather

perfect what is considered in good taste than be merely novel; and he would rather be convincing than shock by being bizarre.

10. The Classicist might also indulge in (and he often did) the techniques of Realism.

We have purposely included a number of descriptive items in the foregoing that are controversial, and some that are obviously borderline or common with other tempers. The author suggests, therefore, that the summary be discussed in the light of the classical music that has been heard. During the discussion, definite composers, specific works and exact portions of those works should be cited rather than generalities or mere opinions. After a worthy discussion has taken place, enumerate your own list of attributes or characteristics of the Classical temper. Then compare those with the characteristics of the Romantic temper, as they have been revealed in previous chapters, especially Chapter XII.

Chapter Twenty-Three

Classical Form and Romantic Content in the Overture

B EFORE we turn to the classical sonata forms as used in the concerto and in chamber music, it will be well to examine a common genre in which the sonata-allegro design is wedded to a programmatic content—the Overture. This is usually an extended symphonic composition, frequently in sonata-allegro form in which, however, both the first and the second themes take on programmatic significances, either from the drama or opera for which the overture might serve as a curtain raiser, or, if the overture is an independent concert piece, from the implications of the literary associations. We have here, then, an interesting fusion of what might seem at first glance to be the irreconcilable elements of "absolute" and "programme" music.[1]

Historical Background of the Overture

The overture goes back to the early Italian operas of the opening years of the seventeenth century. Many of the first operas, including those of Monteverde, were preceded by short instrumental preludes, sometimes little more than a preliminary flourish of trumpets. These were expanded throughout the century, somewhat haphazardly, until the period of Lully, the so-called "father of the French opera." It was he who established the form and mood of the dramatic prelude that served as a model both for his contemporaries and successors.

---

[1] It should be recalled at this time that we have already presented similar works in previous chapters, though for quite different purposes. Among such works were Tchaikovsky's OVERTURE 1812 and his Fantasy-Overture, ROMEO AND JULIET; Mendelssohn's MIDSUMMER NIGHT'S DREAM *Overture*; and Wagner's TANNHÄUSER *Overture*. These might be profitably and pleasurably reviewed along with the contents of this chapter.

In Lully's pattern, which came to be known as the "French Overture," there was first a slow, stately introduction, which was followed by an allegro in fugal style; and a slow section, or minuet, closed the work. Frequently one or another of the popular dance forms of the time was included. Since these dance tunes, too, were generally of a stately, even solemn character, they fitted in excellently with the general lofty style of Lully's overture.

The so-called "Italian Overture" form, due largely to A. Scarlatti, began with a quick movement, followed by a slow, melodic interlude, and then returned to a fast, lively tempo. (One can see here an early foreshadowing of the movements of the symphony of a century later.) Since opera in Italy was an enterprise dependent on popular patronage, while in France it was bound up with the pageantry and ceremony of the Bourbon court, it was natural that the Italian overture was much less "elevated" in style and content than was the French overture.

Until the time of Gluck, the overture had no special relevance to the work it served to introduce. An overture intended for one opera was often used for another, for which it served quite as well. The early eighteenth century, as the student may recall from the chapter on opera, represented a degeneration of taste and style in the form. The frivolous audiences of the day did not quiet down and pay attention to the proceedings on the stage until the entrance of their favourite star. There was a continuous buzz of excitement in the theatre as fashionable personages arrived, greeted their friends, and visited audibly as well as visibly. The composer had little incentive to take much pains with the overture, knowing that it would hardly be listened to.

Gluck and the Classical Overture

It was an Italian working for Louis XIV who had given the overture its start as an art form. It was a German who met his greatest triumph in the Paris of Marie Antoinette a century later who restored it to a lofty place in the art. With Gluck, the overture took an important step toward becoming an integral part of the drama. In the preface to ALCESTE (quoted in an earlier chapter) he says: "My idea was that the overture ought to indicate the subject and prepare the spectators for the character of the piece they are about to see." While he had not yet hit on the idea of incorporating in the overture themes from the work itself—the simplest way of uniting it with the drama—he ran his overtures continuously into the first scene of the opera. In his IPHIGENIA IN TAURIS, the orchestral introduction distinctly foreshadows the storm with which the opera opens and is the most advanced example of unity between overture and the opera itself that had been achieved up to that time, generally speaking; while the introduction to IPHIGENIA IN AULIS is one of the finest examples of the dramatic overture of the period.

Mozart's overture to DON GIOVANNI marked the next forward step. Here the overture was identified with the opera thematically. the introductory andante of the overture presages the music that accompanies the entrance of the statue in the final scene. Similarly, the solemn opening chords for the trombones in his overture to THE MAGIC FLUTE suggest the mystical elements of the libretto. With Mozart, too, the overture took over the sonata-allegro, or first-movement, form, that had now emerged as one of the most flexible and serviceable structures for extended musical works. As a matter of fact, Mozart was fond of "adapting" the form; in his overture to THE MARRIAGE OF FIGARO, he used an abridged version commonly known as the *sonatina form.*

Beethoven, in FIDELIO, continued the process by incorporating themes from the opera in the three LEONORA overtures. Through the two overtures that he wrote for famous plays—to Collin's "Coriolanus" and Goethe's "Egmont—he also opened up the path for the development of the overture into an independent concert piece in strongly dramatic style. What is most interesting here, however, is that in the works of Beethoven especially, the sonata-allegro form came to be freely adapted to the moods and purposes of a programmatic content.

Absolute Form Versus Programmatic Content

In a certain sense, this blending represented a union of fundamentally different elements. The sonata-allegro form is based on the presentation of musical themes, their working out, and their restatement more or less in their original shape. The underlying principle of storytelling or drama, on the other hand, is a combination and working out of the facts or the events to create a situation altogether different from that which existed in the beginning. In a sense, the two ideas are in opposition. That it is possible to reconcile them at all is due to the fact that the overture does not *have* to tell the story—the opera or drama does that—but it can use the dramatic material symbolically, or selectively; that is, it can lift themes with dramatic connotations from the opera or play, and then proceed to work them out along purely musical lines—or nearly so. Since, from an early time, the programme was treated suggestively rather than literally, composers were able to evolve a form that projected the mood of the drama and at the same time lent itself to effective treatment from the musical point of view, structurally speaking.

The Overture of the Romantic Period

Despite his contributions to the development of the overture, Beethoven's genius was symphonic rather than dramatic. It remained for his gifted younger contemporary, Carl Maria von Weber (1786-1826), to open the overture to the diverse influences of the new Romantic style. Weber has often been acclaimed as the father of the German Romantic opera, the precursor of the Wagner of FLYING DUTCHMAN, TANNHÄUSER, and LOHENGRIN. He turned to the legends of the folk, the magic of woodland and mountains, the picturesqueness of local colour and peasant customs. In his operas the overture is part and parcel of the play, not only in regard to musical themes but, even more important, in mood and colour. With him the overture became a subtle tone painting, projecting the audience into the emotional atmosphere of the play. His overtures to DER FREISCHÜTZ, OBERON, and EURYANTHE are justly ranked among the masterpieces in the form.

From Beethoven and Weber the path led directly to the overture of Schubert, Schumann, and Mendelssohn, culminating in the romantic overture of Berlioz and Wagner, of which we studied a notable example in the TANNHÄUSER. The golden period of the romantic overture fell within the first half of the century. With the rise of the Lisztian symphonic poem, the influence of the overture as an independent concert piece waned, for the symphonic poem, with its greater freedom of form, was better adapted to the emotional requirements of the age than a programmatic type of music that still held on to the Classical sonata-allegro form. Within the opera house the overture witnessed something of a decline for another reason. Wagner, in his later works, realized that there was no point in telling the story in the overture if the opera itself was going to do that. In his music dramas he therefore substituted the prelude, a pure mood piece, to establish the emotional atmosphere before the raising of the curtain. The composers at the end of the century steadily reduced the dimensions of the introductory piece. Then, too, the new type of audience in the lyric theatre, coming with a true eagerness and receptivity, made a noisy and protracted curtain raiser psychologically unnecessary. Such a typical end-of-the-century work as LA BOHÈME, for example, has but a few measures of introduction, thrusting the audience almost immediately into the action.

Weber's Overture to "Der Freischütz" (1821)

A decade and a half after the dubious success of FIDELIO, an opera made its appearance that swept Germany as few, if any, operas have swept it before or since—Carl Maria von Weber's romantic folk tale DER FREISCHÜTZ (The Free Archer). To a Germany torn by internal dissension, discouraged in the wake of the Napoleonic conquests, somewhat under foreign domination politically, culturally, and artistically, Weber's opera came like a wonderful awakening, the first victory of a new national art. Based on a legend of the Black Forest, steeped in the folkways and in the very essence of German Romanticism—a love of the mystical and the supernatural—the work completely captured the German imagination. Three generations in Germany have been brought up on its hunting and bridal songs; many of its melodies have passed over into the domain of folk song, and one, the Horn theme heard in the first part of the score, is a popular hymn tune!

The gifted and richly imaginative composer who is today recognized as the father of the German Romantic opera died from consumption at the age of forty at the very height of a brilliant career. Death came to him on December 18 while he was composing and conducting in London, England, and so the first of German nationalists in music was buried in foreign soil. The REQUIEM of Mozart was performed at the funeral service, as it had been at that of Haydn, Beethoven, and Schubert. When Wagner became director of music at the Saxon court, he took an active part in the movement to bring back to Germany the remains of his idol. He arranged the music for the ceremony that accompanied the interment of Weber's body in the soil of his native land and read the oration, one of his more interesting prose works.

By the world at large, Weber is remembered chiefly for the overtures to his three Romantic operas—DER FREISCHÜTZ, OBERON, and EURYANTHE—each a masterpiece in its genre, and for the perennially popular *Invitation to the Dance*. The operas themselves have not retained their place in the usual repertory outside Germany; but the overtures are among the popular orchestral pieces of all lands. The Overture to DER FREISCHÜTZ was successful from its opening night. In his diary, Weber writes that the opera was received with enthusiasm, the overture and folk song were encored, and fourteen out of the seventeen music pieces were stormily applauded. It spread to England and over the Continent at once and was performed in New York as early as 1825, only four years after its first performance. The story of the opera is built around one of those tales of magic and the Evil One of the vintage of "Odine," "Giselle," "La Belle Dame sans Merci," and the fantasies of E. T. A. Hoffmann. The action concerns a young hunter, Max, who almost falls into the toils of the Evil One by selling his soul in return for a magic bullet, but is saved in the end by the love and faith of Agatha, his betrothed. The opera ends in the triumph of young love and the defeat of the forces of evil.

In the quarter century after Mozart's death, composers rapidly came to realize how effective it would be if they incorporated the principal themes of their operas in the overtures. In a short time, the *potpourri* type of overture came into popularity; this is a type in which the composer strings together the "hit tunes" in such a manner that they will be contrasting and pleasing; our "musical comedy" type of overture is very likely to be a potpourri. Weber's overture to DER FREISCHÜTZ, although organized on the solid foundations of the classical sonata-allegro form, exhibits some characteristics of the new type of potpourri, for the subsidiary themes, instead of serving merely as transitional material between the main themes out of which the overture is constructed, are actual tunes from the opera, attractive in their own right as well as dramatic associations. The kind of overture of which DER

FREISCHÜTZ is an example is, in effect, a foreshadowing of the comparatively free organization of the tone poem of half a century later.

More important, Weber's overture is a very crystallization of the mood and atmosphere of his drama. The magic of his orchestration projects in masterly fashion the delicate colours of woodland life, the sinister fascination of the evil powers, and the basic emotional conflict of his story. Weber was much more completely the writer for the stage than Beethoven; his use of instrumental colour to create atmosphere and picturesque effect was developed in him in greater degree than in any of his contemporaries. He thus blazed the trail for the romantic symphonic colourists, for Wagner and Berlioz and Liszt, and for the entire development of the art of modern instrumentation. So many of his innovations lost their novelty through the continual imitation of his successors that we sometimes fail to realize the originality and power of imagination that brought them into being. But, standing as he did on the threshold of the new age, there can be no question that Weber enormously enriched and influenced the course of music, especially operatic and symphonic music.

ANALYSIS. The overture opens *adagio*, in C major, with a mysterious tone C softly (pianissimo) sustained in unison by the strings and woodwinds, creating at once a mood of enchantment—the enchantment of the forest.[2]

Presently a quartet of French horns intones a "Chorale of Faith" of great loveliness and serenity—a symbol of constancy. The tune has been adapted to the words of a popular hymn.

Suddenly the mood darkens: ominous tremolos in the lower strings, the plucking (pizzicato) tones of the double basses and the

---

[2] Compare the opening motive of this work with similar ideas used in compositions listed in footnote 3, Chapter XVI, page 248.

sinister beating of the muffled drum usher in a 'cello passage, creating an atmosphere of eerie foreboding. The tremolos swell to a fortissimo and then die away. We are now ready for the main body of the overture, *molto vivace* (very lively), in a sombre C-minor mode, and played in a brisk, double-time (alla breve) speed.

The first theme emerges from the deepest gloom of the low tones of the 'cellos, in an agitated pianissimo, delineating Max's fear that he may have fallen into the clutches of the Evil One:

The music becomes louder, little by little (*crescendo poco a poco*. and leads to a tumultuous transition in which a striking arpeggio (chordwise) theme and a brusque chordal passage sweep along with almost demoniac energy:

Notice what a perfect psychological and emotional contrast this theme presents to the fearful Max theme, and how effectively Weber has utilized differences in pitch register, change of mode, instrumental tone colour (timbre), rhythm and general melodic contour to project the differences between the two. (How much Wagner owed to Weber!)

After a warning outcry on the horns, repeated thrice, there emerges, *con molto passione* (with much passion), a theme on the solo clarinet, sustained high above the shuddering tremolos of the strings: it is the cry of Max when, on his way to meet the emissary of Satan at midnight to cast the magic bullets, he catches sight of the dread abysses of the Wolf's Glen.

Now the second theme proper appears in the more happy major mode (in the key of E-flat major); it is a broadly flowing melody, expressive of Agatha's love and faith. First given to clarinets and first violins, it is repeated *dolce* (sweetly) by flutes, clarinets, and the bassoons, and its square-cut, regular, four-measure phrase structure and the definite cadence at the end lend a great deal to the feeling of determination and solidity:

The development section that follows combines, in a most skilful manner, fragments of the two subsidiary themes—the arpeggio and chord figures—and the Agatha theme. The brilliant modulations of the music and its headlong pace are irresistible. The recapitulation returns to the home tonality of C minor with the sombre Max theme deep in the bass as before. This section follows the course of the exposition, except that where we formerly heard the troubled clarinet solo before the appearance of the Agatha theme, we now hear a brief reminder of the foreboding that preceded the molto vivace. Then all sadness and fear are swept away as if by magic by the triumphant proclamation of the Agatha theme on the violins and flutes against a jubilant orchestral background leading to the brilliant Coda. It is not difficult to understand the programmatic implications of this musical "speech," and the divergence from the strict form of the reprise is condoned, especially when one hears the second theme proper in the Coda— a very clever manipulation of musical materials, thematic as well as design. Almost all the brilliant Coda comes from the *Finale* of the opera itself; again, a commendable stroke of unusual imagination on the part of Weber. A vigorous repetition of the "sunny" chord of C major, as contrast to the more prevalent, "sombre" C-minor chord, brings this fascinating romantic overture to a most satisfying close.

Beethoven's "Overture Leonora" No. 3 (1806)

Beethoven's solitary venture into the operatic form, FIDELIO, cost him no end of trouble. To begin with, he did not have that flair for the stage that came to Mozart so naturally. Then again, Beethoven's high concept of the ethical nature of music rendered him out of sympathy with the type of story that opera composers of the day customarily chose for their libretti; he professed himself shocked that Mozart should have set plays like DON JUAN and the MARRIAGE OF FIGARO—a view that throws much light on his qualifications as a dramatist. His choice finally fell on a highly edifying story, *Leonora, or Conjugal Love,* based on a novel by Bouilly. The action deals with the self-sacrificing devotion of Leonora, whose husband Florestan is imprisoned in a dungeon through the machinations of the unscrupulous Pizarro, governor of the prison. Leonora disguises herself as a man and under the name of Fidelio—symbol of her wifely fidelity—braves every danger to rescue her husband. The villain is foiled in his plot to kill Florestan by the resourcefulness of Leonora and by the timely arrival of the Minister of Justice, who metes out punishment to Pizarro as Leonora removes the fetters from her husband.

The opera was beset with an extraordinary combination of difficulties from the start. The singers insisted that the music was unsingable—the same complaint that faced Wagner a generation later. What really happened was that Beethoven had introduced a concept of vocal line in advance of his age—and the singers clamoured for what they were accustomed to. The rehearsals were a source of much exasperation to everyone concerned. When the first performance was reached on November 20, 1805, Vienna was in the hands of the French army; Bonaparte was at the Imperial Palace at Schönbrunn, and the capital was deserted by the Emperor, the nobility, and the wealthy patrons of music. The work was a failure, which could not be blamed entirely on the unsettled political situation. Beethoven's friends urged him to revise the book and the score. He was adamant at first, but finally consented. The new version, produced in 1806, made a somewhat more favourable impression; but this time, Beethoven quarrelled with the manager of the theatre and the opera was withdrawn; but he was prevailed upon (in 1814) to make still another revision for a new production of the work. Finally, the opera was launched with a measure of success, in the form in which we have it today.

The opera has caused much division of opinion. Some insist that the nature of Beethoven's genius was fundamentally unsuited to the stage and that FIDELIO is weak in dramatic power. Others maintain with equal insistence that it is one of the most powerful of operas and that not only was Beethoven not lacking in dramatic talent, but he succeeded in fusing the symphonic and dramatic elements of his music with a mastery equalled by few other composers. The actual fate of the opera in the repertory seems to have veered between the two extremes. It has never become a really popular work, yet it has never disappeared altogether from the boards. Of late there appears to have arisen a new interest in it; but it is not unlikely that, in some future time, the opera will be known pretty largely through the overtures Beethoven composed for it.

Beethoven actually wrote four overtures for FIDELIO, three known as *Leonora Nos. I, II and III,* and one known as *Fidelio*—one each for the productions in 1805, 1806, and 1814, and one that did not see the light until after his death. Of them all the LEONORA No. 3, which he prepared for the revised version of 1806, has become the most popular, having established itself in the symphonic repertory as a work of great dramatic power. The so-called FIDELIO overture to this opera has often been termed a symphonic poem. Whatever differences of opinion may exist as to the opera itself, there can be no question that in the LEONORA No. 3, Beethoven projected the very essence of his opera, creating a symphonic drama of fiery eloquence and intensity. Here he was able to think in purely musical terms, undisturbed by the machinery of the stage.

ANALYSIS. The overture opens *adagio,* in the key of C major. A fortissimo chord fades into a sorrowful downward-moving figure on woodwinds and strings, suggestive of Florestan's despair as he descends to his dungeon.

The music modulates from C major down to B minor, then again to A flat, where woodwinds, accompanied by strings, sing the poignant opening measures of Florestan's famous aria in the prison scene in the second act, "In life's springtide, happiness has flown from me."

A transitional passage of great emotional power, rising from a pianissimo mood of foreboding to a fortississimo (*fff*) outburst by the full orchestra and then subsiding to a mysterious pianissimo, launches one into the allegro of the movement proper, in C major, alla breve. The principal theme is played by the violins and 'cellos — a melody of great nobility and courage. Notice the striking syncopated rhythm in the first and fifth measures of the illustration.

After an impetuous unfolding of the first theme and a transitional passage of modulation, the second theme emerges, played by flute and violin (*piano and dolce*), in a tenderly appealing, upward inflection in E major:

This theme is "exposed" and unfolded with great care and skill. The development section is carried out with Beethoven's rich sense of the possibilities implicit in this thematic material. Fragments from the "pleading" second theme are interspersed with hints of the first theme against a seething orchestral background. This culminates in the thrilling trumpet call in the last act of the opera, which signalizes the arrival of the Minister of Justice just as Pizarro is about to carry out his plot against Florestan.

This famous trumpet fanfare is played on the stage during the opera and, usually, behind the scenes (back stage) during a concert performance. Inasmuch as this theme has nothing to do with the musical material of the rest of the Overture, Beethoven was severely censured by his contemporaries; he felt fully justified, however, since the theme comes from the opera itself and serves,

z

in the overture, to maintain the underlying story or programme—one of the compromises between slavish following of the classical form and the freedom of romantic programme music.

The orchestra quivers with excitement; the trumpet call is repeated; then the music surges ahead into the recapitulation. The themes of the exposition are rehearsed, with the second theme transposed to the "home" key of C major, and then the music enters the very moving and dramatic Coda. Here the main themes again come into play and the work comes to a brilliant close with many reaffirmations of the tonic, C-major chord, sounding in the full orchestra. Truly, this is a marvellous synthesis of the classical sonata-allegro form, a real overture for an opera and, over all, a fine example of all these factors used together to provide ideal concert programmatic music.

ADDITIONAL SUGGESTIONS FOR LISTENING

It is hoped that the listener will add to his list Mozart's Overtures to THE MARRIAGE OF FIGARO, THE MAGIC FLUTE, and DON GIOVANNI; Beethoven's EGMONT and CORIOLANUS overtures (especially the last mentioned for study in structure and form); Weber's OBERON and EURYANTHE overtures; Mendelssohn's HEBRIDES and FINGAL'S CAVE. But we know you will derive more pleasure and profit from compiling your own list along the lines of the subject of this chapter.

Chapter Twenty-Four

The Concerto for Solo Instrument and Orchestra

I N THE modern sense, the word *concerto* indicates a composition for solo instrument and symphony orchestra that affords the soloist ample opportunity to display his virtuosity. The word derives from the Latin *concentus*, a species of church compositions, as was probably first used by Ludovico Viadana, in 1602, to describe his motets for voices and organ, which he published as *Concerti Ecclesiastici*.[1] In another and wider sense, the word *concerto* was used in older musical writings to describe a "performing together," that is, a performance in which a number of musicians joined forces in a united, or concerted, effort.

The form of the late seventeenth- and early eighteenth-century concerto was established largely by the composers of the Italian school, such as Corelli, Tartini, Vivaldi, and their musical kin. In this form there was not one soloist, but a group of soloists—strings, winds, keyboard, or any combination of these desired by the composer—who were used singly or together as a contrasting element to the orchestra as a whole. This small group of soloists was called the *concertino*, the remainder of the orchestral players was called the *ripieno*, and together they were called the *concerto grosso*. The form itself came to be known as the *concerto grosso*, and, as such, flourished throughout the eighteenth century. It consisted of a sequence, or collection, of movements in diverse spirits and tempi, such as largo, allegro, andante, with minuets, gavottes, and gigues occasionally interpolated—somewhat analogous to the suite, but depending for its effect on the interplay and contrast of the two groups—the concertino and the ripieno. (For more extended treatment of the concerto grosso, see Chapter XXVII.)

With the rise of the sonata in the period of Haydn and Mozart, the concerto grosso gradually receded in popularity and was

[1] See Grove's *Dictionary of Music and Musicians*, Vol. 1, page 577.

supplanted by the solo concerto, which better served to focus the attention on the solo instrument, its interplay with the orchestra itself, and permitted the latter to indulge in purely symphonic development of the musical ideas in the *tutti* (the orchestra as a whole). This interplay as a dramatic element was heightened when, instead of two groups pitted against each other, a single instrument became the protagonist of the action against the background of the orchestra, just as in Greek tragedy the single character is pitted against the chorus, if we may be permitted that analogy. Viewing the topic thus, one might well say that the concerto drew inspiration not only from the concerto-grosso traditions but also from the opera in which the solo singer alternated with the *ritornellos*, or interludes, of the orchestra. At any rate, it can be seen that previous instrumental forms, together with certain influences which may be traced to the opera, all combined with the new virtuosity on the solo instruments that came to the fore in the late eighteenth and early nineteenth century to produce a flexible, varied, and highly imaginative form. Especially during the period of Mozart and Haydn, when the solo instruments had not yet become important enough to warrant a full evening concert of piano or violin music, the combination of piano and orchestra, or violin and orchestra, became the medium through which such composer-virtuosi as Mozart and Beethoven displayed their powers as executants to their publics. In such an evening, the programme might include—this was a period of Gargantuan programmes—a new symphony or two by the composer, a new piano sonata, several vocal excerpts from a mass or opera, and, to top off the list, the latest concerto!

Mozart played a decisive role in the rise of the solo concerto, developing it as an enormously effective dialogue between soloist and orchestra. He left the form basically as it has come to be known in modern times, in three movements, a fast, a slow, and a fast, with a brilliant cadenza, usually in the first, and sometimes in the last, while the orchestra maintains silence and thus serves to focus further attention on the soloist. In the days of Mozart and Beethoven, when the artist was also the composer, the cadenza was a free improvisation on the themes of the movement. As the art of improvisation waned in favour, the cadenza was written out by the composer, by some famous soloist who had a flair for brilliant improvisation, or by some other composer. Mozart wrote

Double Virginal (Flemish, about 1600)

Ludovicus Grovvelus

between forty and fifty concertos for various instruments: they became the foundation upon which later composers constructed their works. In the piano and violin concertos of his mature period, we find revealed in full his mastery of the inherent style and idiom of each instrument, and his sensitivity to the possibilities of each, whether for soulful melody, dazzling running passages, charm and grace, or technical brilliance.

It need hardly be pointed out that the emergence of the concerto was intimately connected with mechanical improvements in the solo instruments themselves, and in the technical mastery of playing throughout the eighteenth century. This is particularly true of the piano during Beethoven's career. Just as Beethoven expanded the emotional domain of the solo piano in his thirty-two sonatas for that instrument, so he broadened the form of the concerto. In his five piano concertos and one violin concerto, the solo instrument is treated more orchestrally than in the Mozart works; the conflict between the opposing tonal colours and masses is dramatized to the highest degree. (Especially the Beethoven *Concerto for Piano in G major*, Op. 58, or the more popular one in *E-flat major*, Op. 73, called the *Emperor* by someone other than the composer.)

In many of the concertos written during the so-called Romantic Period, broadly between 1800 and 1900, and in subsequent works influenced by the style of that period, one can find many evidences of highly personalized expression within this form. Thus one may discover experiments of the form as a whole and in matters of internal structures. There are also brilliant and colourful orchestration and bravura solo playing, as well as submergence of the solo part into the very web and woof of the orchestra itself—sometimes the solo part is, in reality, just another orchestral instrument. The *tutti* of the romantic concerto is often of the greatest importance as a symphonic entity, as a means of development of thematic material, or as a vehicle for the introduction of new themes that are of more immediate attraction than they are for future organic development. It is not infrequently that one discovers both the romantic and classic tendencies in the same work!

Then, too, this romantic type of music makes frequent use of nationalistic characteristics of melody, rhythm, and instrumental colour, such as one recognizes as Oriental, Gipsy, Spanish, Russian, and the like. Oft times there is an adaptation of actual native folk tunes and native peculiarities, even in the use of indigenous harmony and sound effects. Thus one might continue; but these works and their special effects are much better heard than described.

In view of such a complex situation and natural limitations of space, our immediate task is best accomplished by selecting one or two outstanding and broadly representative works in the concerto form from among the many similar romantic compositions one might hear in concert programmes, over the radio, and by means of gramophone records. While the concertos chosen should readily ingratiate themselves into the listener's favour, they should also afford basic tuition for future experiences.

In that spirit and for that purpose, we have chosen the *Piano Concerto in A minor*, Op. 54, by Robert Schumann, and the *Violin Concerto in E minor*, Op. 64, by Felix Mendelssohn-Bartholdy, for detailed analysis; these also serve to illustrate two different solo instruments.

Robert Schumann (1810-1856)[2]

Surely no one was more to the fore in the Romantic movement in Germany than Robert (A.) Schumann, not only by virtue of his own compositions, but also through his critical writings, personal encouragement, and active aid to worthy young composers (among them, Brahms and Chopin). Born in Zwickau on June 8, 1810, he came to a tragic end near Bonn, the birthplace of Beethoven, on July 29, 1856. He did not come from a musical family, either immediate or remote, as far as we can discover, yet his talent expressed itself in original composition as early as the age of six. His more formalized education began in 1820, first at the Zwickau Gymnasium, then at Leipzig University where he took up a law course. Later, in 1829, he pursued law and philosophy at the University of Heidelberg and studied music on the side—practising as much as seven hours a day at his "hobby."

Schumann lived at the home of Friedrich Wieck, his piano teacher, and continued with his training in composition with H. Dorn at the same time. It was during his strenuous period of piano study that Schumann hit on a mechanical idea designed to strengthen the fourth finger of his right hand—he was determined

---

Ⱶ [2] Some may prefer to reverse the order of the Schumann and the Mendelssohn concertos in this chapter. This is not objectionable.

on a career as a concert pianist; but this contraption only resulted in the crippling of the finger so that his ambition as a piano virtuoso came to an abrupt end. However, as far as the world was concerned, this disappointment found compensation in that his career as a composer now became his chief concern.

The composer was in love with Clara Wieck, the daughter of his piano teacher, which met with the great displeasure of the father. The affair was finally brought to a court of law, with a verdict in favour of the young lovers. Their marriage became one of the most ideal and beautiful romances to be found in art histories—a romance paralleled in many respects by that of Marion and Edward MacDowell. Clara proved to be a great source of inspiration to Schumann, and a flood of songs and piano works flowed from the pen of the happy composer.

Schumann founded and edited the *Neue Zeitschrift für Musik*, for which he wrote many significant essays and criticisms from 1834 to 1844. In 1840, the University of Jena conferred upon him the degree of Doctor of Philosophy for his literary as well as musical achievements. This year was mainly concerned with the composition of his greatest songs, 1841 with his symphonic works, and 1842 with his chamber music.

Schumann lived in Dresden, teaching and composing, until 1850, in which year he unwisely accepted a post as town musical director at Düsseldorf. Evidences of an impending mental trouble began to be manifest, culminating in his attempted suicide by jumping into the Rhine. This forced his incarceration in an asylum near Bonn, and his death followed, mercifully, a few years later, in 1856. Another great composer, whom we have already heard from earlier in this book, Brahms, long a friend of the Schumanns, now became a great source of consolation and friendly aid. Clara resumed her professional public career as a concert pianist, and in that manner, as well as in other ways, carried forward the reputation of Schumann and his music, much as Marion carried forward Edward MacDowell's music in America.

Schumann's Concerto for Piano in A minor, Op. 54

ANALYSIS. Out of the many sympathetic and enthusiastic critiques written about this concerto, we have selected one from *The Art of Music*, a fourteen-volume work edited by Dr. Daniel

Gregory Mason, one of America's foremost composers and scholars.[3]

    The concerto stands as a flawless masterpiece. The themes are inspired. There is no trace of sentimentality or morbidness. The form is ruled by an unerring and fine sense of proportion and line. It is neither too long nor too short. There is no awkwardness, no tentativeness, no striving for effect. No note is unwisely placed. The treatment of both pianoforte and orchestra leaves nothing to be desired, either when the one is set against the other or when both are intimately blended. Though it in no way suggests the virtuoso, it is perfectly suited to the piano, bringing out unfailingly the very best the instrument is capable of.

High praise indeed from a great authority!

    The first movement of the concerto was composed in 1841, the year following Schumann's marriage; the second movement, *Intermezzo*, and the *Finale* were composed in 1845. The initial movement, marked *allegro affettuoso* (lively and tenderly), opens with a forte (loud) chord by the full orchestra and a dashing, impetuous descending solo by the piano.

    The first theme proper appears in the woodwinds and horns. played softly (*p*), and with the theme itself in the solo oboe part. Note well the germinal figures, or motives, marked "A" and "B", for these are developed throughout the three movements; even the principal themes are derived or related to them, as we shall observe. Here is the first theme:

[3] Leland Hall (Ed. in charge), *The Art of Music*, 14 Vols. (New York: National Society of Music, 1915), Vol. 7, page 237. Quoted by permission.

There is much working over the motive "A" of the first theme
between the piano and the orchestra; a rapid octave passage leads
to a *tutti* (full orchestra) which, in turn, leads into a charming duet
(*andante espressivo*, fairly slow and with expression) between the
piano and the solo clarinet, based on the motive "A." This quiet
mood is abruptly dispelled by a reappearance of the opening idea
(Mus. Ill. 1, page 375), and it is bandied about between the solo
instrument and the orchestra; the first theme is heard again, this
time as a duet between the solo flute and the piano, with the
remainder of the orchestra filling in. The first theme (Mus. Ill. 2,
page 375) is heard again in the woodwinds and horns.

The second theme, played by the first violins on the G string,
emerges with the piano affording an accompaniment in true piano
style. It is interesting to see how the composer used the solo instrument as an accompanimental background for solo orchestral instruments, as a solo instrument itself, and as an additional orchestral instrument in the more sonorous *tutti*. Note well the eventual
development of the motives marked "a" and "b" in the second
theme.

The wind theme (Mus. Ill. 2, page 375) is now played by the
piano, at the termination of which the solo clarinet plays (*animato*,
with animation) the ensuing theme, which grows out of motive
"A"; the strings provide the necessary support.

Presently the entire orchestra joins in to make a stirring climax,
at the peak of which the piano comes to its Cadenza (an interpolated solo passage of brilliant character), made largely out of
motives "B" and "A," in that order. The movement quickly
comes to a close.

The second movement, Intermezzo, marked *andantino grazioso*
(rather slowly and gracefully), is an interesting development of the
motive "B" of the first movement, and sets off the piano with a

sort of answering dialogue with the strings. Note this interplay of instrumental colour as well as of thematic development.

This idea persistently recurs, separated by episodical material of a most graceful and lyrical character. The second theme, played so expressively high up on the A string of the 'cellos, is taken up by the clarinet then by the first violins high up on their E strings. The second theme is as follows:

The opening idea (Mus. Ill. 1, above) reappears and is tossed about until a sudden swish of the strings joins the second movement with the Finale, marked *allegro vivace* (fast and sprightly). It will be seen that the first part of the principal theme grows out of the motive "B" of the first movement—another example of Schumann's command of the technical side of his craft.

Soon a marchlike, rhythmic idea is heard (*pp*) in the strings that seems to confound triple and duple metres. This might well be called the second part of the principal theme because of its later importance in the development of the movement.

The piano is soon busy with a running figure that breaks into a *tutti* on the opening theme; but a new theme (the second theme proper) of a lyrical character is played by the oboe over the strings. This idea becomes the subject for "conversation" between the strings and successively the oboe, flute, violins, and the viola. How well Schumann seems to understand the orchestra in this concerto—a refutation of the general opinion to the contrary.

A *tutti* passage leads to a flowing piano passage (closing theme) supported by soft strings, interrupted by the marchlike figure (Ill. 4, page 377). This idea is further extended at some length, leading into a *tutti* return of the principal theme of this movement. Another running theme is heard in the piano:

This is followed by the second theme, which is heard in the woodwinds. A bit of the first theme serves as coda material, and the concerto as a whole comes to a brilliant and satisfying close. Thus we see an ideal wedding of the temper of classicism, as indicated in the technics of form and thematic development, with the temper of romanticism as indicated in the highly individual, imaginative, lyrical, and dramatic emotionalism invested in their use throughout the entire concerto.

We have chosen, for our second illustration of the solo instrument type of concerto, the *Concerto in E minor*, Op. 64, for violin and orchestra by Jakob Ludwig Mendelssohn-Bartholdy, more familiarly known to most of us as Felix Mendelssohn. It was written on September 16, 1844, only three years before his untimely death in 1847. This precocious and prolific composer, who reached a most extraordinary maturity in his compositional art before he was twenty years old, had the singular good fortune among musical geniuses of enjoying a happy and comfortable life, though one must add that he was always extremely busy, and hard working, and occupied posts of the utmost responsibility.

He was born in Hamburg, February 3, 1809, of Jewish ancestry, though for a generation past the family had embraced the Christian faith. At the age of ten he entered the Singakademie, though he had studied violin, piano, and composition before that. It is interesting to note that the very year he entered the academy, his original setting of the Nineteenth Psalm received its first public performance. His home life was not only happy from freedom of monetary woes, but it was a very musical one, for his father saw to it that a small orchestra or an ensemble performed at home every Sunday. Felix thus had an excellent opportunity to hear his own works and to receive training in conducting, which later enabled him to become director of the famous Gewandhaus Symphony Orchestra of Leipzig.

At the age of seventeen, Mendelssohn composed what many consider his greatest work, the overture to A MIDSUMMER NIGHT'S DREAM (see page 117) and the superb octet for strings, Op. 20. The same year he entered the University of Berlin, offering as his evidence of ability a translation of Terence. The next year he composed the opera DIE HOCHSEIT DES CAMACHO. But an amazing experience awaited him at the age of twenty: he produced, for the first time since the composer's death, J. S. Bach's PASSION ACCORDING TO ST. MATTHEW! What a world of inferences might be drawn from that event and the circumstances involved! In 1829 a series of nine musical travels to England were undertaken, and again one might ponder over the influence (yea, stranglehold) that Handel and Mendelssohn have had over English music all these years. His appearances throughout England and the Continent were in the manifold capacities of conductor, composer, pianist, and organist, and he had remarkable success in all. In 1833 he conducted the Düsseldorf Music Festival and accepted the position of Town Music Director. He gave this up in 1835 to become conductor of the Gewandhaus Orchestra in Leipzig, which for so many years stood out as one of the finest symphony orchestras in all Europe. Later he organized and directed the Conservatory of Music at Leipzig (since 1876 it has been known as the Royal Conservatory of Music). On hearing of the death of his beloved and idolized sister, Fanny Hensel, he suffered a stroke and died six months later. His compositions include almost all types save that of opera. His style embraced contrapuntal, classical, and romantic types; and although they have undergone a contemporary eclipse, many authorities maintain that not a few of his best works in each of these types will achieve immortality. Certainly Mendelssohn, both as a person and as a composer, had a vital and tremendous influence on music.

Mendelssohn's Concerto in E minor, Op. 64, for Violin and Orchestra

ANALYSIS. Few musical works have enjoyed such world-wide popularity and consistent favour among the musical elect as has this concerto. Only a few years ago Donald Francis Tovey, the great English musicologist and critic, said of this work, it is "the most remarkable stroke of genius in this most popular of violin concertos."[4] Here classical purity of style and perfection of formal aspects unite with spontaneous melody, fertility of romantic imagination, marked personal expression, and also the elfin lightness of touch that was, perhaps, Mendelssohn's most salient and charming gift.

It was the custom in the more strictly classical tradition of performing solo concertos to have the orchestra play all the way through the exposition and then, at the repetition (signified by the usual "double-bar-and-repeat" sign), to have the solo instrument join in. Some contemporary conductors ignore this procedure, even in the works of the masters.

In the first movement of this work, marked *allegro molto appassionato*, the solo violin is heard in the first theme after an introduction of only a measure and a half. There will be no difficulty in noting its appearance.

This material is worked up into a climactic *tutti*. Then the

[4] Sir Donald Francis Tovey, *Essays in Musical Analysis*, Vol. 3. (Oxford University Press, 1936.) Quoted by permission.

orchestration thins out considerably, the ensuing theme serving as the basis of a transition to the second theme.

The solo violin soars, plays alternately up and down the strings, poises for a moment upon a high G and then B above it, and then down again to the lowest string of the violin (G below middle C), above which the woodwinds (flutes and clarinets) play the second theme proper, softly (*pp*) and peacefully (*tranquillo*). Presently the same theme is picked up by the solo violin.

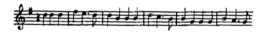

The development section begins with the transition melody, and modulates freely in a brilliant dialogue between the solo violin and the orchestra. Then portions of the first theme are developed by both in turn and, with a sustained, fortissimo chord, the orchestra becomes silent while the solo violin performs a fanciful cadenza. It might be interpolated here that it was once the fashion for the performer to create his own cadenzas as an opportunity to show off not only his manipulative skill but also his compositional talents. However, since Mozart's time (and during it), the composers of the concerti themselves have set down the cadenzas as they desired them.

Mendelssohn's cadenza joins the reprise, or recapitulation, in a very clever manner; the soloist continues with his final arpeggiated figure of the cadenza, while the orchestra brings back the opening first theme in E minor. The reprise is somewhat shortened in comparison with the exposition. The coda achieves exhilarating momentum and ends with a brilliant outburst by the solo violin with the orchestra.

We mentioned in the previous paragraphs some practices pertaining to tradition, both positive and negative. Now, between the first and the second movements of this work, we have another instance. Mendelssohn joined the two movements with a holding tone in the first bassoon; but one most often hears the work with a distinct interruption, due more to applause than to anything else.

At any rate, the second, the slow, movement, marked *andante* (in a slow, walking pace), is very lyrical, filled with breadth and dignity of expression, and quite moving in its simple melodic line—but very difficult to perform correctly here and there. The form is that of an ordinary ternary, or three-part, A-B-A structure. The quiet opening theme is played by the solo violin after eight measures of "till ready" introduction (as Sir Donald Tovey so aptly dubs it).

This theme leads to an agitated middle section, which carries with it not a little feeling of anxiety; but this passes, and the serene and peaceful opening theme reappears. True, Mendelssohn does not sound the depths of human emotions, nor does he attempt to move mountains; it is not that kind of a slow movement. Let us appreciate what the composer does project with such a sure hand—tranquillity and peace and beauty!

The slow movement is, like the first and second movements, not separated in the original score. Mendelssohn placed a hold over the last chord with the solo violin, supported by the strings, entering on the up-beat in what one might call an adjoining interlude (marked *allegretto non troppo*, with movement but not too fast). This interlude lasts for only fourteen measures and leads, without interruption, into the last movement (marked *allegro molto vivace*, fast and with much spirit). A courtly flourish of horns, bassoons, and drums, interrupted four times by a swishlike figure in the solo violin, then the first theme proper appears in the solo violin, embellished with fairylike staccato passages in the woodwinds. The first theme follows:

This sort of exchange of conversation between the solo violin and the woodwinds, with the strings plucking the tones here and there, continues until, with an upward sweep of the violin, the entire orchestra (*tutti*) sounds forth the second theme which vies with the first in sprightliness and vivacity. Sir Donald Tovey calls this a "cheeky" theme!

These two themes alternate in appearance and in development throughout the remainder of the movement, and a brilliant, almost pyrotechnical coda based on the second theme brings this work to a close.

Chapter Twenty-Five

Chamber Music

The String Quartet

THE term "chamber music" once meant that type of music which was played to best advantage in the drawing room, or private chamber, of a person of wealth and high social standing, in contrast to the types of music usually performed in the church or in the theatre.

Later definitions broadened and altered this early meaning of the term somewhat so as to embrace types of music of a more or less intimate nature, capable of being performed in a comparatively small-sized hall, either private or public, and played by a group of solo instrumentalists such as comprise a string or wind duo, trio, quartet, quintet, sextet, septet, octet, nonet, with or without the piano, and having no duplicate, or *ripieno*, parts, as is the case with the symphony orchestra. Mixed groups (wind and string) are frequent, and though vocal parts may be sometimes found in this type of literature (such as Arnold Schönberg's "Pierrot Lunaire" with its *sprech-stimme* vocal part), the term "chamber music" usually is restricted to instrumental ensembles of solo parts, and seldom does the number of performers exceed nine or ten.[1]

Being inherently of an intimate character, chamber music has been naturally selective in its audience, and its comprehension and appreciation much more limited in extent than the type of music heard in the opera, the church, or, in more recent years, in our major symphony orchestra programmes. A great deal of chamber music is likely to be somewhat esoteric and to present real challenge to the abilities of the listener; though we hasten to vouch for the ultimate enjoyment of this form of music if one will make a

---

[1] See the Introduction to *Cobbett's Cyclopaedic Survey of Chamber Music*, by Walter Willson Cobbett. (Oxford University Press, 1929.) We have quoted freely from this monumental and invaluable work, with permission from the publishers.

real effort to listen to it sympathetically, again and again, until effortless appreciation results. Sometimes it is helpful to follow the progress of a work by reading the score; sometimes it is a hindrance. We leave it to the listener to find out for himself.

It might be well, at this point, to compare some of the more salient characteristics of the symphony orchestra of the usual proportions and personnel (about a hundred players) with that of the string quartet consisting of one first violin, one second violin, one viola, and one violoncello (see pages 144 to 146 for description of these instruments). The following list of contrasting characteristics of the two types of music and media of performance is not intended to be exhaustive or inviolable; it is, however, sufficiently general and provocative of desirable thought to warrant inclusion here.

Chamber music is written for and played by a few performers, and thus, instead of the almost infinite variety of tone colours that can be secured from an orchestra, it possesses the concentrated though limited homogeneous quality of a single family of stringed instruments. There are, however, great possibilities for flexibility of performance in the string quartet because of the nature and smallness of the ensemble. The sonorities of the quartet are less than those of the orchestra, and thus the quartet is well suited to intimate recital hall performance; also the listener loses less of the actual production and intention of the composer. The quartet affords far more delicate nuances than are generally obtainable from the orchestra, and thus the listener can delight in an endless variety of lights and shades of expression and sensitiveness of adjustment in intonation that are either limited or impractical in the orchestra. In place of the compelling masses and volume of tone possible in the orchestra, the quartet affords less volume but greater purity of tone and as perfect a blending of tone and ensemble as man can produce. The rhythmic effects of the large symphony orchestra, with its use of exotic, realistic, and often ostentatious percussion instruments, are replaced in the quartet with far more subtle means where the rhythm and rhythmic effects must, perforce, be an inherent part of the music itself rather than a more or less supplementary and additional noise element, as is so often true (and fully justified) in orchestral music. Instead of the blaring forth of themes or the making of them more obvious by means of sharply contrasting tone colour, as is true in the orchestra, the listener has often to discover them in the music of the string quartet amidst a closely woven and intertwined tonal design, a type of writing that might well produce tonal chaos in the orchestra. Finally, the listener has the opportunity of "the enjoyment of the ultimate" in instrumental part-writing in the quartet, and the sheer pleasure of shifting the ear from part to part, to several instruments at once, or to the entire ensemble. This is something that must be experienced to enjoy; and this type of enjoyment, though common both to the orchestra and the quartet, is likely to be more frequent and more intense in the latter than in the former, according to the verdict of seasoned music listeners. It is more or less generally agreed among musicians that chamber music demands more active, more creative, and more intensely sustained interest than do most other types of music. Even the most capable listener finds it necessary to hear a worthwhile quartet over and over in order to appreciate it properly and to "possess" it permanently. Nothing in the way of formalized and detailed study can ever take the place of the listening process. Most experts agree that in some of the later quartets of Beethoven there remain depths yet to be plumbed, even after some 125 years of intensive and discriminating listening.

The comparisons we have just made have been between two musical types; now, in turn, let us contrast them with other art media. A symphony, when played by a large symphony orchestra, may be likened in many ways to a fresco or oil painting of large proportions where the painter deals with gross forms in his composition, large masses of forms and colours, and where he indulges in striking contrasts of content, means, and dynamic action—as though he were painting with a large brush and were concerned with salient rather than minute and subtle effects. A good example of the former type is Michelangelo's "Judgement Day" on the front wall of the Sistine Chapel (and to a less extent, Raphael's "The School of Athens" on page 51); an excellent instance of the small-brush, realistically detailed painting may be seen in the Holbein "Portrait of Georg Gisze" on page 264; and a very striking illustration of economy of means is seen in the ink drawing, Girl in Feathered Hat, by Henri Matisse on page 387 (in a less degree, the Dürer etching of the Doodle-Sack Player on page 148). It should be obvious that each type of art mentioned in the foregoing serves its own peculiar purpose and that anyone who would appreciate them all properly should have to adjust his receptive attitude and judgment of values accordingly. A sculptor, executing such a lofty and spacious work as the "Statue of Liberty" in New York's harbour,[2] had a different purpose in mind and used in working it out means different from those used by a Michelangelo in creating a smaller and more detailed piece such as his "Pietà" (page 333); and the beholder should consider both their similarities and dissimilarities along with the other concomitants of appreciation. When poetry, rather than painting or sculpture, is under inquiry, one does not demand identical appreciator reactions from such typical and divergent forms as a sonnet, a narrative poem, a lyric poem, a folk ballad, an epic poem, and so forth. Quite the contrary, one enjoys the peculiarities of each. So should it be in considering musical types. Since we believe that the reader would be interested in making his own comparisons between the various types of music we have presented thus far, we shall leave that matter for his own accomplishment and, consequently, greater enjoyment.

Girl in Feathered Hat, an ink drawing   Matisse

Most of the instrumental music presented in the text up to this point has involved the use of the huge symphony orchestra. To effect a smooth and gradual transition to the small, comparatively restrained, and more intimate ensemble exemplified by the string quartet, let us first hear Mozart's serenade, *Ein kleine Nachtmusik,* in G major, K. 525.[3] This was written as a *divertimento* "for soloists or a body of players," but it is usually heard on records, and in other performances, as a work for string orchestra—where the original parts are duplicated by having additional instruments

---

[2] By Frederic Auguste Bartholdi, French sculptor, 1834-1904. The Statue of Liberty was dedicated in New York harbour on Oct. 28, 1886.

[3] For 2 violins, viola, 'cello, and double basses *ad libitum.*

of similar kind join in the performance, including the double basses. The serenade was written on August 10, 1787, especially for a gala festivity in Vienna, when the composer was in his thirty-first year.

"Ein kleine Nachtmusik" (*A Little Night Music*), *A serenade for strings*

The overall form of the serenade, constructed with four separate and contrasting movements, is not unlike the complete symphony form; but, of course, it is on a much smaller scale. The first movement, instead of being in the usual sonata-allegro form, is without a real development section and thus is generally styled a sonatina form.[4]

ANALYSIS. *FIRST MOVEMENT: Allegro. G major. $\frac{4}{4}$ time. Sonatina form.* This movement is of a brisk, gay, marchlike character. There is a definite feeling of the gaiety of a social festivity noted by Cobbett. The principal theme is played by all the instruments in unison, in a loud (forte) and spirited manner. Try to follow the use of this and the other themes as they course through the movement, whole or in part, or altered.

The second theme is piano, contrasting its daintiness with the burly good humour of the first.

There is also a third theme, often called a "closing theme" by the theorists, light and gay and altogether charming. Notice how much the trill contributes to this effect.

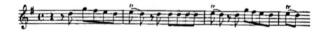

A brief codetta brings us to the double bar at the end of the exposition; the whole section is then repeated.

The development section of the sonatina is so brief as to be practically nonexistent. The recapitulation, or reprise, follows the

[4] Some theorists call this general sort of structure a species of rondo.

hematic sequence of the exposition save that all the themes are now in the home key of G major.

SECOND MOVEMENT: Romanze. Andante. C major. Alla breve. Three-part (A-B-A) form. The second movement, the slow one, is a *romanze*, or *romance*, and, as its name implies, is tenderly lyrical and melodic in character. Here the personal note of the serenade is most in evidence, although the sentiment never becomes deeper than is appropriate for a charming summer evening. Note the inimitable grace of the opening measures, the finish and elegance of the style throughout. Like the themes of the first movement, this one is built on the regular four-measure phrase, two-period formation. There is something well-bred and stately in the bare outlines of such structural regularity.

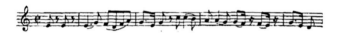

The theme is varied, and, after a bit of adventure, returns in a regular A-B-A pattern.

THIRD MOVEMENT: Menuetto. Allegretto. G major. ¾ time. Minuet and trio form. The minuet is bright and airy in the best eighteenth-century manner.

The trio contains a soaring bit of melody that only Mozart could have written.

After this comes the inevitable *menuetto da capo*, a return to the first section of the minuet proper, without repeats this time and ending at the word *fine* at the close of this section, just before the trio.

FOURTH MOVEMENT: Rondo. Allegro. G major. 4/4 time. Rondo form. This movement is concerned largely with two themes designated as "Theme A" and "Theme B" below. The first and principal idea of the rondo is a jolly and sprightly theme introduced by a group of three ascending staccato chord tones. Note the graceful and typical turn in the second full measure—Mozart was fond of this embellishment. The second, theme "B," is more flowing and legato, but note the syncopations in the third measure of the illustration. What a gay and debonair dance, summery and colourful, the composer has set forth for our enjoyment!

The principal idea returns again and again, its reappearances separated by lively episodical material—the rondo form as we have come to know it by this time. Note how smoothly and inevitably Mozart returns to the main theme, after wandering through related keys and transient moods. The writing is wonderfully clear and perfectly suited to the style and character of the strings. There is a vigorous coda at the close, terminating with a good-humoured cadence passage built on the simple lines of the G-major chord.

It was noted in the foregoing comments about Mozart's work that the five instruments (first and second violins, violas, 'cellos, and double basses) were usually duplicated by having additional players on each part. Now let us listen to a very romantic movement from a well-known work for the string quartet alone—just the solo instruments (and without the double basses), the slow movement, *Andante Cantabile* from Tchaikovsky's Quartet, Op. 11.

Andante Cantabile, from String Quartet Op. 11. B flat. ¾ time. Tchaikovsky

This is a most beautiful and exquisite movement, of great melodic charm and simplicity. The structural design is that of a ternary (A-B-A) main body of three periods of about sixteen measures each (instead of the more usual binary form of the average minuet), plus a trio section. The principal theme, played at the onset by the first violin, is a working out of a Russian folk song that the composer heard his carpenter singing one day. Note its shifting between ²⁄₄ and ³⁄₄ metres.

This theme is "answered" by another sixteen-measure period, which is developed out of the main idea; then the first period is repeated, with four measures added to it to effect a desirable close.

The trio section proper appears after an introductory pair of measures, with the first violin again taking the melodic burden and the 'cello plucking (pizzicato) a reiterated bass part, technically known as a *basso ostinato*. (Do you see any resemblance to an accompanimental figure used in a popular dance-song rhythm?)

After the trio, there is, as in the traditional minuet and trio form, a return to the main section; after which a coda, reminiscent both of the trio and the first theme, brings the movement to a conclusion.[5]

No doubt, by this time, the listener is eager to hear a complete string quartet, and is capable of giving and willing to give it the intense and sustained interest it must receive if he is to get the most from it. One could hardly choose a more fortunate example to begin with than Dvořák's STRING QUARTET IN F MAJOR, OP. 96, with its lilting melodies, lively and contagious rhythms, excellent instrumental writing, unexpected and fascinating harmonies, and its divergent and highly stimulating emotional content—in turn happy, carefree, and gay, sadly sweet and not without sentiment, and often downright poignant.

---

[5] Those who enjoy working out puzzles in musical form will, do doubt, be interested in discovering Tchaikovsky's use of "a ternary form within a ternary form" in this movement. We have merely hinted at it in passing.

String Quartet in F major. Op. 96. Antonin Dvořák

This deeply personal and highly romantic work is more often known by its soubriquet "American," so dubbed because it seems to reflect something of the spirit and atmosphere of the "New World" in which the composer found himself in 1892. (See also page 283 for Dvořák's "NEW WORLD" SYMPHONY.) He had come

String Quartet   *Levine*

to the United States to accept the directorship of the National Conservatory of Music in New York City. However, he yearned for closer contact with folks of his own nationality, and so spent his summers in the Bohemian colony at Spillville, Iowa. No doubt it was here rather than in New York that the so-called "American" spirit affected him.

At any rate, the composer did seem to catch and incorporate in his works enough of the spirit of some American folk songs and folk rhythms to justify a belief on the part of many writers and critics that there was some actual native influence; although one must add that these themes were certainly greatly transformed through the alchemy of the composer's own personal style and individual manner of expression.

Speculating on the influence that this friendly little American-Bohemian village had on Dvořák in general and in the creation of this work in particular, Professor Ottakar Sourek says in Cobbett's work already referred to, "Here, then, is the origin of the fundamental mood which inspired this charming, quickly written (in three days—*sic!*) but detailed work, touched in places with painful yearning, yet with a smiling, idyllic sentiment prevailing throughout. Here, too, is the reason why so many of the ideas in the quartet are simple in substance, and why the themes are frequently exposed in a kaleidoscopic fashion. The quartet is interesting harmonically on account of its swift and unexpected modulations through related and remote keys, in which there is a surprising charm of artifice that only serves to strengthen the fundamental— as it were improvised—style of the whole work." [6]

FIRST MOVEMENT: Allegro ma non troppo. F major. $\frac{4}{4}$ time. *Sonata-allegro form.* Most of this movement is in the spirit of the tempo marking—"lively but not too much so." The first theme, appearing in the viola after two measures of tremolo introduction by the first and second violins, is a happy-go-lucky melody of a simple four-measure duration. Most of the development throughout the movement is concerned with either the syncopated figure of the first measure ("A") or the arpeggiated figure in the fourth measure ("B") of the ensuing illustration of the principal subject. Try to follow these two melodic figures in their development as they are altered or tossed about.

First   Movement

A subsidiary theme appears in the second violin part in the twenty-sixth measure. Being more legato in character, it is somewhat of a foil for the vigorous, dancelike first theme, and also it serves as an excellent, though subtle, anticipation of the second theme.

[6] *Cyclopaedic Survey of Chamber Music,* by Walter Willson Cobbett, 2 Vols. (London: Oxford University Press, 1929). Used with permission. See article on Dvořák.

Presently the music subsides in volume and becomes almost a plaintive whisper, and when it vanishes to a pianissimo (*ppp*), the first violin plays the second theme proper (in A major), which is, no doubt, derived from the first subject.

Soon the development sets in, the viola again dealing with the happy, syncopated idea of the first theme. This figure, by the way, serves for most of the entire section.

The reprise can easily be identified, for the viola announces the first theme as it was when heard in the exposition. Note how Dvořák accomplishes a virtual repetition of material that had appeared in the exposition, yet with artfully different treatment. The second theme appears in due season and as it was in the beginning—though it is now in the home key of F major. A brief coda follows in which the 'cello sings a melody woven out of the second and played high up on its A string; but almost as soon as the arpeggiated figure "B" makes its re-entry, the movement comes to a boisterous and abrupt close.

SECOND MOVEMENT: Lento. D minor. ⁶⁄₈ time. Modified binary form. What a highly personalized and melancholy song this is, as though the singer's heart were breaking through sheer homesickness! "It is," says our informant, "a genuine pearl among Dvořák's lyrical movements, captivating in its lovely, singing melodic line, its depth of sentiment, and the special charm of its pure harmony.[7]

One has only to listen sympathetically to get the real import of the movement; little elucidation is necessary. The design, interesting in its almost naïve simplicity, consists of four balanced periods (a-b: :c-a), each section repeated more or less exactly, excepting the curtailed and modified final period. Note how the insistent accompanimental figure continues in the viola or the second violin (mostly the former) throughout the movement up to the return of the main idea (high on the 'cello), where it is replaced by an alternating arco (bowed) and pizzicato (plucked) chordal accompaniment—not unlike a troubled heart-throb! It is real romantic music. The principal melodic idea of the movement follows:

[7] *Ibid.*

THIRD MOVEMENT: Molto vivace. F major. $\frac{3}{4}$ *time.* This
sprightly movement is evolved out of a single theme in three-four
time and having a strong off-beat accent on the second count. It is
announced at the onset by the second violin and 'cello in octaves.

From here on, Dvořák has shown what genius can do with
simple ideas to produce a most ingenious design and telling effect.
The structure consists of a series of miniature variations on the
single theme; but these are arranged and contrasted in such a
manner, and with the retention of a fundamental $\frac{3}{4}$ metre, that
the traditional minuet-and-trio design is more than merely implied. In reality, also, the movement is basically in two sections
appearing three times in alternation. Note the rhythmic augmentation of the theme in the second section—in the second violin,
then the 'cello, and finally in the first violin. After the "variations," as one might expect, there is a return to the main section,
quite like the da capo treatment in the traditional minuet-and-
trio design. Here is what is meant by rhythmic augmentation: a
drawing out, or elongation, of the time value of the notes.[8] The
theme originally appears as "A"; the same theme augmented as
at "B."

See if you can recognize this compositional technique whenever
it is used in this movement. Also note the exotic flavour throughout, the brusque rhythms, the disposition of the purely accompanimental parts whenever there is a new "variation," and the

___

[8] Composers also use intervallic augmentation, where the original intervals of the
melody are increased. The reverse is rhythmic and melodic diminution, where the
original time values and tonal intervals are made smaller as a means of "development."

characteristic and frequent use of the bare fifths here and there in the accompaniment.

FINALE: Vivace ma non troppo. F major. ¾ time. Rondo form. There is at first a lengthy yet very interesting introduction of some thirty-two measures, characterized by a gaily rhythmic and percussive drumlike accompaniment over which there is more than a sly hint and preview of the delightfully dancelike main theme. This last makes its appearance eventually in the first violin.

This theme is developed, and presently, with no forewarning, the key of A-flat major is jumped into and a subsidiary theme of a lyrical nature appears in the first violin over the drumming, dancelike accompaniment heard in the introduction.

In the midst of this quiet, peaceful, and sustained second section, a choralelike passage appears, which Sourek maintains "is undoubtedly a reminiscence of the Church at Spillville," where Dvořák was wont to play the organ during services.

A lively episode ensues, followed by a reappearance of the main theme, which is interrupted, in turn, by a section that plunges into a series of colourful harmonies.[9]

[9] For those interested in such technicalities, these chords are "borrowed," one might say, from the keys of (F major), D-flat major, G-flat major, e-flat minor, d minor, C major, a minor, and eventually back to the home key of F major.

Thematically, the passage is concerned with bits of the main theme. Soon, however, the subsidiary theme appears; but the persistent and not-to-be-ignored main theme intervenes once more and carries the movement forward through the coda and on to the vigorous and boisterous close.

ADDITIONAL SUGGESTIONS FOR LISTENING

The literature of chamber music is voluminous, and since individual tastes are likely to differ widely, it is difficult to be selective. However, here are a few works that the listener might well add to his repertory as a firm basis for subsequent building: Haydn's *Emperor* Quartet in C major, Opus 76, No. 3; Mozart's Quartet in d minor, K. 421, and the one in C major, K. 465[10] (the quartet with the startling dissonances); Beethoven's Quartet in F, Op. 18, No. 1, of the early period, Op. 59, No. 1, in F, of the middle period, and, for the bold, the quartets from his third period, Op. 127, Op. 130, Op. 131, and Op. 133, the one with the Grand Fugue; Brahms' Quartet in a minor, Op. 51, No. 2;[11] Schubert's *Death and the Maiden* quartet; Debussy's STRING QUARTET IN G MINOR, Op. 10, and Ravel's QUARTET FOR STRINGS IN F MAJOR (written when the composer was only twenty-seven years of age); and from there on into the more contemporary works, the listener may choose as he wills.

Before leaving this chapter, we should like to direct the reader's attention to the quintet—the usual string quartet with an added instrument, either another instrument like that already in the quartet or a basically different type, such as the piano or a clarinet. We urge the reader also to become acquainted with Schumann's QUINTET FOR PIANO AND STRINGS in E flat; Brahms' QUINTET IN B MINOR FOR CLARINET AND STRINGS, Op. 115; César Franck's QUINTET IN F MINOR FOR PIANO AND STRINGS, and Ernest Bloch's QUINTET FOR PIANO AND STRINGS. For other combinations of instruments, and for more modern recordings, the reader is urged to appease his own personal tastes by consulting a good, up-to-date record catalogue.

---

[10] The letter *K* following the opus number of Mozart's works refers to the generally accepted cataloguing of his works by the Viennese editor, Ludwig von Köchel, revised recently by Alfred Einstein, the eminent musicologist.

[11] For more detailed analysis of this work see *Introduction to Music*, by Martin Bernstein. (New York: Prentice-Hall, Inc., 1937.)

Chapter Twenty-Six

The Piano Solo and the Violin and Piano Sonata

The Emergence of the Solo Performer

THE rise of the solo instruments to an eminent place in music is intimately bound up with one of the most interesting developments in the art during the past two centuries—the emergence of the solo performer. From Mozart to Liszt, to Josef Hofmann and Vladimir Horowitz, and from Paganini to Fritz Kreisler and Jascha Heifetz, there stretches a long line of great artists. There are times, even in our own day, when the virtuoso overshadows the composer and many attend a concert to hear Hofmann or Heifetz rather than Chopin or Beethoven. And this is understandable, for these great performers have often exerted a profound influence on music itself: on the steadily rising level of technical skill in performance; on the mechanical improvement of the instruments themselves; on the type of music that composers might write for these instruments; and, most important of all, on the general taste and standards of the musical public at large.

In tracing the rise of the solo performer, it is important to bear in mind that the Middle Ages and the Renaissance seem to have regarded the playing of music primarily as a group activity. One has but to look at the many paintings and sculptures of the period to realize that generally there were three, four, or more persons playing and singing together. (See the paintings of the "Musical Angels" by Fra Angelico, the "Singing Choir" sculptures by della Robbia.) In the magnificently developed choral bodies of the sixteenth century and in the small chamber music groups of the succeeding period, the individual was first and foremost a part of the group; and a great deal of the instrumental playing was in connection with the singing groups, a quite faithful duplication of the vocal parts. Separate instrumental compositions, more often than not, bore the direction, "either for viols or voices."

The rise of Italian opera at the beginning of the seventeenth century of necessity turned the attention of composers to the advantage, from the point of view of dramatic effectiveness, of concentrating the attention on the individual singer. Meanwhile, the interest of audiences, composers, and performers shifted from an almost exclusively vocal art to a much more comprehensive one which included the keyboard instruments, such as the virginal, harpsichord, clavichord (precursors of the modern piano) and, of course, the organ. Here the foundation was laid not only for the development of new instrumental styles, but also for the gradual and eventual emergence of a new type of solo performer. Naturally, it took composers some time to adapt themselves to the needs of the then new outlook and to evolve an effective solo performing style. As with all historical processes, this one advanced through trial and error, through daring experiments and cautious withdrawals, for upward of a century and a half before there finally came into being the general conception of the soloist as we know him today.

It must also be remembered that until the end of the eighteenth century the great solo performers were primarily composers. When one went to hear the famous organists—Buxtehude, Reinken, or Bach—it was in order to hear them play their latest works. When Mozart or Beethoven gave a concert, interest centred on their newest sonata or concerto rather than on their performance of it. Only with the coming of the nineteenth century did there come into widespread acceptance the artist-musician whose function was recognized to be almost exclusively the performance and interpretation of the works of other men. The separation of the two roles was most fruitful for the art. On the one hand, the performer could devote himself completely to acquiring great technical skill and to solving the performance problems of the music in the most finished manner; on the other, the audience, listening to an artist who was exclusively a performer, became ever more critical of the performance and demanded the highest standards. This new attitude toward performance was bound to have a stimulating effect on all branches of the art, including the mechanical perfection of the musical instruments themselves.

Significant advances in musical technique are likely to involve the complex relationship that involves the composer, the perfor-

BB

mer, the listener, and the instrument maker—each of whom influences the others and is, in turn, influenced by them. The great
composer is often ahead of the other three in his technical demands. His more advanced compositions often require a more
advanced style of playing, a finer type of instrument, and a somewhat different attitude on the part of the audience than those that
obtained previously. Once the new types of instrument, performer,
and listener have come into being, the composer who follows is
ready to forge still farther ahead. Sometimes the composer, working in close harmony with a particularly gifted performer or instrument maker, follows their lead (*vide* Paganini and Liszt as
instances of the latter). Such was certainly the case at the end of
the seventeenth century when the achievements of the great Italian
violin makers paved the way for the compositions of Vivaldi and
Tartini. The process is usually a reciprocal one. When we listen,
for instance, to a Horowitz, playing upon a sonorous, modern
concert grand piano, accompanied by a symphony orchestra under
the baton of a Toscanini, broadcasting a Brahms concerto to
millions of listeners, we witness an end-result of long development,
with diverse musical and scientific factors functioning in their
most modern and advanced historical context.

The Piano[1]

For a century and a half, the piano has been one of our most
popular solo instruments. Unlike the string and wind instruments,
the piano is completely self-sufficient, for it is able to play both the
melody and its accompanimental harmony at the same time. For
this reason, it became the favourite household instrument of the
nineteenth century. The ancestry of the piano may be traced back
to the early keyboard instruments of the fifteenth and sixteenth
centuries—the spinet, the dulcimer, and the virginal that were so
popular in Elizabethan England. In the seventeenth century, the
clavichord and harpsichord became the chief instruments of the
keyboard group, a supremacy they maintained until the piano
supplanted them at the end of the eighteenth century. In the
clavichord, the tone was produced by a tangent, generally made
of brass, that was driven against the string and held there. Its tone

[1] More exactly the *pianoforte*, commonly shortened to *piano*.

was metallic and never powerful. Because of the variety of tone possible to it, many composers found the clavichord a most sympathetic instrument for intimate music. In the harpsichord, the string was plucked by a quill, giving a bright, vigorous tone, though somewhat tinkling in quality. The power and character of the tone could not be varied save by mechanical or structural devices. The harpsichord was the favourite instrument for supporting the bass of the small orchestras of the period and for concert use. Since its tone had no staying powers, composers developed a highly ornamented style of writing, full of trills and flourishes and silvery cascades of scale and arpeggio passages that seem to typify the grace and delicacy of the Rococo style.

The piano was perfected in the first decade of the eighteenth century by Bartolemeo Cristofori, a harpsichord maker of Padua (though musicologists point out several previous instances of the instrument). This instrument was called a *Piano e Forte* (soft and loud), to indicate its dynamic versatility, and its strings were struck by a recoiling hammer with a felt-padded head on the end of it. The wires were much heavier than in the earlier instruments. A series of mechanical improvements continuing well into the nineteenth century, including the introduction of pedals to sustain or dampen the tone, the perfection of a metal frame and steel wire of the finest quality, finally produced the instrument we now know, capable of a myriad tonal effects from the most diaphanous harmonies to an almost orchestral sonority, from a liquid, singing tone to a sharp, percussive brilliance.

Frederic François Chopin (1810-1849)

The composer who, more than any other, has come to be regarded as the culmination of the piano style, the "Poet of the Piano," as he is universally known, was Frederic François Chopin, the Polish master who lived for the greater part of his creative career in Paris and who created what still remains the chief ornament of the pianist's repertoire. He was born in Warsaw, Poland, February 22, 1810, and died in Paris, October 17, 1849. The family name was Szopen, but this had been dropped for the more common Gallic and phonetically translated Chopin.[2] His early

[2] See *Chopin, the Man and His Music*, by James G. Huncker. (New York: Charles Scribner's Sons, 1914.)

education was received at the Warsaw Gymnasium together with private musical training from Zywny and Elsner; and so rapidly did be become proficient in playing the piano that he appeared in public at the age of eight. His first essay in composition was published when he was a lad of fifteen. In 1830, after several concerts in Warsaw, he left for Paris—with concert engagements in the large musical centres on his way—and arrived at the French capital a year later. He did not have to wait long to become a social and artistic favourite, and his reputation spread throughout the Continent. Robert Schumann, in his critical articles, hailed him with the now famous "Hats off, gentlemen, a genius!" and Mendelssohn, Berlioz, Liszt, and many other leading musicians, saw in him the divine spark of the real genius. His appearances as a soloist were frequent, and his days were fairly well filled with teaching, so much so that he wrote only a few compositions. His strange friendship with George Sand (Mme. Dudevant) extended from 1837 to 1847, during which period his health failed rapidly because of tuberculosis. In spite of a delicate constitution, he visited England for a concert tour, and he returned to Paris a year later only to succumb to his malady a few months after his arrival. His funeral at the Madeleine was a long and impressive one, during which the celebrated *Requiem* of Mozart was performed—the composer whom Chopin worshipped above all others.

Unlike the other great composers we have studied up to this point, who usually composed for several media of performance, Chopin's genius was almost exclusively devoted to the piano.[3] For him the keyboard comprised the whole magic of realm music—and most experts are agreed that within that realm he was master. Even the shortcomings of the piano—its inability to sustain the tone as do the voice and the wind and string instruments—Chopin, with an intuition bordering on the miraculous, knew how to transform into advantages, by surrounding his poetic and flowing melodies with floating columns of wonderfully figurated harmonies and with the most delicate of traceries and arabesques intertwined. With unerring instinct, he discovered what the piano could do best, and he forthwith applied his seemingly inexhaustible inventiveness to achieve that best. Although he wrote four

---

[3] Chopin's divergences included a Trio for piano, violin and 'cello, Op. 8; a Sonata in g minor, Op. 65, for piano, 'cello (or violin); an Introduction and Polonaise in C major for piano and 'cello, Op. 3; and Seventeen Polish Songs, Op. 74.

sonatas and two concertos, his imagination gravitated naturally to the shorter forms, many of which he himself created and all of which he brought to new levels of development and beauty—the waltzes, nocturnes, preludes, mazurkas, etudes, scherzos, polonaises, impromptus, and ballades that have come to constitute the quintessence of pianism.

In Chopin, the ultraromantic fused with the ultranationalist; he was greatly affected by the sufferings of his native Poland, and in his proud polonaises and mazurkas he voiced his dream of ultimate liberation. His works reveal him as one of the most daring of the experimental harmonists of his time, one of the most original masters of tonal colour and chromaticism, and, strange as it may seem to the uninitiated, a supreme master of the intricacies of the classical as well as romantic internal designs of form and structure (as we shall show presently in the ballade). Schumann called Chopin "the boldest and proudest poetic spirit of our time," and we of today have yet to appreciate him to the full. His hold upon the public of our time is enormous and world-wide. Artists like Paderewski, de Pachmann, Lhevinne, Godowsky, Brailowsky, and Hofmann have built special reputations as "Chopin interpreters." At their greatest, Chopin's works have a refinement, an aristocratic distinction, that remind us of the composer he worshipped—Mozart. He successfully achieved what he called in his early twenties his "perhaps daring but noble resolve—to create a new era in art." As long as the piano endures, its golden age will be synonymous with the noontide of Romanticism—and Chopin.

In spite of the fact that Chopin chose to express himself almost solely through the medium of the piano, he left a comparatively small output for that instrument—some two hundred compositions in all. Yet so constant was he in expressing the noble and the beautiful, that Sir George Grove would have him ranked among the greatest—"because of his breadth of content and the variety of mood, as well as the manner of expression."[4] His superlative musicianship and unerring command of the many and intricate techniques of the craft of composition, especially those pertaining to melodic, harmonic, and structural elements, as well as idiomatic pianistic effects, are unexcelled in the annals of music

[4] Sir George Grove, *Dictionary of Music and Musicians*, 4 Vols. (New York: The Macmillan Company.)

history and seldom equalled. He had a high standard of excellence. There are in his works very few moments of digression that fall to a low quality.

It would be difficult, indeed, to select a more appropriate and expediential work for the moment than Chopin's beautiful Ballade (number three) in A-flat major, Op. 47. This composition illustrates in an eloquent and ingratiating manner the character of piano music in general, and, in particular, Chopin's highly individual style.[5] At the same time, it offers the listener a veritable masterpiece of romantic expression.

Ballade, No. 3, in A-flat major, Op. 47

The word "ballad" (*ballade* or *ballata*) once meant a song to accompany a dance; more usual, however, was the meaning of a folklike song that told a story of a descriptive nature; of love, religion, history, humour, satire, and so forth. Later, when the word was used in connection with the lied, the term designated a narrative song of dramatic character. It was natural that the poet in Chopin should adopt words of poetical connotation for music inspired by and depicting a lyrical mood.[6] We have Chopin's own words to the effect that he had a programme in mind when writing the ballades, for he confessed to Robert Schumann that he had been moved to their creation by the Lithuanian poems of Mickiewicz, the Polish poet;[7] but the composer wisely left the matter indefinite. However, Huneker goes so far as to identify the third ballade as the "Undine" of the set of poems already mentioned.

Another writer (Louis Ehlert) said that this work gave forth the voice of the people, and again ventured his belief that the basic programme of this ballade was a love story. One can cite authority after authority, only to end with the well-founded conviction that any story the listener wishes to concoct for himself—or no story at all—will be quite defensible.

[5] It is not to be inferred that we assume it to be the greatest of the four ballades. We have chosen it, rather, because it best serves our immediate purpose.

[6] The word *ballad* also has the meaning of a simple song, narrative in content and strophic in form, using the same melody for the several verses and, sometimes, having a chorus, or refrain. (The Christmas carol was originally a ballad.) A common contemporary example of the structure is sometimes found in the ordinary popular dance-song. An excellent example of the folk, or traditional, type of ballad is the English and American love song "Barbara Allen" (see page 31).

[7] See also *Chopin, the Man and His Music*, by James Huneker. (New York: Charles Scribner's Sons, 1900.)

The moods of the work are variously described as: aristocratic, gay, graceful, piquant, playful yet ironical in spots, filled with deep passionate emotions, coquettish grace, irresistible charm, sweet contentment (Ehlert), "the composer shows himself in a fundamentally caressing mood" (Niecks),[8] "there is moonlight in his music and some sunlight too" (Huneker).[9] The listener will be interested in comparing his reactions with those just mentioned.

As to the compositional techniques of the work, wonderful things are concealed underneath the surface—as is the case in the best of art. The basic structure of the third ballade may be said to be a freely and marvellously adapted sonata-allegro form, although not precisely according to the strict rules of classicism in the appearances of the main themes, their keys, and their more obvious spirit. But who would have them thus proscribed? That eminent and erudite American composer, scholar, and teacher, Dr. Edgar Stillman-Kelley, was one of the first, if not the first, to observe that the larger and greater works of Chopin adapted the spirit and basic structure of the sonata-allegro form—"sonatified," as he used to say to those of us who were his students.[10] The critic Huneker sees a great deal of contrapuntal skill displayed in the development, or "working out," section of this work. Certain it is that Chopin was sufficiently a master of the Classical form so that he could bend it at will to the best advantage in the expression of his musical and poetic ideas. He adapted the traditional structure and the tendency of the romantic spirit to his material, rather than permitted the material to accommodate the mould, as was too often the tendency of the classical spirit—yes, even in some of the earlier works of Beethoven! Surely the student of harmony, as well as the student of form, will find in this work a veritable mine for exploration—and wonder. The ingenuity and skill shown in the working-out section alone is worthy of the best of thematic "manipulators," and the consummate subtlety shown in many modulatory, or transitional, passages—actual or, more often, feinted—is simply astounding! Of course Chopin does not accomplish these in the same way as the more classically minded, nor was he ever pedantic or academic—but why should he be? He

[8] Friedrich Niecks, *Frederic Chopin as a Man and a Musician.* (1888.)
[9] James Huneker, *op. cit.*
[10] See *Chopin the Composer*, by Edgar Stillman-Kelley. (New York: G. Schirmer, 1913.) This is an erudite and valuable work, not only on the compositional techniques of Chopin, but also on the craft of composition in general.

was a Romanticist. It is enough that he uses all forms, harmonic structures, sequences, and key relationships to the best advantage of his poetical and fanciful moods. He has demonstrated how flexible and adaptable the sonata-allegro form could be, and not a few contemporary composers owe a great debt to him for freeing the form. Let us examine some of these evidences.

The section that would traditionally be the exposition is announced at the onset by the first theme, which is in two sections— "A" as though a woman's soprano voice were singing, and "B" as though a man's bass voice were answering in this imaginary *tête-à-tête*.

After the conclusion of this rather square-cut, eight-measure first theme (though what a poetic and peaceful one it is in spite of its formality!) there follow some seventeen measures of development based upon germinal ideas derived from various portions of the theme itself. Then appears a motive that seems vividly to "bow itself gracefully into our pleasure"!

Then, after eleven measures of this interpolation, the main theme is re-stated much as at first, but ends, finally, with a long sustained *tonic chord* (a chord built upon the key note).

The second subject soon follows, though not in the strict classic tradition concerning key and character. It is a gay and coquettish theme, achieved largely by use of the "hoppinglike," eighth-note rhythmic figure. Note the quaintly nodding octave skip that introduces this theme and that later becomes an integral part of the second subject.

Note also the constant shifting of key feeling throughout this section, so that the harmonies seem to float unhampered by mundane realities—very poetic and imaginative indeed and a harbinger of things to come years and years later!

From here on Chopin displays some facile developmental writing as he toys with the first and then with the second subject in a most dazzling manner, in which rhythms, melodies, and harmonies join in a dancing whirl of scintillating colours and ever-changing forms. It is difficult to know just where the second theme proper ends and where its development begins; but any chance of chaos is averted by a sudden appearance of the second subject, note for note for ten measures as it was first heard. A welcome feeling of having one's feet on the ground (or is it on the glistening ball-room floor?); but this feeling is only temporary, for a clever development of the "bowing" figure previously illustrated interposes; it is suggestive of the reversal of the former figure, as though seen through a mirror.

Again the development, or working-out, resumes—note the sinister and highly contrasting effect of the change of key (into C-sharp minor) with a low, fast-running figure appearing in the bass part.

It is in the next section, which corresponds to the traditional reprise, or recapitulation, that Chopin shows his infallible artistic intuition as well as his rational process, for here he brings back the main theme, first in a foreshadowing, or anticipatory, glimpse, then in full bloom with a greatly altered accompaniment—a real stroke of genius! This is worked up to an impressive climax, only to be interrupted at the close by the reappearance of the fourth musical figure shown above. The second theme is absent in this section, for it has been heard often enough in the working-out section. An affirmative cadence closes this "impassioned love story."

ADDITIONAL SUGGESTIONS FOR LISTENING

The literature for piano solo is exceeded in volume only by that of song, and it is therefore impossible to select a list of suggested supplementary listening that will be comprehensive and universal in approval. After a few suggestions as to what to listen to immediately after the Chopin Ballade just presented, we leave the listener to his own initiative. Try to hear representative works of Chopin in the various forms styled Waltzes, Nocturnes, Preludes, Mazurkas, Etudes, Scherzos, Polonaises, Impromptus, Barcarolles, Fantasies, Sonatas, and, of course, the remaining three Ballades. No doubt you will also enjoy Schumann's *Carnaval*; Liszt's *Hungarian Rhapsodies*, especially number two; Mendelssohn's *Songs Without Words*; Schubert's *Impromptus* or *Moments Musicaux*; Beethoven's piano sonatas, especially Op. 13 (*Pathétique*), Op. 53 (*Waldstein*), Op. 57 (the *Appassionata*) or Op. 27 (*Moonlight*); Mozart's piano sonatas in a minor and a major; Rachmaninoff's *Preludes* in g minor and c-sharp minor; MacDowell's *Woodland Sketches, Sea Pieces, New England Idylls, Etudes* and the *Tragica* Sonata (these works by MacDowell should be on recorded discs by this time); Grieg's *Lyric Pieces, Holbergs Zeit*, and (if recorded) *Sonata* in e minor; Debussy's *Arabesques, Suite Bergamasque, Estampes, Images, Petite Suite* and so forth—consult up-to-date record list; Ravel's *Jeux d'Eau, Pavane pour une Enfant Défunte, Gaspard de la Nuit*, or *Sonatine*; César Franck's *Prelude, Chorale, and Fugue*; *Preludes* by Scriabin; and the more contemporary composers according to taste and availability in gramophone recordings—yes, try Schoenberg's *Concertstück*, Op. 11! However, there will be more fun in compiling your own list than in accepting any we might suggest.

The Violin; the Violin and Piano Sonata; the Trio

For many music lovers, the vibrant, soulful, and sustained tones of the violin are second only to those of the human voice for sheer sensual beauty and capability of stirring one's emotions to their depths.[11] Because its tone can be controlled in its dynamics while being sustained, the violin can achieve melodic effects impossible for the piano; though, of course, it cannot produce the chordal structures and volume of tone of the latter instrument. For these, as well as for other reasons, the violin is not often heard alone as a solo instrument—though there are exceptions as far as actual compositions are concerned. Most notable are the six Sonatas for Solo Violin written by the immortal Bach; but these are difficult, virtuoso pieces, esoteric in appeal, and thus not likely to be heard often in popular concert or radio programmes.[12] However, one can often hear both instruments—the piano and the violin—for in this duo the singing tone of the one is most happily combined and contrasted with the sonority and harmonic possibilities of the other. It is an ideal combination, and composers of European and American countries have written some of their best works for it. Among those who have been successful in writing in a masterly fashion for the violin and piano, few, indeed, have excelled (or equalled) the French composer, César Franck.

César (Auguste) Franck (Liége, Dec. 10, 1822;
Paris, Nov. 8, 1890)

In his biography of this master, Vincent d'Indy (Franck's outstanding pupil) gives several unforgettable pictures of him: one, as he rushes about with his coat-tails flying, giving private lessons—for his fame was not such as to assure him a professorship at the Conservatoire until after the age of fifty. Another picture, and probably the most faithful, is of the master seated at the console of the organ at Saint Clotilde, improvising on that instrument as no

---

[11] Though the exact early history of the violin is a matter of much dispute, there is little doubt that the violin, as we now know it, was a direct and immediate outgrowth of the viol family. (See articles on "Violin" and "Viol" in Grove's *Dictionary*.) The violin was perfected by the great Italian violin makers of the sixteenth century, especially those living in and about the city of Cremona—the members of the Amati family extending from Andrea, born in 1530(?), to Giralamo who died in 1740; the Guarnerius family, extending from Pietro, born in 1626, to "Guarneri del Gesu," who died in 1745; but the greatest debt is due the genius of Antonio Stradivarius (1644-1737).

[12] See page 449 for description and illustration of a *chaconne* (or *ciacona*) taken from one of the sonatas. There is an effective recording of this movement in an orchestral transcription.

one had done quite so well since the time of Bach (a comparison made by no less a master than the Abbé Liszt). His religious spirituality and modesty of character were so marked that he was looked upon as a father by his pupils, who invariably called him "Pater Seraphicus." (It is interesting to note some of those pupils —d'Indy, Chausson, Duparc, Ropartz, Lekeu, and Vidal.) In fact, it was during his music lessons at the organ that Franck imparted his compositional ideas and individual guidance, and thereby virtually created the first modern French "School," especially noteworthy for its contributions to the large symphonic forms and chamber music. (The opera, the ballet, and salon music had been the chief concern of composers before this time.) Still another aspect of wonder concerning this master is brought out by d'Indy, namely, that the bulk of his compositions came *after* he was fifty, and that most of his greatest works (especially orchestral and instrumental) were produced *after* he was sixty: the Symphony at sixty-seven, the String Quartet at sixty-seven, and the Sonata for Violin and Piano at sixty-four! One thinks of Michelangelo, Titian, Tolstoy, and Verdi.

During his early years, however, Franck wrote most of his short works, operas, and choral and church compositions. Especially noteworthy is his immortal oratorio, *Les Béatitudes*, written when he was fifty-seven, an age when most composers have the bulk of their work behind them.

Though Franck was born a Belgian, he came to France at an early age as a student at the Conservatoire and lived so long in Paris that his genius enabled him to become a spokesman for and later a prophet and world figure on behalf of his adopted country.[13] His style in composition is marked by a fortuitous combination of the Gallic traditional preoccupation with ratiocination and the Belgian heritage of deep human feeling and emotion— intuition, if you will. His music is vigorous, with a driving force and dramatic power that is sensed by the novice and learned alike. Always the mystic whenever mysticism could inject itself into such an abstract art as music, he was, nonetheless, keenly alive and sensuous in his own peculiar way. Of course he was a master of his craft, especially in two seemingly divergent aspects, harmony

---

[13] We are aware of the belief held by many of the "moderns" of France. "Franck is not even considered a Frenchman by us," one of the famous group *Les Six* told the author.

and counterpoint, and he had an unusual command of and respect for traditional forms and design—as we shall try to show presently. He used the arts of Bach and the Classicists for his deep romantic feelings, and put his musical ideas into the strictest of contrapuntal species when he chose (as we shall see in the *Finale* of the Sonata); but, on the other hand, he did not hesitate to burst the bonds of chromaticism when that procedure best served his purpose.[14] These altered chords add a colourful and refreshing novelty to the music, even in our day of ultrasophistication in matters concerning harmony, in their individual structures as well as in their unexpectedness and resolutions. But we are anticipating the discussion of the work we wish to present for study.

Sonata in A major for violin and piano

We have chosen this particular work to illustrate the compositional type under discussion for a number of good reasons, of which only a few need be stated. First, of course, it is understood that the work is a masterpiece of its type and style, and one that should be eagerly added to every listener's repertory.[15] The sonata is replete with beautiful melodies that ingratiate themselves at first hearing. Then, too, the work is emotionally gripping, at turns lyrical, dramatic, moody, and compelling; and, at times, it rises to heights of nobility and spirituality rarely equalled and never excelled. The composer is successful in balancing and contrasting the two instruments, with the utmost respect for the peculiarities of each instrument and the effects of their playing together. The violin and the piano seem to vie with each other in bringing to the fore the salient musical ideas of the moment.

Another reason for this choice is that the work presents a large number of opportunities for discovery of subtly concealed

---

[14] Here is a simple example of a chromatically altered chord: if one were to change any one or several of the tones of the simple tonic (first) triad in C major, C-E-G, so as to appear as C sharp-E-G, C-E-G flat, C flat-E-G, C-E-G sharp, C sharp-E flat-G flat, and so forth, while the tonality was still maintained as that of C major, the changed chord might be said to have undergone chromatic alteration. Watch for these chords as they make their appearance in the sonata; they will be salient enough, even for the novice—or should be!

[15] An eminent authority on appreciation, Walter A. Spalding of Harvard University, ventures the belief in his excellent book, *Music: an Art and a Language* (Boston: Arthur P. Schmidt Company, 1920), that this sonata ranks, with those of Brahms, among the finest of its kind. He further opines that it might be declared by some as without an equal!

beauties, and the lover of good music—fairly well prepared through experience by this time—will be handsomely rewarded for the close application of his listening prowess. The listener is warned, however, that some of these challenges are likely to be elusive, but we believe that, with a little guidance, they can be pleasantly and successfully sought out and assimilated at this stage of the listener's development.

It will be recalled that Chopin's *Ballade* involved some nicety of discernment pertaining to compositional features that were not apparent on the surface and that necessitated an advanced accumulation of listening skills to perceive and comprehend properly. So it is with this sonata, only to a still greater degree. (However, the appreciative process can take place regardless of technicalities.)

We have previously mentioned a compositional device known by the term "cyclical," whereby the composer brings about a closer unity among the several movements of a large work, such as a symphony or a suite, by recalling themes, or other musical ideas, that had appeared in previous movements.[16] Now we wish to present another connotation of the word: the evolvement of melodic, or thematic, lines brought about through the development, or extension, of one or more basic, germinal motives—where "the melody seems to grow right out of itself," or where different themes seem to bear all the resemblances one might expect in a close "blood" relationship. Perhaps this meaning can be made clearer by reference to an observation made by d'Indy in one of his three great books on the techniques of composition (*Cours de Composition*), to the effect that the whole structure of this sonata is based upon these three generative motives:

It might be of interest to some to discover the use of these generative motives in the constitution of the principal themes that are used in the different movements, as well as to observe them in the process of "working out," or development, as each movement itself progresses. We hasten to add, however, that such detailed discernment is not at all to be considered a *sine qua non* in

---

[16] See especially Beethoven's FIFTH SYMPHONY, page 310; Dvořák's NEW WORLD SYMPHONY, page 283; and Rimsky-Korsakoff's SCHEHEREZADE SUITE, page 231.

the appreciative process; sometimes it might prove to be just the opposite, for it should be remembered that it is in the aesthetic *effect* of such technical devices, rather than in their *identities,* and the recognition of the same, that the composer achieves his purposes in music as such.

ANALYSIS. *FIRST MOVEMENT: Allegretto ben moderato.*[17] *A major.* ⅜ *time. Sonatina form.* After a wistful four measures of introduction, a mood of elation and freedom is conveyed in this flowing and lilting first theme of triple measure (⅜ time), which is a direct outgrowth of the generative motive "A":

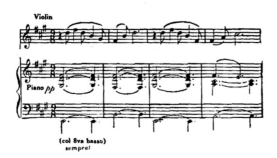

The lyrical and limpid second theme, in the traditional key of the dominant (in this case, the key of E major), makes its appearance in the piano part as an extended section of some sixteen measures. Note that when the violin does enter, it refuses to take up the second theme just presented by the piano—as is the usual practice at this juncture.[18] Instead, the violin persists in the reiteration of the first theme and will have none of the second, leaving that theme exclusively to the piano. Here is the second theme, delightful in melodic flow and lilt, in its harmonic content and its rhythmic design:[19]

[17] *Allegretto ben moderato:* in a well modulated, or moderate, rate of speed that is slower than *allegro.*

[18] The slow movement of the *Piano Concerto in G major,* Op. 58, by Beethoven comes to mind, in which work there is a somewhat similar condition between the orchestra and the solo instrument. There is this difference, however, that there is no "reconciliation" and adoption in the Franck sonata.

[19] Note that the first two measures of the theme (marked with an "X") are repeated in the next two measures (marked with a "Y"), but that the "Y" is sounded up three scale steps (comparing the melodies of both sections, note with note, we have a B in the "X" answered by a D in the "Y" section, A by a C natural, a G sharp by a B, etc.); this device is called a *transposition* or *sequence.* Wagner was especially fond of using it.

There is no working-out, or development, section (thus the form of the movement is styled a sonatina), and the reprise brings back the first theme in the violin, quite like the exposition; but the piano now has a massive, chordal accompanimental figure. The second theme, as in its first appearance in the exposition, is played only by the piano. The two instruments join, with the violin clinging tenaciously to the first theme, soaring and broadening, while the piano brings forth a suggestion of the wistful figure it had in the four introductory measures. Note the dramatic suddenness of the pianissimo (*pp*) in the two last notes—a compact, unified, and delightfully free flowing movement.

SECOND MOVEMENT: Allegro; d minor. $\frac{4}{4}$ time. Sonata-allegro form. The first theme is heard after the three measures of piano introduction. It is an animated and exciting theme, cleverly concealed in the warp and woof of an arpeggiated figure in the piano part. (A development of the generative motive "A".)

The violin picks up this theme, vigorously, along with the piano, and a minor climax appears, which suddenly ends in a very soft (*pp*) passage with a new idea that might be dubbed a secondary theme; but it, too, is soon dispelled by the reappearance of the noisy and bustling first theme. Note, presently, a bridge (or connecting link) passage in the violin, which is based on the first theme of the first movement. This is the transition passage to the second theme, now in the classically proper tonality of F major, and it is heard in the violin—a lyrical theme with a harplike accompaniment in the piano.

Both the first and the second themes are developed, mostly the former. Note the reference to the main theme of the first movement just before the reprise sets in, and also note the somewhat slow (*quasi lento*), pensive and contemplative episode that interrupts and delays—quite teasingly—the reappearance of the principal subject in the reprise. The reprise section will be unmistakable, for the first and second themes (the last now in the key of D major) enter quite regularly. Note again the reappearance of the main theme of the first movement—proclaiming itself as the *idée fixe* of the entire work, and we shall do well to recognize it as such. But see how irresistibly forceful and insistent Franck now makes it! A rather long and extended coda soon ensues, based largely on a rising four-note scale figure (with the violin playing tremolo—a quivering of the bow), reflecting once more the spirit and mood of the principal theme of the movement.

THIRD MOVEMENT: Recitativo-fantasia. Ben moderato. The word *recitativo* was met when the opera was discussed in Chapter VII. It is applied to a kind of musical declamation in which the inflections, accent, and emphasis are closely related to dramatic speech, free of the formal rhythm or regular phrase structure usually observed in song. The *fantasia* usually denotes a fanciful piece, unhindered and irregular in form, and of an improvisatory character in spirit and style. Yet Franck has seemed to combine orderliness of construction with the spirit of freedom, with no sense of restraint.[20] Cobbett ventures an explanation of this seeming

---

[20] Here, as in most worth-while impromptu and improvised speeches, the best are those that are carefully considered and meticulously prepared beforehand.

CC

contradiction in terms and practice; he states that Franck had a greatly developed and almost inordinate respect for the classical traditions concerning form and thus would be disinclined to give this movement a classical title in view of the formal deviations (evidences of the romantic spirit) within the movement.[21]

Along with many other virtues, this movement is distinguished for its long violin solo, which is only sparsely or intermittently accompanied, and which is in the spirit of a recitative improvisation, Again, the violin delays its appearance until after an introduction of four measures on the piano. The tonality eludes fixity in the first theme, for it wanders from d minor to f-sharp minor. The mood is pensive, gloomy, and sad in the accompaniment; which is based upon generative motive "A," while the violin is capriciously wistful, soaring about in running, arpeggiated figures.

A second theme, based on the generative motive "B," now is heard in the violin (in f-sharp minor), and with it a harplike accompaniment in the piano. Note how suddenly and dramatically Franck introduces this theme pianissimo in the midst of a very loud, fortississimo (*fff*) passage. (Franck is not unlike Beethoven in the dramatic use of nuances.) Also observe the first occurrence of the generative motive "C" at the end of this lyrical phrase in the violin:

This lovely *cantabile* (singinglike) melody is extended until there appears an effective quickening and broadening of the mood with

[21] Walter Willson Cobbett, *Cyclopaedic Survey of Chamber Music.* (London: Oxford University Press, 1929.)

a theme in the violin derived from a portion of the second theme of the second movement. Watch for its future use in two of the episodes of the *Finale*—a wonderful glimpse into the secret workings of Franck's compositional style and one well worth the listener's effort to grasp and to hold. We show, first, the source from the second movement:[22]

Here is the theme as it appears now in the third movement—not only pleasing in itself but also another excellent example of the compositional device known as "melodic-" and "rhythmic-augmentation."[23]

The movement is brought to a close with a coda employing a transformation of the *idée fixe*, and the theme last mentioned above. These are worked up to a forceful and impressive climax, fortississimo (*fff*). The final cadence (in f-sharp minor) is of rare and exalted beauty, with its aura of mysticism and spirituality, as the soft, organlike chords intone on the piano high above the earnestly pleading song of the violin. The whole passage contrasts strongly and dramatically with what has gone on only a moment before, as the violin again plays the melancholy and entreating figure it had sounded in the early measures of the movement.[24] Although

---

[22] We are aware that many of these details, here and throughout the text, are likely to be more *immediately* meaningful if one can read the printed score as the music progresses; and the author confesses to conspiratorial intent. However, with careful and repeated listenings, one who is not so trained in notation may attain a comparable understanding. For those who can read musical notation, we refer to page 18, fourth line, third measure of the piano score for the source indicated (G. Schirmer edition).

[23] See page 272 for detailed explanation of these terms.

[24] We suggest that those who can read score compare the passage just described with measures 17 to 22 of this movement.

no words are found in the score, many listeners contend that the close of this movement, though wordless, is nonetheless articulate with beautiful and heartfelt eloquence, a veritable *Miserere mei, Deus!*

FINALE: Allegretto poco mosso: A major. ⁴⁄₄ alla breve. Rondo form.[25] A number of fascinating musical features may be observed throughout this movement. First, it is as joyful and gay as the previous movement was melancholy and introspective. It flows along with themes that are filled with sunshine and gentle—never boisterous —cheerfulness. Then, the gross form of the movement is that of the traditional rondo, composed of three main sections[26] setting forth.and recalling the principal theme (four appearances if one counts the repetition, just before the coda), with intervening free and contrasting episodes and, finally, a coda.

But perhaps this movement is best known for what is generally regarded as the most spontaneous and flowing *canon* in all the literature.[27] The principal theme, used as a canon, is proclaimed at the beginning of the work, without the usual introduction, by the piano, and the violin follows a measure behind.

---

[25] *Allegretto poco mosso:* lively and gaily but slower than *Allegro.* ⁴⁄₄ *Alla breve:* a broad, fast duple measure, to be played as though it were ²⁄₂ time—"double quick" or "cut" time as it is often called.

[26] The sections bringing back the main theme are also known as "refrains."

[27] The *canon* is a form of contrapuntal technique in which a lead-off part (called the *antecedent*) is imitated and repeated, note for note, by another part (called the *consequent* or *answer*) either above or below antecedent, such entries continuing until all the parts have joined in; then all of them proceed together, still imitating each other. The popular songs *Three Blind Mice* and *Row, Row, Row Your Boat* are good examples of canons, which, for obvious reasons, are more particularly called "rounds." The word *canon* comes from the Italian, *canone*, meaning law or rule—for the imitating voice must repeat the lead-off voice note for note. The oldest recorded canon of merit is the lovely *Sumer Is Icumen In*, which is supposed to have been composed in England about A.D. 1240, by John of Fornsete. See *Music in Western Civilization* by Dr. Pau Henry Láng. (New York: W. W. Norton, 1941.) A *superlative* book!

The first episode is another interesting example of counterpoint, with the generative motive "C" in the piano, while the violin plays an embroidery overhead. (It will be recalled that the first appearance of the "C" motive was in the third movement, the fantasia.)

Then follows a sort of banter, or sparring, between the two instruments, in the form of a canon evolved from the principal theme; but this is interrupted by a clever passage in which the "C" germinal motive, just heard in the piano, is now played by the violin and the "embroidery" counterpoint is played by the piano—this is known as invertible, or double, counterpoint. Note the figure in the bass.

The refrain, or reappearance of the main theme, is in the form of a canon, but with the harmonic figuration in the piano greatly changed—another indication of the compositional skill of Franck.

(Canon between Bass part and Violin).

The ensuing brilliant climax is made out of a canon on the first four notes of the principal theme, which sounds forth as though it were simulating loud, clanging bells. The dynamic level is suddenly and dramatically lowered to piano (p), and a theme emerges that had previously appeared in the second movement, constructed out of the germinal motive "A."

A second episode is presently heard. It, too, is based upon the principal subject, but now in the key of b-flat minor, with the violin playing the main theme and the generating motive "B" in the bass part of the piano.

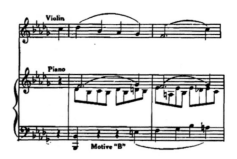

After a resounding interlude on the piano, based upon a portion of the main theme, there is a dramatic entry of the majestic melody from the Fantasia which is almost immediately repeated in a still more grandioso manner. Franck is now building up the climactic section, not only for this movement, but also as the pinnacle for the entire sonata; and he goes about it in a very skilful and confident manner, piling up intensified and agitated emotion, and sweeping one irresistibly along with the music. The third refrain is heard, again in canon, and the emotions are still further agitated as the principal theme is repeated (the fourth refrain, it might be called) with no letup in the onward sweep and passionate fervour. Then one is plunged directly into the coda proper, which is based upon the main theme, in canon, but sounding once more as though the music were coming from giant cathedral bells, proclaiming their joyful message of triumph to the world. The violin trills vibrantly above the clanging and dissonant chords in the accompaniment, which latter eventually turn into what composers call "horn tones," or "horn fifths,"[28] so commonly used in trumpet fanfares.

It is not difficult to conjure up a powerfully triumphant mood picture as these horn-call tones rise higher and higher to the end, punctuated, finally, by a decisive open octave tone on the key note, A.

One is certainly the *richer* for having listened to such a beautifully moving and inspiring work as this and one is most assuredly the *better* for adding it to the treasury of one's memory for unlimited future enjoyment.

ADDITIONAL SUGGESTIONS FOR LISTENING

The listener might begin to enlarge his repertory by playing such violin and piano sonatas as the following: a choice of Bach's Six Sonatas for Violin Alone; Beethoven's Op. 24 in F major, c minor, Op. 30, No. 2, in a minor, Op. 47 (the "Kreutzer"), or the one in G major, Op. 96; Brahms' in A major, Op. 100, or the one in d minor, Op. 108; Corelli's in D major; Dvořák's Sonatina, Op. 100; Grieg's Sonata in c minor, Op. 45; Handel's in A major; Mozart's in C major (K.296), in G major (K.301), in E-flat major (K.302), in C major (K.303), A-flat major (K.304), in e minor (K.305), in G major (K.379), or the one in A major (K.526); Schubert's in A major, Op. 162, and one will be well on his way. However, we wish to point out there that is a steadily enlarging library of records of sonatas for instruments other than the violin—such as those for piano and: flute, clarinet, oboe, horn, viola, 'cello, and others. For further information, consult a good record catalogue.

28

The Trio

However, it is to the *trio* that we wish to direct the listener's attention, especially to trios for piano and strings. Inasmuch as good recordings of such works are none too plentiful, we can only suggest a few titles for a start, hoping that manufacturing conditions will continue to improve along with the increase of listeners' interest. Try the trios by Mendelssohn, especially the one in d minor, Op. 49; Mozart's in E major (K.542), in C major (K.548), and in G major (K.564), and the one for piano, clarinet, and viola (K.498) if recorded; Beethoven's Trio in B flat, Op. 97, and the one in D major, Op. 70; Schubert's Op. 100 in E-flat major; Tchaikovsky's in a minor; Dvořák's in A major, Op. 81; Brahms' in c minor, Op. 101, the Horn Trio, Op. 40, and the one for clarinet, 'cello and piano, Op. 114—but we are already transgressing upon the pleasures and prerogatives of the listener. The foregoing "musts" will provide a good beginning in the right direction, however.

Chapter Twenty-Seven

Bach and the Polyphonic Style
The Reformation and the Baroque

THROUGHOUT the Middle Ages, music found its highest function in the service of the Church. In the colourful ritual that the Roman Catholic Church devised for its holiest solemnities, almost all the arts played an important part. The lofty vaults of the cathedral, the paintings in the chapels, the sculpture and carving and tapestry around the altar, the sensuous appeal of the incense, the pageantry of the processions—all these provided the setting for impressive ceremonials. But a central place in this confluence of the arts was reserved for music. From the thirteenth century on, a long line of brilliant composers created the contrapuntal Masses and Motets that have remained one of the chief glories of sacred art, culminating in the second half of the sixteenth century in the works of Palestrina (1525?-1594), Orlando Lassus (1530?-1594), and Tomas Luis Victoria (1549-1611).[1]

In writing the early type of music for the voices of the choir, composers matched one "point," as notes were previously called, of the soprano against the corresponding point, or note, of the alto, tenor, or bass; in other words, *punctus contra punctum*, or *point counter point*. (Readers may recall this phrase as the title of a popular novel by Aldous Huxley, in which he matches the decisive points in the lives of a group of characters in an essentially polyphonic manner.) *Counterpoint*, therefore, may be said to be the art, or science, of combining several melodies, or parts, simultaneously. As a science, it was carried to great lengths by the medieval masters who were able to combine, with dazzling facility, twenty, thirty, forty, and even more than fifty parts, all flowing on at the

[1] In matters concerning biographical data, dates, etc., throughout this text, we have freely consulted a number of authoritative references, such as Grove's the Oxford *History*, Nef's (Pfatteicher) *Outline of History of Music*; but we have leaned most of all upon Baker's *Biographical Dictionary of Musicians* (New York: G. Schirmer, 4th Ed., 1940).

same time. *Polyphonic* music is based upon the science, or art, of counterpoint and is said to be *contrapuntal*. *Homophonic* music, on the other hand, with a background of chords, is based upon harmony—the art, or science, of the construction and sequence of chords—in which the voices move along in blocks of combined parts. The composers of the nineteenth century. accordingly, thought along harmonic lines as naturally as those of the sixteenth thought in contrapuntal, or horizontal, lines.

Comparing the two musical styles further, we find that the point-counterpoint type of music was conceived as a series of lines flowing along horizontally, and that the harmonic type, on the other hand, consisted of vertical blocks of sound chords in which one combination of several tones, produced simultaneously, proceeded to another such combination. The old music, therefore, was polyphonic, contrapuntal, horizontal, primarily vocal, and choral, and was largely religious. The later music was likely to be homophonic, harmonic, conceived with a horizontal melody against, or along with, a vertical foundation of chordal tones, secular, with the emphasis on the solo voice (as in opera), and became increasingly instrumental. Also the new conception of melody demanded one clear-cut tune impinging upon the hearer at one time, to which everything else was likely to be subordinate. The old conception had presented a melodic confluence of many voices in which the texture as a whole was melodious, even when no one tune dominated.

For purposes of simplifying and highlighting the contrast, we speak of the two styles as though they were diametrically opposed to each other. One needs only to reflect upon the point, however, to realize that often one style imperceptibly shades into, or mixes with, the other. For, in a Mass or motet by Palestrina, with every voice flowing along its own line, if you stopped the music at any one point, a chordlike block of tone would best represent the cross-sectioning. Similarly, even though chords are vertical blocks of tone, as they move along from one point to another, the individual tones are likely to trace horizontal paths, not unlike the voices of counterpoint; and, of course, there are countless instances where the two styles of composition are deliberately compounded, as in Handel's *Messiah*. (See page 109.)[2]

---

[2] It will be recalled that the *Finale* of the César Franck Sonata for Violin and Piano employed the contrapuntal device of the *canon* very frequently. We shall see presently, in Bach's works, another application of this basic device, polyphonic imitation, in the form known as the *fugue*.

This is a good place, perhaps, to reiterate some advice to the listener: Perform the musical illustrations over and over until you have them well in mind. If you cannot read the musical score or play the works yourself, have someone else do it for you; we cannot emphasize too strongly the rendition of the illustrations of music in the text. If they are vocal, sing them—as a group, if you can—and do your best to follow with the eye what the ear is hearing.

The accompanying examples attempt to contrast the basic differences in the two styles of music discussed in the foregoing. Note in the *Doxology* that though the voices other than the melody move along in blocks, or chords, the bass part is melodic and interesting in a horizontal direction; and also note that at any juncture of three or four voices in the *Sanctus*, a chord, or harmony, results.

Musical Examples Contrasting the Two Styles

It is obvious that the concept of *countermelody* that plays such an important part in the orchestral music of the nineteenth century (and into our own time, for that matter) is essentially contrapuntal. So, too, when the composers of symphonies toss a theme from one choir to another, from one combination of instruments to another, or from one solo instrument to another, interweaving it the while with other thematic, or figurated, material, they are thinking in terms of "voices" and interweaving, contrapuntal lines. Beethoven, Wagner, Tchaikovsky, and their compeers developed a high degree of skill in this modern kind of orchestral polyphony, in which the imitations of the melody amongst the different choirs, and the combination with effective counter-melodies, have created a musical texture as richly varied in an orchestral sense as the earlier polyphony had been in choral writing.

However, it should be noted that, in the early stages of the development of instrumental music, the composers treated the instruments as though they were voices. In fact, the old music was likely to have a notation "For Voices or Instruments." Thus, a great deal of the early music for the organ, the keyboard instruments, and the small chamber-music groups during the seventeenth century was polyphonic in style, taking its character from the vocal music. Gradually, as the more pure and individual instrumental style developed, and keyboard instruments were perfected, the music also began to take part in the transition to a homophonic type of thought. This transition was immeasurably accelerated by the fact that instrumental music lent itself excellently to the homophonic style. The organ was ideal for the great blocks of chords that were the foundation of the new style. The violin, accompanied by harpsichord, could be treated like a solo voice with a background of harmony. The harpsichord itself was much better at tracing a melody with one hand and an accompaniment with the other than at tracing several horizontal lines simultaneously. The shifting of the spotlight from vocal to instrumental music meant, in effect, that music had passed from the polyphonic era to the homophonic. By the time of Mozart and Haydn, the shift had been pretty well accomplished.

Bach, coming at the beginning of the eighteenth century, was the composer who best summed up in himself both modes of thought. He was the last and greatest of the polyphonic masters, the culmination of centuries of music history and, at the same time, one of the first great artists in the new instrumental-homophonic style.

Bach and the Reformation

If the style and texture of Bach's music were determined by the historical transition of polyphony into homophony, its content, its emotional wealth and colouring, and its prevailing mood stemmed directly out of the far-reaching religious and social upheaval that Martin Luther set in motion at the beginning of the sixteenth century. We pointed out in the chapter on the oratorio that Bach expressed the spirit of the Reformation in music in the same sense that Milton expressed it in poetry and Rembrandt in painting— in the passionate humanism, the intensity of inner vision, and the almost mystical devotion that transformed art into a purifying experience.

Bach felt deeply about the most significant problems of his life and times—and projected that feeling through his work. Since music was the upwelling of the profoundest convictions and intuitions of the composer, there could, of necessity, be no room for bombast, for mere showiness, for exhibitionism, for cheap sentimentality, for untrue exaggeration and histrionics, as such, and as objective ends in themselves. It is a mistake to think of Bach as a pedantic or unemotional composer. He is, on the contrary, among the most passionate, the most rhapsodical of artists; but his passion and his rhapsodizing happen to be religious rather than theatrical. They are, on that account, nonetheless intense. As scepticism spread through the world, as the spirit of scientific research brought in a new intellectual current, the artist would turn to other sources for the emotional impact of his inspiration. But Bach's age was still fresh and aglow with the memory of men who had died on battlefields to uphold their religious convictions; and this spirit found expression in the art of the time. Thus it is not to be wondered at that Bach's magnificent works for the organ, his monumental Masses (especially the *B-minor Mass*), his five *Passions*, including those according to St. John and St. Matthew, Church cantatas (about three hundred of them!), and other works of his are generally thought of as constituting the peak of Protestant Church music, the loftiest and most enduring monument of all that the Reformation contributed to the aesthetic-spiritual development of modern European culture.

If the music of Bach differed from that of the great Roman Catholic masters, it was a difference not so much between individuals as between two world views. The gentle loveliness of Italian music had culminated in the golden art of Palestrina. Here was mysticism, too, the smooth mellifluous harmonies that transported the hearer to the realm of saints and miracles, a naïveté and tenderness that fitted in with the atmosphere of sacred processions and pilgrimages, of the adoration of relics, of all the exuberance that the Latin temperament brought to religion. The mysticism and the colouring were Italian; the love of sweet melodic effect was Italian; above all, the sensitivity to the powers of the human voice was Italian. The Reformation, with its quest for spiritual values, its slow, dogged search for what it conceived to be the truth, stemmed from the more rugged and more sturdy temperament of the North. Its music was above all a music of inwardness and intensity, of great concentration of purpose; a music of titanic conflict and sublimity. The tenderness here is of the shaken and storm-tossed man rather than that of the child. A shaggy strength infuses the great dissident harmonies of Bach's fantasies, as different from the progressions of Palestrina as the fog of the North Sea is different from the blue of the Mediterranean, or as the Rome of the Sistine Chapel was different from Luther's Wartburg. Bach knew and loved the Italian influence; but he was as German as Beethoven, or Wagner, or Brahms. With every breath he drew, with every note he wrote, he affirmed the deepest convictions, the innermost thoughts and feelings, of the folk that had bequeathed to him his most important heritage.

Bach and the Baroque

The art of the *Baroque*, with its roots firmly planted in the classical traditions of the Renaissance, and with its topmost branches reaching into the Romanticism of the future, is difficult—if not really impossible—to define with an overall, pigeon-hole characterization. However, the term *baroque* has come to designate the general tendencies of European art during part of the sixteenth, the seventeenth, and the first half of the eighteenth century.[3] It was a breaking away from the restraint of the Renaissance, and the movement underwent a number of different influences and stylistic manifestations as the rising-, high-, and ebb-tide of the spirit of the Baroque materialized in several European countries, especially Italy, Spain, France, and Germany. Thus, it is difficult to encompass all the aspects in a paragraph or two, and we shall have to confine ourselves to the more general and salient characteristics, hoping that an enticing glimpse will generate a desire for learning more about them elsewhere.

The essential spirit of the Baroque arose out of a world given over to extremes of self-indulgences: religious asceticism, and extravagant ritualistic ceremonials; deep scientific and philosophical thought, and silly superstitions; noble benevolence, and wholesale crime; dire misery on every hand, and gorgeous and ostentatious display of wealth—a great deal of it recently acquired or ill-gotten. Side by side with leaders of superstitions (*vide* astrology, demonology, witchcraft, and so on) were such men as Harvey, Kepler, Leibnitz, Locke, Newton, and Spinoza.

Naturally, the art expression of the times showed these influences and became more spectacular and dramatic, even seeking to burst the bounds of the medium in which it was conceived and to take on attributes that another and different medium might more fully satisfy. Sculpture often strove for effects that better suited painting, for example, and painting sometimes sought to achieve effects that were inherently the province of the stage. Architecture sought to achieve the plastic forms and spatial illusions that are more usually associated with painting and sculpture.

At its best, Baroque art was a vigorous art, having exuberant imagination, wonderfully elaborate detail, and great emotional fervour. It was intense and dramatic, and, more than had the art of any period before, it strove to incorporate the beholder as a vital part of the creative scheme—*empathy*, as the process is called.

[3] For more detailed analyses of the Baroque art than we can possibly give space for here, read *Southern Baroque Art* and *German Baroque Art* by Sacheverell Sitwell (New York: Doran, 1928); *Art in the Western World* by David M. Robb and J. J. Garrison (New York: Harpers, 1942), Chapters 8, 10, 11, 21, 28, and 29; *Art Through the Ages* by Helen Gardner (New York: Harcourt-Brace, 1936); *Music in Western Civilization* by Paul H. Láng (New York, Norton, 1941), Chapters 9, 10, 11, 12, and 13; *Cultural History of the Modern Age* by Egon Friedell, 3 Vols., translated by Charles F. Atkinson (New York: Alfred A. Knopf, 1931), we refer to Vol. 2 at this time; and the *History of Art* by Elie Faure, translated by Walter Pach (New York: Harpers, 1924), we refer here to Vols. 3 and 4.

The effects of light and shade, of colour and form, of curves con-trasted with straight lines and angles, and horizontal lines cutting off or modifying the effect and function of those that are vertical—all these, along with the subject matter of sensual splendour, dis-play of wealth, free expression of "high living," and ecstasy of sacred as well as profane issue, shaped the Baroque style. Though one should add that these same attributes may not be exclusive to the Baroque and are to be found in the art of other periods, it should be remembered that it is in their combination and emphases, as well as the components and compositional technique, that the period achieves its individuality.

At its worst, the Baroque was likely to be bombastic and in-flated, filled with cheap and maudlin sentimentality, vulgar, often quite degenerate, overlavish and overornate, madly confused and reckless in divergencies and contrasts in the basic content as well as in its manner of execution. However, one should consider both the virtues and the vices of the style when contemplating the Baroque, for the presence of both extremes is a significant charac-teristic in itself.

On page 431 there is a reproduction of a sculptural work, "Saint Theresa in Ecstasy," by one who has been called "the Father of the Baroque," the Italian, Gian Lorenzo Bernini (1598-1680). This work reposes in the St. Maria della Vittoria Church in Rome and depicts a dream which St. Theresa herself has de-scribed.[4] In this sculpture of her dream, the Angel appears before the Saint, with a dart in his hand—a symbol of divine love—and Bernini has caught the moment when the Angel is about to pierce the heart of the sleeping dreamer. The sculptor has shown us a dramatic moment and has greatly intensified the emotion through his means of execution. Note the flamboyant decorations and back-ground of clouds and gilded streamers of light from a heavenly source, the highly decorative and compositional functions of the folds of the draperies, and the impression that the group be-longs to the space surrounding it—heightened by the extended foot and head of the Saint. Note also the play of light and shade, almost as though the medium were painting, and how Bernini has succeeded in communicating a lovely poetic and sentimental religious expression through their means.

[4] Readers who are interested in the biographies of the two saints of like name, though centuries apart, might enjoy *The Eagle and the Dove* by Vita Sackville-West.

Ecstasy of St. Theresa   *Bernini*

In painting, the spirit of the Baroque may be seen in the bold, vigorous, richly ornate, and highly colourful style of the time—though some of these may not be as self-evident as in sculpture, or as positive as in architecture. There is a superabundance of creative vitality in this style of painting, a great deal of the expression of the joy of high living and vigorous health. These attributes may also be seen in the paintings of such artists as Peter Paul Rubens (Flemish, 1577-1640), with his show of action, movement, excitement, and great areas of healthy pink flesh, and in the realism of Michel Angiolo Caravaggio (Italian, 1569-1609).

A sense of showmanship is often indicated in the works of this period, with an almost theatrical play of high lights and bold use of colours and shadows; and now and then there is likely to be not a little outright sensationalism of topic as well as means of expression—encouraged by the Church itself, it might be said, as an effective and legitimate instrument of proselyting. With El Greco (born Domenico Theotocopuli, a Greek, 1541?-1614), the bridge between the High Renaissance and the Baroque was most successfully and definitely accomplished. Along with some of the characteristics already noted, El Greco was much fascinated by and absorbed with nature, with both man and God, and he sought emphasis of his imaginative and creative ideas through wilful distortion of forms and the use of (certain) colours. These become powerfully effective when the sympathetic and understanding imagination of the appreciator functions creatively in contemplation. A reproduction of El Greco's "View of Toledo" is shown on page 433. This was painted late in his life and represents him at the height of his powers. Note the play between the line formed by the crests of the buildings, the contour of the hills, and the winding roads; also note the counterpoint between the forms in the clouds themselves and the patches of ground—and the ominous, foreboding mood that grips one as does a dramatic and tense moment at the theatre; one cannot escape it, and though it is terrifying, one will not avoid it! These are intensified in the original painting through El Greco's use of colour. Such is the fascination of great art, and El Greco is one of the foremost artists in the history of painting. See other works of his in art museums, or, if this is not possible, in good colour reproductions.

In music, one can clearly feel the spirit of the Baroque, sometimes to a greater extent than in the sister arts. This was, of course,

due to the preponderance of the religious feelings of the time and
the adequacy of music to express them. Religion sought for vastness of proportions in its expressive forms, along with a tendency
toward a display of splendour. The music was replete with tonal
colour, frequent and intricate ornamentation, and, often, glorious
bursts of harmonic as well as contrapuntal means. It was often of
the theatre, both literally and figuratively speaking, and the homophonic and polyphonic styles and techniques vied with each other
to produce novel and original effects and overpowering climaxes.
Witness the motets of G. Gabrieli (Italy, 1557-1612), with their
colourful chromatic harmonies (and the same, even to a greater

Toledo   *El Greco*

degree, in the Masses and Madrigals of Gesualdo—1560-1613, Naples). Witness the pompous, brilliant, and elephantine scores of Arazio Benevoli (Italy, 1605-1672), with as many as fifty-three separate parts in a score—bringing to mind the romantic Berlioz who came two hundred years later; and witness the works of Heinrich Schütz (Saxony, 1585-1672), with their continuation of the Italian grand style of choral music, religiously serious and powerfully moving. Then, too, there was the music of George Frideric Handel (Germany, 1685-1759), with its simplicity of melodic line, fresh harmonic backgrounds, lively and rhythmic counterpoint, and, overall, a vigorous and dramatic spirit that is enthralling as it is so often "a loud and glorious sound." (See *The Messiah*, Chapter VIII.) But it is with the incomparable Johann Sebastian Bach that we are most concerned here and now.

Johann Sebastian Bach (1685-1750)

The life of Bach offers less material for romantic legend than does that of almost any other composer. His personal experience was tied in the most immediate way with his art. As with Shakespeare, we have but the scantiest biographical data of an intimate and personal nature. He taught, he played, he wrote the record of his emotional and spiritual growth into his works, and when he had about finished his task, he died.

Biography

Bach was born in 1685, in Eisenach, Thuringia, of a family that had produced, from the time of his great-grandfather, upwards of fifty composers and performers; some of them were among the most illustrious musicians of their time, so much so, that the words "Bach" and "musician" were almost synonymous. He grew up in Eisenach, in the shadow of the stately Wartburg where Luther's translation of the Bible saw the light of day, and where, in the legendary age of the Minnesinger, the gracious Elizabeth had listened to the songs of the noble minstrels and awaited the return of Tannhäuser. Johann Sebastian's father, who was court musician at Eisenach, died when the boy was ten. Brought up by an elder brother who was the organist in a neighbouring town, Ohrdurf, the future composer displayed his gifts early in life. He possessed a beautiful soprano voice, sang in the church and school choirs, and received his first regular instruction on the clavichord from his brother. At fifteen, Johann Sebastian became a chorister at Lüneburg. Here he was able to listen to George Böhm, the organist at St. John's Church, whose playing made a profound impression upon the young musician. This was the golden age of the organ in Germany. For, as long as music revolved around the Church, the organ occupied a central place in the scheme of things. Out of the simple chorale melodies that the congregation sang, the organists of North Germany had evolved a wonderful art of improvising and elaborating upon a theme, the art of the *chorale prelude* and the *chorale fantasy*. It was during his stay at Lüneburg that Bach undertook the famous pilgrimages on foot—he was too poor to go otherwise—to Hamburg, thirty miles distant, to hear Reinken, an outstanding organist of the time. At the age of eighteen, Bach became the organist at Arnstadt; and in 1705, when he was twenty, he went to Lübeck to hear and meet the great Danish composer and organist, Buxtehude, from whom Bach learned so much.

The first important period of Bach's career as a composer coincides with the nine years from 1708 to 1717 that he spent at Weimar as court organist and chamber musician to Duke Wilhelm Ernst. The Duke was passionately fond of the organ and of religious music. This, accordingly, was the period of Bach's great organ works and the early church cantatas.[5] The organ works marked a new epoch in the literature for the instrument. For complexity, grandeur of effect, and richness of texture they far surpassed anything that had been accomplished in the field. In the organ works, the rhapsodical quality of Bach's emotion and his amazing mastery of polyphony combined with all the splendour of the Baroque style to produce works that, in their kind, have never been even remotely approached. To hear a fine organist perform the *Fantasia and Fugue in g minor*, or the great *Passacaglia in c minor* is one of the deepest of musical experiences.

The close of his stay at Weimar—later the city of Goethe and Schiller, and still later of Liszt—was marred by friction with the

[5] A *cantata* is a work for chorus, soloists, and accompaniment, on a sacred or secular subject, in which the lyric drama or story is adapted to music but is not intended to be acted. Bach wrote some 300 of these for the complete Lutheran church-year—about five entire yearly cycles.

Original Manuscript of an "Organ Prelude"   J. S. Bach

Duke. Bach seems to have resented the fact that his master had neglected to offer him the post of *Kapellmeister* when it fell vacant. A man of independent spirit, he asked for permission to leave the ducal service. The Duke, displeased with the manner in which Bach had asked for his release, placed him under arrest and kept him in confinement for a month. On regaining his liberty, the composer joined his next patron, Prince Leopold of Anhalt-Cöthen.

The Prince of Cöthen was as fond of chamber music as the Duke of Weimar had been of the organ. The Cöthen period in Bach's life (1717-1723) is, therefore, the outstanding period of his chamber music composition. He experimented with the secular instrumental style, adapting himself to the combinations of instruments that he happened to have at hand. It was still too early in the development of instrumental style for Bach to apply his inventive faculty to the solution of problems of instrumentation and tone colour; he simply used the instruments already at hand in his parish to accentuate the contrapuntal lines of his musical texture. His works were, however, a contribution of first importance to the evolvement of a distinctive instrumental style. The Cöthen period saw the production of the *Brandenburg Concertos*, the *Suites for Orchestra*, the *Violin Concertos*, and the *Instrumental Suites*. During this period, too, Bach turned to the clavier—we use the term, as he did, to include both the harpsichord and the clavichord—and enriched its literature with such works as the *Chromatic Fantasy and Fugue*, the *English* and *French Suites*, and the *Little Preludes* and *Inventions* that have remained indispensable training material for the young pianist.

At Cöthen, also, he produced, primarily for the education of his older children, the first part of what is to this day one of the most significant works in music, the WELL-TEMPERED CLAVICHORD. The importance of this work is bound up with one of the most pressing problems in the period of transition from the church modes of medieval choral music, through the experiments in the so-called *meantone temperament* (or scale tuning), to the major-minor system of scale tuning of our present-day music.[6] The organization of intervals within the major scale depended on the fact that there

[6] Consult appropriate articles on "Acoustics," "Modes," "Mean-tone," "Equal-temperament," "Temperament," etc., in Grove's *Dictionary of Music and Musicians*, and articles by the present author in Thompson's *International Cyclopaedia of Music and Musicians*.

was only one pattern of whole and half steps, which had to sound the same (and in tune) no matter at what point on the keyboard one might choose to begin. This, in turn, meant that the octave had to be divided into twelve half-steps, each of which was equal in intervallic (ratio) size to all the others. In order to accommodate the harpsichord and clavichord to the needs of the new musical theory, the sharps and flats could no longer be tuned according to the strict natural laws of musical intervals derived from the ratios of the intervals of the overtone series; rather, they had to be shifted or "tempered" so that enharmonics were exactly alike. (Thus, D sharp should be the same as E flat, F sharp the same as G flat, B sharp the same as C, A flat the same as G sharp, and so forth, on our piano.) The WELL-TEMPERED CLAVICHORD was the result of this accommodation to the new system of equal tuning, in which it was possible to have a major and minor key starting from each of the twelve tones of the octave, with the preservation and interchange of enharmonics. To illustrate the artistic and musical possibilities of this new relationship between the keys, Bach wrote a prelude and a fugue in each major and minor key, producing the twenty-four preludes and fugues of Book I of the WELL-TEMPERED CLAVICHORD, to which he later added the twenty-four of Book II. These *Forty-Eight Preludes and Fugues* have become the foundation work for piano and organ the world over.

The death of his beloved wife, Maria Barbara, in 1720 and the desire to provide better educational facilities for his children than Cöthen offered, led Bach to look for a new post. In 1722 he became cantor of the celebrated St. Thomas's school of Leipzig, where the musicians who furnished music for the city's churches were trained. The post, one of the most important in Germany, was first offered to two other composers, neither of whom was available, and was then given to Bach, one of the members of the Council remarking that as the best musicians were not free to take it, it was necessary to accept one "of second rank." Bach pledged himself to lead a modest life, to teach the scholars with devotion, to show the Council all due respect and obedience, to provide music neither too diffuse nor too operatic, and not to leave the town without the burgomaster's permission. He remained in Leipzig for twenty-eight years until his death in 1750. It was here that the third and greatest period of his creative career unfolded.

As at Weimar and Cöthen, Bach's versatile genius adapted itself to the requirements of his employers and to the resources at his disposal. It was his duty, besides teaching the scholars of the Thomasschule their singing and their Latin, to compose music for the church service. It was here that all the influences that had moulded his art—the splendour of the Baroque, the mastery of vocal polyphony that was his heritage from the past, and the spirit of Lutheranism as objectified in music through the chorale—converged to produce his great religious music. The Leipzig period saw the production of the later church cantatas, of which almost two hundred have come down to us, including St. John and St. Matthew Passions, the Christmas, Easter, and Ascension Oratorios, the Motets, the four Lutheran Masses and the great Mass in B Minor. There were also the secular cantatas to celebrate important occasions at the University of Leipzig and celebrations at the court of his royal patron, the Elector of Saxony. Despite his preoccupation with choral music throughout the Leipzig period, he did not entirely cease writing instrumental works. The Italian Concerto, the second book of the Well-Tempered Clavichord, the concertos for one, two, three and four claviers, as well as numerous partitas for harpsichord and clavichord, and chorales, sonatas, preludes, and fugues for organ, and Die Kunst der Fuge, all belong to the final years of his life.

Bach's contemporaries did not have any idea of his true stature as a composer; his life and activity were too circumscribed for his fame to spread as did that of his contemporary, Handel. In a list that Mattheson, the foremost critic of the day, drew up arranging composers in order of their rank, Bach barely made seventh place, Handel fourth. The works of the more favoured men have been all but forgotten. The incident should fill one with scepticism in regard to the judgments that our own critics pass upon our contemporary composers. If Bach impressed his contemporaries at all, it was primarily as an organ virtuoso. In the final decade of his life he achieved even more than local fame in this respect. There is the famous visit he made in 1747 to the court of Frederick the Great. The King, an ardent flute player, was at his chamber music when the arrival of the composer was announced. "Gentlemen, old Bach has arrived!" he exclaimed in some excitement. Bach extemporized on the new pianofortes that were then coming into fashion, astonishing the King with his powers. Frederick played him a subject on which to improvise; Bach forthwith created a fugue in six parts upon it. On his return home, he developed Frederick's theme into a "Musical Offering" that he dedicated to "a sovereign admired in music as in all other sciences of war and peace."

With the exception of rare pilgrimages such as these, Bach's was a life of continual labour; his complete works represent a colossal creative output. A simple, steady man, there were in his life none of the emotional upsets so frequently associated with genius. He found his supreme happiness within the family circle and in the companionship of the second wife, Anna Magdalena—famous because of the notebooks of simple pieces he wrote for her instruction that are now excellent practice material for beginning pianists.

Of his twenty children, several followed in his footsteps. Carl Philipp Emanuel was perhaps the most important composer in the period between the death of Bach and the rise of Haydn and Mozart, both of whom he profoundly influenced. Bach's other sons, Wilhelm Friedemann, Johann Christoph, and Johann Christian, were among the most illustrious composers of their time. In teaching them, as well as a distinguished group of pupils, in discharging his duties as Cantor of the Thomasschule, and in rearing the monumental edifice of his compositions, his life ran its course. As with Milton and Handel, his labours affected his eyesight and he was blind toward the end of his life. He died in 1750, at the age of sixty-five, the last and greatest of the old masters, and, in the opinion of many, of the new as well.

In his own time his art was too much rooted in the past to please his contemporaries. The following age turned so completely to the fascinating ramifications of the new sonata form and homophonic styles of music that the greatest composer of the age was all but forgotten. For the better part of a century his masterpieces lay neglected, until the young Mendelssohn, stirred to highest enthusiasm by an appreciation of their worth, led the way to a true appraisal of the master by his revival of the St. Matthew Passion. The Classical Period had been too dazzled by the "new music" to be able to take the true measure of Bach. It remained for the Romantics, strangely enough, to rehabilitate his works. To an age that is increasingly rejecting the emotional extravagances of the Romantics and the formal elegance of the Classicists, it is to be expected that the music of Bach would offer something enduring and substantial, rich and deeply significant to those of our own time. Relegated to what might have been oblivion until a century ago, the music of Bach has finally taken its rightful place as one of the most potent forces in all "modern" music.

The chorale preludes

For generations, the organists in the Lutheran Church announced to the congregation the chorale that was to be sung. Seated at the organ, their fingers "preluding" seemingly at random over the keys, their musical imagination took wing as they wreathed the simple hymn tune that was to ensue in a new harmonic and contrapuntal setting—purely instrumental in character, but retaining the original melody of the chorale. Thus arose the art of the *chorale prelude*. The chorale preludes of Bach constitute the credo of the inner man, an outpouring of his creative personality. And what Bach had then to say was so deeply, so passionately felt that even now, whether one accepts the particular faith out of which these ecstatic tone poems came or some other creed, the chorale preludes remain by common consent among the most noble rhapsodies of music. We can present only a few out of the many that Bach wrote in this form.

"Christ Lag in Todesbanden" (Christ Lay in the Bonds of Death)[7]

This is an organ prelude on a melody that Bach made and used in his church cantata of the same title, having derived the melody from a popular Lutheran hymn. Grief breathes from the melody, a sense of desolation that in the end gives way to a simple, deep hope and faith that the Lord has, indeed, risen from the dead. There is strength and inner conviction in the music with its beautiful melody and its sombre, rich harmonics. (Note how much more freely and melodically the individual voice-parts move about in the chorale than they do in our average present-day hymn tune.)

[7] The author advises the use of both the original (organ) version of the chorale preludes and the more modern orchestral transcription, so that a proper comparison of values may be made. Also be sure to listen to the original vocal recording of the chorale which inspired the chorale prelude—or better, sing it.

Externally, Bach presents a picture of a simple, earthy man. Yet deep at the core of his nature was the mysticism that, as the years went by, turned his thoughts increasingly to the subject of death and the hereafter. Some of his most moving melodies are built around the thought of his reunion with God, a motif that takes on increasing prominence in his later works. *Komm Süsser Tod* (Come Sweet Death) is truly a song of faith in which the otherworldliness of Bach finds its purest and most serene expression.

"Komm süsser Tod."

In the very effective orchestral transcription by Leopold Stokowski, the melody is played by the 'cellos after an introduction by the double basses. Muted violins wreathe a delicate countermelody high above. The tune is repeated in the woodwinds, finally in the strings, while slowly ascending arpeggios on the harp create a properly celestial atmosphere. Those listeners who are particularly attracted to this form will want to listen to two suggested supplementary preludes, *Sleepers Awake! A Voice Is Calling,* in the beautiful orchestral setting by the Italian Impressionist, Ottorino Respighi; and *Jesu, Joy of Man's Desiring,* in the Stokowski orchestral version; note the significant and flowing countermelody given to the oboe.

Transcriptions of organ works

Since the orchestra has become the principal instrument of our time, just as the organ was in the time of Bach, many great organ works are heard today in modern orchestral transcriptions rather than in their original versions. Also, throughout the long period of the ascendancy of the piano, a number of these organ masterpieces, most of them dating from the first great period of Bach's creativeness during his stay at Weimar, were arranged for piano by Liszt, Busoni, and a number of other master pianists. The listener should be aware of what is Bach and what is the work of the transcriber, and the only way to be so aware is to hear both versions.

The fugue

The *Little Fugue in g minor*[8] is one of the most popular of Bach's fugues. Written for the organ, it has achieved new popularity in the Stokowski transcription. We illustrate only the exposition section.

In the orchestral version of this fugue, the theme is announced by the oboe and is handed about to all the choirs in a series of climaxes that drives forward to the final pronouncement of the subject by the full orchestra. In the course of this development, the theme is shifted from minor to major, then returned to minor, as the orchestra summons up its most brilliant sonorities for the

---

[8] The word *fugue* is derived from the Latin *fuga*, meaning "flight," and the application is warranted because a fugue is actually concerned with the musical exploration (or flight) of a single theme. This theme is treated in imitation, or canonical, style, and is alternately called the "subject" or the "answer" as it enters, part by part (usually in a tonic-dominant, or *doh* and *sol*, key relationship), until all the parts have joined in. Of course, those voices, or instruments, not actually producing the subject or the answer, continue on their way the while, with counterpoint that is appropriate for the moment.

Now after all the voices are in, thus completing that portion of the fugue known as the *exposition*, or *enunciation*, a free and contrasting episodical section appears. This may involve new material or it may develop musical figures taken from the exposition. Such a section is called an *episode*.

Presently the main theme (the subject) reappears in an order different from that which obtained in the exposition. This kind of a section is called a *middle entry*, and the composer may indulge in as many alternations of episodes and middle entries as he thinks his material indicates—or time and length permit.

Then, at the close, the composer might indulge in a fugal device—most common in textbooks about music—known as a *stretto*, which consists of a piling up of the theme at a closer interval of time than that which separated the subject and answer in the exposition, the composer might reduce, or overlap, this succession to a measure or even less. This device is often used to build up a climax or to intensify the emotional effect in general. Then the composer might sound forth the theme in a glorious final presentation, which is often heightened by having a drone, or *pedalpoint*, on the tonic, or the dominant, or both. A punctuating cadence brings the work to a close, and often, if the work is in a minor key, this closing cadence will dramatically put forth the major instead.

Those who enjoy the compositional aspect of the fugue should follow closely the course of the theme. It is a very good practice, and a lot of fun in itself, to sing the theme every time it appears in the composition while the work is being performed. If there is a group listening, all might join in the singing, later discriminating more faithfully with the allocation of "parts."

ultimate crescendo and final cadence in the major; note also the pedal point on the dominant (fifth tone of the scale), three measures before the last. Surely everyone will have enjoyed the thrilling experience of listening to this fugue, and it is hoped that other fugues of Bach also will be heard.

Although the fugue form is rigid in certain aspects and circumscribes the composer to some degree (especially a composer who is motivated by a highly emotional and romantic spirit), there are many opportunities within the structure for wide divergencies and individual expressions of skill. No two fugues are exactly alike. The search for the substantiation or refutation of this statement is bound to be as exciting as it is pleasant.

Bach was in the habit of preceding the more or less strict form
of the fugue with a free or improvisatory piece called, at various
times, a *prelude*, a *toccata*, or a *fantasia*. The prelude and the fantasia
emphasized the element of emotional outpouring; the toccata
(literally, a "touch" or display piece) leaned toward brilliance
and virtuosity. Bach's *Toccata and Fugue in d minor* should be among
the supplementary listening numbers.

Theme and variation forms: the passacaglia and the chaconne

For composers who thought so largely in terms of line as Bach
and those who preceded him, the *theme-and-variation* form offered
rich possibilities for musical invention and display of composi-

tional skill as well as emotional expression. Where Haydn, Mozart, and their successors thought of the variation as an ornamentation or elaboration of the melody, the earlier composers more often retained the melody in its original simplicity and obtained the desired variety in the possibilities of the counterpoint. They thus achieved, in its completest form, the ideal of unity and, at the same time, variety. The *variations on a ground,* or *on a ground bass* (sometimes called a *basso ostinato*), so popular during the seventeenth century, and consisting of a short, distinctive tune of a few measures repeated over and over in the bass, over which the contrapuntal variations became increasingly intricate, culminated in the *passacaglia* and the *chaconne.* The passacaglia, an old and stately Spanish-Moorish dance whose name, according to some, was derived from a phrase, "Passo Gallo," meaning "rooster step," consisted of a solemn melody in triple metre and in the minor mode. This melody was reiterated in the bass against very varied counterpoint in the upper parts. Scholars have never quite agreed as to how the chaconne differed from the passacaglia. Some authorities maintain that the distinguishing feature of the chaconne was in the emphasis on the harmonic character of the theme, while the passacaglia subject was more likely to stress the purely melodic aspect. Until a better definition is agreed upon, the foregoing might well be accepted. In any case, when we use the terms today, we generally have reference to the monumental example of each form that Bach left in the *Passacaglia and Fugue in c minor for Organ* and the *Chaconne in d minor for Unaccompanied Violin.* Both works are frequently heard nowadays in the orchestral versions.

Passacaglia in c minor

By the time that the passacaglia reached the hands of Bach, it had lost its original dance character. The theme on which he built his c-minor passacaglia is a solemn and dignified eight-measure phrase (see the first line of the ensuing musical illustration). Upon this simple theme Bach built a series of twenty "variations," rising steadily in power and intensity, in a structure that for sheer imagination and mastery of technique has never had an equal. (We are able to show only seven of these variations in the illustrations on pages 448 and 449.) At first the theme is kept in the bass, while the parts above it change in ever more intricate contrapuntal patterns. Then we hear it in the uppermost part, while the lower accompaniment shifts about. Then the theme is heard in an inner part, while the counterpoint is woven above and below it. Finally, the work builds up to loud and triumphant pronouncement of the theme, against massive chords and lively, running passages. When the composer seems to have extracted every possible variation, he takes the first half of the theme, combines it with another genial melody, and proceeds to construct a *double fugue* (a fugue on two subjects instead of the usual single theme) that is as worthy and exciting as all that has already transpired in this work—yes, even more so, if that is conceivable. Never before or since has the artistic imagination functioned on such a high, noble, and unsurpassable plane in a similar form; it is the culminating point among giant peaks. Centuries of discipline and experience were necessary before the passacaglia in c minor could come into existence; and, through the ardours of this aesthetic experience and discipline, finally came that freedom which is reserved only for the anointed.

A few pointers for listening might not be amiss here. Note the theme, first of all; memorize it by singing it *along with the performance.* Then observe how this theme repeats itself throughout the piece—if you are playing a gramophone record, hum the theme as it is reiterated, in whatever part it may appear. You may have to try a few times before you overcome the tendency to get lost, to go astray. After you perceive this aspect of the work clearly, go through the composition again and again, noting the more involved tonal patterns and designs that the composer has woven into the richly inventive and highly imaginative contrapuntal fabric. Try to notice what is going on in the other "voices" while the theme is being sounded. With sufficient time and practice, you will be able to hear several principal features going on at any moment as a composite whole, or in such rapid shifts of interest that the effect will be almost the same. However, with all this admonition to observe elements of design, do not lose sight of the aesthetic values of this as well as *all* other compositions to which we have listened. Techniques and craftsmanship of diverse kinds and descriptions have their justification of use and right for being only in so far as they ultimately arouse and achieve aesthetic satisfaction in the listener. Otherwise, craftsmanship is only of

EE

academic interest and of doubtful and even negative value as far as the appreciator is concerned.

The following illustrations show the theme, together with initial portions of seven selected "variations."

Chaconne in d minor

Though the *chaconne* is more often heard nowadays in the orchestral version than in its original medium, it will be well to hear the work as Bach conceived and wrote it *along with* the more modern orchestral transcription. The original of the chaconne is a movement from one of the set of six sonatas that Bach wrote for the unaccompanied violin solo, and, as such, is one of the show pieces for better virtuosi. When one is fortunate enough to hear a great violinist perform this work, one will be moved by that rare blend of pathos, of lyrical intimacy, of nobility and power and complexity all upreared on the tenuous foundation of four violin strings! By all means, listen to Bach's original version. But if that is not possible, the orchestral version will prove to be acceptable to all save the purists because of its Gothic spaciousness, its impressive power, and its architectonic massiveness. Bach's limitless fecundity of invention, his originality of thought, his flowing linear construction—above all, his power to say great things in the greatest way—are apparent in both the *passacaglia* and the *chaconne.*

The Chaconne consists of more than sixty variations on the following theme, which is shown in the original Bach version for violin alone:

ADDITIONAL SUGGESTIONS FOR LISTENING

The complete works of Bach have been published by the *Bach-Gesellschaft* in forty-seven volumes; surely the most diverse tastes should find gratification amidst this monumental output. It will be recalled that other types and forms of Bach's works have been presented in previous chapters—we have reserved the present one for some of the larger instrumental works—thus a review of all his references may be in order. As has been our custom in suggesting supplementary listening, we shall present only a few that seem opportune immediately after the compositions just studied in this chapter.

Of course the listener should become acquainted with more of the preludes and fugues of the WOHLTEMPERIERTE KLAVIER, in two volumes of twenty-four pairs each. First try selections from the two-part and then the three-part *Inventions*; then choose Preludes and Fugues among numbers 1, 2, 4, 5, 8, 9, 16, 21 of Part I and numbers 5 and 9 from Part II of the WELL-TEMPERED CLAVICHORD to begin with; follow along with the "Big" g-minor, "Big" a-minor, and D-major fugues from the more than forty organ fugues. The more daring and advanced will want to make selections from DIE KUNST DER FUGE[9] now obtainable in entirety in records. Then the reader, after hearing a few scattered and selected works in the original or transcribed versions, will have made a good beginning in the literature of Bach with one notable exception—the *concerto grosso*.

The concerto grosso

Bach wrote six of these works, which have become known as the BRANDENBURG CONCERTI[10] (for they were written in 1721 for the

---

[9] DIE KUNST DER FUGE (The Art of Fugue) is a collection of fifteen fugues for solo instrument, two for two claviers, and four canons, presenting almost every conceivable kind of contrapuntal device and variants on a single theme; it is a monumental treatise on the art of fugal writing that was left unfinished at the time of Bach's death. The serious student will find this work an inexhaustible mine of instruction.

[10] The reader is directed to the music volume *Chamber Suites and Concerti Grossi*, edited by Albert E. Wier. (New York: Longmans, Green and Company.) The actual conductor's scores are used.

Margrave of Brandenburg); in them the composer employs a different instrumentation for each concerto. We shall give only a brief description of each:

Number 1, in F major, is for 2 violins (with a *piccolo violino* tuned, according to Grove, a minor third higher than the usual violin), viola, 'cello, bass, 2 horns, 3 oboes, bassoon, and harpsichord. The *Adagio* movement is regarded by many as "one of the most impassioned expressions in music of poignant grief." Note the deviation from the strict form of the concerto by the addition of a minuet, a polacca, and two trios.

Number 2, in F major, is for trumpet, flute, oboe, and violin, with a string band as *tutti*; it is probably the most popular of the six at the moment, no doubt because of the beautiful *Andante* and the very vigorous first and last movements. It is recommended to the listener as his initial venture into these concerti.

Number 3, in G major, is for 3 violins, 3 violas, and three 'cellos to form the *concertino*, with the accompaniment of double bass and harpsichord; the solo instruments play in three groups, and the work, according to the Bach authority, Spitta, contains some of the finest music in German instrumental literature.

Number 4, in G major, is for violin, 2 flutes, with the strings as the *tutti*; note the alternating concerti and *tutti* in the *Adagio*, and the wonderful *accompanied fugue* in the last movement.

Number 5, in D major, is for flute, violin, and harpsichord, with the usual string *tutti*; note the prominent place Bach gives to the harpsichord in this work, especially the many brilliant *cadenzas*.

Number 6, in B-flat major, is for 2 violas, 2 *viole da gamba* (an obsolete instrument slightly smaller than the 'cello, having six strings with frets on the fingerboard; it is held between the legs, hence its nickname, "leg viol") and the 'cello, with the double bass and harpsichord accompaniment. This number requires virtuoso viola players, and the 'cello usually replaces the *viole da gamba*.

It is obvious from the foregoing descriptions that Bach's *concerto grosso* is not to be confused with the *solo concerto*, as we know it today. (See Chapter XXIV.) His works are more like *suites* with a group, or groups, of solo performers, plus contrasting or supporting, or "filling-up" (*ripieno*) instruments. The group of solo performers pitted against the *tutti* is called the *concertino*.

The listener might want to add to his list (if available in recordings at the moment) the concerti grossi by: Corelli, in g minor, the "Christmas Concerto"; Locatelli, Op. 1, No. 2; Vivaldi, Op. 3, No. 11, in d minor; and a superb one, probably one of the outstanding works of our age, for strings and piano, by Ernest Bloch. Of course, no list of concerti grossi would be thinkable without a goodly number by Handel, so we suggest that a choice be made from numbers 1 (G major), 2 (F major), 3 (e minor), 4 (a minor), 5 (D major) and 6 (g minor).

Chapter Twenty-Eight

Impressionism

W HEN Bach had brought the art of polyphony to its pinnacle, the composers who came after, unable to add to
his monumental achievements, struck out in the new
paths offered by homophonic music. After Beethoven had brought
the sonata to its lofty peak, Wagner and Liszt turned in another
new direction that led them to the tone poem and the music
drama. Similarly, it became apparent in the final decade of the
nineteenth century that the last group of Romanticists—Wagner,
Brahms, Tchaikovsky, Dvořák, Rimsky-Korsakoff, César Franck,
Grieg, and others—had, in effect, exhausted the possibilities of
the "grand" style. The young men who came to maturity in the
post-Romantic era had to seek new worlds to conquer. Richard
Strauss adapted the brilliant and virtuoso orchestral techniques of
Wagner and Liszt to the more sophisticated and realistic trends
of his time. Sibelius added to the emotional exuberance of Tchaikovsky the power, concentration, and nationalistic spirit of his
own personality. And Claude Debussy became identified with
Impressionism, setting in motion a force that has exerted incalculable influence on the trends and character of modern music.

Romanticism in music had been strongly influenced by the
Romantic spirit in literature and painting. So, too, Impressionism
in music was strongly determined by trends in the sister arts,
especially those of poetry and painting. In all these arts, Impressionism was a revolt against the emotional extravagance, the fanfare, and the theatricalism of the Romantics gone before. The
name of the movement sprang from the title of a picture of Manet's
—"*Sunrise—an Impression*"—that gave definition to the aims and
ideals of the painters who had broken away in revolt against the
traditionalism and academicism of the older schools. The first
exhibition of the Impressionists in 1870 ushered in one of the most
exciting periods in the history of French painting, dominated by
such men as Edouard Manet (1832-1883), Camille Pissarro (1830-

1903), Edgar Degas (1834-1917), Paul Cézanne (1839-1906), Alfred Sisley (1840-1899), Claude Monet (1840-1926), and Pierre Renoir (1841-1919).

Impressionism in Painting

The Impressionists, working in *plein air* instead of piecing together their recollections in the studio, abandoned the structural and plastic values, the literary or history-telling aims, the intellectual and emotional attitudes of the great Romantic painters. They attempted to capture the fleeting loveliness of the external world, the impression of the moment, the ever-shifting colours, the vibrating atmosphere and elusive contours of a setting where all objects were delicately shaded into one another. They abandoned the fixed attitudes and rigid lines of the academic style for the fascinating interplay of light and colour, the dynamic qualities, and the transparence of a delicate dream world always in flux. They reduced colour to its subtlest gradations; they created a colour technique of shimmering iridescence, a style of subtlety and finesse. In their canvases, all was bathed in light; colours and surfaces swam together in a richly imaginative interplay. Theirs was a "surface art," in many aspects, compared with the emotional richness of the older masters—an art held together by an overall effect of brilliance and animation rather than by the deeper values of emotion, intellect, and structure; but within its limited sphere, it was an altogether revelatory art, opening the way for the refinement and sensitivity that have come to be considered the hallmark of French painting.

For the Impressionists, the momentary excitement of the eye was the criterion of emotional reaction to reality. Although this did not make for depth of understanding or richness of feeling, it did lead to a purely pictorial opulence, a sheer delight in the interplay of light and shadow, of sunshine and luminous greens and reds and blues, that have made Impressionism synonymous with light and brilliance. Certainly no other group of artists ever succeeded in catching so well the sense of spontaneity, of freshness and wonder and delicate nuance. From their canvases innumerable points of colour strike the eye, caught as it were in a state of suspended animation—infinitely deft little strokes that are

Rouen Cathedral   *(Photograph)*

combined in the eye of the beholder to produce the fleeting impression of loveliness (especially in the technique known as *pointillism*). Subject matter, composition, detail, structure—everything is subordinated to the fresh reality of a momentary impression. It has been said that the Impressionists looked at nature

Rouen Cathedral   *Monet*

through a keyhole. What they saw through it excluded, quite often, the third dimensional vision, the profundity of interpretation, the breadth and vigour of the Renaissance and Baroque masters. But they were careful not to pick subjects that required profundity or vigour. Country scenes, river scenes, still lifes, delicate glimpses of Parisian life—the cafés, the ballet rehearsal, the picnic near the Seine, the Latin Quarter, Montmartre and Montparnasse—these fascinated the painters of this school. Thus one may say that the Impressionists were a direct *outgrowth* of Realism. Other influences were felt, such as Oriental art, the physics of light (especially pertaining to colour), the psychology of seeing, and the particularized influences of the sister arts, such as poetry and music.[1]

The Movement in Literature

In literature, the reaction against the pompousness of Hugo and Lamartine, the exuberance of de Musset and George Sand and de Vigny, was no less marked. Charles Baudelaire, strongly influenced by Edgar Allan Poe, led the way toward an employment of qualities of poetic moods and symbols to create a twilight world in which language took on the qualities of music and painting, of perfumes and visions and dreams. Just as the Impressionist painters rebelled against the structural rigidity of academic painting, the Impressionist poets, the Symbolists and Imagists, rebelled against the restrictions of rhyme, verse, and strophe of Classical poetry. The painters abandoned literary moods and intellectual meaning; the poets rebelled against the fixed associations of words. They began to use words for their musical properties, for their elusive combinations of vowels and consonants, rather than for their thought content. Words for them were symbols for the hidden meanings beneath, keys to unlock a world of subterranean associations and dream patterns. Words were tones that started a stream of overtones in the brain, all kinds of subconscious implications that stood to everyday language in the same relation as dreams do to waking life. The Romantics depicted; the Symbolist Impressionist suggested. The Romantic painted in brilliant colour; the Imagist worked his ideas out in delicate pastel tints. Where the Romantic was dramatic, the Impressionist moved in a pale dream of things half said and half seen. Stephane Mallarmé, Paul Verlaine, Arthur Rimbaud, Maurice Maeterlinck—these were the men who created in the final decades of the century a new lyric poetry made up of subtle

[1] See the reproductions of paintings by Degas on page 129, and by Monet on page 456. Note the basis of reality in the Monet work. Observe closely "Nocturne" by the American, Whistler, on page 462.

suggestion and pale twilight colours, of floating images and luminous symbols. One has but to read a few lines, picked at random, from Baudelaire, Verlaine, or Rimbaud to get the richly evocative nature of this poetry.

Like Impressionism in painting, poetic Impressionism was mainly French—one might better say Parisian—in character and inspiration, combining mysticism, sensuality, Bohemianism, the transparence and purity of the French language, the music of words, the subconscious emotional associations of images and symbols, and above all the somewhat exaggerated preciousness of *fin de siècle* sophistication in an altogether distinctive and memorable blend. If there was about this poetry something of the "utterly utter" quality that Gilbert and Sullivan lampooned in *Patience*, it opened up for poetry, like the corresponding movement in painting, a new realm of delicate perception and insight, of fleeting impressions and moods, that cross the borderline between poetry and the other arts, conferring upon words the magic of colour and music.

Impressionism in Music: Claude Debussy (1862-1918)

Musical Impressionism came to such perfect flowering in the art of Claude Debussy that the man and the movement have become indissolubly associated. He was the first of the modern Impressionists; and, despite a host of disciples and imitators, he remains to this day the greatest.

Born in 1862, Debussy entered the Paris Conservatoire when he was eleven, and studied there until his twenty-second year, winning honours in piano and composition. It was during his student years that the future composer spent several summers as pianist to Mme. Nadejda von Meck, Tchaikovsky's patroness.

In 1884 Debussy won the highest honour of the Conservatoire, the Grand Prix de Rome, with his cantata THE PRODIGAL SON. Even in his undergraduate days at the Conservatoire he had constantly chafed at the restrictions of the conventional style of composition. The works he produced during his stay in Rome aroused the anger of the academicians and sounded the note of revolt against accepted usage that was to make him the foremost iconoclast of his time. If in the first phase of his career he vacillated between the influence of his teacher Massenet and the dominating figure of Wagner, after his return from Rome he set himself resolutely on the path to the evolution of a purely French style that would break both with the sugary lyricism of the French Romanticists and with the turgid extravagance of the Bayreuth music drama. A frequent visitor to Stephane Mallarmé's salon, he came into contact with the poets and painters who were the mainstay of the Impressionist movement. Strongly influenced by them, he endeavoured to transplant their aestheticism into the art of music. In 1892 he wrote his *Prelude* to Mallarmé's eclogue, THE AFTERNOON OF A FAUN—the first triumph of musical Impressionism. There now began two decades of creative effort during which he produced the works that won for him the ranking place among the Impressionists—the song settings of poems by Baudelaire, Verlaine, Mallarmé, and Pierre Louys; the three NOCTURNES for orchestra; the piano pieces, especially the two sets of PRELUDES; the STRING QUARTET IN G MINOR; the orchestral suite LA MER; the exotic IBERIA, reflecting Spanish influences; and what has come to be considered by many music lovers as the most perfect opera ever written, his superb setting of Maeterlinck's PELLÉAS AND MÉLISANDE.

In these, as well as in a host of lesser works, Debussy gave eloquent expression to the dominant artistic currents of the turn of the century. Coming at the end of a century of Romanticism, Debussy—to a far greater degree than either Richard Strauss or Sibelius—became the prophet of the new age, the link between the old and the new. His genius was an original one. He revolted not only against the overblown passions of Wagnerism—French in temperament and outlook, he worshipped clarity, limpidity, restraint, balance, and measure—but against what seemed to him the outlived formulas of the Classic-Romantic sonata forms. Just as the poets and painters of Impressionism had abandoned the structural values of the older style, its rigid conventional patterns of grouping and composition, so Debussy set himself to trace patterns in his music that were subtly elusive rather than monumental, that were suggestive and evocative rather than overblown and outright. Blurred outlines, twilight colours, subtle nuances— these became the cachet of the new music. Through strangely exotic, wavering chords Debussy succeeded in conjuring up opalescent visions, impressions, and moods that were the musical counterpart of the misty impressions of Monet, the strange dreaminess of Cézanne, the pearly softness of Renoir, the shimmering subtleties of Seurat. Within their own limited framework these delicate melodies were as sensuous, as tremulous and caressive, as the blatant sonorities of the Romantic school.

The great orchestra of Wagner was not reduced in size but handled with a new delicacy, the brass often muted, the woodwinds used with uncanny effectiveness in low registers, the strings divided; the percussion assumed a new importance, supplying glockenspiel, celesta, triangle and harp, wreathing the tonal mass in a soft luminosity. The melody is shaded, the harmonies dissolving into each other; the details blur and float away in an evanescence that lends an altogether special charm. To a generation brought up on the robustness of Wagner, the homely strength of Dvořák, the rich colouring of Rimsky-Korsakoff, the tempestuous emotional climaxes of Tchaikovsky, this music seemed strange and esoteric.

Many influences besides those of the poets and painters of the Mallarmé circle played upon Debussy. Turning back for inspiration to the glories of French music—he styled himself *musicien français*—he fell under the aristocratic charm of the eighteenth-century masters, Couperin and Rameau. In the Paris Exposition at the end of the century, he heard the exotic effects of the Balinese music, the weird gongs and shifting harmonies of Java and the Far East, and incorporated their strange tones in his colour palette. During his stay with Mme. von Meck, he came in contact with Russian music and fell strongly under the sway of the then unknown genius of Moussorgsky. Upon all these, he managed to lay the imprint of his own personality, of all those qualities that his great contemporary, Anatole France, considered the essence of *l'ésprit gaulois:* clarity, subtlety, precision, objectivity, limpidity, and restraint. Although he relied on titles—often fanciful and poetic ones—to suggest the atmosphere of his creations, he achieved this atmosphere through purely musical means.

This music did not seek to imitate nature; it suggested nature in subtle musical terms. The title was merely the starting point for musical vision and was forthwith left behind. As in the case of Liszt, we get a good insight into the creative horizons of Debussy by examining the titles of his works. Among them we find THE BLESSED DAMOZEL, a lyric poem for female voices and orchestra,

after Rossetti's poem; THREE NOCTURNES FOR ORCHESTRA—
Clouds, Festivals, Sirens; THREE PRINTS FOR PIANO—*Pagodas, An
Evening in Granada, Gardens in the Rain;* THREE IMAGES FOR PIANO—
Reflections in the Water, Homage to Rameau, Movement; a SECOND SET
OF IMAGES—*Bells Across the Leaves, And the Moon Descends on the
Temple That Was, Gold Fish.* Some of the titles of the PRELUDES FOR
PIANO are no less indicative of the Impressionistic influence: *Veils,
What the West Wind Saw, The Girl With the Flaxen Hair, Interrupted
Serenade, The Submerged Cathedral, Dead Leaves, The Fairies Are
Exquisite Dancers,* the *Terrace of Audiences of Moonlight.* There is a
kind of Romanticism in this atmospheric music; but it is a Romanticism so different in spirit from that of Wagner's *Tristan and Isolde*
or Tchaikovsky's *Romeo and Juliet* or Rimsky-Korsakoff's *Scheherezade,* so much more sophisticated and objective, so intellectualized
and distilled, so purged, indeed, of so many of the elements that
we habitually associate with the Romantic temper, that we can
almost consider it the very inversion of Romanticism in many
respects. More than any other musician, Debussy was instrumental in breaking the spell that Wagner had cast upon the late nineteenth and early twentieth centuries, doing so through an exquisite art that, in greater degree than the work of any of his contemporaries, opened the way for subsequent music of the modern age.
At this time, we should also point out Debussy's special contribution to the literature of the piano. Trained as a pianist, he found
a particularly sympathetic medium in the instrument of Chopin;
he became the greatest composer for that instrument after the
Polish "Poet of the Piano," and one of the foremost piano composers of all time. The piano, with its ability to trace evanescent
melodies against floating masses of tone, was indeed an appropriate
instrument for the Impressionistic style. Where Chopin and the
Romantics had exploited to the full its power to sing a melody
against a fluid accompaniment, as well as its harmonic figuration,
and also its flashing sonority and colour, Debussy transformed it
into an instrument of shifting harmonies and twilight colours, of
continually fluxing moods, now dry and crisp and brittle, now soft
and translucent and mysterious. He virtually inaugurated a new
type of piano technique (both manual and pedal) and gave a new
lease of life to an instrument whose golden age had seemed to be
over with the first half of the century.
Frequently associated with Debussy, although he was by no

Nocturne, A Canal in Holland   *Whistler*

The American painter and etcher James Abbott McNeill Whistler (1834-1903) spent many years of his creative life in Paris. His penchant for poetic and musical titles, along with his peculiarly decorative use of colour, tone, and indefinite masses, aligns him with early French Impressionism. Certainly this "Nocturne" successfully conveys the fleeting and vagrant moods aroused by a Holland Canal scene in the misty evening hours.

means the first composer to exploit its possibilities, is the whole-tone scale. The student will recall that our ordinary major scale consists of a pattern of eight tones, spaced a whole step apart except between the third and fourth, and seventh and eighth, tones which are only a half step apart. Debussy found much more congenial for his art a scale composed exclusively of whole steps—a pattern produced on the piano if we play in succession C, D, E, F sharp, G sharp, A sharp and C. One has but to hear this scale to become aware of its exotic and vague implications and its potentialities for bizarre or picturesque effect. Classicism and Romanticism had risen to their peaks within the system of the major-minor scales and their relationships. Wagner and Liszt had loosened the boundaries of key, passing from one tonality to the next in an ever-shifting chromaticism. Debussy took the next step by frequently abandoning the major scale. Needless to say, this very ambiguity of tonality in Debussy's work, which passed freely to and from the conventional major-minor system to the more piquant whole-tone scale system, added not a little to the indefinable charm, the elusive colouring, and the harmonic strangeness that characterized musical Impressionism.

We have, then, in this poet of *fin de siècle* music, an artist of the utmost sensibility, a dreamer of visions. He created no mighty architecture as Bach and Beethoven did, no system capable of development or organic growth (it can almost be said that Debussy *created and exhausted* an entire "school" of musical thought); he treated no vast spiritual issues; he did not plumb the depths of the human soul, nor did he touch its highest moods of exaltation and triumph. But within his style, he wrought patterns of loveliness and brought back the ideals of refinement and beauty to an age that had been dazzled by the bombastic and the grandiloquent. For this, he must be ranked as a not unworthy disciple of the great eighteenth-century masters whom he worshipped.

Prelude to "The Afternoon of a Faun"

This first triumph of musical Impressionism—it has remained Debussy's most popular work—was composed in 1892 when the composer was thirty years old. Inspired by a prose poem of Mallarmé that has been termed a "miracle of unintelligibility," it is, nevertheless, a miracle of clarity, uniting in almost uncanny fashion the simple sensuous tonal beauty of Impressionism, the chastity of style of the antique, and the richness of Debussy's imagination functioning at its most poetic level. Here is the primitive creature, half man, half goat, transported from the sculptures of classical antiquity to the aesthetic subtleties of Parisian life. The result, as might be expected, is a thing of sheer loveliness and utmost sophistication.

Debussy himself explained that his music was intended as an altogether free illustration of Mallarmé's poem, to evoke "the successive scenes in which the longings and desire of the Faun pass in the heat of the afternoon." The poem, published in 1876 with illustrations by Manet, has become known to English readers through the famous paraphrase of Edmund Gosse describing the awakening of a faun in the forest and his attempt to recall his experiences of the previous afternoon. Dreamily he wonders whether it were in dream or in reality that he was visited by nymphs; he seems to see a vision of whiteness among the brown reeds at the side of the lake. The impression fades; he settles in the warm grasses again to seek the dream once more.[2]

The flutes used in their most unusual lower register, sultry oboes, mysterious horns, and antique cymbals mingle in an atmosphere of enchantment. Strangely gliding themes conjure up the dusky land that lies between waking and sleep. The music is drenched in pagan beauty, in glimmering visions of the childhood of man, in the magic of strange forests and forms and visions. Even today, half a century after it was written, the score has retained its delicacy and charm. What it must have sounded like to the ears of those of the 1890's, one can well imagine.

The work, which is free and rhapsodical in form, opens with a sensuous melody announced by the flute in ⅜ time:

The theme is played piano, *doux et expressif* (sweet and expressively) and *très modéré* (very moderately). Nationalist that he was, Debussy

---

[2] See the translation of Mallarmé's poem, "L'Après-Midi d'un Faune," by Aldous Huxley quoted in Addison Hibbard's superb *Writers of the Western World*, page 877. Read the poem *aloud*.

made a point of writing his directions in French instead of the usual Italian.

Silvery glissandos on the harp are heard as the music gets under way. The theme is repeated by a solo flute against a background of tremulous strings. Oboes, clarinets, and French horns weave a limpid tapestry of sound; strange chords emerge and momentarily dissolve; the rhythm shifts back and forth among $\frac{9}{8}$, $\frac{6}{8}$, $\frac{12}{8}$, $\frac{3}{4}$, and $\frac{4}{4}$ time. The music quickens to the beginnings of a crescendo, but it dies away forthwith and the languorous flute theme returns, now decorated with fanciful arabesques. Presently there emerges a new theme on the oboe, plaintive and wayward and rapturous:

In a steady heightening of intensity, marked *toujours en animant* (getting steadily livelier), we reach the third theme announced by the woodwinds, *expressif et très soutenu* (expressive and very sustained), a theme that, according to the French musicologist, Louis Laloy, "speaks of desire satisfied."

Now the music rises to its rapturous climax in a measure of fortissimo that immediately subsides—a departure indeed from the sustained ecstasies of the Wagnerian trumpets and trombones. The first theme returns, *avec plus de langueur* (more languorously). Everything is wreathed in a soft haze; muted horns weave darkly tinted patterns; oboes and flutes scamper about in light, staccato tones. The vision fades; a solo 'cello lingers a while with the flute; the music dissolves into a dreamlike pianissimo; the enchantment vanishes.

The world moves rapidly. Only a generation ago the name of Debussy was synonymous with aestheticism; his music supposedly appealed only to a select few, the "advance guard." Today his melodies reappear as foxtrots or as the theme songs of popular radio programmes. And the supreme citadel of the aesthetes, the AFTERNOON OF A FAUN, has become one of the most frequently played numbers in the symphonic repertoire.

It is obvious that the Impressionist movement at the end of the century represented a drawing together of the arts of literature, music, and painting to a far greater degree than heretofore. For, once the elements of art were used primarily to suggest or symbolize, it was inevitable that the processes of suggestion and symbolism would tend to break down the barriers between the arts themselves so that they might coalesce more perfectly.

This synthesis of aesthetic effect has come to be known as *synaesthesia*, which may be defined as the use in one art of effects and qualities properly belonging to another. In a narrower sense, synaesthesia implies the transference of a sense impression of one kind to a sense impression of another kind. The most familiar example would be the vivid colour associations produced in many people by music. The doctrine played an important part in aesthetic discussion at the turn of the century. Actually, the synaesthesia of the Impressionists was the logical culmination of that drawing together of music, literature, and painting that characterized the early Romantic Period. It carried the alliance of the arts to its farthest extreme—to the point where each not only was influenced by and reinforced the others but actually usurped their images and symbols.

Naturally, the doctrine and practice of aesthetic synaesthesia gave rise to much heated discussion among the aestheticians and aesthetes. The problem continually presented itself: to what extent should one art attempt to function in terms of another? Could it do so at all successfully? Did it enrich music to try to suggest the colour richness of painting, the descriptive qualities of poetry, the "sounds and perfumes of the evening air"? This type of discussion was pre-eminently popular in a period of bold experimentation, when the art-for-art's-sake tendency focused attention on the "how," the manner and technique of art, rather than on the "what," or content.

In listening to typical Impressionistic music, the sensuous appeal of instrumental colours (singly or in combination), the effects of masses of tone and their contrasting values, and the perception of fragmentary and fleeting themes, or melodic figures, are infinitely more important than the discernment of thematic development. This is essentially music for the senses and the feelings rather than for the intellect, and it should make its appeal in the same manner. Thus we have not indulged in minute directions and analyses. Impressionism, above all else, requires a sympathetic and imaginative attitude in listening. The listener is, more than ever before, "on his own."

Maurice Ravel (1875-1937)

The one contemporary of Debussy in France who shared something of his eminence was Maurice Ravel. It is altogether erroneous to consider Ravel, as many have done, a mere collaborator or an imitator of Debussy. Although he was at home in the idiom of Impressionism, the perspective of time reveals increasingly an altogether independent personality, witty and urbane, who, unlike the other French musicians of the period, was able to resist the overwhelming influence of Debussy and strike out on paths of his own. In him, the Impressionistic tendency was united with a stringent Classicism—he was completely sympathetic to the eighteenth-century forms—and to a kind of intellectual detachment, an objectivity that seemed to have descended to him from the Classical masters. The poetic mistiness of Debussy gave place in Ravel to an incisive wit, a tongue-in-cheek sophistication that went far beyond that of the former. The twilight moodiness of the master of Impressionism was replaced in Ravel by a clarity and epigrammatic lightness: where Debussy worked in soft, blending pastels, Ravel turned to the clear outline of the etcher. If Debussy leans to the mystical overtones, the suspended floating masses and hidden meanings that make him in music akin to Proust—was not Vinteuil in "Swan's Way" fashioned after him?—Ravel reveals another side of the French genius, the lightness and grace, the irony and sharp, clear thinking that we find in the writings of Anatole France, for example.

We have already presented Ravel's MOTHER GOOSE SUITE (see page 137) as a splendid example of that composer's feeling for instrumental colour in the symphony orchestra, his charming melodic gift, and his uncanny ability of musical description and characterization.

As an example of Ravel's ability to use these techniques to depict the moods and atmosphere of classical, ancient Greek scenes, while providing actual dance music for a ballet on the subject, we present:

"Daphnis and Chloé," Suite No. 2, for Orchestra

The score itself is the source for the following descriptive action of the three divisions of the Suite, and if it is identified anew with the music as it passes by, the pleasure of listening will be greatly increased. The Ballet was first produced by the Ballet Russe in Paris in 1912, with the great artists Nijinsky and Karsavina taking the leading roles.

1. *Daybreak.* Daphnis lies stretched before the grotto of the nymphs. Little by little the day dawns. The songs of birds are heard. . . . Herdsmen enter, seeking Daphnis and Chloé. They find Daphnis and awaken him; in anguish he looks about for Chloé. She at last appears encircled by shepherdesses. The two rush into each other's arms. . . . The old shepherd Lammon explains that Pan saved Chloé (from the pirates), in remembrance of the nymph Syrinx, whom the god loved.

2. *Pantomime.* Daphnis and Chloé mime the story of Pan and Syrinx. Chloé impersonates the young nymph wandering over the meadow. Daphnis, as Pan, appears and declares his love for her. The nymph repulses him; the god becomes more insistent. She disappears among the rocks. In desperation he plucks some stalks, fashions a flute, and on it plays a melancholy tune. Chloé comes out and imitates by her steps the accents of the flute.

3. *General Dance.* The dance grows more and more animated. In mad whirlings, Chloé falls into the arms of Daphnis. Before the altar of the nymphs he swears his fidelity. Young girls appear; they are dressed as Bacchantes and shake their tambourines (as they dance). Daphnis and Chloé embrace tenderly. A group of young men come on the stage. There is a joyous tumult, and a final, general dance.

Impressionism in Italy

There is no question that the Impressionistic movement was closely identified with France, not only as the place of its inception, but also as the country in which it reached its peak and practically exhausted itself as a movement. However, the French influences were felt in other European (as well as American and a few Oriental) countries, not the least among which was Italy, where the techniques of the French Impressionists (chiefly Debussy) were combined with local romantic nationalism and realism and, of course, the irreplaceable lyricism that has, for centuries, been identified with Italian music.

Ottorino Respighi and his "Fountains of Rome"

French Impressionism was most skilfully combined with Italian tendencies toward fervent nationalism and romantic dramaturgical exposition in the genius of Ottorino Respighi (1879-1936). Of his three Roman musical "essays" THE FOUNTAINS OF ROME (1917); THE PINES OF ROME (1924); and THE FESTIVALS OF ROME (1928), the most popular is THE FOUNTAINS OF ROME. In it the composer shows his great skill in orchestration (he was pupil of Max Bruch and Rimsky-Korsakoff, and early became one of the foremost masters of orchestration). Also he has succeeded in combining the ancient with the modern in his use of old church modes and counterpoint, together with modern harmonic devices and flowing lyricism. Above these, Respighi was immensely successful in portraying intense dramatic feeling and vividly convincing realism. Note, in *The Fountains*, the slowly awakening *pastorale* of dawn in the first section (each section depicts a Roman fountain at the hour of the day when it appeared to the composer to be most effective); the realistic depiction of the precipitate gushing and splashing waterfall that introduces section two (one of the best of its kind to be found in all music); observe the monotonous French horn pedal-point on middle C throughout section two (the "Triton" fountain); and, in section four, the exquisite effect of the dripping water (as though drop by drop) as the setting sun shines and sparkles like jewels through the lazy stream. Note also the final ringing of bells, large and small, coming from all directions, in the last section; one can even distinguish clearly the difference between the "ding" and the "dong" of the giant church bell as it swings to and fro at the very close. Here is picture-painting, story-telling, and an orchestral *tour de force* of the highest order.

The composer attached the following programme to the score:

PART I. *The Fountain of Valle Giulia at Dawn:* The first part of the poem, inspired by the Fountain of Valle Giulia, depicts a pastoral landscape; droves of cattle pass and disappear in the fresh damp mists of a Roman dawn. [Muted strings, oboes, and clarinets serve—just as they did in the days of Liszt—to suggest the diaphanous mists, the murmur of water, the pastoral scene.]

PART II. *The Triton Fountain at Dawn:* A sudden loud and insistent blast of horns above the trills of the whole orchestra introduces the second part, the Triton Fountain. It is like a joyous call, summoning troops of naiads and tritons, who come running up, pursuing each other and mingling in a frenzied dance between the jets of water.

PART III. *The Fountain of Trevi at Mid-Day:* Next there appears a solemn theme, borne on the undulations of the orchestra. It is the Fountain of Trevi at mid-day. The solemn theme, passing from the wood to the brass instruments, assumes a triumphal character. Trumpets peal; across the radiant surface of the water, there passes Neptune's chariot, drawn by sea-horses and followed by a train of sirens and tritons. The procession then vanishes, while faint trumpet blasts resound in the distance.

PART IV. *The Villa Medici Fountain at Sunset:* The fourth part, the Villa Medici Fountain, is announced by a sad theme, which rises above a subdued warbling. It is the nostalgic hour of sunset. The air is full of the sound of tolling bells, birds twittering, leaves rustling. Then all dies peacefully into the silence of the night.

ADDITIONAL SUGGESTIONS FOR LISTENING

We have already suggested a number of additional works by Debussy and Ravel, but we hope that the listener will be prompted to discover additional works for himself. We offer the suggestion that the vocal compositions of both these composers, especially selections from the opera PELLÉAS ET MÉLISANDE, will be numbered among the "finds." It is all well and good to be attracted to the instrumental and orchestral works, but one should not do so at any time at the expense of the songs and choral compositions when they are available—and this goes for composers of the past as well as of the present.

In Spain, Manuel de Falla (b. 1876) has been most apt in adapting the techniques of Impressionism to his native Spanish idioms.[3] Try listening to de Falla's suite for piano and orchestra, NOCHES EN LOS JARDINES DE ESPAÑA (Nights in the Gardens of Spain), in three parts.

Impressionism in England and America has not been as general as in the countries previously mentioned for reasons that need not be gone into here—there are plenty of historical texts available. It is enough to point out one or two compositions as starting points for further investigations on the listener's part. No doubt Frederick Delius (1862-1934) stands out pre-eminently among the Impressionists of England, and of

---

[3] It is to be noted again that the essence of the movement of Impressionism often rests in the *manner* of using the techniques of the various arts even more than in the *entities* of the techniques themselves.

his works, these are suggested for supplementary listening: ON HEARING THE FIRST CUCKOO IN SPRING (this should be the first "must"); BRIGG FAIR; IN A SUMMER GARDEN; SEA DRIFT (on a Walt Whitman poem. See also the work on the same theme by John Alden Carpenter); *Walk to the Paradise Garden*, from the opera A VILLAGE ROMEO AND JULIET; and the tone poem, PARIS. The harmonic counterpoint, vague and changing moods, and fascinating blended orchestral colours are most salient in his works. His compositional treatment of the English folk song is very fresh and interesting.

In America, there are two or three who are, or who have been, generally assigned to this school of composition: Charles Martin Loeffler (1861-1935); and of his works we suggest LA MORT DE TINTAGILES (after Maeterlinck), for full orchestra and *viola d'Amore* (an obsolete viola with added, unfretted, sympathetically vibrating strings). It is believed by many, among them the author, that a number of so-called Impressionistic effects were discovered separately and individually by Debussy and Loeffler. We have yet to appraise this composer properly. Charles Tomlinson Griffes (1884-1920), one of America's most gifted and promising composers, whose career was so prematurely ended. Listen to his symphonic poem, THE PLEASURE DOME OF KUBLA KHAN, and (a "must" at any cost) *The White Peacock* (from the ROMAN SKETCHES, 1917). Here is excellent craftsmanship, a very definite and highly original idiom, extraordinary harmonic colour and invention (it is hard to believe the date of composition!), together with a vigour and strength not usually associated with this style of writing. John Alden Carpenter (b. 1876), one of the best equipped of America's composers; hear especially his SEA DRIFT, a tone poem; and the *Lake* scene from his ballet suite, ADVENTURES IN A PERAMBULATOR—this last should be considered a "must." His works are filled with imagination, vitality, skill of all compositional techniques (he is one of the very few American composers who can think with surety in long, large forms and maintain interest the while), and his works are replete with rhythmic devices that should furnish Tin Pan Alley with ideas for many years to come. Some listeners will want to listen to his ballet-suite SKYSCRAPERS, with its lilting, music-hall tunes and exciting jazz rhythms.

Chapter Twenty-Nine

Expressionism and Other Modern Trends

IN A WAY, we have no need for a special chapter on twentieth-century music, for examples of our age have been scattered throughout the pages of this book. The reason for this distribution can readily be appreciated. Contemporary music stems out of and exists side by side with that of the older schools. It is a part of the living body of the art today; and to segregate it all in a chapter at the close of a book, as has sometimes been done, serves only to establish an altogether artificial barrier around it. From the very first chapter, we have included compositions by contemporary composers in our text to the end that the reader might approach the new music, not as some special and esoteric branch of the art, but as a simple continuation of the musical tradition as applied to the problems and needs of our own time.

At the same time, a few special problems are attached to the technical aspects of some contemporary music that requires a fair background to comprehend; it is to these that we shall now devote our attention.

In the first place, the general tone of contemporary art, whether in music, painting, or poetry, is much more sophisticated than was that of the past, and it demands a far greater degree of comprehension and acuteness on the part of the audience. We have but to compare a poem by E. E. Cummings or Ezra Pound with one by Byron or Shelley, a canvas by Picasso or Gris with one by Ingres or Constable, to become aware of the more sophisticated technical level upon which the modern artist pitches his work (though it is not to be inferred that the sophistication is necessarily an improvement). We must remember that the great artist is almost always ahead of his contemporaries; it generally takes the latter some time to catch up with him. Many of the artists whom we today venerate as "masters" and "classicists" were, in fact, the advance guard, the *enfants terribles* of their times, although it is often as difficult for us to realize this as to visualize our parents as adolescents. Palestrina, Mozart, Beethoven, and Wagner puzzled and shocked their contemporaries; Darwin, George Eliot, Thomas Hardy, and Proust shocked theirs. If the history of culture teaches us anything, it is that we must not be too hasty in our estimates of the artists of our time; posterity may laugh at our limited vision just as we do at that of our forebears. This does not mean, of course, that we should not attempt to evaluate the work of the Moderns and to form judgments in regard to it. But in doing so we should always, as Gladstone exhorted the members of Parliament to do, "entertain the possibility that we may be wrong," either *pro* or *con*.

In the second place, the twentieth-century artist faces a world infinitely more complex, more baffling than any that the past has known. By comparison, the pietistic world of Bach, the beautifully ordered world of Mozart, even the Byronic milieu of Liszt or Wagner, take on an idyllic simplicity. The Modern movement in art came to fruition in the decade of the First World War—a cataclysm much more sweeping than the upheavals of preceding ages. In an atmosphere of bitterness and disillusion, cynicism and world-weariness, the lovely arabesques of the eighteenth century and the Romantic melody of the nineteenth had to give way to new idioms and modes of expression. Modern industrial society, shaken by internal contradictions and universal crises, of necessity had to develop its own language in art—a language compounded of brutal primitivism, of eternal questing for new sensations, of defiant overthrow of many rules and conventions bequeathed to it by the more stable order of the earlier time. It is this revolt against all established usage, this venturesome quest into regions of experience never before accessible to art, that has become the prime characteristic of the twentieth-century artist. Together with poetry and painting, music during the twenties and thirties forsook the well-travelled paths and struck out boldly into new territories. Small wonder that the average music lover, brought up on the good old Classical-Romantic diet, was left in utter bewilderment by the new development.

In the revolt against the Classical-Romantic past, the pendulum, particularly at first, swung to the far extreme. Everything that was connected, however remotely, with the emotional exuberance, the sensuous line, and the literary atmosphere of the nineteenth-century masters was thrown into the discard. While Romantic music had made its appeal primarily to the emotions, the new music became severely intellectualized, taking on at times the semblance of exercises in mathematical ingenuity or abstract logic. While the old music had held before man's eyes the ideal of pure beauty, of symmetry and harmony, the new turned to brutal dissonance, to the cacophony and ugliness that were considered characteristic of the machine age. The idealistic visions of the Romantics, the clouds and waterfalls of the Impressionists, were alike discarded in favour of force and energy. While the old music had striven to be pre-eminently civilized, the new turned to barbaric primitivism, to the elemental passions that alone could provide a new thrill to an effete, "lost" society that felt it had been betrayed by its own supercivilization. Locomotives, turbines, dynamos, football games, and, on the other hand, dances of savages took the place of the enchanted grottos and murmuring forests of the 1850's.

Closely allied with these changes came another, in the internal structure and compositional technique of the music, as a result of which the year 1900 becomes as crucial a date in the history of the art as the year 1600 had been. Then, in the period of Monteverde, the polyphonic texture of medieval church music had given way to a new concept in which one voice, the melodic line, dominated all the others, which became harmonic accompaniment. Then, too, there began that development of tone relationships that culminated in the major-minor key system, given its first mature expression in Bach's WELL-TEMPERED CLAVICHORD and brought to artistic perfection in the symphonies of Mozart, Haydn, and Beethoven. For two hundred years Western European music was dominated by the concept of key, by that intricate system in which the seven tones of the scale centred about the keynote in which the composer sounded the tonic chord at his final cadence again and again, as though to make sure that there could not be the slightest doubt in anyone's mind concerning the home key.

In seeking for new avenues of tonal expression, the Moderns broke down the barriers of key. In *polytonal* music, two or more keys were used simultaneously, creating new effects. So, too, *atonality* made its appearance—music, that is, written in no key at all, in which each tone is quite independent of the others, is its own centre, instead of gravitating to the others according to a well-defined system of key relationships. Polytonality and atonality opened the way to all sorts of experiments, with results likely to be somewhat disconcerting to ears accustomed to the major-minor system.

Similarly, the rhythmic beat, which had held together the flow of the music in a rigid grouping of two, three, four, or six pulses, was now abandoned in favour of a flexible rhythm, which changed continually from one rhythm to the other almost from measure to measure; or, better still, *polyrhythm*, in which two or more rhythms went on simultaneously. It can be readily understood that all these innovations, both in spirit and substance, widened immeasurably the horizons of music and the resources at its disposal; but it is equally apparent that all these changes, especially in the initial period of adjustment, occasioned much chaos, bewilderment, and horror among the conservative devotees of the art.

This does not mean, of course, that every work written in the twentieth century will present such advanced problems as atonality, polytonality, and polyrhythm, or that many of the innovations of the experimental period will survive. On the contrary, many of the leading composers of the present day have their roots, as is natural, in the past and have built their works along the more generally understood lines of the *fin de siècle* period. Throughout this book we have held to the thesis that there are a few basic and elemental stylistic tendencies, or tempers, as we prefer to call them, in all the arts of all time. These we believe to be chiefly what are called Classicism, Romanticism, Realism, Naturalism, Impressionism, and Expressionism, to name but a few of them. Of these, Classicism, Romanticism, and Realism seem to be the most basic and elemental, and the source of many derivations. Further, we contend that these basic tendencies, together with their closely related evolvements, are to be found existing simultaneously throughout art history, in varying emphases in the formulation of current styles.

A "period" in art history may thus be said to be a matter of coincidence of certain tempers and the degree of emphasis they receive by creators of a time or a place. Therefore, an appreciable span of time experienced over a wide geographical distribution might exhibit a number of different periodistic evidences going on simultaneously—as a cross section view of artistic Europe would reveal in 1600, 1800, 1900, or 1950, for that matter. There might be varying lengths of "time lag" between similar movements in different arts if they do not take place at the same time. Some of these tempers might lie comparatively dormant for some time after fulfilling a saliency, or peak function, only to come to life and prominence again (these recurrences are usually designated by the prefix "neo-" [new]; thus, *neo-classicism, neo-romanticism,* and so forth), or they might be combined with one or more subsidiary trends, such as *post-Romanticism, post-Impressionism.*

Of course the idioms of expression, the nature of the techniques, and the means and manner of expression change with the passing of time, from individual to individual, and from place to place. Thus, a Romanticist of 1946 does not express himself with the same means and in the same manner as did one in 1850, though the basic motivating spirit, or temper, may be identical. Too often the critic is inclined to take the idioms of some one age as defining the temper for all time; no greater mistake could be made or injustice done. No such fixed definition or pigeon-hole classification is desirable as a working hypothesis in arriving at a broad appreciation of the arts; any plan should be inclusive rather than exclusive, for there are far too many variables and variants in the history of the social man, the individual lives of creative men, and in the products of both—for such is the history of any art.

It should also be borne in mind that while a period may be known as the "Romantic Period" because of the prominence of the characteristics known as *romantic,* other, and even opposite, tendencies might be coexistent. Thus, during the so-called "Romantic Period" in Europe (broadly from 1800-1900), there were strong evidences of the tempers of Classicism, Realism, Impressionism, and even Expressionism going on in creative spirits as they clung to the more traditional, or became iconoclastic both toward the traditional and the "revolutionary" ideas embraced by the leaders of the time. A cross section of our own age would reveal just such tempers. Then, too, some so-called revolutionary ideas are, in reality, evolutionary, or are even mutations in process, having arrived at no place in particular and being undecided as to immediate or ultimate destination. The actuality of these diverse tendencies at any one time is the life blood of art, without which it quickly shrivels and dies. There can be no health in any of the arts if these several tempers cease their processes of combination, elimination, culmination, and mutation. There can be no vital art when art is static in process or mono-genetic in origin or constitution. In fact, most of the successful creators in the arts might best be classified as "mixed-tempers" types. It is because of these interactions of diverse tendencies that art is able to remain art and to mean many things to all men of all times.

An attempt has been made throughout this book to point out and analyse these tempers as they have constituted the style of a period, a country, a man, and even a single composition; and we have tried to show how best to appreciate them in the works presented for study. It has also been part of our aim to show how the music at the moment became what it was and what influences at large helped to shape it.

This is not too formidable a task when considerable time has elapsed, but the problem becomes an acute one when one contemplates contemporary art. Obviously we are too close to our own time—"so close to the forest that we cannot see it for the trees"—and we can hardly be expected to view the scene of today with any great degree of valid perspective and evaluation. Certainly we cannot, with surety, pick out the persons or tendencies likely to survive our time. But we can know more about what is going on, something as to how the art is compounded, and a little of why it "got that way." We can be a little more discerning than those who too frequently remark, "I don't know much about modern art; but I know what I like—and I don't like modern art."

To bring our task within the realm of possibility, then, let us point out a few composers and their works that are typical of the tempers we have been discussing—a sort of limited cross section of our time—hoping that sufficient interest will have been aroused in the reader so that he will institute his own research and compile his own list of compositions to be heard.

Four Modern Composers[1]

Few composers of our time have had more immediate and widespread influence on other composers than has *Igor Stravinsky*. He was born near St. Petersburg in 1882. Like Tchaikovsky and Sibelius, he prepared himself for a legal career; but his talent manifested itself so clearly that Rimsky-Korsakoff, whom he met when he was twenty-two, advised him to devote himself entirely to music. It was under the Russian master that he received his first systematic training. The teacher's influence has always made itself felt in Stravinsky's brilliant orchestration and sensitivity to instrumental effects. Before many years had elapsed, he was generally acclaimed as one of the foremost masters of orchestration.

Stravinsky came to fame in the years before the outbreak of the First World War as one of the group of brilliant artists whom Serge Diaghileff gathered about him in the Ballet Russe. (For an interesting account of that eventful period, the reader is referred to Romola Nijinsky's biography of Nijinsky, the great dancer, and also Haskell's book on Diaghileff.) THE FIREBIRD, performed by Diaghileff's company in 1910, and PETROUCHKA (see page 133), performed in the following year, established Stravinsky as one of the most original spirits in the hectic pre-war scene. PETROUCHKA has remained the most popular of his works, and in brilliance of orchestration, dramatic power, verve, and melodic richness, it is generally considered his masterpiece.

But it is Stravinsky's ballet-suite, SACRE DU PRINTEMPS (The Rites of Spring), that we wish to recommend to the listener for study in this chapter. It was first produced in Paris in 1913, and its *première* "provoked a scandalous demonstration." The programme of the ballet is concerned with the choreographic representation of the ritualistic spring ceremonies of the pagan and primitive Russian tribes—very romantic and nationalistic, and was prepared by the composer himself, essentially as follows:

[1] Some listeners might justifiably wish to add an American Symphony to the assigned study projects of this chapter. We commend such a spirit and hope that improved recording conditions in the future will permit a wider and more representative choice among American composers than is possible at present.

Our own researches and experiments have indicated several alternate sequences of the suggested listening study as listed in this chapter, such as: (1) Hindemith, (2) Sibelius (or these two reversed), then (3) Stravinsky and finally (4) Schönberg. Still other sequences are possible.

PART I. THE ADORATION OF THE EARTH: Introduction—Harbingers of Spring—Dance of the Adolescents—Abduction—Spring Rounds—Games of the Rival Cities—The Procession of the Wise Men—The Adoration of the Earth—The Dance of the Earth.

PART II. THE SACRIFICE: Introduction—Mysterious Circle of the Adolescents—Glorification of the Chosen One—Evocation of the Ancestors—The Sacrificial Dance of the Chosen One.

(The music lover has probably heard this music in Walt Disney's epoch-making film, "Fantasia," in which the music serves as a background for scenes of primeval monsters.)

The music is brutal in its elemental force, its strange and almost infinite variety of complicated rhythms and metres that change measure after measure—one can easily sympathize with poor Nijinsky when he first tried to dance to it. The orchestration is conceived on a huge scale and is overpowering when in full force, especially when expressed in terms of constant harsh, biting, and unrelenting dissonances and discordant sounds. Here one will find two or three different keys going on simultaneously (this device is known as *polytonality*, as the term itself so well indicates), the brasses, for instance, may be in one key, the woodwinds in another, and the strings in a third; or, again, three brass instruments themselves may be playing in three different tonalities. The rhythmic devices are seemingly inexhaustible and startling in invention and unexpectedness. The climaxes, especially the principal one in the "Sacrificial Dance of the Chosen One," are so vivid, overpowering, and physically exhausting to the listener that only actual hearing can bring appreciation; and the onward rhythmic pulse and drive of the music is unsurpassed anywhere. It is little wonder that no less a musician than Leopold Stokowski has proclaimed this work the outstanding composition of our age. There is little doubt that in this composer the Romantic past is united with the Realism, Primitivism, and Expressionism of the present. Of late years, Stravinsky has evidenced Neo-Classical tendencies. By all means, make the *Rites of Spring* a definite "must" on your list of masterpieces.

We have already described the spirits of Classicism, Romanticism, and Realism, but this is the first time we have encountered the term *Expressionism*. Perhaps we can get a better initial idea of it by turning first to its manifestations in literature and painting.

GG

The great French critic and writer on art, Élie Faure,[2] ventures the opinion that Expressionism is but a "transposition" of the impressionistic way of thinking, that it is an incident of the change from French objectivism to German subjectivism, and, further, that this kind of thinking passes from the plastic to the musical "plane." Impressionism was really based on the exact realities of nature, though expressed by any means at the artist's command; while Expressionism was highly subjective and gave one freedom of means of expressing what one desired to say.

The term, *Expressionism*, has become one of those controversial terms that might well mean different things to different commentators. Originally it was used in antithesis to Impressionism by a group of painters of whom Schönberg's friend, the Russian Kandinsky (1866-   ), was a leader. Instead of concentrating on their impressions of the outer world, the Expressionists looked for material and inspiration in expressing their inner experiences. Instead of deriving their material from nature, the Expressionists sought to lead art into non-representational paths, deriving their forms from the materials of the art—colours, lines, surfaces, sounds, or rhythms—rather than from any attempt to imitate or represent phenomena external to the art. After the GURRE-LIEDER, Schönberg, finding his way toward musical Expressionism, abandoned the methods he had derived from the Romantic programme. Musical design as such began to play an increasing part in his work, as did also a tendency toward cerebral pattern formations as pure architecturally and as devoid of literary meanings as an abstraction of Picasso. The new idiom had enormous influence on many of the younger composers who were in revolt against the Romantic heritage of the nineteenth century.

At the same time, as many commentators have been quick to point out, Expressionism, which bade the artist give expression to his innermost spiritual conflicts and experiences rather than seek inspiration in the forms and images of the world about him— the clouds, leaves, and waves of the Impressionists—opened the way for an even more intense subjectivism, the inner dream world of strange shapes and images that linked Expressionism to the *Surrealism* of the twenties. It can readily be seen that the two possible tendencies within the movement—the one toward an

[2] See Vol. IV of his *History of Art*, translated by Walter Pach. (New York: Harper and Brothers, 1921.)

utterly intellectual, objective manipulation of art materials as pure forms devoid of subjective impressions or meanings, the other toward a most intensive cultivation of the inner moods and feelings of the artist as material for expression rather than the representational bent of Impressionist art—led to diametrically opposite ends. From this conflict arose much of the confusion that attended the discussion of the movement during the twenties. In painting, this dichotomy manifested itself in *Cubism*, which attempted mainly to manipulate art materials in pure, or altogether abstract, nonrepresentational patterns, and in *Surrealism*, which also freed the artist from the trammels of the outer world but only in order to allow him to achieve a more complete expression of his inner creative fancy.

Here the reader is directed to the half-tone reproduction of the painting, "Still Life with Fruit," by my colleague, Vaclav Vytlacil, on page 482, and the one by Pablo Picasso on page 483, entitled "Three Musicians (Three Masks)." This is nonrepresentational art, though, like Impressionistic art, it has its roots and inspiration in realities. The artists are concerned with the play of internal design, the treatment of lines and masses and tones, as well as the evolvement of constructional and compositional germs within the picture. Though realities in nature may have provided the generation, or springboard, for their artistic ideas, they did not seek to re-create or imitate it, nor did they desire that the appreciator should try to discover these realities within the creation, or even retain them mentally when viewing the picture. Both the conception and the arrangement of the forms, as an abstract art, must carry their own aesthetic and emotional values; and in no wise are they to be hindered or bound up with extraneous associations and connotations—even though the artist himself may have been moved, at the onset, by real forms and extraneous associations. What has happened within the artist and how he has expressed his ego concerning the ideas involved, are the important considerations. These seeming contradictions are most likely to be ironed out with sufficient and sympathetic practice; and we leave the works of Vytlacil and Picasso to achieve what the printed word can never do.

The most detailed, comprehensive, and provocative categorical analysis that we have read of the tempers as they are evidenced in literature is by Dean Addison Hibbard of Northwestern Univer-

sity.[3] According to him, in essence at least, Expressionism is
marked by the following: A highly personal and subjective revelation of the writer rather than an imitation of external realities;
the ego of the creator is an essential part of this revelation; the
intellectual element is salient; it may be expressed in abstract art;
it may be fourth dimensional, or mystical in quality; it is psychological, symbolical; it often reflects a spirit of despair and defeat;

Still Life with Fruit   *Vytlacil*

and it seeks to create a new world out of the present chaos. One
may find these same characteristics in other types of literature, to
be sure; but it is, as we have already pointed out in the chapter
on Impressionism, in the coincidence of several of these, the
emphasis placed upon one or more, and the very manner of expressing them and the techniques used, that the real character of
the style is determined. Dr. Hibbard points out such works as

[3] *Writers of the Western World*, by Addison Hibbard (New York: Houghton Mifflin
Company, 1942). Discussion of the Expressionists is to be found on pages 1166-72.
We are greatly indebted to this eminent scholar and teacher throughout much of our
discussion of literature.

Ulysses by James Joyce, *The Hairy Ape* by Eugene O'Neill, and the *Rhapsody on a Windy Night* by T. S. Eliot, among others, as examples of the Expressionistic style.

The composer most often thought of in connection with Expressionism in music is *Arnold Schönberg*. This exponent of so-called

The Three Musicians   *Picasso*

"abstract" art, though once his works were steeped in Wagnerian Romanticism, was born in 1874 in Vienna and is now living in California. It is to be expected that a number of the characteristics pointed out in the media of painting and literature should not apply to music and that the latter should have some that are quite peculiar to itself. This will be self-evident if the listener will hear some of the shorter piano works of Schönberg, such as Op. 11, Op. 23, or Op. 25. But it is his PIERROT LUNAIRE that we wish to offer as a "must" for study in this chapter. (Play as much of this work as time and interest permit.) This work is a setting of twenty-one poems by the French writer, Albert Giraud, for voice and a chamber ensemble involving a solo flute (piccolo), clarinet, violin, 'cello, and piano. The voice part is written in a sort of speaking-singing production of rhythmical fluctuations of tone. The instruments are used in various combinations. In the series of short pieces comprising this work, Schönberg displays adroit use of counterpoint and form which, however, will not likely be apparent to one who cannot read the score, especially in regard to the formal design. As an illustration of his command of the techniques of form and counterpoint, we draw attention to Poem Number 18, *The Patch of Moonlight*, where the piccolo and clarinet play a canon at the fifth (the two instruments imitating each other separated by five scale steps), the violin and the 'cello play another canon at the octave, the piano plays a three-voiced fugue on an augmentation of the first canon theme, and the voice goes on its way the while. At Number 10 in the score, the notes for all the instruments (except the piano, which continues with the fugue) repeat themselves backward, crab-wise, note for note in each part, so that the final notes are the first ones played in the opening measure! This kind of contrapuntal device is technically known as a *canon cancrizans* (crablike: retrograde in motion), and was quite common with the polyphonic composers of the fifteenth and sixteenth century Netherlands School, especially Okeghem (*c.* 1420-1495), and others. From the standpoint of command of polyphonic technique, this is a masterpiece.

Two other characteristics of this work should be singled out for further elucidation. First, as in so many of Schönberg's works (especially in the Sextet, later recorded as a string orchestra piece entitled VERKLÄRTE NACHT), there is a highly personal, psychological, and strongly romantic content and feeling; but it is all said in a technique that is both classical in form and manner and "ultramodern" in harmonic devices. Second, the music will probably sound strange, disagreeable, and even repellent upon first hearing. It might remain forever undesirable to some, in spite of thorough understanding, for appreciation and understanding are not synonymous.

This attitude toward the later music of Schönberg and others of the same school is largely due to the basic constitution of the musical structure, which is variously described as *atonal, abstract, twelve-tone system, Schönbergian-Row,* and so forth. It is difficult to describe in words what is done in the music, but in attempting to do so, we are reminded of a retort made by that great American poet, Edwin Arlington Robinson, when he was asked to define the term "poetry." He replied, in effect, that while it might be impossible to define it in words, everyone would recognize poetry as such when he met it. The most lucid, yet reasonably brief, exposition of the subject that we have met is entitled *Atonality and Polytonality,* written by that learned English writer on things musical, Edwin Evans, and we recommend its reading.[4]

We quote, in part, the definitions he gives of "Atonality": "(1), The negation, deliberate avoidance, or destruction of tonality; (2), the fusion of all tonalities into one, expressed in the twelve-note scale; (3), a state of constant modulation, the horizontal equivalent of vertical polytonality." Later he adds another observation as to the two strongest incentives to atonality: ". . . the allied reactions against harmonic fusion of the texture, and against the subjection of the horizontal or melodic line to harmonic rule." By the term "twelve-tone system," or scale, we mean the utter independence of each and every half step comprising the chromatic scale, or the twelve half steps as equally tempered within an octave.[5] As an insight into the early and romantic works of Schönberg, the listener is directed to that composer's VERKLÄRTE NACHT and to the cantata GURRE-LIEDER, both of which are generally available in good gramophone records.

Whatever may be said in disparagement of Schönberg's compositions, one cannot overlook the tremendous influence ·he has had on modern music throughout the western world, and it is not unlikely that some of these contributions will become permanent.

The third composer we wish to introduce in this chapter is *Paul Hindemith,* born in Germany in 1895, and now living in the United

---

[4] *Cobbett's Cyclopaedic Survey of Chamber Music,* Vol. 1, page 28.

[5] The *chromatic scale* consists of the twelve half steps within the octave (from any key on the piano to the next above or next below is a half step); thus—C, C-sharp, D, D-sharp, E, F, F-sharp, G, G-sharp, A, A-sharp, B and C. In a diatonic scale (our ordinary major scale, for instance), those tones with a "sharp" after the letter in the last sentence would be dependent on, or attracted to, the next higher scale step; thus C-sharp would tend to lead or move to D, F-sharp to G, G-sharp to A and so forth, and ultimately to the key tone. In the so-called "Schönbergian-Row," and the system of composition based on it, there is little or no interdependency, and thus there is no recognition of a dissonance of interval as such. Our musical experience and education is usually toward the establishment of tonal relationship and interdependencies, and it is natural to find music conceived otherwise as strange.

States. Like Schönberg and Stravinsky, he was for many years in turn a Romanticist in spirit and manner, a radical, and later, like the others, a composer infused with the older classical and still older polyphonic styles—of course, never ridding himself completely of his innate Romanticism. The work reserved for study in this chapter is the suite, MATHIS DER MALER (Mathis the Painter), consisting of music selected from the composer's opera of the same title, inspired by the Eisenheim Altarpiece painted by Matthias Grünewald (1480-1530). In this suite, the mastery of all modern devices of counterpoint, harmony, form, and instrumentation is apparent to anyone, as is the conviction that the composer has something vital to say as well as the means in which to say it. This is a modern masterpiece that bears eloquent evidence of the historical verity of continuity and speaks for the evolutionary rather than the revolutionary theory of music. At heart, the composer carries into our own time the romantic past, and he expresses those romantic feelings in techniques of the time of Bach, Stravinsky, and Schönberg—yes, and Hindemith. This is, we believe, the way art has best made its way through the past and will continue to make it in the future. Again, Hindemith is a good example of the tenet that today is composed of countless yesterdays. Other works of this composer are available on records, and the serious listener will want to sample them. There is little need for detailed and extended analysis of MATHIS DER MALER at this time, for the music is self-revealing and the listener has increased his skills of discernment and appreciation sufficiently to be "on his own" with this work.

In all the music of our time, no better example of the currency of Romanticism and Nationalism can be found than the works of *Jean Sibelius* (Finland, 1865). Of his symphonic works, we ask that the listener hear the FOURTH SYMPHONY IN A MINOR, Op. 63, and the symphonic fantasy, POHJOLA'S DAUGHTER, Op. 49. The materials for the latter were found in the *Kalevala* (Finland's national myths; literally, "Abode of Heroes"), and the programme concerns the heroine spinning at the foot of the rainbow. She is sought out and wooed by Lemmin Kainen, the hero of the tales. He is repulsed and, in a godly rage, leaves her. Obviously, this is typical programmatic music, and very romantic in spirit, though the story is told in music that is highly original and of our own time.

Still Life   *Gris*

The SYMPHONY IN A MINOR was said by Sibelius to be "a pro-
test against the compositions of today." What delightful irony! It
is a work filled with beautiful themes, sombre and tragic moods,
sweeping flow and titanic climaxes. There is no mistaking the
peculiar idioms of expression that are his, and it is not without
good reason, and justification, that some critics consider the symphonies of Sibelius to be the best since Brahms; a few enthusiasts,
indeed, would have us go as far back as Beethoven. Nevertheless,

here is a masterpiece that is generally acknowledged as such by the foremost critics of our time, written by a master who already shows unmistakable signs of immortality. Certain it is that a giant is among us, too great to be swayed far in any direction other than his own by contemporary experiments—though he does seem to discover many so-called "modernisms" himself, in spite of his self-imposed isolation from the musical world. It is with almost "divine knowing" that he expresses our time, but he does so in his own peculiar way—a very beautiful way, be it said. After listening to the FOURTH SYMPHONY, the listener will want to go on through the FIFTH, SIXTH, and SEVENTH symphonies, and the VIOLIN CONCERTO which is one of the best in the entire literature.

The works of these four composers illustrate the theses concerning historical continuity that have been set forth and show how Classicism, Romanticism, Realism, Impressionism, and their allied manifestations are to be found in the best works of our time, though expressed in the techniques and general spirit of today. And so, when the expression "Modern Music" is used, it is hardly self-explanatory; unless defined, it may mean all the influences of the past, the motivation by the same tempers with a large amount of traditional means of expression. Rather than seeking to separate the present from the past in order to justify or explain some transient or isolated phenomenon or aesthetic theory, some music historians would do better to realize that these threads, which constitute the warp and woof of history, bind the past to the present and provide the art a surety for the future. As listeners, it is best that we appreciate the good works of all time, including our own, and that we build within ourselves the means of widening the horizon so as to be able to embrace the tomorrow when it comes. Often a work of a contemporary composer acts as a harbinger, and its importance will be recognized by those who are properly prepared.

Of course it is true that new ideas, radical ones if you please, will arise all along the pathway of history. They must make their appearances frequently or the art will die from malnutrition; but these innovations, when they do come, should be viewed, evaluated, and appreciated in proper perspective.

It is not good to limit one's listening exclusively, or even mainly, to one period or one type of music. Too many youthful enthusiasts are satisfied to listen only to a few selected contemporary "radicals" and a far too limited number of types of music. Such practices are to be eliminated by substituting a wider, saner, and more eclectic listening experience. Modern music should include all types of musical tempers as manifested by the creators of all time, else it is not true to itself; for, as we have already shown, creators are now living and working and contributing their bit toward the storehouse of the world's riches in art. These same creators live in the past as well as in the present, and a precious few project into the future. It is the privilege and responsibility of the intelligent listener to know something of them all, and a great deal of a goodly number. Then, and not until then, will personal biases be worth cultivating.

ADDITIONAL SUGGESTIONS FOR LISTENING[6]

The author, throughout this book, has presented a few suggested listening challenges at the close of the chapters. In doing so, he has had in mind a "springboard" rather than a comprehensive listing, believing that, aside from a few samples, it would be better that the listener prepare his own lists. The ordinary difficulties of choice and sequence that plagued the author during the writing of previous chapters are increased in the present chapter by the problems concerning gramophone records—contemporary composers are too often conspicuous by their absence, and often those records that are available are not expedient. However, here are a few suggestions that might well serve as a start (they might even function as counter-irritants!), and they are offered with due apology to any worthy composer who is not included in this necessarily brief and pointed list. (No attempt has been made to arrange them in alphabetical or any other sequence.)

Try listening to the FIRST and the SIXTH SYMPHONIES of Dmitri Shostakovitch; the "CLASSICAL" SYMPHONY (Opus 25), the third PIANO CONCERTO, Opus 26, and the VIOLIN CONCERTO, Opus 19, of Sergei Prokofiev; the SECOND SYMPHONY and SECOND PIANO CONCERTO of Sergei Rachmaninoff; the FIFTH SYMPHONY, *Prometheus, the Poem of Fire*, Opus 60, of Alexander Scriabin; EL SALON MEXICO by Aaron

---

[6] Despite the fact that it is much too soon for any definite critical text on Modern music, there are a number of guide books that will be found helpful during the listener's period of orientation. Among these are *Contemporary Music* by Cecil Gray, *The New Music* by George Dyson, *This Modern Stuff* by Gerald Abraham, *A Music Critic's Holiday* by Ernest Newman, *Twentieth Century Music* by Marion Bauer, *The Problem of Modern Music* by Hans Weissmann, *Modern Composers* by Guido Painnan, *Music of Our Day* by Lazar Saminsky, *Composers of Today* by David Ewen, *Music Ho!* by Constant Lambert, *Our American Music* by John Tasker Howard, *From Madrigal to Modern Music* by Douglas Moore, and *Composers in America* by Claire Reis.

Copland; CONCERTINO for piano and orchestra by the versatile Henry
Hadley; ROMANTIC SYMPHONY, No. 2, by one of the most gifted and
capable of American composers, Howard Hanson; SYMPHONY No. 3,
by Roy Harris, the virile and most completely recorded of American
composers; PAGEANT OF P. T. BARNUM SUITE by Douglas Moore, whose
music is so wholesomely and typically American; ESSAY FOR ORCHESTRA
by Samuel Barber; AMERICAN FESTIVAL OVERTURE by William Schuman; COMES AUTUMN TIME OVERTURE by Leo Sowerby; Arthur
Honegger's outstanding contribution to the expression of Realism,
PACIFIC 231; Alexander Mossoloff's splitting bit of Realism, SOVIET
IRON FOUNDRY; Ernest Toch's FANTASY; Darius Milhaud's question-
able adaptation of American Jazz idioms, CREATION DU MONDE;
George Antheil's realistically noisy MÉCANIQUE; Harl McDonald's
very well done RHUMBA SYMPHONY No. 2; Gian-Carlo Menotti's gay
and vivacious Overture, AMELIA GOES TO THE BALL; Alexander Tans-
man's TRIPTYQUE for string orchestra; THE PLANETS by Gustav Holst;
William Walton's excellent Overture PORTSMOUTH POINT and his face-
tious fantasy, FAÇADE SUITE; Vaughan-William's LONDON SYMPHONY;
John Powell's NEGRO RHAPSODY; and we should have records of many
other worthy American and European composers. Among them should
be Bernard Wagenaar's "Triple Concerto"; selected works by Mrs.
H. H. A. Beach; Burrill Phillips' thoroughgoing American idiom as
seen in McGUFFEY'S READER; an additional number of wanted works
by the eminent American composer-teacher-writer, Daniel Gregory
Mason; of that sturdy, capable, and wonderful craftsman and teacher,
Arne Oldberg; and of that pioneer for American music to whom
America is more in debt than it realizes, Charles Wakefield Cadman;
and additional selected works by Marion Bauer, Charles Haubiel,
Lucas Foss, Harold Morris, Frederick Jacobi, Edwin Stringham and
Dello Joio. We could also wish for a large number of additional recordings of Edward MacDowell, one of the greatest of all American
composers. But we are already transgressing upon the rights of the
reader to enjoy building his own list.

Postscript

*We have attempted in the preceding pages to introduce the reader to a
broad world of music, to help him break down the barriers that might have
caused some of it to seem strange to him, to reveal some of music's inner
workings, its historical traditions, its vocabulary, its luminous, creative
spirits, and to establish a workable philosophy and practice of study for*

general listening. Naturally, any book conceived primarily as an introduction and orientation must contain serious omissions and be limited merely to touching on many vital points that should by right command chapters. Our aim has been to bring the reader to a point where he could and would go on by himself. We shall have succeeded if the listener does, in fact, continue from this point, pursuing the horizons of his curiosity, expanding continually his musical experience, returning again and again to works already known, turning an open heart and mind to new works, and listening for new voices but never forgetting old friends. A rich menu of all kinds of musical styles and forms has been placed before the reader-listener. Of course it is to be expected that preferences and even dislikes shall have been formed; but we hope that these have been tempered with that wisdom which comes from wide traffic with "what is good and beautiful and of excellent report," rather than that existing prejudices shall have been intensified'.

No doubt each listener will want to become better acquainted with certain types of works or with selected compositions, mindful the while that the mere possession of knowledge, facts, and understanding is not at all synonymous with appreciation—though such knowledge is not without value along certain directions of academic study. It is hoped that this aroused listening interest will, in many instances, find fruition in actual performing experience and, perhaps, in the actual creation of music. In order to achieve these desiderata, nothing can ever take the place—nothing can approach it in the slightest degree—of listening to great works of music over and over again until they are really and wholly the "personal" possession of the listener. Thus music can become a vital force in everyday living, making it the happier and the richer for its benign influences.

"But what of the future?" someone might ask. Our answer is that the future will be quite as you, the listener, wish it to be and actively bring it to realization through your own development as an intelligent, discriminating, sympathetic, and eclectic music lover—with a truly creative appreciation of the best in music.

Index

A

A-B-A form, 11, 236, 238
  in folk song, 54
Abduction from the Seraglio, 179, 336
Abraham, Gerald, 224
Absolute music, 185, 275, 282
  vs. programmatic content, 358–359
Abstract art, 483, 484
ACADEMIC OVERTURE, 40
Accelerando, 28
Accent, 27
Ach du lieber Augustin, 39
Adagio, 29
ADVENTURES IN A PERAMBULATOR, 471
Aeolian Mode, 289
AFTERNOON OF A FAUN, 130, 149, 459
Age of Classicism, 180
Age of Reason, 180, 181
Agoult, Countess d', 243
Ah! que Vous Dirai-je, Maman, 40
AÏDA, 86, 227
  excerpts from, 99
  scene from, 85
  Triumphal March from, 13, 14, 26, 154
Albeniz, Isaac, 213, 226
ALCESTE, 87, 357
Alexander Nevsky, 127
ALGERIAN SUITE, 227
Allegretto, 29
Allegro, 29
Allemande, 5
Allerseelen, 69
Amaryllis, 4
AMELIA GOES TO THE BALL, 103, 490
America:
  art song in, 70
  Dvořák in, 282–283
  impressionism in, 470–471
  nationalistic music in, 213
  opera in, 103
America, 43
AMERICAN FESTIVAL OVERTURE, 490
American school, naturalism of, 198
America Sings, 34
Anakreon's Grab, 69
Andante, 29

Andante Cantabile, from String Quartet
  Op. 11, 390–391
Andantino, 29
Andersen, Hans Christian, 65, 132, 213
Anitra's Dance, 116
Antheil, George, 490
Anthems, national, 43
APOSTLES, THE, 113
Appalachian folk song, 34, 36
Arab Dance (NUTCRACKER SUITE), 166, 227
Arabian Nights, 227, 231
Architecture:
  form in, 47–52
  of music, 47–54
Aria, 75, 81
ARIANE AND BLUEBEARD, 208
Arkansas Traveller, 35
Arne, Thomas, 43
Arnim, Bettina von, 305, 313
Arpeggio, 147
  differentiated from scale, 168
Art:
  and religion, 18
  Baroque, 428
  chamber music compared with, 386–387
  classic and romantic elements in, 171–194
  eighteenth-century, 329–330
  form in, 47–51
  modern movement in, 473–474
  nationalism and, 212–214
Art and Revolution, 254
Art in the Western World, 172, 331, 429
Art of Music, The, 375
Art song, 42–47, 55–70
  differentiated from folk song, 55–56
  French composers of, 69
  German composers of, 69
  history of, 56
  romantic love in, 57–58
Art Through the Ages, 429
Art Work of the Future, The, 254
As a Ray of Sunlight, 56
ASCENSION ORATORIO, 439
Ase's Death, 116–117

At Dawning, 70
ATHALIE, 13
Atkinson, Charles F., 429
Atonality, 474, 485
Atonality and Polytonality, 485
Auber, Daniel F. E., 214
Auch Kleine Dinge, 69
Augmentation, intervallic, 395
Aurora's Wedding, 139
AUS MEINEN, 215
Austrian national anthem, 43
Ave Maria, 62

B

Bacchanale, 139
  motif, 260–261
Bach, Anna Magdalena, 440
Bach, Johann Sebastian, 5, 6, 19, 107,
  112, 379, 434–450
  and polyphonic style, 423–450
  and the Baroque, 428–434
  and the Reformation, 427–428
  biography, 434–441
  cantatas of, 22–25
  children of, 440
  chorale preludes of, 441–443
  church cantatas, 439
  fugues, 443–445
  original manuscript of organ prelude,
    436
  religious works of, 22–25
  transcriptions of works, 442–443
Bach, Karl Phillipp Emanuel, 330, 348
Bach-Gesellschaft, 450
Badinerie, 6
Balakirev, Mily, 190–191, 204, 205, 229,
  230
Balance, 49
Balinese music, 460
Ballad, 404
Ballade No. 3 in A-flat Major, 404–408
Ballet, music and, 128–140
Ballet Russe, 132, 468, 478
Barbara Allen, 31
BARBER OF SEVILLE, 80, 81, 84
Baroque, 107, 173
  art, books on, 429
  Bach and the, 428–434
  period, 323
  Reformation and the, 423–450
BARTERED BRIDE, THE, 215
  Overture to, 226

Bass clarinet, 151–152
Bassoon, 152–153
Basso ostinato, 446
BASTIEN AND BASTIENNE, 335
Battle Hymn of the Republic 28, 43
BATTLE OF THE HUNS, THE, 246
Bayreuth, 244, 256
Béatitudes, Les, 410
Beautiful Blue Danube, 2
Beethoven, Ludwig van, 4, 14, 301–316,
    386, 473
  achievement of, 308–309
  biography, 301–307
  birthplace, 303
  deafness, 304–307
  death, 307
  EROICA, 150
  FIFTH SYMPHONY, 153, 310–316
  influence on Wagner, 252
  MOUNT OF OLIVES, 112
  Ninth Symphony, 26
  OVERTURE TO LEONORA, No. 3,
    364–368
  Piano Concerto in G major, 413
  piano sonatas, 408
  Rondino, 53
  SIXTH SYMPHONY, 151, 245
  suggestions for listening, 316
BEGGAR ON HORSEBACK, 123
BEGGAR'S OPERA, 107
Bel canto, 88
*Believe Me if All Those Endearing Young
    Charms*, 39
Bellini, Vincenzo, 84
Bells, orchestra, 159
BELSHAZZAR'S FEAST, 113
Benevoli, Arazio, 434
BENVENUTO CELLINI, production of, 243
Bergomasque Dance, 117
Berlioz, Hector, 69, 198, 202, 243
  Damnation of Faust, 150
  oratorios of, 113
  SYMPHONIE FANTASTIQUE, 150
Beyle, Marié Henri, 334
BILLY THE KID, 140
Binary form, 45–46
Birch Tree, The, 42, 46, 73
Bishop, Sir Henry, 43
Bizet, Georges, 69, 88
  CARMEN, 91–99
  Prelude to L'ARLÉSIENNE, 152
Blanik, 216
Bliss, Arthur, cinema music of, 127

Bloch, Ernest, 452
BLOSSOM TIME, 78
Blue Danube, Beautiful, 2, 214
B-MINOR MASS, 19, 23, 25, 26
Boccherini, Luigi, 330
BOHEME, LA, 86, 99, 100, 360
   excerpts from, 100
Bohemia, 213
   Gypsy music of, 4
Böhm, Theobald, 400
BOLERO, 137, 140
BORIS GODUNOFF, 205, 214, 231
   excerpts from, 101
Borodin, Alexander, 206, 227
   member of "The Five", 230
Bourrée, 5
"Brahmins," 320
Brahms, Johannes, 7, 16, 282
ACADEMIE OVERTURE, 40
   art songs of, 63–64
   biography, 318–320
   Classical Romanticist, 317–328
   composed folk song, 44
   GERMAN REQUIEM, 113
   Lullaby, 42, 44
   Minnelied, 55
   portrait of, 318
   SECOND SYMPHONY, 323–327
Brailowsky, Alexander, 403
BRANDENBURG CONCERTI, 450–451
Branle, 5
Bridal Chorus, 13
Bridal Cortège, 14
Brigg Fair, 471
Brothers Karamazov, The, 126
Bruckner, Anton, 251
Bülow, Hans von, 255, 256, 317, 321
Bury Me Not on the Lone Prairie, 34
Buxtehude, Dietrich, 399, 435
By a Lonely Forest Pathway, 70
By the Waters of Minnetonka, 70

C

Cadence:
   defined, 19
   phrase, period and, 71–74
Cadenza, 166
Ça Ira, 40
Caldara, Antonio, 56
Canon, 418, 424
Canon cancrizans, 484

Cantata, 22
   defined, 275, 436
Carissimi, Giacomo, 56
Carmagnole, 40
CARMEN, 88, 91–99
   scene from, 92
CARNIVAL OF THE ANIMALS, 169
Carpenter, John Alden, 471
   SEA DRIFT, 471
   SKYSCRAPERS, 130, 135–137
Carreño, Teresa, 119
Casey Jones, 34
Castanets, 159
Catholic Church, 82
Catholic revival, 113
Cattle calls, 34
Cavalieri, Emilio del, 106
CAVALIER OF THE ROSE, 101, 267
CAVALLERIA RUSTICANA, 86
   excerpts from, 100, 101
Celesta, 159
'Cello, 145, 146
Ceremony, music and, 11–17
Chaconne:
   defined, 446
   in d minor for unaccompanied violin,
      446, 449–450
Chamber music:
   definitions, 384
   nature of, 384–388
   suggestions for listening, 397
Chamber Suites and Concerti Grossi, 450
Chanson de Mambron, 32
Chant, Hebrew, 19
Chant for the Dead (Kaddish), 19
Chant of the Dead (Dies Irae), 196
Charpentier, Gustave, 88
Chausson, Ernest, 400
CHILDHOOD OF CHRIST, THE, 113
CHILDREN'S CORNER, THE, 6
CHILDREN'S CRUSADE, 113
Chimes, 159
Chinese Dance (NUTCRACKER SUITE), 153,
   167
Chopin, Frederic François, 6, 14, 15, 28,
   213, 401–408
   Ballade No. 3 in A-flat major, 404–408
   biography, 402
   LES SYLPHIDES, 139
Chorales, 22
Choral prelude, 23
   of Bach, 441–443
Chorus, Greek, 128

Chorus of the Pilgrims (TANNHÄUSER), 157
Christian service, debt to Hebrews and Greeks, 19
Christ Lay in the Bonds of Death, 19
CHRISTMAS ORATORIO, 112, 439
Christofori, Bartolomeo, 401
CHRISTUS, 113, 244
Chromatic scales, 211
    defined, 201
    nature of, 485
Church Modes, 36
Cimarosa, Domenico, 80, 88
Cinema, 53–54
    music for, 126–127
Clair de Lune, 69
Clarinet, 150, 151
Classical, 171–175
    defined, 4
Classical art, 330
Classical overture:
    background of, 356–357
    Gluck and, 358
Classical Period, 4, 57
Classical spirit, in music, 330–332
Classical symphony, suggestions for listening, 352
Classical temper, characteristics of, 353–355
Classicism, 198, 475
    and Romanticism, 178–182, 301–316
CLEMENCY OF TITUS, THE, 337, 338
Climax, building, 28
CLOWNS, THE, 86
Coda, 286
    enriched by Beethoven, 308
    symphony, 295–296
Col legno, 144
Come Raggio di Sol, 56
COMES AUTUMNTIME OVERTURE, 490
Comic opera, 77
Comin' Through the Rye, 31, 39
Commedia dell' arte, 80
Composed folk song, 42–47
Concertino, 451
    defined, 369
Concerti Ecclesiastici, 369
Concerto, 369–383
    by Beethoven, 372
    defined, 276
    national characteristics in, 372
Concerto grosso:
    defined, 369
    of Bach, 450–452

Concertstück, 408
Contrabassoon, 153
Contrapunal music, 21, 423–424
Copland, Aaron, 490
    BILLY THE KID, 140
    cinema music of, 127
COPPELIA, 139
COQ D'OR, 14
Corelli, Arcangelo, 369
Coriolanus, 358
CORONATION CONCERTO, 337
Coronation March, 13
"Coronation of Napoleon and Josephine," 12
Countermelody, 116, 426
Counterpoint, 423
Couperin, François, 330
Courante, 5
Cours de Composition, 412
Cowboy songs, 34
CREATION, THE, 306, 345, 346
    choruses from, 112
CREATION OF THE WORLD, THE, 139, 490
Credo, 19, 25
Creole songs, 32
Crescendo, 27, 28
Crucifixus, 19, 25
Cubism, 481
Cui, César, 227
    member of "The Five", 230
Cummings, E. E., 472
CUNNING PEASANT, THE, 282
Cyclical compositional technique, 240, 309, 412
    in NEW WORLD SYMPHONY, 284
Cyclopedic Survey of Chamber Music, 384, 393, 416, 485
Cymbals, 159
Czechoslovakia, music in, 3 (*see also* Dvořák; Smetana)
Czerny, Karl, 242

D

Dance:
    folk, 35, 36
    form in, 52
    music and, 1–10
DANSE MACABRE, 150, 159, 196, 198
    analysis of, 200–204
Dance music, American, 284
Dance of Death (Liszt), 202
Dance of the Sugar Plum Fairy, 159, 165

Dance of the Toy Flutes (NUTCRACKER SUITE), 149, 155, 167
DANCE SUITES, 5
"DANCING PEASANTS," 3
DAPHNIS AND CHLOÉ, 149, 468
Daquin, Claude, 330
DAUGHTER OF THE REGIMENT, 84
DEATH AND LIFE, 113
Death and the Maiden, 57, 62
DEATH AND TRANSFIGURATION, 268
Death is Like a Cool Still Night, 63
Death of the Lovers, 70
Debussy, Claude, 6, 213, 214, 251, 453, 458–467
    AFTERNOON OF A FAUN, 130, 149, 463–467
    art songs of, 69–70
    piano solos, 408
    RHAPSODY FOR SAXOPHONE AND ORCHESTRA, 152
    titles of works, 460–461
Decrescendo, 27, 28
Deh vieni, non tardar, 81
De Koven, Reginald, 78
Delibes, Léo, 130, 139, 152
Delius, Frederick, 470–471
    THE MASS OF LIFE, 113
DESERT, THE, 227
Deutschland über Alles, 346
Development, symphony, 294
Devotion, 69
Diaghileff, Serge, 132, 133, 478
Dictionary of Music and Musicians, 36, 266, 267, 275, 369, 403, 437
Dies Irae, 196, 203
Diminution, rhythmic and melodic, 395
DINORAH, 87
Disney, Walt, 479
DON GIOVANNI, 88, 334, 337, 358
Donizetti, Gaetano, 84, 102
DON JUAN, 266
Do Not Go, My Love, 70
DON PASQUALE, 84
DON QUIXOTE, 266
"Doodle-sack Player," 148, 387
Dorn, H., 373
Double bass, 146
Double virginal, 371
Dove Sono, 81
Doxology, 19, 425
Drama and opera, 83
Drame lyrique, 87
Dream in the Twilight, 69

DREAM OF GERONTIUS, 113
Dresden Amen, 25
Drinking song, 32
"Drink to Me Only With Thine Eyes," 31, 36, 37
Driving Sawlogs on the Plover, 34
Dry recitation, 80
Dukas, Paul, 196, 207–211, 263
    biography, 208
    SORCERER'S APPRENTICE, 153, 208–211
Duparc, Henri, 410
    art songs of, 69
Duple meter, 2
Durchkomponiert, 55
Dvořák, Antonin, 3, 213, 280–300
    biography, 280–282
    composed folk song, 42
    LARGO (NEW WORLD SYMPHONY), 150
    nationalism of, 281
    String Quartet in F major, 392–397
    SYMPHONY "FROM THE NEW WORLD," 280–300
Dynamics, 26–28

E

EASTER ORATORIO, 439
"Ecstasy of St. Theresa," 431
EDEN, 113
EGMONT, 308, 358
1812 OVERTURE, 192, 214, 218–221
    compared with FINLANDIA, 225
Ein kleine Nachtmusik, 388–390
Eisler, Hans, 127
EL AMOR BRUJO, 130, 131
ELEKTRA, 101, 267
Elgar, Edward, 11, 14, 147, 213
    oratorios of, 113
ELIJAH, 106, 112
ELIXIR OF LOVE, 84
Elsa's Dream, 90
Emotional expression, volume and speed in, 26–29
Empathy, 429
EMPEROR JONES, THE, 103
EMPEROR STRING QUARTET, 346
Enchanted Flute, The, 149
ENCHANTED LAKE, THE, 226
"Endless melody," 89
Enesco, Georges, 226
England, 213
    impressionism in, 470–471
    oratorio in, 107, 111, 113

English folk song, 30–32, 36
English horn, 150
EN SAGA, 222
Entr'acte music, 114
Enunciation, fugue, 443
Episode, fugue, 443
ERLKÖNIG, DER, 55, 59–60
Eroica, 15, 150, 306
Essays in Musicol Analysis, 380
Et Resurrexit, 19, 25
Euryanthe, 89
　overture to, 359, 361
Evans, Edwin, 485
Evening Harmonies, 70
Even Little Things, 69
Exoticism in music, 227–241
Exposition, 286
　fugue, 443
　symphony, 292
Expressionism, 265, 472–490
　defined, 480
　Schönberg, 483–485
　Stravinsky, 478–479
　suggestions for listening, 489
Extase, 69

F

FAÇADE SUITE, 490
Fagotto, 152
FAIR AT SOROTCHINSK, THE, 205, 206
Falla, Manuel de, 470
　EL AMOR BRUJO, 130, 131
FALSTAFF, 86
Fantasia, fugue, 445
Fantasia and Fugue in g minor, 435
"Fantasia" (Walt Disney), 209, 479
Farewell of Wotan, 262
Farmer in the Dell, The, 55, 72
Fate motif, Beethoven's, 311, 314
Fauré, Gabriel, art songs of, 69
Faust, 67–68
FAUST (Gounod), 88, 202
　excerpts from, 100
FESTIVALS OF ROME, THE, 469
FESTIVAL PIECE, 246
FIDELIO, 306, 308, 358, 366
FIFTH SYMPHONY (Beethoven), 153
　analysis of, 310–316
　announcement of, 310
Finland, 213, 222–226
FINLANDIA, 214, 222–226, 269
FIREBIRD, THE, 132, 139, 478

First-movement form, 286, 291–296
　diagram, 295
　enriched by Beethoven, 308
"Five, The," 230
Flamenco songs, 40, 73
Flea, The, 55, 67–68
Flute, 149
FLYING DUTCHMAN, THE, 91, 243, 252,
　253, 255
Folk dance, 2, 35–36, 39, 73
Folk song, 30–39
　A-B-A pattern in, 54
　American, 32–34
　composed, 42–47
　differentiated from art song, 56–57
　English, 30–32, 36
　French, 40
　German, 40
　Irish, 39
　Italian, 40
　nationalism and, 30, 35–36
　nineteenth-century, 42–44
　Russian, 40
　Spanish, 40
　work song, 32–35
FORCE OF DESTINY, THE, 86
Forest Murmurs, 262
Forgotten Village, The, 127
Form and structure, 47–54
For Music, 69
Fornsete, John of, 418
Forte (*f*), 28
Fortissimo (*ff*), 28
FORTUNE TELLER, 78
Forty-Eight Preludes and Fugues, 438
FORZA DEL DESTINO, LA, 86
Foster, Stephen, composed folk song, 16,
　43, 55, 73–74
FOUR ELEMENTS, THE, 247
France, 213
　oratorio in, 113
Franck, César:
　art songs of, 69
　biography, 409–411
　piano solos, 408
　Sonata in A major for violin and piano,
　411–421
　THE BEATITUDES, 113
Franz, Robert, 69
FREISCHÜTZ, 89
　overture to, 163, 359, 360–364
French-Canadian folk song, 32
French folk song, 40

French horn, 155–156
French opera, 86–88
French overture, 357
French Revolution:
 influence on Beethoven, 301
French Romanticism, 69
French round dance, 4
Fries, Count, 302
Friml, Rudolf, 78
FROM THE CRADLE TO THE GRAVE, 246
From the Fields and Groves of Bohemia, 216
From the Land of the Sky-Blue Water, 70
Fugue, 424
 of Bach, 443—445
Funeral Hymn for a Hero, 245
Funeral March, 14, 28, 150
Für Musik, 69

G

Gabrieli, G., motets of, 433
GAIETÉ PARISIENNE, 139
Galuppi, B., 348
Gasperini, 254
Gaudeamus Igitur, 40
Gavotte, 5
GENOVEVA, 243
German, Edward, 226
German dance, 5
German folklore, 89
German folk song, 40
German lied, 321
GERMAN REQUIEM, 319, 321
German Romanticism, 63, 64, 360
 influence on music in America, 283
Germany, 213
Germinal motive, 247, 257, 322
Gershwin, George, 78–79, 152
Gesualdo, 434
Gewandhaus Symphony Orchestra, 379
Ghys, 4
Giannini, Vittoria, 103
GIDEON, 113
Giga, 5
Gilbert and Sullivan, 79
Giono's Harvest, 126
"Giselle," 361
Git Along Little Dogie, 34
Glazounov, Alexsandr K., 139, 165
Glière, Reinhold, 140
Glissando, 144
Glockenspiel, 159
Gloria, 19, 21, 22

Glorification of Venus motif, 26
"Glorified speech" type of singing, 93
Gluck, Christophe Willibald, 86, 246
 and the classical overture, 357–358
Godowsky, Leopold, 403
God Preserve Our Gracious Emperor, 43
God Save the Emperor, 346
God Save the King, 43
"Going Home," 287, 290
GOLDEN AGE, THE, 140
Golliwog's Cakewalk, 6
Gong, 159
Goodbye Old Paint, 34
Good Night, 69
Gossec, F., 348
GÖTTERDÄMMERUNG, 256, 262
Gounod, Charles, 69, 88, 101, 128, 202
Grace notes, 235
GRAND CANON SUITE, 226
Grand opera, 81–103
 and drama, 83
 church background of, 82
 French, 86–88
 Italian, 84–86
 secular background of, 82
Grand style, 453
Gregorian Chant, 21
Gregory the Great, Pope, 21
Grieg, Edvard, 14, 213, 214, 226
 art song of, 64–65
 composed folk song, 39
 Ich Liebe Dich, 55, 65
 piano solos, 408
Grimm brothers, 213
Ground Hog, The, 34
Gruenberg, Louis, 103
Guion, David, 2
Guiraud, Ernest, 93
GUNTRAM, 268
GURRE-LIEDER, 480, 485
Gute Nacht, 69
Gipsy
 Hungarian, 44, 73
 influence on Dvořák, 281
 music, 4
 song and dance, 40–41
Gipsy Love Song, 78

H

Hadley, Henry, 490
Hageman, Richard, 70, 103
Hallelujah Chorus, 111

Handel, George Frideric, 107–113, 434
  great oratorios of, 107
  influence on Haydn, 346
  THE MESSIAH, 109–111, 424
Hanson, Howard, 103, 490
Hark, Hark the Lark, 57, 60–62
Harmonics, 144, 208–209
Harmonie du Soir, 70
Harmony:
  melody and, 15–17
  nature of, 16
Harp, 146–147
Harp That Once Through Tara's Halls, The, 39
Harris, Roy, 490
HARY JANOS SUITE, 226
Haydn, Franz Joseph, 4, 330, 332, 344–352
  Austrian national anthem, 43
  biography, 344–347
  My Mother Bids Me Bind My Hair, 56
  oratorios of, 112
  romantic characteristics of, 182
  SURPRISE SYMPHONY, 348–352
  teacher of Beethoven, 302
Hebrew chant, 19
Hedge-Rose, 61, 62
Heidenröslein, 61, 62
Heifetz, Jascha, 398
HENRY THE EIGHTH DANCES, 226
Hensel, Fanny, 379
Herbert, Victor, 78, 103
HERO'S LIFE, A, 266
"Hiawatha's Wooing," 287
High Up on Old Smoky, 34
Hillbilly tunes, 34
Hindemith, Paul, 196, 485–486
HOCHZEIT DES CAMACHO, DIE, 379
Hoffman, E. T. A., 163, 202, 245, 252, 361
Hofmann, Josef, 403
  as solo performer, 398
Holst, Gustav, 113, 490
HOLY CHILDREN, THE, 113
Home on the Range, 31, 34
Home Sweet Home, 43
Homophonic music, 21, 424
Honegger, Arthur, 490
  cinema music of, 126
  oratorios of, 113
HORA NOVISSIMA, 113
Horn, 155–156
Horowitz, Vladimir, 398, 400

Humoresque, 281
HUNGARIA, 246
Hungarian Gipsy, 4, 73
Hungarian Rhapsodies, 213, 243, 408
Husitska, 281
Hymn, 18, 19
HYMN TO JESUS, 113
Hymn to the Dead, 203
HYMN TO THE NIGHT, 91
Hymn to the Sun, 227
HYMNUS, 281

I

IBERIA, 226
Ich Grolle Nicht, 55, 62
Ich Liebe Dich, 55, 64–65
IDEAL, THE, 246
If Music Be the Food of Love, 56
Il Etait un Bergère, 40
I'll Not Complain, 55, 62
IL MATRIMONIA SEGRETO, 80
Im Herbst, 69
Impressionism, 453–471, 475
  in America, 471
  in England, 470–471
  in Italy, 468–470
  in literature, 457
  in music, 458–471
  in painting, 454–457
  suggestions for listening, 470–471
Impromptu (FINLANDIA), 223
Improvisation, 370
In a Summer Garden, 471
In Autumn, 69
Incidental music, 114–127
INCREDIBLE FLUTIST, 139
Indian Love Call, 78
INDIAN SUITE, 119, 121–123
Indian themes:
  in MacDowell's works, 121
  in NEW WORLD SYMPHONY, 283
Indy, Vincent d', 113, 152, 410
Instrumental choral prelude, 23
Instrumental-homophonic style, 427
In Summer Fields, 63
Interlude, 114, 143
  comic opera as, 77
Intermezzo, 114
  comic opera as, 77
Intervallic augmentation, 395
In the Hall of the Mountain King, 116
In the Steppes of Central Asia, 227

Invitation to the Dance, 361
I PAGLIACCI, 86, 100, 105
IPHIGENIA IN TAURIS, 358
Irish folk song, 39
Irish Washerwoman, 35
Isle of the Dead, The, 196–197
ISRAEL IN EGYPT, 107
Italian Concerto, 439
Italian folk song, 40
Italian influence on music, 428
Italian opera, 84–86
Italian overture, 357
ITALIAN SYMPHONY, *Finale* of, 28

J

Java, music of, 460
Jazz, 4, 152, 490
    trumpet players, 155
Jeanie with the Light Brown Hair, 43
JEPHTHA, 107
Jesu, Joy of Man's Desiring, 19, 23, 442
Jig, 5
Joachim, Joseph, 319
John Henry, 31, 34–35
JUDAS MACCABAEUS, 107
JUDITH, 113
JUPITER SYMPHONY, 337
Just a Song at Twilight, 70

K

Kaddish, 19
Kalevala, 486
Kandinsky, Vasili, 480
Karsavina, 133, 468
Kelley, Edgar Stillman, 113
Kentucky folk song, 36
Kern, Jerome, 78
Kettledrums, 158
Keyboard instruments, 399
KHOVANTCHINA, 205, 231
KING AND COLLIER, 281
KING DAVID, 113
KINGDOM, THE, 113
KING'S HENCHMAN, THE, 103, 123
KISS, THE, 215
Kiss Me Again, 78
Köchel, Ludwig von, 397
Kodály, Zoltán, 226
Kol Nidrei, 19
Komm Süsser Tod, 442

Korngold, Erich, 127
Koussevitzky, Serge, 133, 279
Kreisler, Fritz, 4, 53
    as solo performer, 398
KUNST DER FUGE, DIE, 439, 450
KUOLEMA, 115
Kyrie, 19, 21, 23

L

Labelling, perils of, 178–179
La Flute Enchantée, 149
L'Africaine, 87
La Mort des Amants, 70
Landler, 39
L'APPRENTI SORCIER, 208–211
Largo, 29
Largo al factotum, 81
LA SERVA PADRONA, 80
Lassus, Orlando, 22, 423
Last Rose of Summer, The, 39
LA TOSCA, excerpts from, 100
LA TRAVIATA, 86
L'Automme, 69
LA VESTALE, 87
LA VETA NUOVA, 113
Lead Kindly Light, 19
Legato, 12
LEGEND OF ST. CHRISTOPHER, 116
LEGEND OF ST. ELIZABETH, 244
Leit motifs, 240–241, 323
Lekeu, Guillaume, 410
Lento, 29
Leoncavallo, Ruggiero, 86, 100, 105
LEONORA overtures, 358, 364–368
LE PROPHÈTE, 87
    Coronation March from, 13
LES PRÉLUDES, 29, 245
    analysis of, 246–249 |
    programme for, 247
LES SYLPHIDES, 139
Letter, The, 127
Lhevinne, Josef, 403
Liadov, Anatole K., 226
LIBUSSA, 215
Liebestod, 182–184
Lied, 57
    Brahms, master of, 321
Lieutenant Kije, 127
LIGHT OF LIFE, 113
Light opera, 75–81
    operetta and, 75–81
Linden Tree, The, 57, 62

L'Invitation au Voyage, 69
Liszt, Franz, 29, 119, 199, 202, 213, 242–250, 401, 453
  as solo performer, 398
  biography, 242–246
  HUNGARIAN RHAPSODIES, 44
  influence:
    on Smetana, 215
    on Strauss, 263–265
  LES PRÉLUDES, 245, 247–249
  oratorios, 113
  symphonic poems, 245–246
Little Fugue in g minor, 443–445
Little Preludes, 437
Loeffler, Charles Martin, 113, 471
Logger's Boast, The, 34
LOHENGRIN, 13, 151, 253, 255
  Prelude to, 25, 29, 90
  production of, 243
London Bridge is Falling Down, 55, 71–72
Londonderry Air, 39
LONDON SYMPHONY, 490
Long, Long Ago, 17
Lorelei, Die, 40
LOUISE, 88, 101
Louisiana, folk song, 32
LOVE, THE MAGICIAN, 131
Love, Thou Pure Impulse, 81
Love's Ban motif, 261
Love's Old Sweet Song, 70
Love Song, 63–64
Love songs, 57–58
Love Went A-Riding, 70
LUCIA DI LAMMERMOOR, 84, 102
LUDMILLA, 281
Lullaby, 42, 44
Lully, Jean Baptiste, 86, 130, 356–357
Lumberjack tunes, 32–34
LUTHERAN MASSES, 439
Lyric drama, 87

M

MACBETH, 267
MacDowell, Edward, 119–123, 213, 374, 490
  art song of, 64, 68
  piano solos, 408
  The Sea, 55
  titles of compositions, 120
Macfarren, Natalia, 26
McGUFFEY'S READER, 490
MADAME BUTTERFLY, 86, 100, 227

Madrigals, 142
MAGIC FLUTE, THE, 88, 337, 338, 359
Mahler, Gustav, 251
Maid-Mistress, The, 80
MA MÈRE L'OYE, 130, 137–139
Mandoline, 70
MANFRED, 243
MANON, 88
  excerpts from, 100
March:
  ceremonial, 11
  nature of, 12
Marche Militaire, 11, 14
March (NUTCRACKER SUITE), 164–165
Marco Polo, 127
Mariage des Roses, 69
Marlborough, 31, 32
MARRIAGE OF FIGARO, 80, 88, 337, 358
Marseillaise, 43
  in 1812 OVERTURE, 219–221
Maryland, My Maryland, 40
Marxsen, 319
Masaniello, 144
Mascagni, Pietro, 68
Mason, Daniel Gregory, 375, 490
Massa's in de Cold, Cold Ground, 43
Massenet, Jules, 69, 88, 100, 227
Masses, 423
  of Bach, 427
MASS FOR GRAN CATHEDRAL, 244
MASS FOR POPE MARCELLUS, 19, 22
MASS IN B MINOR, 439
Master Singers, 56
MATHIS DER MALER, 196, 486
Mattheson, Johann, 439
MA VLAST, 215
May Night, 63
MAYTIME, 78
MAZEPPA, 246
Mazurkas (Chopin), 213
Mean-tone temperament, 437–438
MÉCANIQUE, 490
Meditation, 70
MEISTERSINGER, DIE, (The Master Singers), 89, 91, 155, 256
Melody and harmony, 15–17
Mendelssohn, Felix, 13, 25, 28, 106, 378–383, 408
  biography, 378–379
  CONCERTO IN E MINOR, 378, 380–383
  MIDSUMMER NIGHT'S DREAM SUITE, 117–118
  oratorios, 112

Mendelssohn-Bartholdy, Jakob Ludwig (*see* Mendelssohn, Felix)
Menotti, Gian Carlo, 103, 490
Mephisto Waltz (Liszt), 202
MERRY MOUNT, 103
MERRY PRANKS OF TILL EULENSPIEGEL, THE, 156, 268–274
MESSIAH, THE, 107, 109–111, 424
Metre:
  differentiated from tempo, 28
  duple, 2
  triple, 2
Meyerbeer, Giacomo, 13, 87, 253
Mezzo forte (*mf*), 28
Mickiewicz, influence of, on Chopin, 212, 404
Middle Ages, religious music in, 21
MIDSUMMER NIGHT'S DREAM, A, 13, 379
  Nocturne, 155
  Suite, 114, 117, 118
Mighty Fortress Is Our God, A, 18, 19, 25
Milhaud, Darius, 139, 490
Military march, 11
Miniature Overture (NUTCRACKER SUITE), 164
Minnelied, 55, 63, 64
Minnesingers, 56
Mississippi Sawyer, 35
MLADA, 206
Mlle. Modiste, 78
Moderato, 29
Moldau, The, 214, 216–218
Molloy, James, 70
Monodic music, 21
Monteverde, Giulio, 356, 474
Moonlight, 69
Moonlight Sonata, 278
Moore, Douglas, 490
Moore, Thomas, 39
MORAVIAN DUETS, 281
Morning, 116
Mort de Tintagiles, La, 471
Mossoloff, Alexander, 490
Motets, 394
  of Gabrieli, 404
MOTHER GOOSE SUITE, 130, 137–139, 467
  Beauty and the Beast, 153
Motion pictures, 53
  music for, 126–127
  operettas, 77
Motives, leading (leit motifs), 257
MOUNT OF OLIVES, THE, 112, 308

Moussorgsky, Modest, 213
  biography, 204–205
  member of "The Five", 230
  Night on Bald Mountain, 196, 205–207
  Song of the Flea, 55, 67–68
Mozart, Wolfgang Amadeus, 4, 88, 178, 330, 473
  as solo performer, 398
  biography, 335–338
  church music of, 112
  compared with Wagner, 183–184
  concertos by, 371–372
  Ein kleine Nachtmusik, 388–392
  influence on Chopin, 403
  MARRIAGE OF FIGARO, 80
  piano sonatas, 408
  role in rise of solo concerto, 370
  romantic characteristics of, 182
  SYMPHONY IN E-FLAT MAJOR, minuet from, 183, 184
  SYMPHONY IN G MINOR, 151, 339–344
  The Violet, 56
Müller, 232
Mürner, Thomas, 268, 269
Music:
  and the dance, 1–10
  architecture of, 47–54
  as personal expression, 55–74
  Impressionism, 458–471
  sentence structure in, 71–74
Musical comedy, 77
Musical revue, 77
Music drama, elements of, 83
"Music of the future," 244, 265
Mute, 146
Muted tones:
  horn, 156
  trumpet, 155
My Heart at Thy Sweet Voice, 199
My Mother Bids Me Bind My Hair, 56
My Old Kentucky Home, 43, 214
My Peace Thou Art, 62

N

Narrative, tone painting, and mood, 195–211
Nationalism:
  and the arts, 212–214
  Dvořák (*see* Dvořák, Antonin)
  folk song, 30, 35–36, 43
  in concertos, 372
  in music, 212–226

Nationalism (*Cont.*)
  Sibelius, 486
NATOMA, 103
Naturalism, 198, 475
Negro influence, folk song, 32
NEGRO RHAPSODY, 490
Negro themes:
  in NEW WORLD SYMPHONY, 283, 284
  in SKYSCRAPERS, 136
Neo-classicism, 476
Neo-romanticism, 476
Nevin, Ethelbert, 70
NEW CROOKED DEVIL, THE, 344
NEW YEAR'S EVE IN NEW YORK, 152
NIGHTINGALE, THE, 132
Night on Bald Mountain, 196
Nijinsky, Romola, 132, 478
Nijinsky, Waslaw, 132–133, 468, 478
NOCHES EN LOS JARDINES DE ESPANA, 470
Nocturne, 69, 117–118, 155
Nocturne, defined, 118
None But the Lonely Heart, 65–66
NORMA, 84
Norway, 213
Norwegian Bridal Procession, 14
NORWEGIAN DANCES, 226
Nur Wer Die Sehnsucht Kennt, 65–66
NUTCRACKER SUITE, 162–170, 240, 268
  Dance of the Sugar Plum Fairy, 159
  Dance of the Toy Flutes, 149, 155

O

OBERON, 89
  overture to, 359, 361
Oboe, 150
O Descend Upon Us, Night of Love, 91
"Ode to Joy," 26
Offenbach, Jacques, 139
Of Mice and Men, 127
Oh Come, Do Not Delay, 81
Oh Promise Me, 78
Okeghem, Jean d', 484
Oldberg, Arne, 490
Old Black Joe, 40
Old Chisholm Trail, The, 34
Ol' Man River, 78
On a Screen, 70
On Hearing the First Cuckoo in Spring, 471
Onward Christian Soldiers, 19
On With the Play, 100
Op., 232
O Paradiso, 87

Opera, 75–103
  differentiated from oratorio, 104–106
  grand, 81–103 (*see also* Grand opera)
  in America, 103
  light, 75–81
Opera and Drama, 254
Opera buffa, 76, 80
Opera comique, 87
Operettas, 77–79
  and light operas, 75–81
  motion-picture, 77
  romantic, 78
Oratorio, 104–113
  by American composers, 113
  in England, 113
  in France, 113
  nature of, 104–106
  of Classical Period, 112
  of nineteenth century, 112
  of twentieth century, 113
  THE MESSIAH, 109–111
Orchestra, the, 141–170
  advanced by Beethoven, 309
  arrangement of, 160–161
  brass choir, 154–158
  concerto for solo instrument and, 369–383
  Debussy's handling of, 460
  development of, 141–143, 186–187
  in action, 162–170
  percussion instruments, 158–160
  scoring, 162
  string choir, 143–147
  symphony, 385–386
  woodwind choir, 147–154
  writing for, 161–162
Orchestration, 161–162
Ordinary of the Mass, 21
ORFÉO, 246
Organists, famous, 399
Organ works, transcriptions of, 442–443
Oriental drums, 158
Orientale, 227, 230
ORPHEUS, 246
O Sole Mio, 43
OTELLO, 86
Overture, 114
  classical form, romantic content in, 356–368
  development of, 359–360
  French, 357
  historical background of, 356–357
  Italian, 357–358

Overture (*Cont.*)
 MIDSUMMER NIGHT'S DREAM, 117–118
 nature of, 192
 of Romantic Period, 359–368
 potpourri type of, 361
 suggested listening, 356, 368
 to Tannhäuser, 258–261
OVERTURE SOLENNELLE *1812* (*see 1812 OVERTURE*)

P

Pachmann, Vladimir de, 403
PACIFIC, 231, 490
Paderewski, Ignace, 403
Paganini, 400
 as solo performer, 398
PAGEANT OF P. T. BARNUM SUITE, 490
PAHJOLA'S DAUGHTER, 226
Palestrina, Giovanni Pierluigi, 19, 22, 423, 424, 428, 473
 Pope Marcellus MASS, 19
Paloma, La, 43
Parry, Charles Hubert, 113
Parsifal, 261
Passacaglia, 323
 defined, 446
Passacaglia in c minor, 435, 446–449
Passion oratorios (Bach), 112, 379
Patch of Moonlight, The, 484
Pathetique, 15, 189, 278
Payne, John Howard, 43
PEER GYNT SUITE, 116, 214
PELLÉAS AND MÉLISANDE, 88, 470
Percussion instruments, 158–159
Pergolesi, Giovanni, 80, 132
Periods in art history, 475–477
Peter and the Wolf, 143, 144
Peter Gray, 289
PETER IBBETSON, 103, 123
PETROUCHKA, 130, 132–135, 157, 478
 scene from, 134
Phantom Double, The, 62
Phillips, Burrill, 490
Phrase:
 defined, 19
 period, and cadence, 71–74
Phrasing, 71–74
Pianissimo (pp), 28
Piano, 159–160
 development of, 400–401
 literature for, 408
 Debussy's contribution to, 461

Piano (p), 28
Piano solo, 398–408
Piccolo, 149–150
PICTURES AT AN EXHIBITION, 205
Pierné, Henri, 113
Pierrot Lunaire, 384, 483–484
PIGHEADED PEASANT, THE, 282
Pilgrims' Chorus, 91, 259, 261
PILGRIM'S PROGRESS, 113
PINES OF ROME, THE, 214, 469–470
Pison, Walter, 139
Pizzicato, 116, 144
Planer, Minna, 252
PLANETS, THE, 490
Pleasure Dome of Kubla Khan, The, 471
Poetic Meditations, 246
POHJOLA'S DAUGHTER, 486
Point counter point, 423
Poland, 213
Polly Put the Kettle On, 35
Polonaise, 5, 12, 213
Polonaise Militaire, 12, 14
Pomp and Circumstance, 11, 14
POPE MARCELLUS MASS, 19
Pop Goes the Weasel, 35
Polovtzian Dances, 230
Polyphonic music, 21
Polyphonic style, Bach and, 423–424
Polyphony, 21
Polyrhythm, 475
Polytonality, 474–475, 479
Porgi amor, 75
PORGY AND BESS, 78–79
PORTSMOUTH POINT, overture, 490
Post-impressionism, 476
Post-Romanticism, 183–476
Post-Romantic Period, 207, 267
 composers of, 453
Potpourri type of overture, 361
Powell, John, 490
Prelude:
 by Wagner, 261
 to LOHENGRIN, 25, 29
 to PARSIFAL, 25
PRÉLUDES, LES, 29
Prelude to Act I (LOHENGRIN), 90
Preluding, 441
 defined, 23
Presto, 29
Primitive drums, 158
PRINCE IGOR, 230
Procession, 69
PRODIGAL SON, THE, 458

Programmatic content, absolute form, *vs.*, 358–359
Programme music, 184–187
  examples of, 185
Prokofieff, Sergei, 143, 144, 489
  cinema music, 127
PROMETHEUS, 246
Puccini, Giacomo, 86, 99–100, 227
PULCINELLA, 132
Purcell, Henry, 56
Pure music, 185

Q

Quartet from RIGOLETTO, 102
Quintet, 397

R

Rachmaninoff, Sergei, 489
  piano solos, 408
Radicati, 305
Raff, Joseph Joachim, 119
Railroad songs, 34
Rameau, Jean Philippe, 86
RAPPRESENTAZIONE DI ANIMA E DI CORPO, LA, 106
Rasbach, Oscar, 70
Rasoumowsky Quartets, 305
Rathaus, Karol, 126
Ravel, Maurice, 140, 213, 467–468
  BOLERO, 137
  DAPHNIS AND CHLOÉ, Suite No. 2, for Orchestra, 468
  Enchanted Flute, The, 149
  MOTHER GOOSE BALLET, 130, 137–139
  piano solos, 408
Realism, 171, 198, 475
  Richard Strauss and, 263–274
Recapitulation, symphony, 294–295
Receuillement, 70
Recitative, 81
  defined, 93
RED POPPY, 140
Reformation:
  and the Baroque, 423–450
  Bach and, 427–428
"REFORMATION" SYMPHONY, 25–26
Refrains, 418
Register, defined, 60
Reinken, Jan, 399
Religion:
  art and, 18
  music and, 18–29

Reményi, Eduard, 319
Reprise, symphony, 286, 294–295
REQUIEM MASS, 338, 347, 360, 402
Respighi, Ottorino, 231, 442
  FOUNTAINS OF ROME, 469, 470
Reveille, 154
RHAPSODIE, 321
RHAPSODY FOR SAXOPHONE AND ORCHESTRA, 152
RHAPSODY OF ST. BERNARD, 113
RHEINGOLD, DAS, 156, 157, 256, 261
RHUMBA SYMPHONY, No. 2, 490
Rhythm, 7–10
  defined, 7
Ride of the Valkyries, 262
RIENZI, 252, 253
RIGOLETTO, 86
  Quartet from, 102
Rimsky-Korsakoff, Nicholas, 14, 165, 206, 213, 226, 227–241
  biography, 229–231
  SCHEHEREZADE, 130, 151, 153, 231–241
RING OF THE NIBELUNG, THE, 89, 255–256
Ripieno, defined, 369
Ritardando, 28
Rites of Spring, The (see SACRE DU PRINTEMPS)
Ritornellos, 370
Ritter, Alexander, 265
Ritual Fire Dance, 130, 131
River, The, 127
ROBERTA, 78
ROBIN HOOD, 78
Rococo art, 330
ROMANIAN RHAPSODY No. 1, 226
ROMAN SKETCHES, 471
Romantic composers, 182–185
Romanticism, 57, 198, 475
  and Classicism, 178–182, 301–316
Romanticists, 175
  last group of, 453
Romantic movement, 242
  in music, 182–187
Romantic operetta, 78
Romantic Period, 4
  overture of, 359–368
ROMANTIC SYMPHONY, 490
Romberg, Sigmund, 78
ROMEO AND JULIET, 100
ROMEO AND JULIET OVERTURE, 188, 190–194
Rondino, Beethoven's, 53
Rondo, 4, 6, 42, 277

Room for the factotum, 81
Rosary, The, 70
ROSE-MARIE, 78
ROSENKAVALIER, DER, 101, 267
Rossini, Gioachino, 80, 81, 84
Round dance, 4
Rounds, 418
Row, Row, Row Your Boat, 418
Rubinstein, Nicholas, 191, 219
Rule Britannia, 43
Rumania, Gipsy music in, 4
RUSALKA, 281
RUSSIAN EASTER OVERTURE, 226
Russian folk song, 40
Russian music, 213
    influence on Debussy, 460
Russian Sailors' Dance, 140
Russian Symphony Society, 230
RUSTIC CHIVALRY, 86

S

SACRE DU PRINTEMPS, 139, 478-479
SADKO, 227
ST. ELIZABETH, 113
ST. JOHN PASSION, 22, 439
ST. MATTHEW PASSION, 22, 439, 440
ST. PAUL, 112
ST. PETER, 113
Saint-Saëns, Camille, 69, 88, 100, 106, 152, 227
    biography, 199-200
    CARNIVAL OF THE ANIMALS, 169
    DANSE MACABRE, 150, 159, 196, 198, 263
SALOMÉ, 267
    excerpts from, 101
SALOMON SYMPHONIES, 345
SALON MEXICO, EL, 489
Salon music, 286
Saltando, 144
Sammartini, G., 348
SAMSON ET DELILAH, 88, 100, 106, 227
    excerpts from, 199
Sanctus, 19, 25, 425
SANTA FE TRAIL, THE, 226
Santa Lucia, 40
Sarabande, 5
Sarka, 216
SAUL, 107, 113
Sax, Adolph, 152, 400
Saxophone, 152
Scale, defined, 168

Scale tuning, 437-438
Scarlatti, A., 357
SCARLET LETTER, 103
Scarlatti, Domenico, 330
SCHEHEREZADE (Ravel), 149
SCHEHEREZADE (Rimsky-Korsakoff), 130, 149, 229
Scherzo, defined, 118
Schönberg, Arnold, 384, 408, 480, 483-485
Schonbergian-Row, 485
Schubert, Franz, 11, 14, 112
    art songs, 57
    composed folk song, 44
    Der Erlkönig, 55, 59-60
    Serenade, 55
Schuman, William, 490
Schumann, Clara, 320
Schumann, Robert, 243, 373-378, 408
    and Brahms, 319
    art songs of, 62-63
    CONCERTO FOR PIANO IN A MINOR, 374-378
    Ich Grolle Nicht, 55, 62
    judgment of Chopin, 402, 403
Schütz, Heinrich, 434
Scoring, 162
Scotch snap, 31, 39
Scriabin, Alexander, 489
    piano solos, 408
Sea, The, 55, 68
Sea Drift, 471
SEASONS, THE, 112, 139, 345
Secco, 80
Secrecy, 69
Secret Marriage, The, 80
Sentence structure in music, 71-74
Sequence, 413
Serenade (Carpenter), 70
Serenade (Schubert), 55, 57-59
Serenade (Strauss), 69
Sextette from LUCIA, 102
Shadow Song, 87
SHANEWIS, 103
Shape of Things to Come, 127
Shelley, Harry Rowe, 113
Shepard, Arthur, 152
SHICKSASLIED, 321
Shostakovitch, Dmitri, 140, 489
SHOW BOAT, 78
Sibelius Jean, 114-116, 213, 214, 453, 486-488
    composed folk song, 42

Side drum, 158
SIEGFRIED, 212, 214, 256
Singspiel, 76, 88
SKYSCRAPERS, 130, 136, 152, 471
SLAVONIC DANCES, 3, 213, 281
SLAVONIC RHAPSODIES, 281
Sleepers Awake! A Voice Is Calling, 442
SLEEPING BEAUTY, 139
Smetana, Bedrich, 3, 213, 215, 226
    biography, 215–216
    The Moldau, 216–218
Smith, David Stanley, 113
Smoke Gets in Your Eyes, 78
Snare drum, 158
Société Nationale de Musique, 200
SOLEMN MASS, 308
Solo instrument and orchestra concerto
    for, 369–383
Solo performer, emergence of, 398–400
Sonata, 276–78
    defined, 275, 276
Sonata-allegro, 276
Sonata-allegro form, 286, 291–296
    contributors to, 348
    diagram, 295–296
    enriched by Beethoven, 308
    first movement, 299
    Haydn's influence on, 348
Sonata form, 276
Sonatina form, 358
Song of India, 227
Song of Love, 78
Song of the Flea, 55, 67–68
Song-play, 76, 88
Songs My Mother Taught Me, 281
Song to the Evening Star, 91
Sorcerer's Apprentice, 196
    analysis, 208–211
Sordino, 146
Sousa, John Philip, 12, 14
SOVIET IRON FOUNDRY, 490
Sowerby, Leo, 490
Spain, 213
Spanish folk song, 40
Speed, volume and, 28
Spiccato, 144
Spontini, Gasparo, 87
Staccato, 12
Stainer, John, 113
Stamitz, Johann, 330, 348
Ständchen, 69
Stanford, Charles Villiers, 113
Stars and Stripes Forever, 12, 14

Star-Spangled Banner, The, 43
Steiner, Max, 127
Stokowski, Leopold, 442
    arrangement of orchestra, 160
STONE GUEST, THE, 231
Strauss, Johann, waltzes of, 2
Strauss, Richard, 101–102, 198, 251, 453
    and Realism, 263–274
    art songs of, 69
    biography, 265–268
    MERRY PRANKS OF TILL EULENSPIEGEL,
        THE, 156, 268–274
    suggestions for listening, 274
Stravinsky, Igor, 139, 231, 478–479
    Neo-classical tendencies of, 479
    PETROUCHKA, 130, 132–135
Stretto, fugue, 443
String choir, 143–147
String quartet, 384–397
    compared with symphony orchestra,
        385–387
    Haydn, "father" of, 347
Strophic song construction, 31
Structure and form, 47–54
Styles, interrelationship of, 332
Suite, defined, 114–115, 277
Sullivan, Arthur, 79
Sumer Is Icumen In, 418
Sur le pont d'Avignon, 40
SURPRISE SYMPHONY, 348–352
Süssmayer, Franz, 338
Swan, The, 169, 199
Swan Bent Low, The, 68
Swanee River, 43, 55, 73–74, 214
SWAN LAKE, 139
SWAN OF TUONELA, 226
Swing Low, Sweet Chariot, 285
SYLVIA, 130, 139
Symmetry, 49
Symphonias, 143
Symphonic operas, 88
Symphonic poem, 195–211, 242–250
    nature of, 196
SYMPHONIE FANTASTIQUE, 150, 202
Symphony, 278–280
Symphony:
    classical, 329–355
    defined, 276
    fourth movement, 298–299
    Haydn, "father" of, 347
    romantic, suggestions for listening, 328
    second movement, 296–297, 299–300
    third movement, 297, 299

Symphony (*Cont.*)
whole, schematic outline of, 291–300
Symphony orchestra, compared with string quartet, 385–387
Syncopation, 284–285

T

Tabor, 216
Tales from the Vienna Woods, 214
Tales of Hoffmann, 139
Tambourine, 158
Tannenbaum, Der, 40
TANNHÄUSER, 253–255, 359
excerpts from, 91
Grand March from, 13
Overture to, 258–261
Paris edition, 261
production of, 243
Tartini, Giuseppe, 369, 400
Tasso, 245
Taylor, Deems, 103
THROUGH THE LOOKING GLASS SUITE, 123–126
Tchaikovsky, Peter Ilyitch, 139, 213, 214, 227, 240, 263, 453
Andante Cantabile, from STRING QUARTET, Op. 11, 390–391
1812 OVERTURE, 29, 218–221
FIFTH SYMPHONY, 293
FOURTH SYMPHONY, 42, 46
None But the Lonely Heart, 65–66
NUTCRACKER SUITE, 149, 159, 162–169
Chinese Dance, 153
Dance of the Flutes, 155
PIANO CONCERTO IN B-FLAT MINOR, 188
ROMEO AND JULIET OVERTURE, 188, 195
SIXTH SYMPHONY, 15, 156
The Birch Tree, 42, 46
"Temper," use of, 173
Tempo, 26–29
Tenebrae factae sunt, 19, 21
Ternary form, 36–37 (*see also* A-B-A form)
within ternary form, 391
THAÏS, 227
excerpts from, 100–101
Theatre, music in, 114–127
Theme-and-variation form, 445–450
THEME AND VARIATION ON A THEME BY HAYDN, 321
Theme transformation, 245

They Are Over, 81
Thousand and One Nights, A, 227
Three Blind Mice, 290, 418
THUS SPAKE ZARATHUSTRA, 266
Thy Beaming Eyes, 68
TILL EULENSPIEGEL, 156, 268–274
Timbre, 141
To Anacreon in Heaven, 43
To a Water Lily, 119
To a Wild Rose, 119
Toccata and Fugue in d minor (Bach), 444, 445
Toch, Ernest, 490
Tone colour in music, 141–170
Tone poem, 196
Tonic chord, 406
To Rest, to Rest! 69
TOSCA, 80
Toscanini, Arturo, 323
arrangement of orchestra, 161
To the Sea, 68
Train That Never Pulled In, The, 34
Transcription of organ works, 442–443
Transposition, 413
Traum durch die Dämmerung, 69
Trees, 70
Tremolo, 144, 236
Trepak (NUTCRACKER SUITE), 166
Triangle, 159
Trio, 422
Triple metre, 2
TRISTAN AND ISOLDE, 6, 89, 91, 152, 255, 256
Liebestod, 182, 183
Triumphal March from AÏDA, 26, 154
TRIUMPHLIED, 321
Trombone, 157
Troubadours, 56
Trouvères, 56
Trumpet, 154–155
TRYPTYQUE, 490
Tuba, 157–158
Turkey in the Straw, 2, 35
Tutti, 372, 376, 378, 380
defined, 370
Twelve-tone system, 485
TWO WIDOWS, THE, 215
Tympani, 158

U

UNFINISHED SYMPHONY, 78
Unity, 49–50

V

Valhalla motif (Das Rheingold), 156
Valse Triste, 115
Variations on a ground bass, 446
Vaughan-Williams, 490
Verborgenheit, 69
Verdi, Giuseppe, 13, 78, 84, 102, 214, 227
Vergebliches Standchen, 44
Verismo, 100
Verklärte Nacht, 484, 485
Vesti la giubba, 100
Viadana, Ludovico, 369
Victoria, My Love, 56
Victoria, Tomas Luis, 423
Victory Song of Miriam, 112
Vidal Paul, 410
Village Romeo and Juliet, A, 471
Villon, François, 70
Viola, 145
Violet, The (Mozart), 56
Violin, 144, 408–409
    and piano sonatas, 421
Violin Concerto in D (Brahms), 319
Violoncello, 145–146
Virginal, double, 371
Vittoria, Mio Core, 56
Vivace, 29
    movement, 239
Vivaldi, 369, 400
Vlatava (see "Moldau")
Voi che sapete, 81
Volume, and speed, 26–29

W

Wagenaar, Bernard, 490
Wagner, Cosima, 243, 256
Wagner, Richard, 6, 13, 14, 17, 25, 200,
    212, 213, 243, 453, 473
    biography, 251–257
    compared with Mozart, 183–184
    contributions to music, 257
    Götterdämmerung, Siegfried's call,
        156
    literary works of, 254
    Lohengrin, 151
    operas of, 88–91
    Siegfried:
        dragon theme, 157
    suggestions for listening, 261–262
    Tannhäuser, overture, 157
    Tristan and Isolde, 182

Wagner as Man and Artist, 257
Wagnerian festival, 243
Wagnerites, 320
Walküre, Die, 91, 256
Walton, William, 113, 490
    cinema music, 126
Waltz, ancestor of, 39
Waltz in C-Sharp Minor, 6
Waltz of the Flowers (Nutcracker Suite),
    168–169
Wanderer, The, 62
War March of the Priests, 13
Wearing of the Green, The, 39
Weber, Carl Maria von, 89, 212, 213,
    359–361
    Freischütz Overture, Der, 163
Wedding March, 13, 14, 117, 118
Weinlig, Theodor, 252
Well-Tempered Clavichord, 438, 450,
    474
We Won't Go Home Until Morning, 32
What One Hears on the Mountain,
    246
When I Bring You Coloured Toys, 70
When I Have Sung My Songs, 70
White Peacock, The, 471
Who Is Sylvia? 62
Wieck, Clara, 374
Wieck, Friedrich, 374
Will You Remember? 78
Wolf, Hugo, 69
Wolf-Ferrari, Ermanno, 113
Woodland Sketches, 119, 121
Woodwind choir, ranges, transpositions
    of instruments, 154
Working out, 294
Work songs, 32–34

X

Xylophone, 159

Y

Yablochko, 140
Yankee Doodle, 289
You Who Know, Tell Me, 81

Z

Zueignung, 69
Zur Ruh, zur Ruh! 69

Printed in the United States
142753LV00004B/78/P